The Godfather.
Boss of Bosses.
Only he knows where
the bodies are buried.

"Those who want to understand the mentality of organized crime in the U.S. must read this story by the former 'Father' of one of New York City's so-called five families."

—*Publishers Weekly*

"If you enjoyed the book *The Godfather*, or the subsequent motion pictures derived from it, *A Man of Honor* will lead you from the romantic fiction of the Mafia to its reality . . . Bonanno has probably written the most factual and fascinating account ever provided on the early days of the Mafia in the United States."

—*Seattle Post-Intelligencer*

A MAN
OF HONOR
JOSEPH BONANNO

A MAN OF HONOR

The Autobiography of "The Boss of Bosses"

JOSEPH BONANNO

with Sergio Lalli

PUBLISHED BY POCKET BOOKS NEW YORK

PICTURE CREDITS

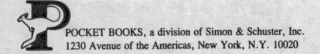

POCKET BOOKS, a division of Simon & Schuster, Inc.
1230 Avenue of the Americas, New York, N.Y. 10020

ISBN: 0-671-50042-2

First Pocket Books printing February, 1984

10   9   8   7   6   5   4   3   2

POCKET and colophon are registered trademarks
of Simon & Schuster, Inc.

Printed in the U.S.A.

Acknowledgments

THIS BOOK would not have been possible without the energy of many people who helped transform an idea into a finished product. Their encouragement, assistance and criticism has helped me in one way or another, some without recognizing the importance of their comments.

I want to thank the people at Simon and Schuster: Michael Korda, editor-in-chief, for recognizing the true me in the book; John Herman, my editor, for his suggestions and refining the manuscript, and Vincent Virga for a brilliant photo section. Additional thanks go to Frank Metz for developing the jacket; Eve Metz for turning a set of manuscripts into a beautifully designed book; Elaine Marion for her sensitive understanding; and Julia Knickerbocker for her enthusiastic support. The constant enthusiasm of my literary agent, Frank Cooper, encouraged me at times when he was the sole reader.

Another early reader, whose counsel I greatly appreciated, was my lawyer, Alfred (Skip) Donau III.

Credit for manuscript typing (and for catching most of the spelling errors) deservedly goes to Diana Ossana.

At one stage or another, the book became a true family project. I wish to thank my son Joseph, my daughter, Catherine, and my son Salvatore for their loving efforts in this project, especially Salvatore (Bill). To my daughters-in-law, son-in-law and grandchildren, my thanks for their understanding and support. Special thanks to my grandson, Joseph Gregory, whose presence relieved me of many mundane chores. Marie-Therese Kupelian was like a member of the family, listening to my stories at the dinner table and offering encouragement.

My gratitude to Sergio Lalli—writer, critic and loyal friend, who stuck with it from beginning to end—who at times agreed with me, argued with me, cried with me, laughed with me and with his help made this difficult task easier.

Finally, I wish to thank my loyal and faithful Doberman, Greasy, for his companionship and who shares with me, in the December of our years, the loving memories of Fay.

J. B., Sr.

January 25, 1983
Tucson, Arizona

WITH PROFOUND ESTEEM AND MEMORIES OF LOVE,
TO MY HUMBLE, LOYAL AND DEVOTED WIFE, FAY—

WITH INFINITE AFFECTION, TO MY CHILDREN,
SALVATORE, CATHERINE AND JOSEPH—

WITH PRIDE IN OUR NAME AND HOPE FOR A BETTER
FUTURE, TO ALL MY GRANDCHILDREN—

I LOVE YOU ALL

Contents

Introduction

I WISH TO PROVIDE an honest portrait of myself and of my times so that you may judge for yourself what kind of man I am.

My name is Joe Bonanno. I am seventy-eight years old and a grandfather. I've often been described as a gangster, a racketeer, a mobster.

I'm supposed to be, or to have been, or to have wanted to be, the "boss of all bosses" . . . whatever that means. At one time or another, I have been accused of trying to "take over" New York, California, Arizona, Wisconsin, Colorado, Alaska, and choice provinces of Mexico and Canada too.

I am not unmindful of my past. Who knows better than I my mistakes and my accomplishments? This book does not attempt to foist apologies or to deny facts. To arrive at a balanced picture of a man, one must make a thorough examination.

Most of my reputation has been a product of exaggeration and ignorance. A great deal of it is complete balderdash. Life is richer, deeper and infinitely more complex than its representation in the mass media. Therefore, if you have picked this up expecting to read the confessions of a no-good, no-account Sicilian, or if you expect a chronicle of blood and mayhem, pass this book on to someone else. I have put too much time and care into these memoirs to have them consigned to the category of cheap thrills. I want to be understood for a change.

I have had many problems with that—being understood. The biggest regret of my life is that I have never totally mastered English. I can manage all right for everyday use, but I cannot speak with wit or elegance. It is a failing I share with many an immigrant.

I claim no distinction in my adopted language. The words come to me sometimes in English, sometimes in standard Italian and sometimes in the Sicilian dialect of my hometown. Occasionally, I throw in a word or two of French. I speak a hybrid language.

To make myself understood, I have enlisted the help of a scribe to write this book. Through him, I can express myself in proper English. Since I am an educated man, it should not altogether amaze you that I can think long thoughts and that I can quote from famous books. All too often, Sicilians are made to sound doltish, simply because they have faulty diction. In their native tongue, those same Sicilians can be eloquent.

Even so, there was a difference between most of my fellow Sicilians and me. I was luckier than most, in that I had a formal education which included college.

Among my Sicilian friends, in America, I was always singled out as a man of learning, if for no other reason than my ability to recite from *The Divine Comedy* or to expound on a few passages from *The Prince*. Most of the men I knew in the New World were not what you would call bookish. Men such as Charlie Luciano, Albert Anastasia and my cousin Stefano Magaddino were baffled whenever I would slip a literary allusion into our conversations. When I spoke Italian, they often complained that I used words they did not understand. They had grown up in the impoverished fields of Sicily or in the tenement streets of America. Their language was coarse and expedient.

My friend Vincent Mangano, when exasperated over one of my intellectual flourishes, would say,

—Peppino, but with you, we have to look things up in the books. How do you expect us ever to finish our meal?

Since I shall recollect many conversations throughout this book, I want to explain my method when I quote people. If the quotation is verbatim—let us say from a newspaper clipping or from a trial transcript—I shall place the words between quotation marks or indent them in the usual fashion. At other times, as for the example above, I shall precede the words with a dash to indicate that the quotation is an approximation of what was said. I will emulate the Greek historian Thucydides, who wrote in the foreword to his chronicles:

"As to the speeches, it is hard for me to recollect the exact words. I have therefore put into the mouth of each speaker the sentiments proper to the occasion, expressed as I thought he would be likely to express them, while at the same time I endeavored, as nearly as I could, to give the general purport of what was actually said."

Whatever your opinion of me, the truth is that I am the last survivor of an extinct species and of a bygone way of life. I have known people from both extremes of life. I have seen virtue and I have seen depravity. My life is full of ironies. Very often, when I review my life and juxtapose all its diverse elements, all I can do is laugh—the sardonic laughter of one who has seen much and has lived to tell the story. It was a triumph in itself to have survived the Volcano—my figurative name for New York City. Most of the old boys died in the turmoil. I'm still here.

Thank God I can still laugh!

I'm also thankful that I still have a good memory. The past is more vivid to me now than ever before, and the patterns of my life seem clearer because I can see them from a greater distance.

And perhaps, if I tell my story faithfully, you will learn not only about me but also about yourselves and the society in which we live.

That which we are, we are . . .
Made weak by time and fate, but strong in will
To strive, to seek, to find, and not to yield.

—*"Ulysses"*
Alfred, Lord Tennyson

BOOK I

The
Odyssey

1

MY EARLIEST CHILDHOOD MEMORIES ARE NOT OF MY NATIVE
Sicily, but of America.

When I was three years old, my father, my mother and I
(their only child) moved from our hometown of Castellammare
del Golfo to the United States. We settled among other Sicilian
immigrants in the Williamsburg section of Brooklyn, where
we lived on North Fifth Street and Roebling, not far from the
East River.

Across the river was a place called New York City. Down
the block was the elementary school where I would begin my
education. We spoke English there. At home, we spoke Sicilian. Other ethnic groups lived around our neighborhood—Jews,
Poles, Armenians. The cops were Irish. The beer vendors were
German.

The Sicilians all complained about the cold weather. Back
home, it was almost always warm. In America, we saw snow
and slush for the first time. You had to burn wood to keep
warm in the winter. If a horse-drawn fire engine trundled down
the street, I would follow it to the fire and collect scraps of
wood to bring home.

The reason for my father's departure from Sicily in 1908
has always been something of a mystery to me. A story I later
heard from relatives was that my father left to avoid prosecution. The case against him was eventually dismissed, but by
that time, we had already moved to the New World.

In Sicily, a place that had not yet entered my young consciousness, my father was known as a "man of honor"—words that meant nothing to me then but were to become the touchstone of my life. He was the head of the Bonanno clan—the leading family of Castellammare. That responsibility, which he could not escape, placed strict limits on his life in Castellammare. So I imagine that as proud as he was of his tradition, he at least partly welcomed the move to America.

The Castellammarese immigrants remained a tight-knit community in the New World. They had come with energy and high hopes, but everything they owned was in a suitcase. They had to look out for one another and cooperate. For example, if an immigrant needed money he could not expect much help from a conventional bank. Most Sicilian immigrants could not show any credit or collateral for a loan. However, they had what they called the Italian bank. Some of their own countrymen had money to lend them, if no one else would, and these men acted as neighborhood bankers. Their interest rates might be higher than the establishment bankers charged, but at least you could do business with your own people. They did not give you the cold shoulder. You had to pay up on time but that's true of everything. Even so, with the neighborhood banker you could get an extension on your loan, perhaps by doing him a favor. Everyone has his talents.

The Williamsburg neighborhood also had something called the Italian lottery. It was a cheap game that offered a big jackpot. For a very small bet you stood to gain a thousandfold if you were lucky. It was incomprehensible to most immigrants and other poor folk that such a lottery was illegal. If you were rich and could afford to bet money in a gambling casino, or if you played the stock market, you were safe from the law. If you were poor and bet a penny, it was illegal. It was a strange country.

Americans were difficult to fathom. Drinking beer and whiskey was okay, but drinking wine, which Sicilians made in their basement stills, was considered the exotic habit of "foreigners." We couldn't imagine that someday they would be so foolish as to prohibit the drinking of alcoholic beverages altogether!

Since he was a Bonanno, my father's reputation preceded him to America. The Castellammarese immigrants in Brooklyn looked up to him, as their relatives had in Sicily. Downstairs from our apartment, my father opened a pasta factory to satisfy the neighborhood demand for fresh macaroni and spaghetti. Across the street from the pasta shop, he opened a tavern. In the rear of the tavern was a small kitchen. Customers could always count on a big pot of stew bubbling with potatoes, green vegetables, pig's knuckles, tripe and maybe even some lean meat.

They referred to my father as don Turridru. In my language, Turridru is an affectionate nickname for Salvatore, just as Peppino is a nickname for Giuseppe. "Don" is equivalent to the English "sir."

I remember being told a story of the relationship between my father and his friends at the tavern. One evening a Castellammarese brought a friend, who was Italian but not Sicilian, to don Turridru's tavern. The customers already in the tavern guessed the man was not Sicilian because, upon entering, he did not pay his respects to don Turridru. The Castellammarese, however, immediately made his way to don Turridru and asked for his blessing.

The Castellammarese and his friend sat at the bar. They drank all they wanted. The Castellammarese put a check on the counter. Don Turridru picked up the check and deposited it in the big old cash register behind the counter.

The puzzled stranger asked his friend,

—Aren't you going to ask for the change from your check?

—Don Turridru knows best, the Castellammarese said stoically.

—But you have change coming to you!

—And what do you expect me to do? That's the way it is around here.

The seemingly high-handed conduct of the tavern owner rankled the stranger.

—What if you had come into the tavern with just a few coins instead of a big check? the non-Sicilian asked.

—Then we could still have drunk here all night.

—And what if you came in here with no money at all?

—Ah! said the Castellammarese. It wouldn't have made any difference. We could have still drunk here all night. You see, don Turridru is my friend. In the winter, when I often don't have any checks because there is no work, I can come here to

4

drink and to eat all I want from the big pot. Don Turridru pays for it then . . . that's the Sicilian way.

When I was seven years old and in the second grade, my father would take me to the nickelodeon to watch Neapolitan moving pictures. He would tell me stories. He told me the inventor of the telephone was not Alexander Graham Bell, but an Italian named Antonio Meucci who used to live in Brooklyn as we did and was an owner of a candle factory across the bay in Staten Island. In that same candle factory worked Giuseppe Garibaldi, the Italian liberator, who was in political exile at the time.

—Garibaldi came to the New World just like us, my father would say.

My father said that while in the New World, Garibaldi also went to Uruguay and helped liberate it from Brazil. When he was in the United States and the Civil War broke out, Garibaldi sent a letter to Abraham Lincoln, offering his services to the President.

My father would talk about America, of how rich it was and of how much more time it would need to mature and to be truly great.

—Perhaps in another hundred years, this country will be civilized, he would say.

Like everything else he said to me at that age, I would only partly understand. The full significance of his words became clear to me later in life.

One evening, my father had a long talk with me. He said we were going back to Sicily. He looked serious, and it was because of his grave face rather than the announcement itself that I cried. He held me sympathetically, but was in firm control of his emotions. Even when I was a seven-year-old, my father addressed me in a dignified manner. He said,

—You are a Bonanno. Be proud.

His voice soothed me, and I stopped crying.

Castellammare del Golfo is situated deep inside an emerald gulf at the western tip of Sicily. The name means "castle by the sea," and there is an ancient castle in the center of the town's waterfront.

I was home again in the land of *mezzogiorno*—the land of

midday, where people sang in their misery and their joy, where the sun was your constant companion and the hot and dusty sciroccos blew across the sea from the Libyan desert. In the wind, you could smell grapefruits and lemons.

I had lots of exploring to do. I would walk up to the top of the ancient castle and look out at the open sea, green toward the shore and blue in the distance. Playing hooky from school to go swimming was a constant temptation. One day, after missing school, I came home looking rather disheveled. My mother told me to take off my shirt. After I stripped to the waist, she licked me on the shoulder.

—I taste salt! she said. You went swimming, didn't you?

Then she spanked me. Naturally, I did not like being slapped, but I never resented the spankings from my mother. The more she spanked me, the more I loved her.

On the way home from La Playa, the town's main beach, I would linger to hear the fishermen singing while mending their nets. If a fisherman on the beach needed a bucket and ladle to empty the bilgewater from his boat, he would make a lilting aria out of it:

—So-oome-body bring me the bu-uuu-cket and la-aa-dle, ple-eee-ease!

The peasants who worked the hills behind Castellammare spoke a totally different dialect. They sounded lyrical even when talking to their donkeys and sheep. The fishermen and the farm peasants could barely understand each other; and if you went to a neighboring town, yet another dialect would tickle your ear.

I had some difficulty at first speaking solely in Italian. I must have impressed my new schoolmates with my English, and I must have taught them slang words, such as "swell" and "okay." But after a while, English words slipped out of my vocabulary altogether.

My new friends called me Peppino instead of Joe or Joey. I told them all about my trip across the ocean, and we played many games. The top of the castle was the deck of our ship, and it seemed natural for me to take command. I knew about ships. I ran a tight ship, too; strict discipline aboard. I swore to go down with the ship, if it sank, all the way down to the bottom of the sea, where the fishes could enjoy me.

* * *

The reason for my father's return to Sicily was vague. But I later learned that he was needed home because the old rivalry between the Bonannos and the Buccellatos, the two major factions in town, was festering once again. This ancient family feud had molded my father's character and had framed his life.

At the end of the 1800s, the Bonanno House was preeminent in the Castellammare region. The family owned land, cattle and horses. In comparison with other families, the Bonannos were well off. They wielded vast influence.

The family leader was my grandfather, Giuseppe Bonanno. My grandfather had four sons. All of them would inherit part of his wealth, but only one of them—the one with the necessary qualities—would assume his power and position. He would lead the family.

Giovanni, the oldest son, showed little inclination for this role. He moved to Tunis, where he became a very successful farmer and rancher. Among his vineyards and Arabian horses, Uncle Giovanni probably led the most peaceful life of all the Bonanno brothers.

The second son, Stefano, was a quiet and devoted family man. Upon his father's death, he promised his mother that in order to take care of her he would never marry. Uncle Stefano had a calm and modest disposition, and he acted as adviser to his younger brother, Giuseppe.

Giuseppe, the third son, had the necessary inward resources, coupled with a natural extroverted charm that made him popular. Uncle Peppe was a leader of men, and the family's mantle of power fell on him.

One of the stories I remember about Uncle Peppe involved his indoctrination of a young disciple. One day he abruptly and without any explanation ordered the young man to take off his jacket and shirt, for he was going to get a beating. The order stupefied the young man, because he had done nothing to provoke my uncle. What could it be? What had he done to deserve a punishment? Confused though he was, the young man dared not disobey my uncle. He dutifully stripped off his clothes and kneeled. My uncle then repeatedly thrashed him over the back with a plaited bullwhack.

—Not a sound, not even a peep, my uncle admonished while administering the beating.

When it was over, my uncle told the young man to wash.

7

He helped to gently towel-dry the young man, and then smeared lemon juice on the welts raised by the whiplashes. This stung sharply but it prevented infection. My uncle didn't appear to be at all cross with the young man.

Before the young man had a chance to ask about the nature of his wrongdoing, he beheld my uncle blithely taking off his own jacket and shirt.

—Take the whip and give me twice as many lashes as I gave you, my uncle instructed.

—Mind you, my uncle added when the young man hesitated, if you don't whip me as hard as I whipped you, I'll give you a second beating.

The young man whipped his master, and afterward helped to dress his wounds.

—You understand how it is? the older man asked the younger. It's one thing to say you're never going to talk against your friends, but it's quite another not to talk when someone is beating you. I wanted to see how well you took a beating.

As for the youngest son, my father, Salvatore, his future was mapped out largely by his mother. He was sensitive and intelligent, and his mother wanted to spare him intrigues, vendettas and feuds. It so happened that one of my grandmother's first cousins was a monsignor. The church was an accepted and certainly the safest form of social advancement. Clergymen held power in their own right. My grandmother, therefore, sent her youngest son to study at a seminary so he could become a priest.

If the Bonanno family was the dominant power in the Castellammare region, the Buccellato family was the rival power. The Buccellatos were trying to expand their sphere of influence, and this inevitably set them at loggerheads with the Bonannos.

Feuding played a large part in Sicilian culture not because people relished it, but because they were fighting for their very survival. Centuries of overcultivation have depleted Sicily's soil of its richness; most of the island has been deforested. There is not enough rain. It is hot and dry most of the year, and arable land is at a premium. Sicily was stripped of its natural resources by conquerors, who also took the choicest land, leaving the scraps to the natives. Since there were more mouths to feed than there were scraps, the natives often fought among themselves to get their share.

Sicilians have come to look upon poverty, scarcity and death as constants in their lives. The have-nots will do almost anything to escape this misery, and the well-to-do will fight in order not to sink back into it. In some respects, the feuding resembled the range wars among cattle barons in the American West. In western Sicily, as in the American cowboy frontier, men fought over cattle because cattle made a man rich. The sons of a longtime ranching family were easy to distinguish in Sicily. They ate more meat than the general population and consequently grew to be taller than the rest. For instance, the Bonanno brothers were all six feet tall or better.

In the countryside behind Castellammare, there was not enough good grazing land. Ranchers could not afford to fence in their property, so they had to let their cattle feed on common pasture used by other ranchers. These conditions almost invited rustling, and thefts of cattle resulted in retaliations. One skirmish brought on another, foray followed foray, confusion abounded.

If the Bonannos did not find a natural explanation for an event, they blamed the Buccellatos, and vice versa. For example, the Bonannos and their supporters were never willing to believe that the death of Stefano Bonanno was purely accidental. One day as he was winding his way up a narrow mountain trail on his mule, Stefano came upon a bend where a rockslide had made passage impossible. The startled mule must have skittered and reared up. My uncle's body was found on the side of the mountain. Who was to say that the Buccellatos or one of their cohorts had not intentionally arranged the rockslide beforehand, knowing that Stefano Bonanno was going to ride up the mountain that day? No one could prove it, but suspicions persisted.

The chief ally of the Bonanno family was the Magaddino family, headed by Stefano Magaddino. At one point in this struggle, Felice Buccellato, the patriarch of the Buccellato clan, orchestrated a scheme which resulted in Peppe Bonanno and his right-hand man, Stefano Magaddino, being sent to jail. The case against them succeeded because of the collusion of a bribed law officer. For a time, Peppe and Stefano were sentenced to house confinement on a prison island off the coast of Sicily.

After their release, Stefano Magaddino did not put anything beyond the guile of Felice Buccellato. The Bonanno ally said that Felice was not even beyond hiring criminals and bandits to fight his battles.

—His name should be "ruination," Stefano Magaddino would say of Felice, whose name in Italian means "felicity."

One night, Peppe Bonanno was awakened by one of the caretakers of his house. My uncle was in the second-story bedroom and the man was calling him from the ground floor, part of which was used as a stable. The caretaker shouted for help in disengaging two fighting horses. When Peppe went downstairs, a rifle boomed. When the rest of the household hurried down to investigate, they found Peppe Bonanno dead.

Uncle Peppe's murder caused my father, who had grown restive with seminary life, to reexamine his plans. His Latin and Greek studies, his musings over *The City of God*, suddenly seemed frivolous exercises. He heard the call, the ancient call, both dreadful and enchanting—the call to action. The siren call of the old Tradition beckoned him.

Salvatore had the choice of thinking only of himself or of taking care of others. Since he was studying for the priesthood, he had a perfect excuse for shunning the grimmer duties that awaited him. He could have remained in cloistered selfhood and gone on to become a rosy-cheeked pastor. He could have been more self-centered, placing personal tranquillity over sacrifice. Instead, he chose to help his family. If we were to ask a man such as my father who he was responsible for, he might answer, as I would answer, "For as many people as need me."

My father, then only twenty-one years old, devised a brazen plan that would dissolve his obligations to the church and bring him home, regardless of his mother's objections. He showed up in Castellammare in possession of a gold candelabrum which belonged to the monsignor. The monsignor wasted no time in expelling him from the seminary.

Salvatore had come home, but he was inexperienced in the affairs of men. His father and older brothers were not at his side, so the role of guide and counselor to the fledgling fell to Stefano Magaddino, the most stalwart and most feared of the Bonanno followers in Castellammare. A gruff, burly and uncomplicated man, Stefano Magaddino had been one of Peppe

Bonanno's closest friends and was known to friends and foes alike for his toughness and bluntness.

Not long after Salvatore Bonanno returned home, two members of the Buccellato clan met their death. The people of Castellammare had their own idea as to who was responsible, but they kept it to themselves. Salvatore was seen more and more, in the town square, in the social clubs, in the fields. He had grown into a fine-looking man with deep-set eyes and a rakish handlebar mustache.

In 1903 he married Catherine Bonventre, a girl educated by nuns in a convent. Catherine's mother was Stefano Magaddino's sister. Thus the marriage solidified the bonds between the Bonannos and the Magaddinos.

After I was born, on January 18, 1905, my father, in a bid for lasting peace, asked his archenemy Felice Buccellato to be my godfather at my baptism. Buccellato agreed, and the villagers called me the "dove of peace."

Three years later, my father left for America. While my father was away, Stefano Magaddino became the leader of the Bonanno faction. Felice Buccellato resented the Magaddinos' rise to power, which he felt had come at the expense of his own family. Tension rose. Relatives and friends implored my father to return to Sicily to accept his ancient responsibility. The social order was disintegrating.

2

I USED TO LOVE TO RIDE MY PONY TO THE GREEK TEMPLE AT Segesta.

This magnificent Doric temple, about ten miles out of town, overlooked my family's farm in the hill country behind Castellammare. The temple roof is missing, but all its thirty-six columns are standing. The side lintels and the front and rear pediments are also intact.

The color of the temple would change with the progress of the sun, from a soft gold at noon to a bronze at sunset. Swallows nested inside the temple, and green lizards darted in and out of the masonry cracks. Orange poppies grew on the hillside. You could hear the bleating of sheep and the lowing of cows. On rainy days, I would roam through the temple grounds foraging for snails, which my grandmother fried in garlic.

The temple was built on a lofty spot in the countryside in honor of Demeter—the Greek goddess of agriculture. The goddess' altar is missing from the temple; as throughout the entire island of Sicily, conquerors and invaders have come and gone through Segesta with devastating regularity. All that remains of the Greek town itself is scattered stone blocks. Grass and shrubs cover the dead city.

Although it is easy for outsiders to list Sicily's foreign invaders, it is difficult for them to fully appreciate what this perpetual turmoil did to the Sicilian character. It is one thing to understand, and yet another to feel. But let us just run through the list of invaders: Greeks, Phoenicians, Carthaginians, Romans, Vandals, Byzantines, Saracens, Normans, Angevins, Aragonese, Bourbons, fellow Italians and the Allied army during World War II. No wonder that Giuseppe Tommasi of Lampedusa, the Sicilian author of *The Leopard*, called Sicily "that America of antiquity." The island has a stew of races. Wandering through Sicily you will encounter not only people with raven hair and olive skin, but also blonds and redheads, people with the palest of skin and people with tawny skin, Latin faces, Asiatic faces, African faces and Celtic faces. The latest additions to this diversity are the black-skinned children that American GIs left behind during World War II.

Sicily has been buffeted by foreign influences for well over two thousand years. The Arabs alone, for example, remained for about three hundred years—a full century more than the United States of America has been in existence. It is obvious that without a genius for survival, Sicilians would have long ago lost their identity. Greek genius built the temple at Segesta, but Sicilian genius made it possible to endure subjugation and to survive long after the Greek town fell to ruin.

Out of necessity, Sicilians put all their talents and energy into creating a life-style of survival, a peculiar and distinctive way of life that over the years became Tradition. Prevented from participating in the rule of their own land, Sicilians withdrew all the more into their own families. Everyone inside the family was a friend, all outsiders were suspect. Unable to understand the many strange customs and languages foisted on them by their conquerors, Sicilians took comfort in their own parochial dialects and customs, developing their own shibboleths or investing common words with double meanings. Exploited by colonial laws and cheated by greedy public officials, Sicilians developed their own folk laws and their own business practices. Frustrated and angered by the inequities of state justice, Sicilians adopted a personal sense of justice which placed the responsibility of conduct and punishment on the individual and the family. This subcultural system of justice did not overthrow the official order, but existed alongside it. In an unjust world, it was necessary to create one's own justice.

A Sicilian of the old Tradition gives his highest allegiance to his family. Outside of that, however, he's proudly independent. He knows how to look after himself. As the Sicilian proverb says, "The man who plays alone never loses." Above all, he is intensely aware of himself, like a stallion in the wild.

On my family's farm downhill from Segesta, we used to

keep a stable of spirited Arabian horses which we would obtain from my Uncle Giovanni. Those Arabians were our pride. I had my own Arabian stallion as a young man. Probably the highest compliment you can pay a man's horse in Sicily is to describe the horse as *mafioso*. As an adjective, the word has many connotations, but all share the same general import: spirited, brave, keen, beautiful, vibrant and alive.

Let us say two Sicilian wagon drivers happen to meet each other at the foot of a hill. One might say to the other:

—Let's race up the hill. I'll show you which horse is *mafioso*.

A horse may be said to be *mafioso;* so can an apple or a woman. So can a man.

Not long after my father returned from America, he became enmeshed in a problem unrelated to the feud with the Buccellatos.

A rancher who owned land near the Bonanno property had been murdered and my father was accused of conspiracy to commit the crime. He was innocent, but the prosecution's principal witness was a man willing to testify that he had heard my father talk about the murdered man in unfriendly terms. It was a tenuous case which could have gone either way. In the absence of hard evidence, the outcome of the trial would depend on who made a better impression on the witness stand.

The witness on whose testimony the case hinged was another neighbor rancher by the name of Vetrano, who had a wife much younger than he. She was pretty, and he kept her in virtual seclusion on his ranch, playing a suspicious Othello to her innocent Desdemona.

I remember my grandmother taking me across the mountains to Trapani, the capital of the extreme western province in Sicily, where my father's trial was being held.

My grandmother told me that she went to talk to her son in prison during the trial. He told her the outcome of the trial was uncertain. He admitted that he might be found guilty if his lawyers did not impeach Vetrano's testimony.

—My lawyers are useless in this matter, my father said. Vetrano has it in for me.

—But why? my grandmother said. Why does he hate you?

My father told her that jealousy had turned Vetrano's mind.

14

When my father came back from America, he had made it a point to visit the nearby ranches and reacquaint himself with his neighbors. When he visited Vetrano's ranch, he did not find the owner home and so he chatted amiably with his comely wife. Who knows how she later spoke of the charming young don Turridru? Who knows how her suspicious husband interpreted her words?

—You mean Vetrano thinks you and his wife . . .

—What else?

—What are we going to do, my son?

—We are going to fight deceit with imagination. Please do as I say. Speak to the midwife in Castellammare. She is your friend. We need a small favor from her. . . .

In those days, midwives would visit married women to examine them, check on their pregnancies and administer to their periodic needs. It wasn't surprising, then, that donna Crocifissa, the midwife, should show up at Vetrano's ranch to examine his wife.

—Just routine, nothing to worry about, the midwife assured Vetrano's wife. Suppose you lie down and let me look at you.

After the examination, donna Crocifissa went directly to see her good friend Vita Bonanno. The midwife described the young wife's private anatomy. My grandmother then relayed the vital information to her son.

The following day Salvatore Bonanno requested permission to address the court himself.

—Your Honor, my lawyers have done the best they can, my father said. They are the two best lawyers in Trapani, as Your Honor well knows, but the infamy against me is so great that even they cannot help me.

My father's lawyers were just as amazed as the spectators and the judge at this pronouncement. Both lawyers were capable professionals, but they did not know what was on their client's mind. If they had known, they probably would not have gone along with my father's risky idea, for it involved unorthodox methods and absolute panache in execution.

—Your Honor, I ask the Court's forgiveness for having held my tongue so long, my father said, rising to his feet. I confess that I never thought this sorry business would get this far. I thought the infamy against me would have been cleared up by now. I can assure this Court, and every man here, that if it were not for the outrageous lies spoken against me, I would ordinarily rather face death than say what I have to say.

It was his duty, the judge told him, to bring forth all the evidence.

—Out with it, the judge ordered, in less flowery language.

—Very well. I have remained quiet up to now because I did not want to compromise one of the fairest flowers in Sicily, if not the whole world. This woman is the wife of my accuser, Vetrano.

My father pointed to Vetrano and stared at him for dramatic effect. Then he continued:

—The reason for this man's perjury against me is very simple. He hates me because his wife has cheated on him.

The courtroom swelled with hubbub. The judge kept rapping his gavel. Vetrano kept banging his fists on the railing, red in the face and slobbering at the mouth. My father looked serene.

—This is v-very serious, said the flustered judge. And ir-re-regular.

—For my indiscretion with this lady, my father continued, I am fully accountable to God. But I do not see any wisdom in allowing myself to be vilified and sent to prison for what is, after all, a common occurrence between men and women.

Suddenly, my father turned around to face his accuser, scoffing him.

—Look at Vetrano now. Why, he cannot even bring himself to speak coherently.

It was true. Vetrano seemed to be in the throes of an epileptic seizure.

—Signor Bonanno, the judge snapped, he is not on trial, you are. . . . Can you prove you went to bed with his wife?

The question sent a wave of lewd anticipation through the suddenly hushed crowd.

—Your Honor, it pains me to admit that this lady and I were caught up in a moment of passion, an unpremeditated moment. Reason abandoned us. The act seemed quite innocent at the time.

—Yes, yes, the judge said, but this is not the time for a hymn on fleshly desire.

—Your Honor took the words right out of my mouth. What lovely flesh, what strong legs, and such a firm bottom. As for her breasts . . .

—Excuse me, the judge interrupted adamantly. What is your proof, sir?

My father approached the bench. He told the judge in a whisper that an examination of the young woman's private anatomy would reveal the presence of an exquisite brown mole directly above the cleft.

A subsequent court-ordered examination of the woman confirmed the presence of the mole—which had been discovered originally by the midwife. This revelation caused a furor in the trial and undermined the prosecution's case. My father was acquitted.

The trial soon became known throughout the entire Castellammare region. Whenever Vetrano passed, street urchins would make the sign of the devil's horn, the sign of the cuckold, behind Vetrano's back.

My father's destiny took its final turn with the outbreak of World War I. He was drafted into the Italian army early in 1915 and assigned to the artillery. His regiment was sent to the Austrian border, where it was in the thick of the fighting. In one battle, almost all the men in the regiment were wiped out; my father was one of the few survivors, but he was badly wounded. Before Christmas of 1915, he came home to recuperate. Complications set in, and a month later, he knew he was dying.

My father's death scene was calm and deliberate, and for me, at the age of eleven, dreadful. Near the end, he invited people into his bedroom for a last word or blessing.

How helpless my father must have felt during his last moments. He knew he would be leaving his wife without a husband and his son without a father. In addition, his family would be battling for its existence against a stubborn local enemy.

He asked my mother to fetch him some writing paper. In a feeble handwriting, he scrawled a pithy message to his nephew Peppino in the army. I later found out that he urged his nephew to take his place back home when he could.

Then he called for me. I was led to my father for the last time. He spoke to me. On other occasions, I knew how to react to his words. This was different. I did not know what my emotions should be this time. All I knew was that I should get as close to my father as possible. He instructed my mother and Uncle Stefano Magaddino to take good care of me. His last words were:

—Your name is Bonanno. Always be proud of your name. He died while clutching me to his bosom.

3

I HAD BEEN ACCUSTOMED TO SEEING MY GRANDMOTHER IN black mourning clothes. Now my mother joined this sodality of women in black. There was also a black ribbon on the front door of our house.

At eleven years of age, I already began developing an awareness of life's ambiguities, its contradictions and ironies. Death had become a reality. People could go away by taking a ship across the ocean. Or they could be right in front of you, holding you, and go away all the same. I grew up steeped in a sense of loss, but I also continued gaining from life. Sad moments gave way to happy ones. The same force in life that took away also gave generously.

School was a relief from the sometimes grim atmosphere at home. Now, more insistently than ever, my mother urged me to study. If I studied, I could become a professional and would not have calluses on my hands. A man who can avoid hard labor is very smart. Luckily, I had a quick mind in school, and the prospects seemed good that later in life I would not have to roughen my hands.

On the way to school, my friends and I used to walk past the cobbler's shop. We called the owner Maestro Marco, a title usually reserved for skilled artisans and teachers. Maestro Marco had a big nose and an ugly face. However, there were compensations in his life. He was very proud of his ability to read. He always kept a newspaper in his shop.

—What's the latest news on the war? we would ask him as we passed his shop.

To be asked to explain something in the newspaper made

him very happy. He would reach for the newspaper, ceremoniously unfold the pages, wet his lips and begin reading an account of the latest battle against the Austrians.

On one occasion, when Maestro Marco read about a heavy artillery barrage, this inspired my friends to pop off a complementary series of raspberries and farts. Some of us imitated the sound by pressing our lips to our hands and blowing. Those more skillful in the art of flatulence fired away the real thing.

The outraged cobbler stormed out of his shop bawling and cursing at us, a leather strap in his hand. We had gone too far—we had violated the most solemn activity in his life.

—Scoundrels, ruffians! he called out after us as we scattered. You impudent scamps! Is this the respect they teach you in school?

He pursued us to our school and went straight to the principal's office. We could hear the cobbler's vituperation from the hallway.

Later that morning, the principal called all the boys to an assembly. After telling us of the cobbler's complaint, the principal asked for the culprits to turn themselves in. No one budged. Sicilian boys are trained from birth to obey their elders. It took all our willpower not to break ranks.

The principal threatened to punish all the boys if someone didn't tell him the names of the culprits. Since we had been blabbing about nothing else that morning, half the boys knew who the offenders were and the other half had a pretty good idea. While the principal waited, my friends and I kept watch over the younger boys and those weaklings who might inform on us. If one of the boys showed signs of breaking down, we would stare him into silence or kick him in the shins. In true Sicilian fashion, no one squealed. The principal let us off with a stern lecture on propriety.

In my grandfather's time, Sicily was under the dominance of the Bourbon dynasty, a royal family of Spanish and French ancestry. Italy itself was like a jigsaw puzzle with the pieces owned by various powers.

Because of this patchwork of foreign domination and internal weaknesses, Italy was the last major country in Europe to be unified under a native ruler. The unification movement was spearheaded by King Victor Emmanuel II and his brilliant prime minister, Cavour. It could not have been accomplished, however, without the leadership and inspiration of the Italian patriot Giuseppe Garibaldi.

Garibaldi catalyzed the unification movement by enlisting a volunteer army to liberate Sicily. These volunteers, a motley crew of idealists and zealots, wore a distinctive garb and became known as the Red Shirts. In 1860 Garibaldi's enthusiastic band, some one thousand strong, landed in Marsala on the west coast of Sicily.

Although the Red Shirts were vastly outnumbered by the Bourbon army, they had the backing of the populace. Men of my Tradition, such as my grandfather, sided with Garibaldi in order to overthrow the hated Bourbons. The ranks of the Red Shirts also swelled with Sicilian youngsters, the *picciotti,* the young ones.

You can imagine what a stirring tale this made when I heard from my elders how, for example, during one famous victory Garibaldi tricked the Bourbons into believing the Red Shirts were more numerous than they actually were. The *picciotti* gathered cattle and sheep from the countryside and herded the animals in front of the enemy at a distance . The animals raised such a cloud of dust that the Bourbon soldiers, thinking a huge army was marching toward them, fled before the battle even started.

With the invaluable aid of the local insurgents, most of them men of my Tradition, Sicily was liberated, paving the way for the unification of Italy. But if Garibaldi and the men of my Tradition collaborated in ousting the Bourbons, they did so out of different impulses.

Garibaldi wanted to forge an Italian national state, which had never existed. (Some wags insist that it does not exist today.) However, the local insurgents were mainly interested in a little more freedom to run their own affairs. The men of my Tradition knew that as far as Sicily was concerned, nothing changes basically. They had gotten rid of the House of Bourbon only to make themselves subject to the House of Savoy. One ruler departs, another takes his place.

The concept of nationhood never stirred them deeply. It was a vague concept that required men to give their highest loyalty to an abstract entity, the nation, rather than to their families, which were flesh and blood. It would require young men to fight foreign wars on behalf of the national state, to fight strangers from whom one had never received a personal affront or injury, to fight people one didn't even know.

Sicilians are among the most idealistic people on earth, but they are not abstract. They like things on a human scale. Even in the smallest business transactions, they like to deal with each other man to man, eyeball to eyeball. It is no different when they fight. They take fighting very personally. They believe in personal, not abstract, honor.

In this regard, the story of the Sicilian Vespers bears repeating. The story describes another insurrection, this one when the island was under French domination. During Easter week of 1282, while the people of Palermo were making their way to evening worship (vespers), agents of the treasury waited outside the churches to apprehend tax debtors. The agents handcuffed and dragged many citizens to jail, publicly shaming them by slapping their faces—an intolerable insult.

As it happened, a young lady of rare beauty, who was soon to be married, was going to church with her mother when a French soldier by the name of Droetto, under the pretext of helping the tax agents, manhandled the young lady. Then he dragged her behind the church and raped her.

The terrified mother ran through the streets, crying,

—*Ma fia, ma fia!*

This means "My daughter, my daughter" in Sicilian.

The boyfriend of the young lady found Droetto and killed him with a knife.

The mother's cry, repeated by others, rang out through the streets, throughout Palermo and throughout Sicily. *Ma fia* soon became the rallying cry of the resistance movement, which adopted the phrase as an acronym for *Morte alla Francia, Italia anela*—"Death to France, Italy cries out."

This was the version of the Sicilian Vespers story as told to me. Scholars now consider parts of the story to be legend or folklore. That may be true, but so what? The important element of the story is not its factual veracity, but the Sicilian spirit which it exemplifies. It speaks to me to this day of the living ideals of personal honor, personal justice and personal dignity.

The years between the unification of Italy and World War I have been described as the golden age of my Tradition. The new rulers were willing to tolerate or make accommodations with men of my Tradition in exchange for their political support.

Although they acted separately in pursuit of their own goals, men of the old Tradition, as a group, composed a sort of shadow government which existed alongside the official government. In the western part of Sicily, where the old Tradition was strongest, "men of honor," as they were called, flourished as they never had and probably never will again. The rustic culture of the island condoned the activities of these "men of respect." The king of Italy might rule the island, but men of my Tradition governed it.

These men usually came from the middle class. Some of them owned land. Some of them had a monopoly (or were trying to acquire one) in a particular business enterprise. No matter how they made their living, however, they usually had influence or control over jobs. This gave them leverage to influence votes for politicians. One could also turn to these men for solutions to personal problems, for the redress of wrongs. They assisted friends in need and were implacable toward enemies.

To be sure, some of these men abused their power or perverted it for personal gain. But the Tradition I am describing would have never endured without the backing of the people. And it had the people's support because, in the main, the Tradition worked in practice.

"Men of honor" were essential to Sicilian society in their capacities as brokers, facilitators and arbiters. But to serve as a middleman, a "man of respect" needed more than personal courage. He needed friends, in all places and at all levels. His effectiveness depended on his network of friendships.

To deal effectively with city hall, for example, one had to have a friend there. Consequently, if someone asked a favor from a "man of honor," let us say to expedite some legal papers, he could tell the supplicant:

—Rest assured, you shall have your papers tomorrow. I have a friend in city hall and he will do me this favor.

By performing such favors, large and small, the "man of honor" made himself indispensable.

If, for example, someone asked the "man of honor" to recover a stolen ring, the "man of honor" needed some connection among bandits and brigands in order to negotiate for the return of the ring.

The "man of honor" handled such a task realistically and with aplomb. He could not very well charge up the hills and shoot every bandit in sight. There were too many bandits in Sicily for that! First of all, he would ask for a marginal sum of money from the man whose ring was stolen. Then, through his connections in the demimonde, the "man of honor" would find out who stole the ring and buy it back for a sum less than its actual worth. He also kept part of the money from the ring's owner as a commission. As a result, the owner got his ring back, the bandit made money and the "man of honor" performed a favor and got a commission.

Those who did such favors were variously referred to as "men of honor," "men of respect" or "men of order." Such men were also said to be "qualified"—they were qualified in all aspects of life, qualified to deal with all types of people. Usually, these men used diplomacy, astuteness and friendly persuasion; sometimes, however, they resorted to violence.

My mother was a gentle, modest and devout woman. Having come from a family of eighteen brothers and sisters, she was unused to loneliness. The loss of my father devastated her and she became sickly and thin. Five years after his death, she died . . . of a broken heart.

My grandmother Bonanno, herself a widow, lived on to the age of ninety-seven. She could often be heard reciting the rosary, or talking to herself out loud. Sometimes in the midst of her monologues I would hear the name of a Buccellato who had just passed away. It was as if she were keeping count of the enemy dead on her rosary.

Not long after my father died, open war broke out with the Buccellatos, sparked by charges and countercharges of cattle rustling. The Buccellatos decided to ambush Uncle Stefano Magaddino and his nephew. The nephew was killed, but Uncle Stefano escaped. After that, all the casualties were on the Buccellato side.

One evening, I overheard my grandmother muttering over her rosary:

—In a sack, they found him in a sack . . . and now they don't want to open the casket.

24

There had been a funeral in town that day for one of the Buccellatos. The coffin was kept closed. The man buried that day, I later found out, was Felice Buccellato. My godfather's body had been found in a gully. The body was in a burlap sack, hacked to death and too horrible to look at.

I was too young to assume a position of responsibility, so Uncle Stefano's brother, Giuseppe Magaddino, became my guardian and the administrator of my father's estate. Also, after my mother's death, since my grandmother was too old to take care of me alone, I went to live with my mother's side of the family, in the household of Grandfather and Grandmother Bonventre. Nonna Bonventre's maiden name was Magaddino, so in this household I came under the direct influence of Uncle Stefano, the unchallenged head of the family.

In adolescence, I was more introspective and self-reliant than most boys. I wavered between extremes. My moods ranged from melancholy to rage, from romanticism to practicality. They had told me my father had died in the fight against oppression. I saw the world as a battleground between noble causes and evil forces. I burned with idealism. I reveled in the chivalrous stories enacted by the armored marionettes in the puppet theater. Sitting in a dark room watching fantastic battles, I became the paladin Rinaldo, fighting the noble war against the heretic Moors.

My grandfather, Martino Bonventre, was a very religious man who went to church every morning. He wore an earring on his right ear, and on special occasions he liked to wear the tricolor sash popular among Garibaldi's followers. Although a farmer by occupation, his avocation was mending broken bones. Even licensed doctors would recommended patients with broken bones to Martino Bonventre. He had a special way with cleansing wounds and preparing salves. He would not hesitate to get up in the middle of the night to answer a call for help. Everyone called him a benefactor.

There were three Magaddino brothers: Stefano, the leader; Giuseppe, the administrator and diplomat; and Giovanni, the black sheep who had gone off by himself on his farm. (Their names were the same as the three oldest Bonanno brothers.)

I did not see Uncle Giovanni much. He and Uncle Stefano

did not see eye to eye on many things. If I asked Uncle Stefano about his brother Giovanni, he would say:

—He's doing all right by himself in the mountains. Let's not talk about him.

Uncle Giuseppe, my legal guardian, was a smart and reasonable man. He acted as Uncle Stefano's counselor on family matters and he was probably the only man who could calm him when he became angry. He also had a reputation as a lady's man, a pursuit that Uncle Stefano considered frivolous.

—We need his mind, Uncle Stefano would say of his brother, but we also need an iron fist.

Uncle Stefano—he of the reddish-blond hair—was that iron fist. Everyone showed him respect; he was a father figure to me. He was a gruff and intimidating man, but boys liked him because he spoke his mind, because he was forceful and direct, and because he told war stories. From Uncle Stefano I learned how to present one's face to the world.

Uncle Stefano undoubtedly considered it his role to pass on the Tradition to those who would soon be men, especially to those in whom he recognized the spark of leadership. When I and some of the Bonventre brothers would walk alongside him, he would stick his hand in my pocket. That way he could be sure I was always close enough to hear everything he had to say.

I have never known a man to be so sure about everything. Doubt and hesitation were for other men; Uncle Stefano was unequivocal. That did not make him infallible, but it certainly made him decisive. At the same time, Uncle Stefano's bluntness made him the scourge of the town.

If, while walking down the street, Uncle Stefano encountered a quarreling couple, he did not hesitate to step in and give them a piece of his mind.

—What's the matter with you two, shouting like that in the middle of the street? How is a man supposed to take a quiet walk? Why don't you wash your clothes inside your house?

Uncle Stefano was not a man to be trifled with or giggled at, despite his eccentric habits.

Regardless of whether he was entering a house or leaving it, Uncle Stefano's greeting and farewell were always the same. He would always say *"Arrivederci"*—which means "So long," or "I'll see you again." No one had the nerve to question Uncle

Stefano's vocabulary except his brother Giuseppe. Whenever Giuseppe reminded Uncle Stefano of his odd habit of saying *"Arrivederci"* all the time, Uncle Stefano would puff up and reply:

—Hello and goodbye, it's all the same.

One evening, we heard the familiar *"Arrivederci"* and in strutted Uncle Stefano, beaming with pride and showing off his wardrobe.

—Does anyone notice anything different about me? Something in my wardrobe? Look carefully!

We were afraid to speak.

—Peppe, have you nothing to say to your brother?

Uncle Giuseppe stroked his chin.

—That's a nice-looking vest you're wearing, Stefano.

—You don't make sense! This is the same old vest I've been wearing for who knows how long! Uncle Stefano bellowed. Then he began to pace about the room.

—You must all be blind! How did everyone become blind all at once?

Finally, Uncle Stefano blurted out:

—Look, here, on top of my head. I've been to the hat shop. Open your eyes, you blind fools!

He twitched off his hat and held out the beret.

We had all spotted the beret from the beginning. We had refrained from mentioning it, however, because the beret's color made Uncle Stefano look ridiculous. The cap was black. In Sicily, black is the solemn color worn only for mourning. To wear black for fashion's sake, or for any other reason, is to make a mockery of death. Uncle Stefano knew that. What had likely happened was that he had bought the beret hastily and probably thought it was a dark blue or a dark brown.

As he held out his beret like a dead bird, Uncle Stefano must have realized his blunder, for he made a wry face. Since he was a proud man, however, he did not want to admit his mistake and make himself look foolish. He had his reputation to protect. When he looked up at us, his eyes twinkled as he said:

—I know it's black, but every so often I remember my father's death. And I wear black to honor his memory

. . . what do you think, that I'm like you ungrateful children who forget their father six months after he's buried? Stefano never forgets.

Over a lifetime, a man has many sons, sons of the flesh and sons of the heart. Uncle Stefano made me a son of his heart. Aside from teaching me the value of being affirmative, Uncle Stefano also endowed me with a love for our Tradition. He spoke of it lovingly and zealously. He said Tradition was the bulwark against chaos.

If a man is in a fight, he would tell me, then he must fight to the end. But a man must be careful with violence. Once he uses violence, it can be used against him.

He stressed how important it was for a man to have friends.

—I've always been the Bonannos' right arm, he would say proudly.

Later, when I was in America and a budding leader myself, I sent Uncle Stefano a photograph of me in shorts. Relatives later told me how Uncle Stefano would lovingly take out the snapshot and address me, as if I were there:

—Be true, Peppino. Look over both your shoulders. Keep to your inner light. . . . My, what good-looking legs you have, young buck!

I had approached the age when I had to choose a career. Since both my father and mother were dead, the choice was entirely mine and the decision weighed on me all the more. I was almost seventeen years old and almost a man.

The world beyond my village was coming into my ken. The Treaty of Versailles had been signed by the great powers. Sober men swore never to repeat such a catastrophe as World War I.

I did not know what awaited me in the greater world. But I knew that Castellammare itself could not hold me for long.

I still enjoyed eating mullet and sea bass, I still savored fruity sherbet and creamy pastry, and I still relished sheep's cheese and pungent wine from my hometown . . . but I also wanted to expand my tastes.

I still marveled and participated in the cycle of feasts and celebrations. On Ascension Day, the villagers would place the statue of the Madonna on a boat and row out into the gulf.

Everyone sang and waved flags. Those in high spirits would jump in the water with their clothes on.

On the feast day of the town's patron saint, the Madonna of Succor, her statue was paraded in the streets. People wore cockades and broad sashes around their waists. Pennants flew from the housetops. There were horse races.

But for all its wonders, life in Castellammare was very provincial. Life there wasn't always comfortable, either. I could not discount the strife and contention that I saw. Now that I was coming of age, there was even bickering among my relatives over property settlements.

It was the open sea that inspired my most lasting fantasies. The sea liberated me. Even death out at sea seemed enchanting.

A maritime career seemed to hold the most promise. I did not want to become an ordinary sailor, however; I wanted to become a sea captain. I wanted to travel and win renown. Most of all, I wanted to command men.

4

THE FIRST STEP IN BECOMING A SEA CAPTAIN WAS TO ATTEND
the nautical preparatory school in Trapani for a year to bone
up on technical subjects. The most notable part of the year,
however, was the extracurricular lesson I learned in how to
conduct an amorous liaison.

Her name was Virginia, a jaunty and pretty girl from a
school nearby. We got out at the same time, and I often saw
her walking home. She had large, dark, coquettish eyes and
at first we would smile at each other from opposite sides of
the street. Before long, we were actually walking alongside
one another, holding hands and chatting frivolously. We might
have had lusty dreams about each other, but we never got
further than kissing on the cheek.

One day Virginia's father, who was one of the leading
bankers in Trapani, caught her writing a torrid love letter to
me. Like all Sicilian fathers, he was strict, and there was no
telling what retribution he would demand if he thought his
daughter's virtue had been compromised. In Sicily, at least at
that time, the mere suspicion of dishonor was enough to taint
a virgin's reputation and bring shame on the father.

Even the innocent gesture of holding hands with Virginia
was a mark against me. We had held hands in public. People
had seen us. Only engaged couples held hands in public. If
that wasn't enough, Virginia's letter, written in schoolgirl romantic fervor, made our friendship seem like the love affair
between Antony and Cleopatra.

Only one man was qualified to settle such an unseemly
affair. Virginia's father consulted his brother don Ciccio—a

"man of honor" and a champion of violated virgins. I learned about this from don Totò, another "man of respect" in Trapani, who knew me and my family. Don Totò informed me of the gravity of my indiscretion. I admitted my foolishness and repented having been so free with Virginia. But I hastened to add I had not tampered with the girl. Her purity was intact.

—Peppino, you've heaped a mess on yourself, don Totò intoned ruefully. You've provoked a father's ire. You should have known better. Listen to me, when you court a girl you have to seduce her father as well.

—But I wasn't courting her, I protested, at least not in the way her father thinks.

—You're going to have to be a man about it. You have to come with me to see don Ciccio. It's up to him.

I prepared for my conference with don Ciccio as if he were Solomon. I went over how to greet him and ask for his blessing. I memorized a humble speech replete with apologies. I scrubbed myself and wore my best clothes. I promised myself that if I got out of this predicament unscathed, I would never look at another almond-eyed woman as long as I lived.

Don Totò escorted me to don Ciccio's house.

—Is this the young man? don Ciccio said, averting his eyes and addressing only his friend don Totò.

—Yes, don Totò said, the same young man the father wants dead.

A lump about the size of a watermelon rose in my throat.

—He is full of contrition, don Totò added. I might also note, although it doesn't mitigate his offense, that he comes from an honorable family. He is the only son of Salvatore Bonanno of Castellammare.

Don Ciccio kept ignoring me.

—My friend, he told don Totò, if you pledge for him and if he comes from such a distinguished family, this young man can't be all bad. There might be some hope for him if he learns to control his appetites.

I felt like hugging don Ciccio for his profound understanding of human nature.

—As always, don Totò answered, don Ciccio speaks wisely and magnanimously.

—Sit down, my friend, don Ciccio said, allowing himself a faint smile. Here are sweets and coffee.

Don Totò sat next to the host. I remained standing, like a
sentinel. I was there only to listen and benefit from their remarks.

—It will take all my powers to appease the father, don Ciccio
remarked after the two made themselves comfortable. You
should have seen how angry he was. For a moment I thought
I would have to give my niece away in matrimony to this young
man. It was a choice between vengeance or matrimony. I'm
glad I didn't have to choose.

I thought I detected don Totò winking.

Don Totò later assured Virginia's father that his daughter
had not been violated and that no harm should come to me.

After a year in Trapani, I was accepted at the Joeni Trabia
Nautical Institute in Palermo. I was a college man. I felt wonderfully alive, keen, cocky and curious. I was on my own,
with a flat of my own and my own late-night companions. In
the morning, when I opened my shutters, I gazed out over
Palermo.

Palermo is an old, beautiful and varied city. Its seaport lies
at the foot of Mt. Pellegrino, which Goethe called the most
beautiful promontory in the world. Inland, the countryside opens
into what is known as the golden valley, because of the numerous citrus groves. The climate is semitropical, and as you
walk around the city you see bougainvillea, clematis, palms
and water-lily gardens. The city's architecture is a study in
contrast—Norman palaces, baroque villas, high-rises. It is also
a city of convents and monasteries. Situated almost in the center
of the Mediterranean Sea, Palermo, like Sicily itself, has been
abused by and has benefited from the traffic of mankind.

My ancestors played a part in this varied history. A Bonanno
once was mayor of Palermo. The Villa Bonanno still stands;
just outside Palermo, in Bagheria, is the Villa Palagonia, built
in 1715 by order of the Prince Gravina Bonanno.

When I had my family tree traced at the archives in Palermo,
I received a document bearing the Bonanno family seal: a crown
above an emblem showing a black leopard, its right paw raised.
According to the document the Bonannos came to Palermo
from Pisa at the end of the thirteenth century because of a
dispute with the ruling faction in Pisa.

Monreale, a suburb of Palermo, is known for its exquisite

Norman cathedral, the bronze doors of which were made by the artisan Bonanno Pisano (Bonanno of Pisa). Perhaps it was this Bonanno who, upon returning to Pisa after his Monreale commission, first began regaling his family with stories of Sicily.

My studies went smoothly. When I read or listened to lectures I always sought to understand the big picture. Consequently, homework was just a matter of filling in details—easy enough but tedious. I was never interested in studying for its own sake, but if a teacher called on me in class and asked me to improvise on a theme, I would shine.

All my teachers, from elementary school on, complimented me on my memory. To this day my friends wonder how I can remember poems, proverbs, anecdotes and jokes from my childhood. It probably has something to do with the rich oral tradition in Sicily. On an island where the official language changed periodically depending on what foreigners were in power, my people learned to store information in the safest place of all: in their minds.

Our curriculum at the nautical institute included both technical and liberal arts courses. I studied English, and I still have the English reader we used: *The Boundless Sea*. It was edited specifically for naval cadets, and contains wonderful excerpts and passages about the sea. You could flip through its pages and read about the storm that scattered the Spanish Armada on its way to attack England; or about the lighthouses, one on the European coast and one on the Asian coast, that illuminate the Strait of Bosporus; or about the Battle of Trafalgar and how Lord Nelson, mortally wounded, bravely continued the fight to victory and then, as death was approaching, told his chaplain, "Doctor, I have not been a *great* sinner."

I lived in a boardinghouse. Across the street was a small clothesmaking shop, which employed seamstresses. In warm weather the girls would sit outdoors, gabbing and singing, with the garments they were sewing on their laps.

My roommate and I would watch them from our apartment window. When it was very hot the girls would raise their skirts above their knees and unbutton their blouses, thus unknowingly revealing themselves to our covetous eyes. It was useless to try to study. When we couldn't contain ourselves any longer, we'd stick our heads out the window and lewdly flick our tongues at them.

Because of their numbers and our youth, the girls were not frightened by our taunts. And because they felt safe, they felt bold enough to exchange gibes with us:

—Ah, you naughty rogues, they would say. How's the scenery from up there? See something you like? Go on with you, go on. Take a dip in the sea, you pups.

In my spare time, I indulged my many interests. I cultivated a taste for good opera, the more flamboyant the better, and I became a fancier of fine women—the more discreet the better. I also played the boulevardier at times and paraded around town in the white uniform of a naval cadet.

There was also a serious side to my nature. It was the early 1920s, and I was not unmindful of the ominous overtones of the Fascist regime, which had just come to power under Benito Mussolini. When Mussolini was making his way up, it wasn't clear what he was all about. He wanted to keep the workers from Communism; that pleased the industrialists. He wanted to capture colonies for Italy; that pleased the chauvinists. He wanted to restore order, clean house and make the trains run on time. He passed himself off as a genuine leader.

—I would rather live one day as a lion, Mussolini liked to say, than one hundred days as a sheep.

That sounded stirring and noble. Little did we know that the speaker was made of straw.

He had come to power after his party followers, the Black Shirts, marched on Rome. It was later discovered that during this famous march, *il duce* was awaiting developments in a town near the Swiss border, in case the Fascist show of strength in Rome failed.

Mussolini was a cowardly man pretending to be a tough guy. I've seen a few tough guys in my day, and I think I have a measure of expertise on the subject. When I say tough guy, I mean it in a complimentary sense: a forceful man who sticks to his principles. A true tough guy, whether you agree with him or not, knows he is superior to most men. The phony tough guy lacks this sense of security; he has to bully people so he can hear them say he is superior. Mussolini was a bully—a phony tough guy.

As a student in Palermo, I kept a wary eye on the Fascists, especially since men of my Tradition were beginning to see the true Mussolini and were predicting he would bring despotism to Italy.

My college idyll lasted until 1924, my third year at the maritime college. I was more desirous than ever of earning a license that would allow me to enter the merchant marine. But that year a tempest would tatter my sails and toss my ship in unknown waters.

Now undisputedly in control of the national government, Mussolini sought to eradicate all dissent and to install a totalitarian regime.

His picture appeared everywhere. His sayings were inculcated into children at school. There were Fascist slogans to recite and Fascist anthems to sing. There were Fascist social clubs and uniforms. Fascism tried to regulate every aspect of life. Italy would become an orderly state, but at the expense of humanity.

Men of my Tradition reviled Mussolini, once he showed his true colors. "Men of honor" realized that he was no different from the tyrants their ancestors had fought in the past. As far as Mussolini was concerned, he couldn't abide stubborn resistance to his rule from a group of men he considered archaic. With his mania for absolute control, he couldn't coexist with men who did not worship him and who constituted a subcultural ruling order themselves.

Mussolini went about cleaning Sicily of its "mafiosi." He appointed a special prosecutor with special powers to remove "reactionary elements" that were hindering Sicily's "progressive evolution." The special prefect for Sicily was Cesar Mori, who claimed that the island's "mafioso" tradition was keeping its people mired in a feudal society. Mori spoke like a contemporary sociologist; but when it came to hunting down men, he did his job as well as any medieval grand inquisitor.

Men of my Tradition were imprisoned in droves, often on the flimsiest charges. They were tried and sentenced with utter disregard for their civil liberties. Many men were forced to flee to America. Many went underground or became insurgents. Some twenty years afterward, these same partisans would aid and welcome the invading Allied army during World War II.

In the meantime, the Fascists were supreme. At the nautical college, word came down that students would be required to sing the Fascist hymn each morning. We were told the merchant marine was as vital to the country as the navy, and that as students we were expected to do our patriotic duty by joining the Fascist Party. As a sign of support for Mussolini, we were to wear black shirts for our school uniform.

These measures offended me, and I protested them vociferously. Other students rallied around me, and became political activists. The authorities called us radicals. For me, the spontaneous revolt against repression sprang from the same rebellious urges that had motivated men of my Tradition in the past. In addition, my rebellion was laced with romanticism, as I compared myself with storied Sicilian rebels such as Coreolano of the Forest and the Blessed Pauls. Mine was an inconsequential rebellion next to theirs, but it was just as sincere.

To dramatize our cause and to activate the more acquiescent students, we activists urged everyone to refuse to wear a black shirt to school. We made fun of the idea of changing our shirts from white to black.

The day all the students were to stop wearing black shirts arrived. My fellow activists and I went to school early that morning and waited at the gate to gauge the response. Even I, the leader of the protest movement, could not have hoped for more. Just about all the students wore white shirts that day.

Our antics irritated school officials, whose jobs were at stake if they didn't curry favor with the Fascists. The school director tolerated our protest for a day. But he warned us that if we didn't wear black shirts from then on we would be suspended or expelled.

It was too much to ask the students to risk their careers for the sake of a black shirt. The overwhelming majority abandoned the boycott. Out of a student body of about three hundred, only seven of us refused to wear the black shirt.

Because of my continued resistance, I was suspended from school for three months. If I didn't want to be expelled, I had to show up again wearing a black shirt.

I returned to Castellammare. Returning with me to the village was my cousin Peter Magaddino, the son of my guardian and my constant companion after I moved into the Bonventre household. He was my age, and his father urged us to keep together and always help one another. When I went to school in Palermo, Pete did the same, as much to be close to me as anything else. He too enrolled in the nautical institute, and was suspended during the black-shirt protest.

Some of my relatives advised me to reconsider my position; they didn't want me to throw away a career so easily. But I was nineteen years old, impulsive and idealistic, and with no parents to restrain me. I had sworn not to wear a black shirt and nothing could make me change my mind.

If I couldn't go back, I had no choice but to go forward. I was not afraid to travel and start anew in another land. When I told Pete my intentions, he cast his lot with me. We prepared to embark for the United States.

5

MY FIRST STOP OUTSIDE OF SICILY WAS TUNIS. I REMAINED there several months as the guest of my Uncle Giovanni while waiting to be joined by Pete Magaddino, who was still trying to get a passport.

Uncle Giovanni was very proud of the horses he raised, and the walls of his house were covered with award ribbons. He was the last of the Bonanno brothers of Castellammare. He was naturally concerned about my welfare and offered to help me if I wanted to settle in Tunis. He had even lined up a prospective fiancée from a rich family. I was tempted to stay, but I rejected his offer, as kind as it was. It would have been very easy for me if I had accepted. I would have settled into a comfortable bourgeois life, but a life without adventure.

After Pete Magaddino caught up with me in Tunis, we both went to France, from where we hoped to sail for America. In Paris I stayed with my cousin Salvatore Bonanno, Uncle Giovanni's son, for a couple of weeks. Paris was a great treat for a nineteen-year-old, and with my cousin, who was a sculptor, I went to cabarets and music halls and drank cognac—the beginning of a lifelong habit.

My cousin suggested I enroll in school in Paris, but nothing could deter me from following my western star. A complication had arisen, however, that made the journey westward somewhat problematic. Neither Pete nor I had a visa to enter the United States.

There was a quota system to enter the United States, and we would have to wait several years to obtain a visa. Our impetuosity to see America didn't allow us such a lengthy delay. I had a student passport and, if I had tried, I probably could have obtained a temporary visa. Pete, however, didn't even have a passport. He had tried to obtain one while I waited for him in Tunis. After trying for several months he had left Sicily without one, fearing that if he didn't catch up to me then, I would leave Tunis without him.

From Paris, we went to Le Havre and arranged for passage on the ship *Liberté,* which was bound for Havana.

Pete and I spent a month in Havana until we could arrange safe conduct across the hundred miles of water that separates Cuba from the United States. A small fishing boat took us from Havana to Tampa, Florida.

Because of a mixup, we couldn't land on the mainland immediately. We had to wait overnight on a sliver of marshy land off the Florida coast. Another boat picked us up in the morning. Once we were on the mainland, a vehicle transported us to the Tampa train station. With other aliens, Pete and I took a train to Jacksonville. We wanted to try to make it all the way to New York.

In Jacksonville, we wanted to spend the night in a hotel, from where we could contact relatives. I left Pete in the train station while I went to hail a taxi. There were immigration guards at the station entrance. They grabbed me and took me to a detention center. Later, Pete was also brought there. It looked as if our luck had run out. I was allowed to make a telephone call. I called my Uncle Peter Bonventre in Brooklyn; he was my mother's brother. Three agonizingly slow days passed. Then, as we were about to be transferred to another detention center, we were released. Someone had posted $1,000 each for Pete and me.

Outside the immigration center, we were greeted by two men. One I recognized from Castellammare, but the other was a stranger. They could have been Laurel and Hardy for all I cared. It was simply great to be free. The stranger was a short, plump man who, after I had risen to the top in New York, liked to quip that he was the first one in America to know Joe Bonanno. This man's name was Willie Moretti.

As I later found out, my call to Uncle Peter Bonventre in Brooklyn had resulted in a call to my cousin Stefano Magaddino of Buffalo. My cousin Stefano was the son of Giovanni

Magaddino and the nephew of Uncle Stefano Magàddino, the elder. Cousin Stefano, upon learning of our plight, dispatched two of his men to rescue Pete and me.

After getting out of the detention center, Pete and I were taken to a hotel. Willie Moretti had a surprise for us. It was probably the best gift two virile young men could receive. Waiting for us in our hotel rooms were two American girls, both of them pretty and both of them willing . . . to help improve our English.

BOOK II

The Castellammarese War

6

MY AUNT MARIETTA MADE ME A BIRTHDAY CAKE WITH TWENTY candles on it. The cake was for a surprise birthday party that my aunt and uncle held for me on January 18, 1925. Since I had been in America a little more than a month, the party was also a welcoming to my new home and to my new country.

I lived at my uncle's house in Brooklyn. Uncle Peter Bonventre was a humble immigrant barber. He and Aunt Marietta treated me like a son, although they had two sons and a daughter of their own. Their children, by the way, grew up to fulfill the immigrant dream: The daughter became a schoolteacher, one of the sons became a doctor, and the other son became a professor of theology.

During my first months in America I still thought of myself as a college student. I dawdled and daydreamed, went to the movies and generally frittered away my energies.

Indolent and aimless though I was, I nonetheless felt confident in my potential. I believed in myself. I thought, as many young men that age think, that I could be good at just about anything. The problem was what to devote myself to. I could inspire myself all I wanted to with shining dreams of greatness, but I had no skill, barely spoke English and wasn't making a living.

My Uncle Peter didn't pressure me in the least, even though I wasn't paying him for food and lodging. Although he wouldn't have wanted any payment anyway, he did want me to think about my future. One day I asked his advice about work.

—I don't know of any jobs for nautical students, Uncle· Peter said, but I can teach you how to be a barber.

I listened respectfully, but I suppose my face couldn't hide my disappointment. Uncle Peter's intentions were good. He wanted to keep me off the streets and out of mischief. However, cutting hair didn't seem to augur a great future. Without slighting him, I refused his offer. I thanked him for his kindness and hospitality. The best thing I could do now, I told him, was to move out of his house. I wanted to be on my own.

I moved to a boardinghouse in Brooklyn's Williamsburg-Greenpoint section, where I had lived as a boy. How good it felt to walk down the streets and hear the familiar dialect of my hometown. It wasn't difficult to make friends, considering all we had in common. Besides hailing from the same village, we all shared the momentous experience of having disrupted our lives to move to the United States. Besides, the Castellammarese in Brooklyn were familiar with the Bonanno name and eagerly sought my company. People invited me to their houses or to their social clubs.

The Castellammarese tended to stick together. We had our own distinct neighborhoods, not only in Brooklyn and Manhattan, but also in Detroit, Buffalo and Endicott, New York. Not only did we all know each other, but we were often related to one another. Among ourselves we spoke Sicilian. English was handy but usually unnecessary to our lives. We asked nothing from anybody. We took care of our own. In all our ethnic neighborhoods, we established a branch of the Castellammarese Society of Merit, our version of the Kiwanis or Rotary clubs to help the needy, celebrate feast days and remember our heritage.

In order to get ahead, we had to cooperate with each other. The first-generation immigrants, in particular, had no other choice. They had little if any funds. They could not "buy" themselves into American society. They also suffered from discrimination, because the mainstream culture was Anglo. These conditions induced immigrants to band together so they might utilize whatever resources they had, which was mainly manpower.

Our life-styles centered on our Family. A Family (with a

capital F to distinguish it from one's immediate household), in the Sicilian usage of the term, is a group of people, allied friends as well as blood relatives, held together by trust in one another. Regardless of their varied individual activities, Family members support each other any way they can in order to prosper and to avoid harm.

We instinctively congregated around a Father, the patron around whom we revolved like spokes around a wheel hub.

History had already taught us that the greatest avenue of upward mobility was not so much talent—talent was universal—as it was friendship, what Americans call connections.

When I arrived in America, the two most important Castellammarese figures were Stefano Magaddino of Buffalo and Gaspar Milazzo of Detroit. They had arrived in America earlier in the century and had initially settled in Brooklyn, where the original and the largest Castellammarese colony existed.

As my cousin Stefano and Gaspar Milazzo made their way up, they came in conflict with rival groups within our world. Very often these rivals were friends and relatives of enemies in Sicily. The Magaddino family was not alone in having members in America; the Buccellato family did also. They were archenemies in Castellammare, and archenemies they remained in Brooklyn.

As Stefano and his friend Gaspar were walking out of a store in Brooklyn one day, someone shot at them but missed. During the ambush, two innocent people were killed. To Sicilians of my Tradition, revenge is a personal responsibility. Not long after this careless incident, several Buccellato men were shot to death. Thereafter, the Buccellato clan would no longer play an important role in the affairs of my world in America.

Police suspicion fell on Stefano and Gaspar, who removed themselves from Brooklyn. Stefano went to Buffalo and Gaspar to Detroit. They wound up staying in these cities and setting up their own Families, but both continued to maintain close ties with the large Castellammarese community in Brooklyn. The Brooklyn Family was left in the hands of Cola Schiro, a bland, compliant man who depended on my cousin Stefano for his position.

The fact that I was Stefano Magaddino's cousin greatly facilitated my passage into this immigrant society. Still, it was

up to me to take advantage of my opportunities. Two of my
earliest friends were Gaspar DiGregorio and Giovanni Romano.
Gaspar's mother and my cousin Stefano's mother were sisters.
(In America, Gaspar was later to marry Stefano's sister.) I
didn't know Gaspar in Castellammare, but I did remember
Giovanni, who was a playmate of mine and the son of a sheep
rancher.

Giovanni, Gaspar and Gaspar's brothers had a bootlegging
operation going. That wasn't so unusual because at the time
there must have been two or three stills per block in Williamsburg. It might well have been the home-distillery capital of the
world. Gaspar and Giovanni, eager to have a bright and well-
connected man at their side, asked me to join them, and I didn't
hesitate to say yes.

The second decade of the twentieth century in America was
a fabulous era. Calvin Coolidge, the nabob of prosperity, was
President. Babe Ruth, the Sultan of Swat, whacked sixty home
runs. Charles Lindbergh flew the *Spirit of St. Louis* across the
Atlantic nonstop. Gene Tunney, a college kid, took the heavy-
weight crown from Jack Dempsey. Rudolph Valentino, a tango
dancer who could barely speak English, became the most
famous man in America; and then, at the height of his silent-
movie career, died of stomach ulcers.

The 1920s had it all. It had flappers and outlandish automobiles. It had Art Deco and jazz music. It had prosperity.
And it had Prohibition. Congress had ushered in the 1920s by
passing the Volstead Act, which made the manufacture, distribution and sale of alcohol illegal.

Prohibition was championed by the rural ladies of America,
who considered booze the cause of dissipation among their
menfolk. These ladies of the Women's Christian Temperance
Union had no confidence in their men's ability to resist temptation.

But that was only the surface motivation behind Prohibition.
In the larger picture, Prohibition was the reaction of rural America against big-city America—where the booze came from,
where the immigrants swarmed, where factories hummed, where
fashions and books and magazines and movies came from,
where all sorts of alien and new influences began their journey
and spread across pristine America.

America, in other words, was growing up. It was leaving its arcadian past, becoming more urban and more urbane. Prohibition was a resistance to this change. Immigrants understood Prohibition to be a mere rite of passage. Prohibition seemed to them very peculiar, something Americans would get over in time.

In the meantime, however, Prohibition provided a splendid and accelerated opportunity for immigrants to make money. It was the newcomers to this land—the Jews, the Irish, the Poles, the Germans, the Sicilians—who took the lead in bootlegging.

To these teeming masses of immigrants, Prohibition was the golden goose.

The basement distillery that gave Giovanni, Gaspar and me our livelihood was a relatively small operation. In our neighborhood, many of these stills grew out of the homespun stills that we Sicilians frequently built to make wine for personal consumption.

Our still was in the basement of an apartment building. Across the street, one of Gaspar's brothers, Matteo, had a garage which was used to load the whiskey into delivery trucks. A tunnel led from the still to the garage. Nino, Gaspar's older brother, had the contacts with the politicians and the police that ensured no government interference in our operation. All the Irish cops took payments. A uniformed policeman would walk down the street and, on seeing a truck being loaded with contraband whiskey, would suddenly whistle and do an about-face.

The tolerant relationship between the police and the bootleggers existed not so much because of bribery as because of a similar attitude toward Prohibition. The Irish cops of the day, as well as the public at large, adopted a laissez-faire attitude. I remember one police lieutenant in our neighborhood who told us bluntly that he would look the other way at bootlegging, but if he found any of us carrying guns he wouldn't hesitate to arrest us or chase us out of the neighborhood. That's the way it was, at least originally.

When I first got into bootlegging I thought it was too good to be true. I didn't consider it wrong. It seemed fairly safe in that the police didn't bother you. There was plenty of business for everyone. The profits were tremendous. And let's face it, especially for a young man, it was a lot of fun.

Shortly after I joined my friends, Gaspar's brother Nino must have noticed that I always wore the same dark-brown suit. It was my only suit, the same one I had worn when I entered the United States. One day, while passing the Kronfield Clothing Store, Nino led me inside to buy a suit for Gaspar. Since I was about the same build as his brother, he told me to try one on.

—Looks good, Nino said as I modeled the suit. Looks very good on you.

—But are you sure this is right for Gaspar?

—Well, now that you mention it, Nino answered, feigning astonishment, it looks a lot better on you than it ever would on Gaspar. Why don't you keep it? Gaspar can buy his own suits.

Nino had planned that all along, of course. He bought me my first suit and also my first overcoat in America. Soon I was making more than enough money to buy my own things, and later that year I bought a big, dark-gray Hudson. This was a bootleggers' delight. It was fast and it had special compartments under the floor for stashing one-gallon cans of whiskey.

My friends and I, being young, single and flush, enjoyed ourselves to the fullest. We'd go watch the fights at St. Nick's Arena, or go to the movies or the theater. We also had our regular dance halls and nightclubs. It seemed that the more money we made, the more we were broke . . . but never for long.

Gasparino was the most spendthrift. He squandered money on clothes, entertainment, cars, gambling—he loved billiards. He also was absentminded, forgetting where he left his hat, forgetting where he parked his car, forgetting what he did with his money. But he was a good-natured guy who made us laugh, very often unintentionally.

My other associate, Giovanni, was much more moderate and a tireless worker. In making whiskey, Giovanni had the skill of an alchemist. He took his responsibility seriously. One night, a sleepy Giovanni insisted, over our objections, on going down to the basement to prepare a shipment of whiskey for the next day.

The order could easily have waited an extra day, but Giovanni was a punctilious businessman. As tired as he was, he went downstairs to the still. It wasn't for the money that Giovanni returned to his work. We really didn't need more money. Giovanni simply was a conscientious worker. He always liked to meet his obligations.

That night an explosion rocked the building. Giovanni had apparently dozed off at the job. Alcohol spilled on the floor and flowed under the burner, igniting the still. A screaming Giovanni ran out into the street. His clothes, flesh and hair were on fire. He slapped himself and rolled on the ground to smother the flames; onlookers tried flogging him with their jackets. But Giovanni didn't live past that night.

Giovanni's death put me out of the bootlegging business temporarily. At about the same time another incident drove me into the bakery business.

I had met a young man who knew me from Castellammare, and I had written my name and address for him on a slip of paper. This fellow was shot to death in my neighborhood. Who knows why? On discovering the slip of paper with my name on it, police began to inquire about me. My biggest worry was that they might find out I was an illegal alien. Police also began inquiring about Giovanni's death, since they weren't sure it was an accident. I thought it prudent to lie low and let things cool off.

My Uncle Peter Bonventre was worried about my getting mixed up with the wrong crowd. Out of fatherly concern, he suggested I talk with another uncle, Vito Bonventre, who owned a bakery and might be able to employ me.

At this juncture of my life, since I had not been in the bootlegging business long enough to have truly tested myself, I wanted to prove both to myself and to my solicitous uncle that I was a reliable, responsible individual.

I went to see my uncle the baker and asked to work with him. Since he didn't know me that well, he didn't know what to expect from me.

—I can relieve you of some of the labor, I told Uncle Vito. That will free you to take care of administration. You'll see. I won't let you down.

He was skeptical, of course. He knew I had been a student, unaccustomed to the hurly-burly of business or to physical labor.

—I work hard, he stammered. This is hard work. I don't

think this is the kind of work for you. . . . Excuse me, Peppino, but I want to know something. Have you ever worked?

—This would be my first regular job, I answered.

It took a little doing, but we eventually came up with an arrangement. He made me a partner, agreeing to let me pay him a little at a time for my share of the business. I agreed to drive the delivery truck, freeing him to supervise the bakery as a whole. But I was also free to expand the business if I could. We shook hands on it—that was our contract.

Uncle Vito had taken a chance on me, but he wasn't being utterly reckless. Although I had never labored, I was bright and industrious. I had a glib tongue, which was useful to me as a salesman. I had a sure and easy manner. He needed a go-getter to expand his business, something he had been unable to do despite his excellence as a baker.

During 1926 I dedicated myself to the bakery business, and business did indeed improve. I used the friendships I had made to good advantage, through a connection here, a contact there, a favor in return for another consideration. I didn't know anything about bread, but I knew my way around people. People considered me likable and charming. I enlarged the bakery, increased sales and added delivery trucks. My uncle could hardly keep up with me.

Later, when I was ready to go on to something else, I thanked Uncle Vito for giving me a chance and I returned my share of the business to him without any recompense. I had mainly wanted to prove myself.

I did not fool myself that I would remain a breadmaker for long, and I was always on the lookout for other possibilities.

At a café one evening, I ran into a friend who was sitting with another man I didn't know. My friend was the personal secretary of an opera singer. The stranger, I learned, was a drama coach.

—A professor of acting, explained my friend, who was a bombastic sort.

The "professor" was Italian and spoke only makeshift English. Since the movies were silent then, the professor's lack of English fluency was not a hindrance to the practice of his art. He made a living turning out character types for silent movies, many of which, in those days, were made on movie lots in Long Island.

—Hey, professor, what do you think? my friend said. Is Peppino a type, or is he a type?

—He has strong features.

—He's handsome, my friend added. Another Valentino.

—Go on, go on, I said in embarrassment and secret delight.

—But he's right, you know, the professor said to me. You have a good face, winsome but strong.

—If you two keep flattering me like this, I said, grinning, I'll feel obliged to pay for your drinks.

—I'm not kidding, though, my friend said. If you could only sing, you could play the lead in *La Forza del Destino*.

Although I scoffed at the idea then, before long I enrolled in evening classes while still working at the bakery. The professor had a studio near Union Square. The studio was equipped with a victrola and an odd-looking motion-picture camera on a tripod. Six or seven other students attended classes with me.

Silent movies demanded skill in dramatic pantomime. Italians seem particularly adept at this. It is a national trait.

—Make your emotions come out through your face, your body, your movements, the professor would tell us as he gave us dramatic situations to enact. Remember, make your face the map of your heart.

During our first session, the professor asked me to walk across the room. It seemed a strange request, but I walked, as I always walked, without affectation or stiltedness.

—Will you look at that, the professor cried out. You're a natural, Peppino. Never change that walk. Always walk like that.

He used to say I was *vispo*, which means lively or vivacious. He would typecast me sometimes as a tough guy and sometimes as a lover. He said he loved my face and my big ears.

Movie acting seemed easy, I thought. You just had to be yourself. But, among my classmates, I was surprised to see how difficult it was for some of them to act naturally. One girl in particular caught my eye. She strained and labored at her scenes and moved like a stiff mannequin rather than the comely girl that she was. I forget her name but not her loveliness. She was slim and had long, dark-brown hair that swayed behind her like the tail of a horse. We often found ourselves paired in romantic scenes. No matter how passionate the scene, she always felt tense in my arms. Moreover, she moved lethargically, unsure of herself.

—She needs some loosening up, the professor would whisper to me, poking me in the ribs.

I took her to the movies, and once I met her parents. We might have kissed and petted, that nameless girl and I, but my passion for her sputtered. I couldn't keep anything burning for her. She possessed all the physical assets but lacked the fire within.

The end of our romance, such as it was, coincided with my waning interest in acting. Even though I enjoyed it and the teacher praised me, I had a cavalier attitude toward acting. I considered it a divertissement more than anything else.

I began to skip classes, and eventually I dropped out. I didn't really want to live in the fantasy world of films. Shortly after I stopped pretending I wanted to be an actor, the real world captured all my attention. And the real world was fantastic enough.

My life took a decisive turn at the end of 1925 when Salvatore Maranzano, a hero of mine in Sicily, immigrated to the United States. When I was a boy, Maranzano was a chief warrior under Uncle Stefano Magaddino in Castellammare, and he too had fought against the Buccellatos.

Afterward, Maranzano sought his fortune in Palermo, where he quickly established himself as a man to watch, a shrewd merchant in the food business, a man on the rise, a bold man and a ready fighter, an apostle of the old Tradition. When Uncle Stefano visited me in Palermo while I was a college student, he often took me to Maranzano's office and we would join him in a midday meal. Maranzano was married to the sister of don Totò of Trapani.

Many daring and romantic stories surrounded Maranzano. One of them told of how Maranzano confronted his enemy, a swordsman by the name of Calantra, in a Palermo park. Maranzano had lured Calantra to the park by taking evening rides in his carriage. One evening Calantra's carriage pulled up next to Maranzano's. Calantra was about to unsheathe his sword when a knife sailed from the adjacent carriage. The wounded swashbuckler retreated.

This renowned "man of respect" had now come to America,

fleeing the same insufferable political climate that had turned me into an exile.

I attended a dinner that many Castellammarese friends in Brooklyn gave to welcome him. We embraced heartily and kissed.

—When your father was alive, Maranzano told me, I always followed him.

—Yes, don Turridru, I said, enthralled by him.

—And your Uncle Stefano was my teacher.

—Yes, don Turridru.

—Peppino, you understand me.

—Don Turridru, I . . . I . . . yes, don Turridru.

I felt honored and privileged just to be near him. I suppose it was like falling in love, only it was between men. When I was around Maranzano, I felt more alive, more alert, more called upon to fulfill my potential.

He was a fine example of a Sicilian male: robust, about five feet nine inches tall, full-bodied but with no excess flaccid flesh on him, deep-chested, with sturdy muscular arms and legs. He was said to be able to snap a man's neck with his thumbs and to leap amazing distances.

Maranzano was handsome. He could make his face smile sweetly, or he could look severe enough to make you tremble. He liked fine clothes. He dressed like a conservative businessman, preferring gray or blue suits, soft pinstripes on the blues. He didn't wear any jewelry other than a watch and his wedding band.

His voice . . . ah, his voice. What an important aspect of a man, his voice. We remember voices, it seems to me, more than we do faces. Sound seems to be more ancient than sight.

He had a sweet voice, not at all gruff or basso profundo. His voice had an entrancing echolike quality. When Maranzano used his voice assertively, to give a command, he was the bellknocker and you were the bell.

Maranzano could make everyone in a crowded room think he was talking to him individually. He tailored his speeches to the mentality of his audience. To a simple audience, he spoke in parables; to a more intelligent audience he proclaimed ideas. He knew how to interlace a speech with humor, and, when called for, he knew how to soar poetically or come down suddenly and fiercely on a single crucial word.

Maranzano spoke mainly in Sicilian, but he knew several other languages, including Latin. His Latin he learned while studying to be a priest; Maranzano, like my father, had once attended a seminary school. Perhaps that was why he was such a strict one for manners and decorum. He was as punctilious as an archbishop.

After his welcoming banquet to America, I began seeing more and more of Maranzano. While he waited for his wife and children to join him in America, he lived in an apartment near Fourteenth Street and Second Avenue in Manhattan. We often went to the movies together. He especially liked westerns.

I found him irresistible, he found me refreshing. I was twenty-one years old, and he was about forty. He must have liked having a disciple around him. I liked being around a man of experience. He could talk to me on a high level, as he could with few others among the Castellammarese because they lacked schooling. With me, Maranzano could expand and elaborate and not stint in his vocabulary.

—Only you understand me.

—Yes, don Turridru.

7

My Uncle Peter Bonventre, always looking out for me, invited me to a little family gathering. At the party I was introduced to several young ladies, among them Fay Labruzzo, or Fanny as some called her—a gracious girl with whom I exchanged only a few words.

Uncle Petrino must have watched us contentedly, although at the time I didn't realize his intentions. I come from a Tradition where one of the father's highest duties is to take part in his son's choice of a wife. Nowadays, this practice is considered meddlesome, even cruel, but it doesn't have to be. Uncle Petrino was like a father to me. Even when I saw through his adroit and gentle scheming, I did not resent it.

My uncle's scenario became perfectly transparent after he asked me to accompany him when he paid a visit to his good friend don Calorio, Fay's father. Calogero Labruzzo—don Calorio—came from Camporeale, a town about seven miles inland from Castellammare. He was fairly well off. He owned a six-story building on Evergreen and Jefferson streets, in the Bushwick neighborhood. On the corner of the building was a butcher shop which Mr. Labruzzo used to operate but then rented to another butcher after suffering a heart attack. The building contained apartments, but the ground floor was entirely devoted to a ladies' clothing factory, operated by Mr. Labruzzo's son-in-law and his daughter Marian. Adjacent to the building was Mr. Labruzzo's private house.

Calogero and Mari'Antonia Labruzzo had five sons and six daughters. Fay and her sisters worked in the clothing shop. It was Fay's job to check the seamstresses' final product to see that it conformed to pattern. She made alterations with dazzling speed. When she was satisfied, she straightened out the dress on the wooden dummy and tapped the shoulder with the back of her fingers.

When Mr. Labruzzo saw us, he bustled around us, saying:
—How good to see you. Why didn't you tell me you were coming? Marian, look who's here. But why are we standing around? Let's go in the office. No, I have it. Let's go to the house, just next door. Someone run to the house and make some coffee. This way, please.

I did not have a change to talk with Fay, but we gave each other a look of instant and total understanding—I don't know how else to put it. Everything was clear, without the need for words. We knew what was happening. Everything was going along as generation upon generation of Sicilians had seen to it that it should. Fanny and I responded silently, letting things take their course.

Falling in love is just as much a process of self-recognition as it is of discovering another person. I still had much to discover about Fay, and I did my exploration during our courtship. But before that, in how she simply presented herself or in the way she flicked her fingers expertly at a well-made dress, I recognized her to be the embodiment of an image I've always carried in me, the image of the kind of woman I would want to fall in love with. I've always loved Fanny, even before we met.

In any case, it would have been unseemly for Fanny and me to converse openly without the formal approval of her father. Mr. Labruzzo had a reputation for being one of the strictest, most hidebound and hotheaded Sicilian fathers around. His outbursts of rage were legendary. At the slightest provocation he would slap his children (it didn't matter how old they were). He tolerated no insubordination.

Don Calorio's temper would often get away from him. Pity the wretch who happened to insult don Calorio when the old man carried his walking cane, for he would administer a bastinado before the offender could utter a word of apology. If his walking cane was not available, don Calorio would just as swiftly snatch his shotgun or his butcher knife. The old man scared people. It was not unusual for people who didn't know him well to think that don Calorio was a bit crazy.

Mr. Labruzzo had to be handled just right, and during our first encounter I was duly polite and attentive to his tender emotional constitution. Intense discussions between Mr. Labruzzo and Uncle Petrino must have followed that initial get-together. Soon, Fay and I were sounded on our feelings toward each other. The initial impression was mutually favorable. Even astrology seemed to favor us. We were both born in 1905, I at the beginning of the year and Fay at the very end, December 31. It was all clear then. There had to be a *conoscenza*—the ancient custom wherein a suitor, through his sponsor, formally announces his intentions to a girl's father.

When Uncle Petrino and I went to the Labruzzo house, we found Mr. Labruzzo alone in the parlor dressed in his fancy suit. All the children were upstairs. After stepping into the room to greet us, Mrs. Labruzzo also left. Uncle Petrino stood by my side. It was up to him, as my sponsor and stand-in for my father, to open the ceremony:

—My nephew Peppino, who comes from an upright family, as you well know, don Calorio, and whose good character I can vouch for, would like to express, in accordance with our custom, his good intentions toward your daughter Fanny, of whom he speaks with unqualified admiration and whom he would not dare approach without the consent of her dear father.

The chest of Calogero Labruzzo swelled. He stuck out his lower lip and nodded approvingly. Then he cleared his throat:

—When a young man shows respect for the father, the father may rest assured he will show respect for the daughter.

Mr. Labruzzo then turned to me and spread out his arms.

—I am honored to give my consent. Come, kiss me.

Then the entire family was invited into the parlor. Mrs. Labruzzo and the children, all of whom had been merrily awaiting the moment, rushed in. Mr. Labruzzo called for drinks and sweetcakes. Fay, dressed prettily, sat in a chair beside me during all the commotion. She blushed and smiled, reminding me of a blossoming rose.

Within a short time after his arrival to America, Maranzano established himself as an expert entrepreneur. In its own way his was a classic American success story. He built up an import-export business, had real estate holdings and had considerable interests in the bootlegging industry. He recirculated his profits, becoming a financier. He made connections and soon had well-placed friends in all circles of life.

In business matters, Maranzano loved perfection. He took great pride in his ledgers, his account books, his records and files. All his books had to be in order, each entry had to be immaculate—an exquisite tapestry of numbers.

By this time, I had left the bakery to go to work for Maranzano. I should more properly say that he called me to him and I answered the call. I gladly accepted not just because of the job but also because I expected my life with Maranzano to be an adventure.

My job was to check and keep an eye on Maranzano's whiskey stills. I was his traveling representative, visiting his stills in Pennsylvania and upstate New York. The job had many facets. Each still had a local manager who was part owner in the business with Maranzano. I had to make sure that supplies were coming in as scheduled, that everything was running smoothly and everyone was on the ball. If one of our stills was raided by the police, I bailed out our people.

Maranzano kiddingly referred to me as his "chemist." The only thing I knew about chemistry was that you shouldn't fall asleep over a fire. Whereas before I had been connected with a small neighborhood still, I now was an overseer of Maranzano's interstate operation. I began carrying a pistol.

Since bootlegging was an illicit enterprise, popular as it was, we couldn't turn to the government for protection or for settling disputes. We had to protest ourselves, and when necessary I undertook missions for Maranzano that required the use of force.

Fires, by the way, whether by accident or because of sabotage, were fairly common at stills. One of Maranzano's stills once caught fire and was partially destroyed. Maranzano assigned me and a couple of his men to find out who had done it, since we suspected sabotage. Through various tips we discovered someone who knew who the culprits were. We didn't even have to touch him. A graphic description of the human legbones was enough to make him want to talk. We relayed the information to Maranzano. Our leader probably entrusted the job of retaliation to someone else. Maranzano had many connections. He didn't tell me everything.

Another common occurrence was the hijacking of delivery

trucks by rival bootlegging groups. One of our numerous transfer points—where whiskey shipments were stored for pickup and distribution elsewhere—was at a barn near Wappingers Falls, New York. When one of our trucks didn't arrive at this barn, Maranzano ordered me and three others to scour the neighboring farms for the truck.

For the transport of alcohol we used vehicles disguised as milk trucks or fruit trucks or, as in this case, furniture-moving trucks. We searched all the farms in the area that night, but we had no luck. One of our last stops was at a remote farm. We turned off our headlights and parked a safe distance from the barn, leaving one man at the wheel. Three of us then walked quietly to the front of the barn. The furniture truck was inside. We also heard voices, but we couldn't tell how many men were in the barn. The three of us drew our pistols and rushed inside, surprising two men, who hid behind hay bales and began firing on us. We wounded one of them, but the other escaped through the back. We drove the furniture truck away.

The truck's recovery gladdened Maranzano, but he reminded us that if we had taken a moment to plan our assault of the barn we would have positioned a man behind the barn to prevent any escape.

I now drove a six-cylinder Paige, dark-gray and very fast. I owned new suits, new shoes and new overcoats. I was making good money. I moved to a new apartment. I had Maranzano. I had Fanny. Those were the flush times.

Pretty soon I even invested some of my own money in a still, which I and my partners operated independently of Maranzano. Operating a still was a matter of having capital, having connections and having protection. I had these, but as yet I wasn't a member of a Family.

I was much like a squire in the service of a knight. Maranzano was my knight. My association with him was like an apprenticeship to see if I had the necessary qualities to be accepted into the society of honored friends—that is to say, a Family.

Because of his position in Sicily, Maranzano was accepted into the Castellammarese Family in Brooklyn when he immigrated. Of course, since I was an apprentice, this was not something Maranzano discussed with me directly. Until one is accepted as a Family member, one's affiliation is private knowledge. Nonetheless, I could draw my own conclusions, and I looked forward to the day when I too would be inducted into the Family. My whole history had prepared me for it.

It must be understood that when I speak of my old Tradition I am referring to an all-embracing way of life governed by certain values and ideals. One practical aspect of this way of life is the forming of clans, or Families, for the mutual advantage of their members. It is this phase of my Tradition which Americans usually refer to as the Mafia. A Sicilian may believe in the principles of his Tradition, but he might not want to join a Family. That's his choice. Such a decision is not taken lightly, because becoming a member of a Family entails not only privileges but corresponding duties.

It is during his apprenticeship stage that an aspirant learns of these duties and is given tasks to test his mettle. My missions for Maranzano, for example, were not only part of my job but were also little tests by which Maranzano could decide whether I had the inner stuff to become a Family member. Obviously, obedience to one's superiors was one of the duties of a Family member. Silence was another cardinal duty. One had to learn to keep a secret and not betray one's friends. Also, for young men especially, one had to learn to curb one's desire toward the wives and women relatives of friends. Becoming a Family member, therefore, made one strictly accountable for one's actions, and it also required that one be ready, if necessary, to bear arms to protect the Family's interests.

Because of my heritage, I took all this for granted. I knew the ground rules even before they were explained to me, and I yearned for the day when I too would find distinction as a "man of honor."

At my private still my partners complained about receiving persistent calls from a strong-arm blockhead by the name of Mimi, who was trying to intimidate my partners into giving him a payoff. When he came by again, I was waiting for him. I could tell right away he was a dolt. He made animal-like noises and grunts, and heaved his body around the room like an obnoxious braggart.

I told Mimi he could shake down anyone else but to leave my business alone. He said I was in his territory. I said I was my own man.

—That's a lot of crap, answered Mimi.

I didn't seem to be getting through to the numbskull.

—I'm independent, I said. Now get out.

—You can't talk to me like that, Mimi bawled. I'm connected.

—All right, I won't talk.

I raised my hand in front of his head. I clenched my hand into a fist. Next I slowly lifted my thumb vertically and extended my index finger horizontally to represent the outline of a pistol. Mimi seemed fascinated. He didn't get my message right away. He was looking at me as if I were a magician about to pull the ace of spades out of my sleeve. I curled my index finger, my trigger finger. With my fist a few inches from his temple, I squeezed my finger rapidly six times. Mimi flinched back.

—Who the fuck do you think you are? he cried out.

Mimi blustered out of the building, issuing catcalls and curses and vowing that I would hear from him again.

Although I didn't know it at the time, Mimi was a member of the Castellammarese Family in Brooklyn, and he had apparently decided on his own to try to collect money from my still in exchange for protecting my operation. A still operator, as I said, usually needed such protection in order to survive; indeed, a still operator often sought such a connection for his own welfare. However, Mimi didn't know I too was connected to Maranzano, a member of his own Family.

If society is in good order, disagreements like that between Mimi and me do not have to lead to blows, as they might have in this case. These disputes can be resolved peacefully and according to custom. If I had been a nobody with no connections my argument with Mimi would have been left for us to settle on our own, but because I was with Maranzano and because I was a cousin of the powerful Stefano Magaddino of Buffalo, I was given the privilege of airing my case in "court." A hearing was convened before a panel of qualified men.

The arbitrator of the hearing was Vito Bonventre (not my uncle the baker but a second cousin of the same name). This Vito Bonventre was a group leader within the Family, and my still was in his district. Mimi's older brother, also a Family member, acted as his counsel for the "trial."

My counsel was to have been Stefano Magaddino, who kept

an active interest in the Castellammarese Family in Brooklyn. Although this trial was a relatively minor affair, Stefano had come from Buffalo to shower me with his benevolence. He was also trying to impress me with his influence and win my gratitude.

At the hearing, however, it was Maranzano who stole the show by speaking on my behalf. Maranzano berated Mimi for not bothering to check who I was before trying to bring my still under his protection. If Mimi had checked with his superiors he would have learned that I was with Maranzano and couldn't be interfered with.

In my world there was a distinction between what constitutes extortion and what does not. One must remember that in the economic sphere one of the objectives of a Family was to set up monopolies as far as it was possible. For instance, if a Family member owns a bakery all the other members tend to give him their patronage and support. If two Family members are bakers, they are not allowed to own bakeries on the same block, for that would be bad for both their businesses. They would be competing against each other. Therefore, one baker will be allowed to flourish in one territory and the other baker in his own territory.

If an outsider, a non-Family member, locates his bakery near a Family member's bakery, then the Family baker is within his rights to try to drive the competing baker out of business or to try to arrive at some accommodation with him. What is seen as extortion from the outsider is viewed as self-protection by the insider.

Unless one understands these monopolistic practices it is too easy, and erroneous, to simply ascribe them to criminal conduct. That Americans, of all people, don't fully appreciate this process shows a great blindness on their part. For a long time, for example, several American oil companies enjoyed a monopoly on Saudi Arabian oil whereby these companies set the price of oil and prevented other companies, French or British let's say, from enjoying the same privileges. In a sense, then, the cartel companies exercised their "extortion" options, all to the benefit of their customers, the American people, who paid a lower price for gasoline.

A skeptic will say that what the oil companies did was entirely different than what we did in our world, but I see them as similar, with the difference being that one is played in the arena of the neighborhood and one in the international arena.

Mimi, then, in wanting to maintain his sphere of influence, was wrong not so much in picking on me as in picking on the wrong man.

—Let's look at the facts, Maranzano said in my defense. The fact is that Peppino told Mimi to go to hell. If Peppino has the nerve to tell a guy like Mimi where to go, obviously Peppino doesn't need protection. The inescapable conclusion is that Peppino can protect himself. Logic is logic.

If I hadn't had the support of Stefano Magaddino and Maranzano I doubt if even Maranzano's droll mockery would have won the day for me. Since I did have their backing, however, the arbitrator ruled that Mimi had overreached himself and that I would be allowed to operate my own still unmolested by anyone in the Family. Mimi skulked out of the room, and he never gave me any more trouble.

If Stefano had hoped to impress me at the hearing, he was outclassed by Maranzano. Although Maranzano did not pose a challenge to Stefano, who knows what secret resentments Stefano began to form toward the newcomer to America?

Maranzano kept his opinion of Stefano to himself, but he did give me hints of how he felt. Once Maranzano told me cryptically that Stefano would someday give me trouble. I didn't understand. I didn't know the dark side of either Maranzano or Stefano yet.

Nonetheless, by the end of the hearing, Stefano knew, by Maranzano's vigorous defense of me and by my transparent admiration of him, that I was to be considered a disciple not of Magaddino but of Maranzano.

The mere fact that I was allowed to participate in a Family court—a singular privilege for a non-Family member—indicated the confidence these men had in me. I continued to serve Maranzano ably, and I felt the day when I would become a member growing closer, although no one expressly told me so.

One evening a friend of mine invited me to dinner at his house. He was about my age and also worked for Maranzano. On entering the house I saw many important men of the neighborhood and some I didn't recognize. We smiled at each other. One by one they embraced me and kissed me on the cheek.

Though they were all Sicilians, I had never particularly

connected these men with each other before, since they had different pursuits and came from different walks of life. That they should congregate in one room could only mean one thing—they were all members of the Family. Maranzano was among them, and the understanding smile between him and me gave me the greatest satisfaction.

It was understood then. I had passed my apprenticeship. I understood the covenants that binded us together. I was a Bonanno and I understood our Tradition thoroughly. Hardly anything had to be said. After a toast for good health, we sat down for dinner.

I was a member of the Castellammarese Family.

Mr. Labruzzo had given me his consent to call on his daughter Fay in the evening at her house. I also was permitted to take Fay on chaperoned dates on the weekend.

Fay was good-humored about these restrictions. She had an accommodating, generous disposition. Everything about her, her thoughts, her movements, her sentiments, was natural and spontaneous. A lively girl. A girl of loyal affections. Trusting.

Fanny and I both needed a good sense of humor, for throughout our courtship we were seldom left alone. At the beginning, we were always under the watchful eyes of her father. Suitors had to obey stringent house rules. Mr. Labruzzo's policy was that young men calling on his daughters couldn't stay at the house past eight o'clock in the evening. During my first house call, on a Sunday afternoon in 1928, Fanny whispered to me,

—What's worse is that Papa remains in the parlor the whole time and you can't talk about anything. When he starts to yawn, that's the signal to clear out.

—How would you like to take a ride in my sports car?

—Don't talk nonsense, Fay said. That's never been done before.

In the parlor, Mr. Labruzzo, contrary to his conduct with other suitors, greeted me exuberantly, as if I had come to see him instead of his daughter. This raised a few eyebrows among the women. Don Calorio had never acted this way before.

Mr. Labruzzo must have heard good things about me. But I did not want him to like me solely because of my recommendations. I wanted to establish a personal bond with him. I well remembered the advice of don Totò of Trapani, who had told me that if I wanted to win the daughter I would have to win the father as well.

—I trust you are in good health, I said to Mr. Labruzzo while the women prepared some refreshments. You look well, that's for sure. •

—You think so? Mr. Labruzzo said. You should have seen me before my heart attack.

—But that's in the past, don Calorio. Today you're healthy and fit. Today is a fine day.

—Fine day, Mr. Labruzzo repeated, jutting out his chin and nodding.

—It's such a lovely day, I said casually, that I drove here in my convertible.

—A convertible, you say?

—Yes, it's out front. Come look, you can see it from the window.

Mr. Labruzzo peered through the parlor window.

It was a sleek Buick roadster—a dandy, high-performance car, dark brown and cream, a two-seater, with a rumble seat over the trunk.

—That must have cost a fortune, Mr. Labruzzo remarked as he gaped at the sports car.

—Why don't we go outside to take a closer look?

The women were returning to the parlor, plates and trays in hand, just as Mr. Labruzzo and I were going out of the room, chattering about the car. Our chummy behavior absolutely floored the women. They quickly forsook their plates and trays to trail after us, but followed us no farther than the front porch, from where they observed the strange goings-on.

Mr. Labruzzo walked around the car, admiring its sleek lines. I invited him to sit behind the wheel. When he opened the car door, both of us were startled by wailings from the front porch.

—No, Papa, the Labruzzo children clamored. Don't do it, Papa. Remember your heart!

—Calogero, for heaven's sake, don't! screamed Mrs. Labruzzo.

They all evidently thought Mr. Labruzzo was going to take off for a drive by himself.

—Mari'Antonia—and all of you—shut up! Mr. Labruzzo shouted back.

I told Mr. Labruzzo that I would deem it a privilege if I could take him for a ride.

—In fact, I added, I came over this afternoon expressly to ask you and Fanny if you wanted to take a ride.

—Have you spoken of this to Fanny? he asked.

—No, I wanted to ask you first.

Mr. Labruzzo smiled gratefully.

—You did well.

Mr. Labruzzo shouted for someone to fetch him his jacket and ordered Fay to get ready to take a ride in the sports car. As I opened the rumble seat, Fay sidled over to me and asked:

—How are you two lovebirds doing?

—Trust me, I said, with a wink. I know what I'm doing.

We were interrupted by Mr. Labruzzo, who was trying to clamber into the rumble seat.

—You must sit up front, I said.

—I wouldn't think of it, Mr. Labruzzo said as I led him to the front passenger's seat.

—I wouldn't have it otherwise, I insisted.

Once he was snugly in place, Mr. Labruzzo bellowed to his wife:

—Mari'Antonia, see what a fine future son-in-law I have?

Now that they were assured he wouldn't be driving, Mr. Labruzzo's children and his wife seemed glad to see him off for the afternoon. They waved enthusiastically as we glided away in the Buick.

On passing any pedestrian whom he knew, Mr. Labruzzo would greet them with a regal flourish of the hand. At one point in our ride, he began to hum. I could feel a song coming on. Beneath his forbidding, blustery exterior, there was another side to Mr. Labruzzo. He was a man of unrestrained sentimentality, excessive in bliss as he was in anguish. When he was offended, don Calorio would explode in anger; when he was pleased, he would break out in song. He had a fine voice.

Sensing that he was in his musical mood, I told Mr. Labruzzo that I had access to tickets for concerts and operettas.

—I know how well you love good singing, I said. Perhaps you would do me the honor of allowing me to take you to an operetta some day?

Mr. Labruzzo turned his head back to address Fay.

—Are you listening? See what a fine son-in-law I'm going to have?

To the astonishment of his family, his son-in-law Jimmy in particular, Mr. Labruzzo did not chase me out of the house at eight o'clock when I called on Fay. Not only that, but he frequently invited me to stay over for supper. He would leave Fay and me in the parlor unattended, as long as the door was slightly ajar. He even allowed us to go to the moving-picture shows alone.

Fay gibed that her father and I were true sweethearts. Some two or three months after we were formally introduced, Fay and I became engaged. The wedding was set for 1929.

8

BOOTLEGGING WAS NO LONGER A FLEDGLING COTTAGE INDUS-
try. At first, the marketplace had been dominated by small,
independent still operators. Each competitor tried to gain the
advantage over the other; some grew bigger, some failed, some
were satisfied merely to hold their ground. By the last quarter
of the 1920s, consolidation began. The bigger firms gobbled
up the smaller ones. The intense competition brought about
mergers. The same thing happened in the bootlegging industry
as later happened in the food-retailing industry when large
supermarkets displaced small grocery stores.

In our Sicilian world, the A & P of bootleggers was Joe
Masseria, who was the head of his own Family.

In New York City, there were five Families, which had
formed spontaneously as Sicilian immigrants settled there. The
number five was not preordained; it just worked out that way.

The dominant Family was that of Joe Masseria. At one time
or another, this Family included Peter Morello, Charlie Luciano, Joe Adonis, Frank Costello and Augie Pisano, to mention
just a few.

The second major Family was headed by Al Mineo (his real
name in Italian was Manfredi), an avowed ally of Masseria's.
This clan included Tata Chiricho, Joe Traina, Vincent Mangano, Frank Scalise and Albert Anastasia.

These Families had interests both in Manhattan and Brooklyn. The Bronx, however, was the domain of the third Family,
that headed by Tom Reina. In this Family were such men as
Gaetano Gagliano, Tommy Lucchese and Steve Rondelli. Because of Masseria's power, Reina had to be careful not to offend

him, and he generally toed the Masseria line. But it was a relationship based on convenience rather than on likemindedness.

The fourth Family had interests in Brooklyn and, to an extent, in Staten Island. At the outbreak of the Castellammarese War, this Family was headed by Joe Profaci and his right-hand man, Joe Magliocco. Profaci's sympathies were with the Castellammarese, but his Family would never take part in the war directly. Maranzano urged Profaci to remain officially neutral and to act as an intermediary with other groups.

The fifth Family was the Castellammarese clan of Brooklyn and Manhattan.

Masseria was a Sicilian immigrant, but in America he was known as "the Boss." His English nickname was something new, and, in hindsight, it reflected the subtle changes already transforming our Tradition in America. The title "boss" represented a corruption of the title "Father." It's regrettable that in America the term "boss" became the more popular of the two. The terms are not interchangeable. "Father" describes a paternal, kinship-oriented relationship between a leader and his followers. "Boss" connotes a relationship between a master and his servants or his workers. The growing use of the word "boss" when referring to "Father" was one of the earliest indications that in America relationships between a leader and his followers had more of a business than a kinship base. The word "boss" represented a new reality.

Maranzano eschewed the word altogether. He had his own nickname for Masseria. He called him "the Chinese" because of Masseria's bloated cheeks, which, at a distance, made his eyes seem like narrow Oriental slits. Masseria was a squat, chubby man. Success had considerably widened his girth—as a younger man, he must have been leaner. In the early 1920s, he had engaged in several well-publicized street gunfights from which he had miraculously emerged unhurt. He gained a reputation as a man who could dodge bullets. More than once, Masseria escaped from close-range ambushes.

At the height of Prohibition, through a combination of intimidation, strong-arm tactics, bullying and tenacity, Masseria attained a dominant position in the Sicilian world of the Volcano. Masseria's Family was then the most powerful in New York.

Though he was known as "Joe the Boss," his insatiable appetite could have won him the nickname "Joe the Glutton." He attacked a plate of spaghetti as if he were a drooling mastiff. He had the table manners of a Hun. Some people eat a lot because they feel happy; others stuff themselves because they are nervous. Most people thought Masseria ate because he was content, but Maranzano believed Masseria was the nervous type of eater, an incomplete man inside—the glutton in him compelled to feed his belly as the bully in him was compelled to feed his ego.

Maranzano also believed that Masseria was the type of man who, under intense pressure, would get crazier and crazier and fatter and fatter.

—As long as he doesn't bother us, Maranzano would tell me when the subject came up, what do we care?

I couldn't help comparing my beloved Maranzano with the oaf Masseria. Masseria was vulgar, sloppy and puffy. Maranzano was refined, taut and intellectual.

As yet, Masseria had left the Castellammarese alone, although he had stretched his tentacles throughout the city. I'm sure that at least part of the reason Masseria hesitated to mess around with us was that we Castellammarese, in the face of oppression, were an intractable lot. In western Sicily, the men of Castellammare were renowned for their refusal to take guff from anybody.

To trace the origins of the Castellammarese War, one has to bring on stage Al Capone, the Neapolitan whose surname, in Italian, means a castrated male chicken.

Sicily and Naples, as well as the rest of southern Italy, used to be ruled by the Bourbon dynasty. This dominion was called the Kingdom of the Two Sicilies from 1815 to 1860. Nominally, the kingdom had twin capitals, Naples and Palermo, but the Bourbon kings mainly stayed in Naples. Sicilians believed all Neapolitans were rascals anyway and the reviled Bourbons might as well live among them.

In the New World, the numerous Sicilians soon began to dominate affairs among fellow Italian immigrants. Our superiority rested just as much on social structure as on numbers. Our clan system gave us great solidarity and afforded us advantages in our enterprises. Many outsiders tried to copy the

Sicilian ways, but since they didn't fully understand our Tradition, the result usually was a caricature. Neapolitans, for example, went in for loud clothes, roughhouse and maudlin outbursts of violence. The archetypical Sicilian, in contrast, is stoic, self-possessed and given to violence only to restore order, not out of display.

Whether it was desirable or not, the assimilation of Sicilians with non-Sicilians occurred freely in the melting pot of America. An example of this trend was Al Capone, a non-Sicilian who was accepted into our world but who was never representative of our Tradition.

Capone originally was from Brooklyn. He had gone to Chicago in the 1920s at the invitation of his close Neapolitan friend Johnny Torrio and with the consent of Frankie Yale of Brooklyn. Yale was a group leader in Masseria's Family, and it can be assumed that Capone's relocation to Chicago had the blessing of "Joe the Boss."

Capone, remembering where he got his start and where his support came from, must have passed along a fraction of his vast bootlegging revenues to Masseria.

Once he established himself in Chicago, Capone was at odds with the top Sicilian already in Chicago, Joe Aiello. In 1929, Joe Masseria went to Chicago at Aiello's invitation to hold a clarification parlay. They met in the basement of Aiello's house. Also in attendance was Gaspar Milazzo, the Castellammarese stalwart from Detroit. Milazzo was the godfather of Aiello's son, an indication of the close friendship between the two leaders. It was through Milazzo that the Castellammarese learned what happened at this meeting.

Aiello told Masseria that he considered Capone an intruder in his city. Masseria offered a typically stupid response. He offered to check the ambitious Capone in return for the rights to the east side of Chicago. Aiello would retain his sphere of influence over the west side of Chicago and everything west of the city.

Masseria was merely offering to exchange his direct presence in Chicago for Capone's. The bit about giving Aiello everything west of Chicago was ludicrous. Aiello had enough on his hands in Chicago. What would he want with Dubuque, or Sioux Falls?

Aiello blew up at Joe the Boss and told him to go back to

New York before it got unsafe for him in Chicago. The parlay was over.

In a dither, the fat man returned to New York and immediately spread the word that Joe Aiello was crazy and that he, Masseria, had narrowly escaped with his life. He encouraged the rumor that he had avoided assassination in Chicago. This was his pretext for seeking vindication.

Instead of curbing Capone, Masseria encouraged him to compete with Aiello. In the fight against Capone, Aiello teamed up with the Irish Bugs Moran clique. Such a Sicilian-Irish combination was a surrealistic turn of events possible only in America.

It was also said that Masseria, in his zeal to have Capone carry on the fight against Aiello at all costs, had promised to recognize Capone as Father of his own Family if he won. It was all too much.

Next, Masseria sought to deprive Aiello of his ally in Detroit. Masseria promised to split up the country with Gaspar—whatever that meant—if he would betray Aiello.

Masseria's plans shocked Gaspar Milazzo, who felt doubly insulted at Masseria's suggestion that he should betray his *compare* Aiello. After a conference in New York, Milazzo spurned Masseria's offer and returned to Detroit, keeping his good friend Stefano Magaddino of Buffalo abreast of developments.

Maranzano didn't like the way things were shaping up. According to Maranzano, Masseria was trying to force Milazzo to take sides not only to defeat Aiello, but also to drive a wedge among the Castellammarese—a prelude to subjugation.

Milazzo's rebuff must have rekindled all of Masseria's latent hatred for the recalcitrant Castellammarese. Arrogantly, Masseria demanded that both Gaspar Milazzo of Detroit and Stefano Magaddino of Buffalo come to see him in New York.

Gaspar and Stefano refused to kowtow to him, and this infuriated Masseria all the more. He vituperated against all Castellammarese, calling us unruly and thick-skulled.

Up to then, Masseria had been keeping his insults on the personal level. Now he was disparaging the honor of Castellammare itself.

Who did this fat man think he was?

* * *

Don Calorio Labruzzo was full of vim and spice when it came to protecting his interests.

He guarded his property like a badger. He also had six daughters to protect. And as if this wasn't enough, lately he had a basement still of his own to guard. Wishing to share in the cornucopia of Prohibition, Mr. Labruzzo had implored me to help him set up a modest still of his own. I obliged him and we became partners.

This association increased his estimation of me. He said I had the double virtue of making him happy and rich. Mr. Labruzzo treated me not only as his son-in-law but also as his confidant. He placed such extraordinary trust in me that even though I wasn't yet married to Fay, he deeded me all his property.

Through correspondence from relatives in Sicily, he came to suspect that someone was trying to swindle him out of property he owned on the island. On an impulse, which is how he usually did things, Mr. Labruzzo decided to go to Sicily and settle the matter personally, even if it involved bloodshed. Mr. Labruzzo eventually was talked out of this crusade before he departed. But while making secret preparations for his trip (he didn't want to alert his enemies of his mission), he drew up a new will, in which he stated that if anything should happen to him and if he should never return, all his property should be placed under my guardianship. Don Calorio did this because he knew I was strong enough to safeguard his property on his family's behalf and to take care of his interests.

When I received the papers from Mr. Labruzzo's accountant, I went directly to the Labruzzo home, seeking an explanation. Not finding don Calorio at home, I told the rest of the family what he had done. I showed them the document.

They were astonished and vexed. The children complained:

—Papa's crazy.

—Papa said when he dies I would get his property.

—You're not even our brother-in-law yet.

—Papa's really gone out of his mind this time.

I told them to quit their chattering and denunciations.

—At the moment I'm busy, I said, feigning indifference. You can all remain in your home for the present. But maybe one day I'll chase you out.

No one dared make a peep now. They gaped at me uneasily.

Then, as I had their full attention, I ripped up the papers in front of them.

—All this means, I said, referring to the will, is that your father would die for me and I would die for him.

After this incident, the Labruzzo family looked upon me as their protector—a man who could be counted on to rescue don Calorio from his own folly.

One day, hoping to catch the vandal who had damaged several mailboxes, don Calorio grabbed his blackthorn cane and hid behind the stairwell of his apartment building. Presently a teenager came along and began tampering with the mailboxes. Don Calorio sprang from his watchpost and cudgeled the vandal, gashing his skull.

—Go home, don Calorio shouted as the boy ran away, and tell your father he's a cuckold.

Don Calorio thought no more of the matter and went to the butcher shop in the same building. A little while later, he looked through the shop window and saw the vandal's father walking toward the shop. Don Calorio scurried down a tunnel—a maze of tunnels had been constructed under his building—and took an underground passage to his house next door.

As it happened, I entered his house moments later. I was there just for a social visit, not aware of his predicament. Don Calorio was very agitated and kept his hands behind his back.

—Peppino, he said, it's good to see you. You're the favorite of my heart. I would sell myself for you. But just at this moment you have to excuse me, for I must have a word with someone outside.

Mrs. Labruzzo came running into the room, carrying a shotgun and screaming:

—Don't pay any attention to him, Peppino. He wanted to take this shotgun with him, but I wouldn't let him have it. Please talk him out of it, Peppino, please!

—Never mind the shotgun, don Calorio scoffed. This will do.

And from behind his back he brandished a knife almost as long as his arm.

—He's crazy, his wife wailed.

Mrs. Labruzzo bawled out the entire story for my benefit. At the same time, like a background chorus, Mr. Labruzzo hurled invective after invective at the cuckold and at the cuckold's son and at the cuckold's wife and at all of the cuckold's relatives on both sides of the Atlantic.

Although the situation might seem ludicrous to an outsider, it was definitely possible that both don Calorio and the vandal's father might injure themselves willy-nilly.

—Sir, I told don Calorio, you insult me by wanting to go outside to deal with this man yourself. Now that I'm here, you should wait inside while I go outside to kill this cuckold for you.

I had given don Calorio the opportunity to back out of the confrontation without losing face. Mr. Labruzzo blessed me and, addressing his wife, said,

—Mari'Antonia, see the kind of son-in-law I have?

I had no intention of killing the vandal's father, but at least I had neutralized don Calorio. I went outside, followed by Mr. Labruzzo's son-in-law Jimmy. We learned that the vandal's father had entered the butcher shop, but on not finding Mr. Labruzzo there he had returned home.

We went to the man's house and knocked on his door. Finally, a woman opened the door. She looked very frightened of us.

—Where's your husband? I said. I understand he wants to see Calogero Labruzzo.

Before I could finish, the woman broke down in tears.

—No, please, don't hurt my husband. He didn't mean anything by it. He was just coming over to apologize to don Calorio for our son's shameful behavior. Please don't hurt him. He's a good father. He went over to apologize. You have to believe me. He wouldn't think of harming don Calorio!

—Enough! I ordered. You look like a sensible woman. I'm inclined to believe you. But to prove you're not lying, your husband must come before don Calorio himself.

The husband, a meek man, had hidden himself under his bed when the two strangers knocked on his door. At his wife's urging, he crawled from under the bed and came with us to the Labruzzo house.

On seeing the vandal's father, don Calorio shouted,

—Ah, cuckold, you dare show your face in my house?

The miserable man apologized for his son's vandalism and begged forgiveness from Mr. Labruzzo.

—You're a wretch, don Calorio said. It's my son-in-law

you have to thank for saving your life. If it was up to me, I would have cut your throat. But I'm satisfied and I forgive you.

Don Calorio called for wine and then, as if nothing had happened, he began to sing.

I had intended to get married sometime late in 1929. My choice for best man was Salvatore Maranzano. He graciously accepted, even though at one time he had asked me if I might be interested in marrying his daughter. I felt honored, but it was too late for me to reconsider. I was already too much in love with Fay to turn my back on her. And how could I possibly abandon the cantankerous don Calorio?

In light of the tense situation in our world, however, Maranzano urged me to delay my wedding date. He was right. It was no time to be getting married.

My work sometimes exposed me to hazardous situations. Sometimes I was in danger of my life; occasional showdowns were unavoidable. I accepted this risk. It didn't seem any different from the risk of violence that any "man of respect" in Sicily accepts as a matter of course. I was not frightened by the risk. If anything, it made me feel even more alive. During normal times, I didn't consider this risk of violence an obstacle to getting married or raising a family.

If war broke out, however, I didn't want to expose Fay or her family to danger, or myself to compromise. If war broke out and if I was married, my attention would be divided between Fay and the war. If it came to war, young men such as myself would bear the brunt of the fighting. I wanted to spare Fay the possibility of becoming a young widow or of having to take care of a maimed husband.

To be absolutely fair to Fay, I decided to give her the choice of either waiting for me, possibly for a long time, or of breaking off our engagement altogether. It was a difficult decision, for I loved her dearly.

After I told him of my precarious circumstances, Mr. Labruzzo said he was in favor of postponing the wedding, but he was adamantly opposed to breaking off the engagement.

—If I were a younger man I'd be right there with you on the front lines, he said.

Then he clasped me to his chest and said he loved me for wanting to spare his daughter possible heartache and suffering.

Still, it was up to Fay to have the final word.

—Don't you want to marry me? she asked after I explained the situation in private.

—It's because I love you that I'm giving you a chance to be free.

—You're my first love, she said.

—But I might get killed.

—Is what you do so dangerous?

Fay knew about my position with Maranzano, but didn't know all of it.

—I could get killed, I repeated. Do you understand?

—Yes. But I don't understand everything.

—I can't promise you anything, Fay. Not at this moment.

—You're my man.

—It's up to you to decide. If I should stay alive, then . . .

—I'll wait for you, of course, she interrupted. I'll wait for you. You're mine.

She sobbed as we kissed goodbye.

I wouldn't see her for another nine months.

Early in 1930, Gaspar Milazzo was assassinated in a Detroit fish market. The bereaved followers of Gaspar cried out for revenge.

In Chicago, fighting had already started between Capone and Aiello. Capone, Masseria's confederate, was getting the best of Aiello.

In Buffalo, Stefano Magaddino put his Family on alert. Masseria had invited Stefano to New York City for a clarification parlay concerning Milazzo's death. Stefano, suspecting a trap, refused.

In New York City, the biggest tinderbox of all, the air crackled with static electricity. A sense of foreboding gripped the Castellammarese in the city. We had no doubt that Masseria was responsible for Milazzo's slaying. But what could we do about it? Masseria was a formidable enemy. In terms of resources, manpower and allies, Masseria had a huge advantage over the scattered Castellammarese clans. He was Goliath and we were David.

In Brooklyn, the Castellammarese held a Family meeting.

The head of our Family was Cola Schiro, a compliant fellow with little backbone. Stefano Magaddino had used Schiro as a sort of puppet ruler in Brooklyn. During times of peace, Schiro was adequate. He appeased people, being extremely reluctant to ruffle anyone. He was well off monetarily and was getting on in years.

War frightened Cola Schiro. At our Family meeting, Schiro therefore spoke in favor of neutrality. He was all for temporizing.

Maranzano, with whom I attended the meeting, winced at Schiro's attitude. He had already told me he considered Milazzo's slaying as being tantamount to a declaration of war against all Castellammarese.

Maranzano had done his own investigation into Milazzo's death, and he was very interested in noting the reaction of Joe Parrino, who was in our Family. Joe's brother, Sasa Parrino, had left Brooklyn to join Milazzo's Family in Detroit. When Gaspar Milazzo was shot down in the Detroit fish store, Sasa Parrino was also killed with him. In the grisly language of assassinations, the double slaying could have been intended as an intimidating message both to the Castellammarese in Detroit and the Castellammarese in Brooklyn, since Sasa had been one of us.

And yet, at our Family meeting, Sasa's brother Joe didn't seem all that disturbed at his brother's death.

—What am I to think? Joe Parrino said. My brother's death was an accident. Sasa happened to be with Gaspar in the fish store and they both got shot.

After Parrino's statement, Maranzano took the floor for the first time. Before speaking he waited for absolute silence.

—I want to point out that according to my information Gaspar's body had five bullets in it.

Then Maranzano paused, looked around the room and let his gaze linger on Joe Parrino.

—But Sasa's body, Maranzano continued, had six bullets. It was no accident.

The meeting room awoke with commotion: buzzing of voices, fidgeting, coughing, oaths, murmurs.

—Silence, silence.

Maranzano's voice pealed sonorously through the hubbub.

—*E una sporca macchia sul' onore di Castellammare.*

It's a dirty spot on the honor of Castellammare, Maranzano said. It was as if he were sounding our battle cry.

With his pithy declaration that the honor of Castellammare had been violated, Maranzano performed the essential duty of a leader before battle: He inflamed us with the conviction that we were right and the enemy was wrong.

—What shall we do, don Turridru? Cola Schiro peeped, even though he was our leader.

—Why ask me? Maranzano replied. I'm just a soldier.

Maranzano was a pure warrior leader.

By this I don't mean that he was a war lover, but that he had the instincts and inspirational traits that you would want to have in a leader in time of war.

Maranzano knew what had to be done.

If you've ever been in battle, you know that in the face of danger most people take cover and wait to see what everybody else is doing. But one man, the pure warrior, knows what to do. He just does it. Everyone else on the battlefield looks at him and says,

—That man looks like he knows what he's doing.

Soon, everyone on the battlefield follows the natural leader, the pure warrior, him who has showed them what has to be done. And they follow this man regardless of his rank.

Maranzano also possessed an uncanny ability for always remaining alert. This trait is more remarkable than it sounds. War veterans know that the hardest part of war is not the actual fighting but the waiting. You spend a lot more time shuffling here and there in war than you do actually fighting. It's precisely during these tedious lulls that most soldiers entertain gloomy thoughts, lose their enthusiasm and come to the irrefutable conclusion that war is indeed hell. Everybody grouses, everybody wants to go to sleep. Only one man, the pure warrior, is off in the corner oiling his rifle, arranging his gear, darning his socks.

Everybody feels like going over to him and saying,

—Hey, what is it with you? Let up.

But in his heart everybody knows the pure warrior is right. The pure warrior is alert only to the present. And everybody starts cleaning his rifle.

Lastly, Maranzano believed in himself. Most people don't really believe in themselves. Everybody makes himself inconspicuous when the captain asks for volunteers for night patrol. But one man, the pure warrior, has already rubbed burnt cork on his face. He believes winning the war is his personal responsibility.

Maranzano quickly saw where the coming war was going to take place. In a war between the Castellammarese and the Masseria conglomerate, the main theater of action would be in Masseria's home field, in the capital, in New York, the Volcano.

And yet, the Castellammarese in New York City were not making any preparations.

With this in mind, Maranzano traveled to Buffalo to confer with Stefano Magaddino. He took me along to this meeting, as well as Gaspar DiGregorio, who, by this time, had also joined Maranzano's coterie.

My cousin Stefano looked careworn. With contemptuous bravado, Masseria had given Stefano a month to appear before him in New York. Masseria threatened to condemn Stefano if Stefano didn't show up.

—He actually uses the word "condemn," don Stefano, said Maranzano as he told my cousin the latest developments in New York City.

—Condemn me, will he? Stefano fulminated. I'd like to see him do that. Why doesn't Masseria come to see me in Buffalo? I'll take good care of him if he does. I'll blow his brains out.

—The fact remains, Maranzano said, that no one in New York is making any preparations.

—What about Schiro?

—Bah, Schiro, Maranzano answered disdainfully, as if to dismiss the need for further explanation.

—That's true, Stefano agreed. Schiro wouldn't be any good in this situation.

With Gaspar Milazzo's death, Stefano was the senior chief among the Castellammarese clans. As the standard-bearer, it was up to Stefano to do something in defense of all of us.

—We have Vito Bonventre in Brooklyn, Stefano said, referring to my second cousin, not my uncle the baker. But he's weak and loves his money too much. . . . We need someone to take charge in New York, all right.

Whatever reservations he might have about Maranzano (and already I suspected he was jealous of Maranzano), Stefano also recognized that for the greater good he had to submerge his personal feelings. For the present crisis, Maranzano obviously was the man of the hour.

As a result of this meeting, it was understood that Maranzano would spearhead the campaign against Masseria in New York. In essence, that made Maranzano the supreme commander in the New York theater of war. Since the Castellammarese in New York would do most of the fighting, it was also agreed that Detroit and Buffalo would supply Maranzano with money, arms, ammunition and manpower.

Maranzano had gone from being "just a soldier" to wartime commander-in-chief.

9

NO ONE IN NEW YORK AS YET KNEW THAT MARANZANO HAD committed himself to war against Masseria, not even the people in our Family in Brooklyn. People in Masseria's camp, meanwhile, were trying to persuade Maranzano to remain neutral. The other side had already singled out those Castellammarese who might give them special trouble. As a result, Maranzano was invited to a friendly meeting with Masseria himself and with Peter Morello, don Petru, the second most important man in Masseria's family.

Maranzano needed more time to prepare for war and to assemble an "army." He couldn't afford to defy Masseria just yet. If word got out that Maranzano was the designated war leader of the Castellammarese, Masseria could have moved swiftly against him before Maranzano could fortify himself. To stall for time, Maranzano decided to attend the meeting with Masseria and Morello.

When Maranzano informed his personal staff of his decision, we recognized what a big risk he was taking. Tête-à-têtes with "Joe the Boss" had a history of ending badly. The meeting could be a trap, in which case Maranzano would be going to his own execution. Even if it didn't come to that, Masseria and Morello might try to pin him down, force him to show his hand. Maranzano would need to be in total control of himself.

—Will you carry a gun? one of us asked.

—No, no guns, Maranzano said. But I am going to take along Peppino.

The others looked at me with a mixture of admiration and sorrow, as if to say,

—What a lucky bastard! What a dead stiff!

The announcement stunned me as much as anyone, because Maranzano hadn't discussed it with me beforehand. In a split second I thought I saw my whole life pass by. If it's my destiny to die, I resolved on the spot, then I'm ready. In the glow of that moment, I would have followed Maranzano to perdition.

Afterward, when Maranzano and I were alone, he said he was going to the Masseria meeting alone. He had announced I would be going with him to show the others how much faith he had in me.

—If something does happen to me, Maranzano said gravely, they'll know who my favorite is to lead them.

—Thank you, don Turridru, I stammered, I feel honored, but . . .

—But what? You don't have to come with me.

—But . . .

—But nothing. It might be dangerous.

—Please, don Turridru. Don't deny me the honor of being at your side no matter what happens.

Maranzano grabbed me forcefully by the shoulders and gave me a bear hug. Then he smiled, an arch smile. Now I understood his little charade. It was another one of his effortless lessons in leadership which I would store and use later in my own career as a leader. Maranzano knew he could order me to go with him, but he wanted to see if I wanted to go willingly.

The following day, the day of the meeting, I picked up Maranzano at his home, being extra sure I was on time. Maranzano always harped on punctuality. He didn't say anything to me in the house. I was starting the car when he finally spoke:

—*Andiamo e ritorniamo.*

Let's go and let's return.

At the meeting, which was held at a private house in uptown Manhattan, Masseria and Maranzano exchanged greetings in the Sicilian manner: cheek-to-cheek, one eye looking at the man and the other eye looking over the man's shoulder. They and Morello sat at a table by themselves, while I and a couple of Masseria bodyguards sat to the side. Espresso coffee was served, the steam spiraling out of the demitasse cups.

Masseria lit a big cigar. He was wearing an expensive-looking suit which nonetheless made a sloppy appearance on him. His belly protruded from under his half-opened vest. His collar was unbuttoned and his tie loosened. One of his shirt sleeves was buttoned on the wrong holes.

Puffing away on his fat cigar, Masseria made a few opening remarks. Maranzano never smoked, and I imagine he must have felt uncomfortable having to inhale all the smoke and hot air coming out of Masseria, who struggled through a rambling monologue, not being able to speak in either good English or good Sicilian. He touched on all sorts of things, but his salient observations were these: that Gaspar was dead and nothing could bring him back to life; that Stefano Magaddino was as good as dead if he didn't show up in New York; and that Salvatore Maranzano was alive and doing very well in business. Further into the matter Masseria did not care to go. He liked to keep things simple. As for the finer points of the discussion, Masseria said,

—Let don Petru talk for me.

Masseria sat back, yielding the floor to his second, Peter Morello. This Morello had a deformed right hand, from which he got his nickname, "the Clutch Hand." There was nothing of the buffoon about Morello. He had a parched, gaunt voice, a stone face and a claw.

Morello was Masseria's brain trust, his chief adviser and chief strategist. If was probably Morello who had advised Masseria to try to neutralize Maranzano. Morello, who was from the Sicilian town of Corleone, had known Maranzano when Maranzano lived in Palermo; he knew of Maranzano's reputation as a warrior.

—Thank you, Mr. Joe, Morello said, nodding slightly at Masseria, who grinned smugly.

Morello congratulated Maranzano, first of all, on his success in America. These repeated references to Maranzano's success were intended to point out that continued success would depend on whether Maranzano had the right friends. Then Morello said he wanted to clarify some recent events which Maranzano, being a Castellammarese, no doubt must be concerned about.

—The Milazzo slaying, Morello admitted, was from our part. We can't deny it.

But Morello accused Milazzo and Aiello of plotting to kill "Mr. Joe." And since Stefano Magaddino had refused to talk with Masseria, Morello continued, there was every reason to suppose don Stefano didn't like Mr. Joe either.

—Perhaps you, Morello told Maranzano, can go to don Stefano and put in a good word for Mr. Joe. Tell him to come see Mr. Joe. We just want to clarify everything, that's all.

Maranzano gave no indication of what he really thought of the suggestion.

—I'll see what I can do, Maranzano said coyly. But really, don Petru, I'm just a soldier in the House of Cola Schiro, as you know. I have no authority.

—Try, try, Masseria bellowed out of a cloud of smoke.

—Do try, don Turridru, Morello reiterated. Something must be done.

—It can't hurt to try, Maranzano said. But I can't promise anything.

—If something isn't done, Morello said, there might be bloodshed. And if there is fighting, I think the wisest course for an intelligent man such as yourself would be neutrality. On that we can all agree.

—We understand each other, Maranzano said.

The two had been treating each other gingerly and tactfully. Suddenly, Morello leaned closer to Maranzano and, dropping his voice to a lower pitch, said:

—If you're fooling us, your fight will be against me. In Sicily you never fought against anyone like Petru Morello.

Maranzano replied quickly in a calm, level voice:

—And you have never fought against anyone like Turridru Maranzano.

They stared at each other for an instant and then tried to smile, to make it appear they had only been kidding.

—What a bunch of comedians, you two, Masseria declared.

The meeting officially closed with the drinking of Marsala cordials.

Masseria heard no more from Maranzano, and when the deadline passed for Stefano Magaddino to go before Joe the Boss, Masseria threw a tantrum. Those stubborn Castellammarese had defied him again. He called us troublemaking rebels. Our informants told us Masseria had vowed to "eat those people like a sandwich."

Despite his failure to entice Magaddino into a meeting and

despite his failure to woo Maranzano, Masseria still held the advantage. His grand strategy, no doubt devised by Morello, had been successful so far. To subdue the already warring Castellammarese in Detroit, Masseria had given support to a non-Castellammarese leader, Cesare Lamare, and had urged him to set himself up as the new head of the Milazzo Family. In Chicago, Capone had emerged as the top man; the fighting there continued, but Aiello had not been seen for months. Masseria had not been able to stir dissension in the Magaddino Family; that Family remained intact. But Magaddino was safe as long as he remained in Buffalo. By isolating him in Buffalo, Masseria kept Magaddino away from the upcoming action in New York City.

Now it was time for Joe the Boss to assert himself in regard to the Castellammarese in Brooklyn. Masseria demanded and received a $10,000 tribute from Schiro. Morello must have been behind this move, for it reflected a deft touch. If Masseria had killed Schiro, his Family would surely have sought revenge. However, by intimidating Schiro, a timid man, Masseria stood to domineer us all.

After paying the money (buying his life), Schiro went into hiding. His disappearance disheartened the rank and file of our Family. He had left us without word, without explanation. What did it mean? Why should we fight when our own Father was not around to fight?

The Masseria people spread the word that the Castellammarese's own Father had abandoned them. Meanwhile, Maranzano, still busy preparing a strategy of his own, not only saw through the Schiro maneuver but also accurately predicted where Masseria would strike next.

It was Maranzano's theory that Petru Morello, whom he always gave credit for Masseria's moves, would next strike against the one among us who had the means to help finance a war against Masseria. Having disgraced our official leader, Maranzano thought, Morello would then want to eliminate one of our leading rich men. That would be Vito Bonventre, my second cousin, an affluent bootlegger. Next to Schiro, Bonventre was probably the most wealthy Castellammarese.

When Maranzano warned Bonventre to take precautions, Bonventre reacted skeptically. It must be remembered that Maranzano's scenario was just a theory; he didn't have any solid information to back it up. Also, although he had fought many battles in his younger days, Bonventre was at the stage in life when joining another fight seems more tiresome than glorious.

Bonventre wouldn't change his daily routine. His relatives also urged him to take a few simple precautions, just in case, but Bonventre would not listen. He said he was old and respected, that he had made many friends and that no one would dare touch him. He couldn't believe that Masseria would try to kill him.

Two days after Maranzano's warning, Vito Bonventre was shot down outside his home garage.

What must be appreciated is that war among civilians, such as I am describing, is ever so much more ambiguous and enigmatic than a war between nations. It was a more unnerving war in that you had to worry both about your enemy and about the police. You had to leave your family, you had to abandon your business and you had to put your life in danger—not a pleasant prospect for any man, least of all a rich and complacent gentleman. As in any war, it was mainly the young and unattached who did the fighting.

Without Schiro and Bonventre, our Family lacked its two most important pivots. Maranzano now had to step to the fore in order to avoid disintegration. He therefore called a Family meeting in Long Island. To discourage shirkers, Maranzano let it be known that all Castellammarese should attend, whether or not they were sick, old or on a stretcher.

At the meeting, Maranzano stressed that Masseria had made it clear that he wanted to eliminate or subdue not only our leaders but all Castellammarese.

—He has condemned all of us, Maranzano said. He wants to eat all of us like a sandwich. If you choose to stay out of the fight, it will gain you no safety. Masseria will only devour you in time. Masseria intends to subjugate us all. You can't make a separate peace with him. He is insatiable.

If Maranzano overstated Masseria's avarice, he did so to motivate and unify us. Like any good coach, he frightened us a little in order to make us bolder.

At the end of the speech, Maranzano suggested that we choose a commander for the upcoming fight. In one sense, Maranzano's suggestion was purely rhetorical. Schiro was gone,

Bonventre was dead. Who else would we turn to but Maranzano?

But the request was also a shrewd bit of diplomacy. Maranzano could easily have announced that he already had Magaddino's approval to be our war leader. But that wasn't Maranzano's way. He wanted to find out if we voluntarily wanted him as our war leader. He wanted us to take responsibility for making him our chief.

We held a vote. Few of us knew that Maranzano already had the blessing of the other Castellammarese clans. But we overwhelmingly voted for Maranzano in any case.

Before disbanding, Maranzano had a few words with each group leader individually. He had already thought out how each one of us could be helpful in the war. Each was asked to pledge his allegiance to the war in defense of our honor.

Maranzano was ready.

He shunned his home and office. No one, except those closest to him, knew where he would be from one day to the next. He designated several places, most in New York and one in Long Island, as "safe houses" where he and his personal staff would find shelter, food and supplies. No one knew ahead of time in which of these houses Maranzano would spend the night.

Maranzano divided his "army" into squads and designated a leader over each group. Each "soldier" pledged to totally obey his squad leader. Only these group leaders knew who the other group leaders were and their whereabouts.

He also established an extensive system of supplies. Some people were responsible only for supplying our hideouts with food and equipment. Others were responsible only for delivery of ammunition.

Maranzano and his personal staff rode in armored cars. These cars, two Cadillacs outfitted especially for us in Detroit, had special metal plates on the sides and bulletproof windows. Maranzano's Cadillac was always preceded by the other Cadillac. Sometimes a third car would ride behind his car, making it nearly impossible to ambush our leader.

If anyone was foolhardy enough to attack our vehicles, we were more than capable of defending ourselves. We carried pistols, shotguns, machine guns and enough ammunition to fight the Battle of Bull Run all over again.

Maranzano would sit in the back seat of his car with a machine gun mounted on a swivel between his legs. He also packed a Luger and a Colt, as well as his omnipresent dagger behind his back.

Just as the President of the United States has his Secret Service men, the King of England his palace guards and the Pope his Swiss guards, so did Maranzano have his personal bodyguards and staff.

We called ourselves "the boys of the first day" because we were with Maranzano from the start.

During the war, I acted as Maranzano's chief of staff. Needless to say, I didn't attain that position by being a spectator. I had to prove myself by undertaking dangerous missions. Most of the time, people had to go through me first before they could see Maranzano. Maranzano could entrust me with a diplomatic mission, in addition to entrusting me with military assignments. I rode in Maranzano's car, in the front passenger seat.

Maranzano's driver was Charlie DiBenedetto. Charlie had a quick mind and a fluent tongue. Born in America, he was the best English-speaker among us. If a policeman stopped our car for some reason, you could count on Charlie to talk his way out of it. Like the rest of us, Charlie could handle a gun without embarrassing himself.

The lead escort car would usually contain Gaspar Di-Gregorio, Bastiano Domingo and Vincent Danna. Gaspar was a deliberate and fussy soldier, almost the opposite of what he was in normal life. For example, before an engagement, Gaspar would usually take the longest of all of us in selecting a firing position. He would examine and reject several covers before finally choosing one that met his stringent standards concerning line of sight.

Gaspar's snail's pace would usually spur Bastiano to make some wisecrack:

—Whenever you're ready, Gasparino. Take your time. If the rest of us start without you, it doesn't mean we don't like you. . . .

Bastiano, or Buster, was the quickest to set up and the best shot among us. He could shoot from any angle and from any direction. His specialty was the machine gun, with which he was a virtuoso.

Vincent we referred to as "Doctor." He and I had been school cronies in Castellammare, where Vincent's father was a pharmacist and his uncle was a doctor. Medical know-how seemed to run in the family. Vincent acted as a sort of medic for us, in addition to being a sharpshooter.

We also had a sixth musketeer among us, Joe Stabile. Joe owned one of the homes we used as a safe house. A sharpshooter extraordinaire, Joe volunteered for many missions. We were all tall, except for Joe, who was short. Once during the pandemonium of a street brawl in which he took part, Joe escaped arrest by crawling between the legs of a cop.

To keep track of enemy movements, Maranzano utilized taxi drivers, among whom he had many friends. Hacks roam the streets at all hours. They make excellent spies.

Within our Family, only a minority were combatants. The majority were noncombatants such as bakers, butchers, undertakers, masons, doctors, lawyers and priests. They all pitched in, helping us out with their special skills. We all saw nothing wrong in us Sicilians settling our differences among ourselves.

In order to chip away at Masseria's support in New York City and elsewhere, Maranzano would stress that the war was not only to defend the honor of Castellammare but also to free everyone else from servitude and slavery to Masseria.

Maranzano's challenge to Masseria soon had its effect on the fence straddlers. In private, Tom Reina of the Bronx expressed admiration for Maranzano, the only one who had the guts to stand up to Joe the Boss. An informant within Reina's Family relayed these sentiments to Reina's *paesano* from Corleone, Peter Morello. And Morello reported it to Masseria.

Early in 1930, Tom Reina was shot to death in the Bronx. As he had done in Detroit, Masseria quickly backed one of his own supporters to take charge of the Family. In this case, Masseria endorsed Joe Pinzolo to become the new Father. In the meantime, Gaetano Gagliano, a member of the Reina Family, formed a splinter group within the Family in open opposition to Masseria and Pinzolo. Gagliano's group attracted Tommy Lucchese, Steve Rondelli, John DiCaro and others.

At the same time that Maranzano was trying to draw defectors from Masseria's side, he also had to extirpate quislings within our own Family.

After Cola Schiro went into hiding, Masseria had supported Joe Parrino to become the new Father of the Castellammarese clan. That tactic failed when we elected Maranzano as our leader. Parrino was a despicable sort. For a chance at becoming Father, Parrino was willing to serve a tyrant. He was also willing to overlook the slaying of his brother, who was shot with Gaspar Milazzo in Detroit. Joe Parrino was shot to death in a restaurant.

The inability of Masseria to gain a foothold in the Castellammarese Family in Brooklyn and the erosion of his influence in the Reina Family were minor setbacks. Masseria still reigned supreme. His chief adviser, Morello, felt so safe that he openly went to his office every morning. The Castellammarese were thought to be in disarray and on the defensive. No one expected them to strike.

Maranzano used to say that if we hoped to win the war we should get at Morello before the old fox stopped following his daily routines, as Maranzano had already stopped doing. Once Morello went undercover, Maranzano would say, the old man could exist forever on a diet of hard bread, cheese and onions. We would never find him.

Morello never got a chance to go on such a severe diet. He went to his Harlem office as usual one morning, along with two of his men. All three were shot to death.

Masseria had lost his best man, the brains of his outfit. "The Clutch Hand" was gone.

At the outbreak of the war, Maranzano had sent Al Capone a message warning him not to meddle directly in the New York conflict. Although Capone had supplied Masseria with money, Capone was too busy fighting Aiello and his supporters to do anything else. Until the end of summer in 1930, therefore, Capone had not sent any reinforcements to Masseria.

After Morello's death, however, Masseria leaned on his allies all the more. In exchange for Capone's more direct help, Masseria went ahead and accepted Capone, the Neapolitan, into our Sicilian orbit.

In September of 1930, Maranzano received a tip that some of Capone's people were to arrive in New York, perhaps as many as a dozen men, reinforcements for Masseria. They were supposed to rendezvous in an office building on Manhattan's Park Row. We didn't know how reliable the information was, but just to play safe Maranzano prepared a welcome for Capone's men.

The rendezvous was supposed to be held in a spacious office room. A locked door separated this large room from a smaller adjacent room. Maranzano's plan was for me, Bastiano Domingo and Charlie DiBenedetto to hide in the small room and wait for our out-of-town visitors. At the proper time, we were to kick down the door and welcome everyone to the Volcano. We loosened the door hinges ahead of time.

For this mission we needed "fresh" machine guns—weapons that could be abandoned on the spot and not traced to any of us individually.

On the day of the ambush, Charlie went to pick up the machine guns. I waited for him in the park in front of City Hall, which borders Park Row. City Hall is located just about at the entrance to the Manhattan side of the Brooklyn Bridge. After picking up the weapons, Charlie was supposed to pick me up. Buster was going to meet us outside the Park Row building.

It was a Thursday. I remember that because every Thursday a band would play on the park pavilion in front of City Hall. I listened to the band that pleasant afternoon, idly watching the office workers and strollers.

It had been almost a year since the Wall Street stock market crash. The economic boom of the 1920s was over. Prohibition itself had but a short time to run. Franklin Roosevelt was governor of New York and being mentioned as a Democratic candidate to run against President Herbert Hoover. I supposed most people were worried about the hard times ahead.

Uppermost on my mind, however, besides my immediate mission, was winning the war and getting back to my sweetheart, Fay Labruzzo. After not having seen her for nine months, I had impetuously gone to her house late one night. I told Fanny how much I had thought of her and declared she had grown lovelier during my absence. Her father wanted to hear all the news about the war. Don Calorio said he would like to meet Maranzano one day. I couldn't take a chance on staying very long. . . .

I abandoned my reveries when I saw Charlie's car pull up to the curb. I dashed to the car, but I had barely opened the door and sat down when I heard the bark of policemen:

—Hold it, you two. You're under arrest.

Since I didn't have a gun permit, the first thing I did was take my pistol off me and stash it under the seat. When I looked up, police detectives had us surrounded.

Buster watched the arrest from across the street but was helpless.

The detectives, as I later found out, were homicide investigators working on a machine-gun slaying unrelated to the Castellammarese War. In the course of their investigation, they had staked out a suspected machine-gun supplier. By coincidence, this was the same man who was getting us our machine guns from Detroit. When the police saw Charlie's car entering and leaving the building, they followed the car to Park Row. When I got in the car, they decided to apprehend both of us. They thought they had stumbled on a lucky break, but they didn't know who we were or what the machine guns were for.

Charlie and I were driven a short distance to New York City police headquarters on Centre Street. Inside the car, police found one pistol, three machine guns and about six hundred rounds of ammunition. At my preliminary interrogation, I told the police that I was listening to the band music at the park on my day off from work. I was about to take the trolley car across the bridge to Brooklyn when I saw my friend Charlie and decided to catch a ride with him.

I was then left alone in a room for about half an hour. Charlie and I had been segregated and I didn't know what was happening to him. I couldn't imagine how the police had found out about the machine guns. Had someone snitched on us? What were the police after? I was in the dark and totally on my own.

Presently, two tall and hefty detectives came in my room and began taunting me:

—Oh, so you're the guy with the machine guns.

I didn't say anything. Without warning and with no trace of emotion, the two policemen began working me over. They punched me, kicked me, kneed my head and threw me on the floor. They struck me repeatedly until I was nearly unconscious. Then they raised me from the floor and flopped my bruised body on the chair next to the solitary table in the room. They left.

Two other detectives entered shortly thereafter. One of them said,

—What's happened here?

He took off my jacket and used it to wipe my blood off the floor. I started to mumble a reply when his colleague grabbed the chair from under me and crashed it across my shoulders and neck. I passed out.

It must have been around midnight when I received my next visit. This time, three detectives entered the room. Two of them didn't say anything. The third did all the talking. He wore eyeglasses.

—I just came on duty, he said, and I'm sorry for what happened. It's not right. If I was here this wouldn't have happened.

He identified himself as a captain. He had a suave, even-tempered manner.

—How do you feel? You want anything?

It hurt to talk. I shook my head sideways, my lips curling derisively.

—It's my duty to question you, the captain with the eyeglasses continued. What I want to know first is your name. What's your name?

—Joseph Bonanno.

—What work do you do?

—I'm learning how to be a barber.

—And where do you live?

—4009 Church Avenue, Brooklyn.

—What's your name?

—Joseph Bonanno.

—You're lying.

—I'm telling the truth.

—So why do you have two names?

The captain was referring to the two licenses I carried. One was my driver's license, which was under the name of Joseph Bonanno. When I went to work for my Uncle Vito Bonventre, the baker, I took out a chauffeur's license because I had to drive trucks. The chauffeur's license was under the name Giuseppe Bonventre. The name Bonanno didn't mean anything to the police. However, my distant cousin Vito Bonventre (with the same name as my uncle the baker) was known to the police as a "mafioso" and a leader of the Castellammarese clan in Brooklyn. Since his death was publicized, police also knew that Vito Bonventre had been slain in what they described as gang warfare. The police figured that I was a Bonventre and that Bonanno was an alias. If my name was Bonventre, as they thought, they assumed that I also was mixed up with gang warfare and I could provide the police with valuable information. In nabbing me and Charlie, the police thought they had found a way into the maze of Sicilian warfare current in New York. It seemed like a big break for them.

—My name is Joseph Bonanno.

The Captain looked down on me dubiously. Unknown to me, while I had been unconscious, police had questioned my Uncle Peter Bonventre, whose address, 4009 Church Avenue, was on my driver's license. Before the war my uncle and I had agreed that if anyone ever asked him who I was he should say I was his apprentice barber.

—What's your uncle's name? the detective said.

—Bonventre.

—Then your name is Bonventre.

—My name is Joseph Bonanno.

The captain said he wanted to help but that my replies were beginning to agitate him.

—How can I help you if you don't cooperate? he said. Don't you realize you could go to prison for a good long time?

The telephone rang. Its shrill jingling seemed to irritate every nerve in my body. The captain answered and mainly listened to the person at the other end. Periodically, the captain would alternately say,

—Ah huh. . . . Right. . . . Ah huh. . . . I see.

He hung up and turned to me.

—You know what that was about? the captain said. That was about your friend Charlie. He's a nice boy, that Charlie. He's going to tell us . . . everything.

The captain circled me, giving me time to absorb this information. Although I didn't know how Charlie was being treated, I had to believe that Charlie was not going to betray me, just as he had to have faith I wouldn't betray him. Silence and trust were virtues inculcated into us by our Tradition. And yet, since we were both young, we had never really been tested. Would we live up to our principles under actual duress?

As it turned out, Charlie was undergoing a somewhat easier test of his manhood than I was. While I was being pummeled unconscious, Charlie was leading police on a wild goose chase.

Charlie, the glib musketeer, had told police he was from Buffalo on a visit to New York City. A friend of his in Brooklyn, Charlie told police, had lent him his car for the day. Charlie said he drove the car to Manhattan, went sightseeing and paid quick visits to several places, including the building being observed by the police. On the way back to Brooklyn, Charlie told police, he noticed a friend in the park at City Hall and stopped to give him a ride.

Charlie swore he didn't know anything about the machine guns that police had found wrapped in a blanket on the floor by the back seat. Those guns must have been there all along. Charlie said when he picked up the car he hadn't even looked at the back seat. The first time he saw the guns, Charlie told the police, was when the police searched the car.

Why don't we go to your friend in Brooklyn? the police told Charlie. Okay, Charlie replied, anything to please the police.

Once they drove to Brooklyn, Charlie pretended to be lost. He said all the apartment buildings in Brooklyn looked alike. And the streets in Brooklyn were confusing. After all, he was from Buffalo. On and on they drove, and around and around, never finding their destination.

I didn't find out about Charlie's escapades until later, of course. At the time, the captain wanted me to think that Charlie was cooperating with the police. The captain even received a second call about Charlie.

—That was from the Empire Street station, the captain said after the second call. Charlie's taking us to see his friend in Brooklyn. Charlie's a real nice boy. He doesn't want to spend his life in prison. You know what Charlie told us? He told us you know everything. You see, you're ruined.

—I'm tired, captain, I said in my first voluntary statement of the night. I want to say this one last time. My name is Joseph Bonanno, my address is 4009 Church Avenue . . .

Before I could continue the captain mimicked me, saying,

—4009 Church Avenue. 4009 Church Avenue. From now on I'm going to call you Mr. 4009.

The captain began pacing. I was weary and becoming defiant. He was weary and reaching the threshold of his patience. His face looked sterner. Time for him to drop the nice-guy pose. In an angry, loud voice, the captain said:

—Charlie's going to go free and you're going to jail. Do you hear me? We're going to send you away!

I didn't answer, having decided to ignore him from then on. But the captain made it difficult to do that. He suddenly took out his gun and pointed it directly in front of my lips.

The man was bluffing, but a nervous twitch of his finger and it would have been all over for me.

—Are you going to talk? the captain demanded, putting the tip of his pistol in my ear.

I had now reached the point where I almost didn't care what happened as long as these police stopped tormenting me. If I was going to die, I told myself, I was going to die without giving my captors any satisfaction.

—Go ahead, I shouted, shoot.

He slammed the butt of his revolver on my nose. On impact, my nose felt as if it were flying across the room while my face was trying to pull it back. My rage made me forget everything but retaliation. I struck with my fist, landing flush in the captain's eye. The lens of his eyeglasses shattered and blood oozed out of his eye socket. After my fist landed, my leg instinctively shot up and I kicked him in the groin.

That's all I remember. The other detectives in the room grabbed me. Everything went black.

In the morning, a lawyer hired by Maranzano came to police headquarters and arranged for Charlie and me to be released on bond. But we had to appear later that same day before a magistrate for a hearing.

Charlie briefly took me to a hospital to have my wounds checked. My face was puffy and bluish. My broken nose canted to the left.

Our lawyer swore up and down that the police would not get away with it. He said we would have our retribution in court. This sort of thing isn't supposed to happen in America, he assured us.

The late morning papers had already printed a story about our arrest. In the articles, I was identified as Joseph Bonventre, alias Joseph Bonanno. Police had told reporters I was suspected of being a machine-gun runner for Al Capone. At that time, because of all the publicity he had received, the public automatically associated machine guns with Al Capone. The allegation that I worked for Al Capone seemed plausible both to the police and to the naive reporters.

To this day, whenever newspapermen search for something to say about me during Prohibition, they refer to me as a gun runner for Al Capone. And although I've just now explained how this error originated—a ludicrous mistake considering that during the Castellammarese War Al Capone was on the *other* side—I'm certain that long after I'm dead reporters will continue to refer to me as a gun runner for Al Capone.

When Charlie and I showed up at the courtroom later that day, I noticed the captain had a black eye and a bandage over his eyebrow. I recognized several other detectives in the courtroom. They all looked serious but slightly disoriented, as if it was the morning after a night of revelry.

Our lawyer wasted no time in telling the judge that during my detainment the night before, the police had assaulted me.

—Tell the court how this happened, the judge instructed me.

—Your Honor, my lawyer doesn't know the true story. He thinks I was beaten. But what actually happened was that while I was being booked last night I accidentally fell down the stairwell and broke my nose.

The magistrate scowled and snuffled.

I never had any intentions of accusing the detectives in court. It wasn't in me to squeal on anyone, not even a cop. What good would it have done anyway? I think everyone in the courtroom realized I was prevaricating.

After my statement, the prosecution huddled and then the state attorneys had a few words with the detectives. By holding my tongue, I let the prosecution off the hook. Theirs was a weak case to begin with. Instead of a celebrity case, they were stuck with two unknowns, me and Charlie. When they understood I wasn't going to make any trouble for them, they realized my silence was contingent upon them not making trouble for

Charlie and me. The prosecutor told the judge he wasn't ready to press charges against us.

This unexpected twist made the magistrate very grumpy. He said we were all wasting his time. He told me he didn't believe my story but there was nothing he could do if I didn't speak up. He was forced to dismiss the case.

This ordeal at the hands of the police was one of my proudest moments. I had remained silent in the face of physical danger. I had not betrayed my friends. I had proven to myself that I would not break under pressure.

What's more, because the newspaper accounts referred to me as a gun runner for Al Capone, everyone in my world knew without doubt that I had kept my mouth shut.

My friends, my relatives, and, most important of all, Maranzano praised my valor. I had lived up to the principles of my Tradition. Charlie DiBenedetto also received praise, but it was fainter than mine. After all, I was the one who got the lumps. Charlie didn't even get scratched.

—One of these days, I would tease Charlie, I'm going to give you the beating you missed.

Charlie called me that "one and only notorious gun runner for Al Capone, Joseph Bonventre."

—You expect anyone to believe your real name is Bonanno? Charlie would say. If I had a name like that, I'd change it too.

He would kid me constantly about my broken nose. He would stare at it, reflect and then say,

—I don't know, Peppino. Maybe I should hit your nose from the other side to make it look even.

Indeed, even after it healed, my nose made me look like a pug, and in 1937 I underwent an operation to straighten it out a bit.

Maranzano rewarded Charlie and me with a little rest and recuperation. He had us check into a private sanatorium in Long Island, where we shared a room. Charlie and I were under orders to behave and to enjoy our vacation. The sanatorium food was lousy, lacking all tang or zest. That's what I remember most about the place. Our therapy, such as it was, consisted mainly of alcohol rubdowns administered by young female attendants.

10

MARANZANO WANTED TO ACHIEVE A BREAKTHROUGH IN THE war before Christmas of 1930.

After the death of Peter Morello, Masseria went into hiding. Even Joe the Boss himself had to worry about his safety. Nothing had gone right for him lately. He had lost Morello, and this was followed by the loss of Joe Pinzolo, the man Masseria had supported to head the Reina Family after the slaying of Tom Reina. People within the Reina Family eliminated Pinzolo. The Reina Family could no longer be counted on to aid Masseria. After Pinzolo's death, the leading members in that Family were Gagliano, Lucchese and Rondelli.

At this stage of the war, Masseria used Al Mineo as his chief strategist. Mineo was the head of his own Family and was Masseria's closest ally among the Sicilian clans in New York.

Part of Mineo's strategy was to keep Masseria as inconspicuous as possible. By this time Joe the Boss had lost his personal effectiveness. He had made too many false moves, sought too many needless confrontations and offended too many people. But although his personal stature had diminished, Masseria was important as a figurehead, as a symbol for that coalition of interests that would suffer if Joe the Boss lost the war.

The other part of Mineo's strategy was to get at Maranzano directly. Up to then, Masseria had tried to isolate the Castellammarese from the other Families and had tried to sow disunity among the Castellammarese. With the advent of Mineo as Masseria's war adviser, the strategy was simply to eliminate

Maranzano, since it was obvious he was the one man the Castellammarese could not do without.

The war now became a race between Masseria and Maranzano to see who would knock off the other one first.

At our safe houses Maranzano usually had a room and bed all for himself, while the rest of us shared sleeping accommodations. One night, at one of our smaller houses, there were not enough beds for all of us and so I slumped in a chair. I had nearly dropped off to sleep when Maranzano noticed me.

—Tomorrow there's a lot of work to do, he said. Tonight you're going to sleep with me.

He took me to his room, but I couldn't fall asleep right away. I watched Maranzano loading shotgun cartridges. I watched him weigh the black gunpowder on a small scale and fill the cartridges with pellets. Maranzano eschewed store-bought shotgun shells—he liked to prepare them himself. He did it the last thing every night, before turning in.

He performed the loading of the shotgun shells as if it were a sacred ritual, with great precision, even elegance. It had been almost a year since we had gone to war, and yet Maranzano's fervor had not abated. The single-minded intensity of the man was uncanny; it frightened you a little. As I observed him, I wondered if this man had a weakness, a flaw like the rest of us. Did he have moments when he completely lost control of himself? Did he suffer from obsessions or illusions? Was it possible for him to break? Or was he superhuman?

I said nothing. Sitting on the bed, watching him fill the cartridges, I became entranced with Maranzano, who concentrated totally on what he was doing. Then, without looking up at me, he began a hushed monologue. There was a trace of reverence in his voice as if he were reciting his creed.

—To kill a rabbit, to kill a deer, to kill even a bear is simple. You aim steady and you shoot. But man is the hardest animal to kill. When you aim at a man, your hands shake, your eyes twitch, your heart flutters, your mind interferes. Man is the hardest animal to kill. If possible you should always touch the body with your gun to make sure the man is dead. Man is the hardest animal to kill. If he gets away he will come back to kill you.

I had heard bits and pieces of Maranzano's admonition before, but never with such a tone of finality. He didn't say anything else after that. I lay down on the bed, watching him load cartridges by lamplight until I dozed off. Sometime during the night I got up to go to the bathroom. Everyone was sleeping. Shuffling past the living room, I saw a light and, on adjusting my eyes, I focused on Maranzano sitting on a chair and cleaning a gun. Around him, on the floor, lay a dozen other weapons. Maranzano was cleaning and oiling all the guns. He looked content, in his element. He looked up when he heard me, and in a low, sardonic voice, Maranzano said,

—We're going to stick it to them up the ass.

A lucky break occurred for us in late October 1930.

Masseria had been seen entering an apartment building in the Bronx.

The tip had come from Tommy Lucchese, the second leading member of the Reina Family, second only to Gaetano Gagliano. Lucchese, like almost everyone else involved in the war, had recruited fresh soldiers. One of these recruits was Joe Valachi, a man outside our Tradition. It was Valachi, I believe, who had actually spotted Masseria going into the Bronx building. Lucchese then relayed the information to Maranzano.

I must digress briefly here to say a few words about Valachi, because in the public mind he has assumed a role way out of proportion to the actual part he played in the war. The American public first heard of Valachi in the early 1960s when he appeared before the McClellan Committee of the U.S. Senate. What the public and the police know about the Castellammarese War is still largely based on what Valachi told them. This has resulted in a great deal of distortion. Valachi did not see the entire picture and he was an unreliable interpreter of events.

For instance, Valachi identified Joe Profaci as being one of Maranzano's sharpshooters. In fact, Profaci was the Father of his own Family. Profaci did not actively fight in the war, and if he had he certainly wouldn't have been a sharpshooter, which is a task for a soldier, not a general. After the war, Profaci became a good friend of mine. He told me he had never met Valachi in his life. Obviously, Valachi was confused or was trying to embroider the truth.

Valachi also identified me as being his "godfather." I never met or talked to this guy, either. How could I be his "godfather"?

Valachi also talked about a certain "Buster of Chicago," and I gather he must have been talking about Bastiano Domingo. But Valachi describes Buster as being six feet and weighing two hundred pounds. In fact, Buster was a very thin man. If he weighed two hundred pounds, he had to be wearing three fur coats, all of them dripping wet.

I don't want to belabor the point. Valachi, as an observer, often claimed more than he knew. The fact was that he was a newcomer, performing a low-level job. Most important, Valachi was a stranger to our Tradition. He was a petty thief who had served time in prison. He was recruited because the war demanded fresh bodies, new faces. Many of these new recruits were non-Sicilians like Valachi, whose parents, I believe, were from the Naples region. In the long run, this assimilation proved debilitating. These people, the newcomers, the non-Sicilians, were not born into our culture. It was not something they had absorbed over a lifetime. They had to be instructed about our Tradition. To expect Valachi to act as a reliable guide to our Tradition, as the police, the press and politicians did, was like asking a new convert to Catholicism in New Guinea to explain the inner workings of Vatican City.

To get back to our story, after he was recruited into Lucchese's group, Valachi's main job was to rent an apartment across the street from an apartment building in which lived Steve Ferrigno, a henchman of Al Mineo's. The surveillance of Mineo's lieutenant paid off in an unexpected way. One day, either Valachi or Dominick Petrilli, another of Lucchese's men, spotted none other than Joe the Boss Masseria entering Ferrigno's building.

When word of this reached Maranzano, he sent three of his musketeers to the Bronx and they rented another apartment across the courtyard from Ferrigno's building. They waited in ambush, expecting Masseria to come out sooner or later.

The detection of Masseria, who had been in hiding for months, was a timely break for our side. Just about this time, the Castellammarese side lost Joe Aiello of Chicago. Earlier in the year, to escape harm from Al Capone, Aiello had sought and had been given refuge in Buffalo by Stefano Magaddino. However, against the advice of Magaddino and Maranzano,

Aiello didn't remain in Buffalo but returned to Chicago. Shortly after he returned there, Aiello was shot to death. Capone's chief rival had been eliminated, and Capone—a Masseria man—had Chicago to himself. That meant trouble for us if the war continued a long time. It made the deadly mission in the Bronx all the more imperative.

The wait lasted days and days, stretching into weeks. Still, no sign of Masseria. Had he left the building through a secret passage? Had he fled during the night? The sharpshooters waited. Then, just as it seemed Masseria had given everyone the slip, Mineo was seen entering the apartment building. That indicated Masseria might still be there.

One morning, shortly after daybreak, several men came out of the building, including Ferrigno and Mineo. Masseria was not among them. Maranzano had already decided that if Masseria eluded our ambush, the sharpshooters were to at least fire on Ferrigno and Mineo. The sharpshooters did their job.

Afterward it was learned that Masseria indeed was still inside the building but had delayed coming out that morning for some unknown reason. Masseria's personal luck was still holding out. Nonetheless, the death of Mineo was a crippling blow.

The ambush gave Maranzano the decisive breakthrough he had sought. Joe the Boss had a limited number of meals left to eat in this life.

We celebrated our latest victory, and the end of another year, with a week-long party around Christmastime at a farm in upstate New York, near Hyde Park. In addition to Maranzano and his personal staff, the party was attended by Stefano Magaddino and some of his men from Buffalo; by Joe Zerilli and some of his men from Detroit; by Gaetano Gagliano, together with Lucchese and some of his men from the Bronx; by other leaders from Brooklyn; and even by some early defectors from the Mineo Family, such as Frank Scalise and Joe Traina.

From Detroit we heard that the man whom Masseria had backed to lead the former Milazzo Family, Cesare Lamare, was no longer among the living. The situation in Buffalo had remained stable, with the people there remaining solidly behind Magaddino. In Chicago, although we had lost an ally in Joe Aiello, it didn't seem likely that Capone would seek a protracted fight with the Castellammarese in light of Masseria's waning fortunes.

In New York City, it was a particularly tense time for people in the Mineo Family, which in terms of numbers was the largest in the city. Frank Scalise had been among the first to defect from that Family and openly to embrace Maranzano's cause. Another defector, although he came later, was Vincent Mangano, an old-fashioned gentleman who had established himself on the Brooklyn waterfront.

Another member of the Mineo Family who was to join our side was Carlo Gambino, at that time a low-ranking member. Before he defected, Gambino had drawn the ire of Tommy Lucchese—for what reason I don't know. An attempt was made on Gambino's life, but the gunman mistook Carlo's look-alike brother for his target and shot the wrong man. Carlo's brother partially lost his ear but didn't die. Ironically, after the war, Carlo Gambino and Tommy Lucchese became good friends and their children intermarried.

With the Mineo Family splintered, Masseria grew more dependent on Charlie "Lucky" Luciano, the only group leader in Masseria's own Family who had the resources and the brains to salvage him. I didn't know much about Luciano, who up to then had operated independently with his associate Meyer Lansky, and was absorbed by Masseria into his Family. At first, Luciano had mainly contributed his business acumen to Masseria; consequently, Luciano was untouched by the war during its initial stages. As far as I know, Luciano didn't become a significant factor until the very end of the war.

Early in 1931, Maranzano let it be known through various intermediaries that he would not seek vengeance on Masseria supporters or soldiers once Masseria was eliminated. In other words, Maranzano was telling the other side that the quickest way to end the war and save their lives was to take care of Masseria themselves. Masseria, it must be remembered, was hiding, and it probably would have taken us a long time to find him. The quickest way to get Masseria was through his own people.

After Maranzano announced his intentions of not seeking retribution, Luciano came to see Maranzano at a private house in Brooklyn in the spring of 1931.

This meeting gave me my first opportunity to meet Charlie

Luciano. He was a thin man with a full head of black hair and a scarred and pockmarked face. He walked obliquely, lurching slightly to the side. His Sicilian was scant, but what words he knew he spoke well. He usually expressed himself in American street slang. But he was not a big talker; he liked to get to the point without any flourishes. Luciano had an ardent, intelligent look about him.

Vito Genovese, an early member of Luciano's clique, accompanied him to the meeting.

Maranzano and Luciano engaged in one of those classic Sicilian dialogues in which every word carried manifold implications but nothing is stated directly.

—Do you know why you are here? Maranzano asked.

—Yes.

—Then I don't have to tell you what has to be done.

—No.

—How much time do you need to do what you have to do?

—A week or two.

—Good, Maranzano said. I'm looking forward to a peaceful Easter.

Before ending the meeting, Maranzano received assurances that Luciano and not one of his subordinates would take personal responsibility for the success of the mission. If Luciano failed, it was understood that Maranzano would continue to consider him his enemy. Luciano thus had a very positive inducement to see to it the job was done right the first time.

Joe Masseria was shot to death in a restaurant. He had just finished a big meal. He died on a full stomach, and that leads me to believe he died happy.

As the newspapers reported in April 1931, Masseria was cut down by gunmen who had entered an Italian restaurant in Coney Island where Joe the Boss had been dining with friends. After dinner, the papers reported, Masseria's table companions all left the restaurant except for Charles Luciano, who remained to play cards with Masseria.

Luciano told police that he had gone to the bathroom and was washing his hands when he heard gunfire. When he returned to the dining room he saw Masseria slumped on the table.

Was the enemy vanquished? Did that mean the war was

over? It took a while for the news to sink in. Yes, Joe the Glutton was dead. He had eaten his last supper.

My glee on hearing the news was in marked contrast to Maranzano's stateliness. He allowed himself a smile, but otherwise he did not gloat or act exuberant. The careworn lines on his face hinted of work that had yet to be done. He knew from experience that it was not yet time to rest.

Maranzano taught me that although the enemy is dead, the war is not over until the victors and survivors both establish a firm peace. He used to tell me that winning the war was the easier task. Winning the peace was a lot harder.

The impression given in accounts of Maranzano by unreliable observers is that after Masseria died, Maranzano proclaimed himself ruler of all the Sicilian clans, or as the expression goes, "boss of all bosses." This view of him is vulgar and superficial.

All Fathers are equal in that each has sovereignty over his Family. But among themselves, Fathers are obviously different. Some Fathers, because of their probity or power, attain greater influence and are consulted more than others. In Sicily we would refer to such a man, one who has gained the respect of all the other Fathers, as a *capo consigliere*—a head counselor, a chief adviser. Among the men who occupied this informal position before the advent of Masseria were Tata Aquilla of New York and later Gaspare Massina of Boston.

To be more precise, however, it is incorrect to think of these leaders as occupying a *position:* They did not hold a formal title; they did not perform a job with prescribed duties and remuneration. A *capo consigliere* is not an executive or an administrator. He is a figurehead whose influence among other Fathers derives not from the imposition of his will on them but from their willing cooperation with him. More than anything, the role he plays stems from a willingness in men to congregate around a greater man. In doing so, every man finds his place in relation to the greater man and thus friction is avoided. The result is harmony and a well-ordered society. The *capo consigliere*, in the ideal at least, is at the disposal of the lesser men. He is there for their benefit and not to gain anything from them.

Men being flawed creatures, this arrangement doesn't always work the way it is supposed to. Some leaders, such as Masseria, decide they can impose themselves by force. They think they can gain a position of eminence by dominating and subjugating those around them. We call such leaders tyrants, and consider their ascension to power illegitimate. Masseria forced his way to the top by enslaving others. That's what Maranzano was referring to when he said the Castellammarese War was a war of liberation for all.

Although Masseria was a tyrannical leader, he was the figurehead, the top man, around whom most of the other leaders, by necessity, had to cluster and align themselves. Now that he was gone, someone had to take his place. Someone else had to establish a new status quo, a new pecking order, so there would be no confusion, so there would be order, so there would be harmony. This is the way it has always been.

After Masseria's demise, the Castellammarese hailed Maranzano as their hero. Maranzano was the victor of the most cataclysmic conflict ever to disrupt our world in America. With the victory came a new order of affairs in our world. The balance of power and influence had shifted from Masseria to Maranzano. In order for our world to get back to normal, for us to continue our lives in peace, the various Fathers of the Sicilian Families had to realign themselves within this new reality.

Consequently, after the war there immediately followed a series of meetings in which Maranzano and the other important men of our world acknowledged among themselves the new state of affairs. A new constellation was coming into being.

In New York City, the alignment process had largely taken care of itself. Because of the war, the five New York Families all acquired new leaders. The Schiro Family was now led by Maranzano, who chose Angelo Caruso as his second-in-command during peace. Caruso was the leader of a strong non-Castellammarese group within our predominantly Castellammarese Family. Maranzano had chosen Caruso in the interest of Family unity, to balance the ticket as it were. The Reina Family now recognized Gagliano as their Father, with Tommy Lucchese under him. Frank Scalise became Father of the Mineo Family. In the Masseria Family, Luciano had taken over, with Vito Genovese as his second. Lastly, the leader of the fifth Family remained Joe Profaci, with Joe Magliocco at his side. All the leadership changes had the blessing of Maranzano.

The new Family leaders had all been either allies or supporters of Maranzano during the war. They already recognized Maranzano as their central axis. Thus, when all of them got together for the first time they no more than confirmed what they had already established with Maranzano separately.

Although the leadership alignment in New York was clear, there were fuzzy spots outside the city. Some out-of-town Families had participated directly in the war and some indirectly, some for and some against Maranzano. Other Families had remained neutral. The leaders of these various clans had to be told how matters stood in New York, and for this reason Maranzano arranged a meeting in May 1931 at a resort near Wappingers Falls, New York.

Into a large room sallied perhaps three hundred men from all over the country. At the front door stood four of Maranzano's musketeers, each carrying arms. Everyone entering the room was frisked for guns and checked to see what Family they represented. All exits in the room, except for the front door, were either boarded or blocked. The guests were told that once the meeting began no one could leave the room for any reason. If someone had to go to the toilet, one of the musketeers had to escort him. The most important guests, the Fathers, sat randomly at a very long table; the rest of their entourage stood.

Maranzano took a place at the head of this very long table. He smiled benignly as each guest found a seat of his choice. After the shuffling and chattering died down, one could hear a faint, rumbling noise, like that of a motor. The droning got closer and closer until the sound of it seemed to fill the room. It was the unmistakable buzzing of an airplane.

—The plane is circling the grounds, Maranzano said when heads turned to him for an explanation. The plane is armed with machine guns and bombs. Please remain in your seats. We're about to start.

Maranzano had hired the pilot, the son of someone in our Family, to circle overhead and be on the lookout for police cars. But the guests, who didn't know that, probably thought the airplane might be used against them. It was precisely to

impress these people—the uncommitted and the undecided—
that Maranzano was being theatrical.

—In front of me, he said, I see many nice people with good
expressions on their faces. I also see people with pale, frightened faces. I don't want anyone to fear me. If you don't want
to stay here, raise your hand and you'll be allowed to leave.
If you remain here under false pretenses, then you're not worthy
to be at this meeting and you deserve to die.

The stunned audience hardly had time to protest when Maranzano stood up and slowly walked down the length of the
long table. As he passed each leader, he examined his face.
He then reassigned them to different seats.

—I want no one to look down, Maranzano said as he went
down the table. Everyone should look me in the eye.

When Maranzano had rearranged the seating, he returned
to the head of the table and said,

—On my right is the honest line. And on my left is the
dishonest line.

Peals of exclamations and protests rang out from the men
on both sides of the table. One man wailed,

—Don Turridru, I'm honest.

And he removed himself from the dishonest line to sit across
the table.

The room was all in uproar . . . and the airplane droned
monotonously overhead.

—All right, declared Maranzano, enough! Sit down all of
you, it doesn't matter where. Only your conscience knows what
side you're really on. But what's past is past. What's important
now is peace.

After he talked to them as a group and explained the causes
and results of the Castellammarese War, Maranzano spoke to
each leader individually. Each leader thus had the opportunity
to appraise Maranzano and in turn be appraised by him; each
had the chance to align himself in his own fashion with the
new top man in New York City, the new man around whom
national politics in our world now crystallized.

This meeting in upstate New York was but the prelude to
a national convention in late May of 1931 in Chicago—our
first national conference.

It is important to underscore that the nature of this meeting
was political. These men weren't coming together to sign con-

tracts, or to form criminal cartels, or to organize illicit enterprises. Neither were these men going to Chicago as vassals paying tribute to their new master. It wasn't like that at all. The convention was held mainly to allow everyone to identify and place himself within the new political constellation in our world.

The meeting itself was a showcase. The actual work had already been accomplished behind the scenes. Maranzano, for instance, had already been in contact with every major Father in the country. The only loose end in the national political picture was Chicago.

Through emissaries, Maranzano and Capone arrived at the following understanding: Maranzano would affirm Capone's place in Chicago and Capone would affirm Maranzano's supremacy in the national scene.

After this rapprochement, Capone offered to host the upcoming national convention. Since Capone was being so solicitous and since Chicago was centrally located and more convenient to get to, Maranzano chose to hold the national convention there.

Maranzano invited me to accompany him to Chicago. These were among the happiest times for both of us. I had not only survived a war but had even won distinction in it. I had been the chief aide of the victorious general. Through him I was now coming in contact with all the most important Fathers of our world. I was proud to be Maranzano's favorite *picciotto*. Though I was only twenty-six years old, some people were already referring to me as don Peppino. I was young and optimistic, and soon—after all these peace conferences—I would be getting married.

Before departing for Chicago, I remember that Maranzano and I had a drink with Charlie Luciano at a Manhattan hotel. Luciano asked Maranzano if it was possible to take Meyer Lansky along to Chicago. Lansky was the financial whiz behind Luciano's success. But Lansky was a Jew and could not take part in our Tradition.

—All right, Maranzano agreed, but he can't be in the room with us when we meet.

A Sicilian of the old school would not even have thought about taking a Jewish friend along. But that was Charlie Lucky for you—he wasn't locked in by traditional ideas.

We all boarded the same train for Chicago. In Buffalo, Stefano Magaddino and his right-hand man John Montana and Pete Magaddino, my cousin, also got on the train. Maranzano got off the train to make a phone call. A half hour passed; Maranzano didn't return. The train was scheduled to leave the station momentarily. It was unthinkable to abandon Maranzano.

Montana got off the train. Montana was an illustrious man in Buffalo. He owned the cab company, and at one time he was the city's deputy mayor. When he returned to our compartment, Montana told us he had arranged for the train to wait until Maranzano came back. This exhibition of clout impressed us greatly. After Maranzano boarded again and we were on our way, my cousin Stefano beamed with pride.

—See what kind of men I have under me? Stefano said. John can stop trains.

Although they behaved in the most amicable manner, I wondered how Maranzano and Stefano really felt about each other. Before the war, Stefano had been the more prominent of the two. Now, Maranzano had surpassed him. What did Stefano really think about this reversal? Did Stefano resent Maranzano's glory? And what about Maranzano? Before the war, he and Stefano hadn't seemed to like each other personally. Did Maranzano foresee any problems with Stefano?

Capone was an extravagant host. The convention was held at the Hotel Congress, which I think Capone owned. He picked up the tab for everyone's accommodations and provided the food, the drink and the women. He sent Maranzano a gold watch studded with diamonds. Capone also gave us his unimpeachable assurance that the police would not meddle in our business while we were at the hotel.

Capone was a chunky man with a flashing smile. Despite his grisly reputation, now that I met him and could make my own opinions, I found him to be a rather jolly fellow, at least on this occasion.

We held many parties and informal get-togethers at the hotel. But there was only one meeting that really mattered, and that was held in the hotel basement. Maranzano, acting as master of ceremonies, welcomed the few hundred people there; only the VIPs had been invited to this exclusive gathering. First off, Maranzano recited the annals of the Castellammarese War.

He then apprised us of the reconstitution of leadership in New York, introducing the new Fathers one by one. After a round of applause, Maranzano spoke glowingly about Capone, referring to him at times as Alfonso. Although Capone used to be of the Masseria faction, Maranzano said, he now wanted peace and the enjoyment of a society of friends. In so many words, therefore, Maranzano recognized Capone as the head of the Chicago Family. All clapped.

Once all the major leaders had been recognized and confirmed by the congregation, the gathered leaders had their turn to show their respect for Maranzano. Capone gave a speech praising Maranzano. We all applauded, acclaiming as much the man as what he stood for. Here was the man who, because of his preeminence, once again made it feasible for all of us to return to normal activity. We hailed Maranzano.

I, as well as the other members of Maranzano's wartime staff, had been with him on a daily basis for about a year and a half. We all looked forward to returning to "civilian" life. We had dropped everything to follow him into war. Now we had to think about our future. None of us worked in any of Maranzano's businesses anymore. For example, my job as supervisor of Maranzano's stills ended with the war. Maranzano had promised us that when the war was over he would take care of us in some manner. Perhaps he would set us up in business or give us some money.

We all expected some reward once things finally settled down. In the meantime, we were still at Maranzano's call, although we weren't necessarily with him every day. After the war and the peace conferences, we on his staff slacked off. For Maranzano, on the other hand, the pace seemed to grow more hectic. He was coming in contact with a great many more people than ever before. He had to divide his time among a variety of new concerns that were not his worry when his only duty was to the Castellammarese. Visitors besieged him. It's possible that Maranzano got less rest during peace than during war. He had stepped into the grand arena of national politics. I don't think he anticipated what an exhausting life that entailed.

Then, too, Maranzano had to give some time to his own businesses, neglected during the war. As I've mentioned, he had real estate holdings and an import-export food company.

He also owned a fleet of fishing boats and a processing plant south of Ocean City, New Jersey. And he owned a farm in upstate New York. In his early days, Maranzano had an office at Lafayette and Spring streets in Manhattan. After the war, befitting his new status, Maranzano moved uptown on Park Avenue, where he rented an office suite on top of Grand Central Station. At his imposing office, Maranzano was most proud of his business records, which his accountants assured him could withstand the most meticulous IRS review.

In June of 1931, a banquet was held in Brooklyn to honor Maranzano and his war staff. Many leaders from Families other than ours attended or sent representatives. The banquet was a fund-raiser of sorts in that people felt it appropriate to bring gifts. It was no different really from when, let's say, the President of the United States is the honored guest at a $100-a-plate dinner. Likewise, no one was forced to contribute money to Maranzano at our banquet, though it was considered good form. And why not? Maranzano and we on his war staff had risked our lives by going to war. We had been on the front line of action. Many of the people at the banquet never had to sacrifice as we did. And yet, they had benefited from our struggle.

I don't know how much money was raised at the banquet; I wasn't the program director. Shortly after the banquet, however, Maranzano asked me privately if I would hold on to $80,000 for him. He said if he needed the money, he might ask for it back. He also said he might add to the amount and have me distribute it among the war staff.

His request perplexed me. Why me? Why should I hold on to it? I assumed this money had been raised at the banquet. I didn't want to be responsible for this money if it didn't belong to me. Maranzano wasn't giving me the money; he was asking me to save it for him. With that much money from Maranzano in my care, the rest of the war staff might think that he and I had made some sort of private arrangement. I didn't want to arouse ill feelings among the others.

The strange incident showed me an ambiguous side of Maranzano, a side he hadn't exhibited to me before. Was his request to hold on to the money an equivocal way of showing me favor above the others? Did he want to test my trust in him? I didn't know what was on his mind.

I didn't take the money from Maranzano. He seemed neither angry nor pleased. He didn't mention it anymore.

By midsummer I was free at last to attend to my personal business. The mood of the other staff members was petulant. Gaspar, for one, grumbled about Maranzano's tardiness in rewarding us for our war service. I assured him, as well as the others, that when Maranzano settled his own affairs he would be in a better position to show us his gratitude. Anyway, it's not that we were without money altogether. During the war, it was not uncommon for Maranzano to slip me maybe $500 a week without my asking for it. The others also received pocket money. All in all, we were not wanting, and we certainly had good prospects, being as close as we were to such an important man.

My main preoccupation, in any case, was not Maranzano but my sweetheart, Fay Labruzzo, whose company I now once more enjoyed. I put everything else in back of my mind in order to resume my courtship of Fanny. We scheduled our wedding for October 25. Maranzano was to be my best man.

By August of 1931 I had stopped going to Maranzano's office every day. I checked in mostly by phone in case Maranzano needed me.

Maranzano seemed to be more comfortable as a warrior than he was as a statesman. Part of the reason I revered him as a war leader was his ability to drive a straight line through the most tangled mess. This was Maranzano's forte, his directness and vigor. Leadership during peacetime, however, demands different talents, which I think Maranzano possessed to a lesser degree. During peace, during normal domestic times, the successful statesman must possess a pliant disposition, an accommodating nature, an instinct for pleasing the greatest number of people and antagonizing the least, an ability to take a circuitous line around problems and perhaps avoid them, instead of inviting problems by butting heads with every contrary or dissenting view. In this respect, Maranzano had qualities that made him a great conqueror but a mediocre statesman.

Maranzano was also hindered by his very demeanor and style. He had an aristocratic, almost imperious manner that chilled many people. Maranzano was capable of affection and humor; on first impression, however, most people thought him austere and forbidding.

I was at a dinner once with some friends. We were waiting for Maranzano to show up. At the table was Angelo Palmieri, a friend of mine from Stefano Magaddino's Family. Don Angelo had brought a box with him to the table. We asked him what was in the box and he said it was a $100 felt hat. Whatever for? we inquired. Angelo said that the last time he had been in town he had been to see Maranzano at his office and had said something to displease Maranzano.

—He got so upset that for a moment I thought Maranzano was going to kill me, don Angelo explained. Tell me, is he still angry at me? Is this hat going to do any good? I want to give it to him.

We all derided Angelo for his exaggerated fears and his squeamishness.

—Laugh all you want, he said, dismissing our lightheartedness. But I'm going to give him this hat anyway to make things up between us.

No doubt Maranzano had gotten angry at don Angelo, but Palmieri didn't have to fear for his life. The incident did show what a frightening impression Maranzano could make.

Angelo had touched on something about Maranzano that was becoming more and more frequent—flareups of temper.

Once, on walking into his office, I noticed that Maranzano had a somber look, as if he were brooding over something. He had his thumbs cocked under his suspenders, which he repeatedly raised off his chest and then let slap back.

—You don't look like yourself today, I said casually.

—What's that? Maranzano barked, glaring at me. Are you pestering me, too?

Maranzano's testiness peeved me. I walked straight out of the office, muttering to myself rather than criticizing Maranzano.

As I was washing my hands at a small sink in the waiting room, I looked up and saw Maranzano's reflection in the wall mirror in front of me. It startled me to see him suddenly appear. I jerked up and wheeled around.

—Oh, it's you, don Turridru.

Maranzano laughed and kissed me on the cheek.

—What do you expect from me today? he said by way of apology. It's been a bad day.

Maranzano's irritability indicated he was under great pressure, but I was not privy to the specific causes of his distress. By late August I was an infrequent visitor to his office. When I did stop into the office, Maranzano was always preoccupied and in the company of an expanded circle of friends. Two of his new confidants were Frank Scalise and Tommy Lucchese.

One day, after not having seen Maranzano for about two weeks, I impulsively barged into his office, but I regretted it the moment I observed the scene inside. I beheld Maranzano clasping the head of his friend John DiCaro. From the furious look on Maranzano's face and the frightened look on DiCaro's face it didn't appear the two men were about to kiss. It seemed more likely that Maranzano was about to insult DiCaro. There was a third man in the room, Frank Scalise, pale in the face. After my abrupt entrance, Maranzano glowered at me. Then he dropped his hands from DiCaro's head and seemed embarrassed; Scalise, meanwhile, haltingly uttered some reassuring words about everything being fine. DiCaro asked Maranzano's pardon and Maranzano said all was forgiven. Who knows how the scene would have turned out if I hadn't walked in? After Scalise and DiCaro left, Maranzano showed me a half-smile and said,

—This stays between us. The incident is closed.

But it wasn't, and Maranzano himself brought it up again. Maranzano lived on Avenue J in Brooklyn. Charlie DiBenedetto and I shared an apartment on Avenue H. Maranzano invited me to his house one evening. During our conversation he asked:

—Do you remember the last time you were in my office?

Although I knew he was alluding to the DiCaro incident, I remembered his injunction not to talk about it and so I answered,

—I don't remember.

He gave me a reproving look.

—All right, I added. I don't want to remember.

—That's kind, Peppino, but let's talk about it anyway.

Maranzano then gave me the background to the scene I had stumbled upon. He said he had called DiCaro to the office to rebuke him and to humiliate him in front of Scalise. DiCaro's sin was that he talked too much. DiCaro had heard Maranzano express his discontent over Stefano Magaddino. Foolishly DiCaro repeated what he heard to Gaetano Gagliano. Such information, if it had reached Magaddino, might have been taken very badly and might have sparked an open row between Magaddino and Maranzano. But the information didn't spread. Gagliano had told his right-hand man, Lucchese, who then brought it back to Maranzano. That's how Maranzano had found out DiCaro had been babbling. Lucchese had done Maranzano a favor.

That Maranzano and Magaddino were not getting along didn't surprise me. Outside his presence, Maranzano used to refer to Magaddino as the rustic. At the same time, Stefano would complain behind Maranzano's back. The two men seemed to be headed for collision, but until then I didn't realize how close to it they already were.

By telling me about the DiCaro situation, Maranzano had voluntarily disclosed to me the same delicate information that he didn't want DiCaro to repeat. He was testing me to see how I felt about any possible move he might make against my cousin Stefano. This gave me a queasy feeling. The matter seemed repulsive to have to think about, especially during my pre-nuptial euphoria. But even so, how could I possibly bring myself to support, or even simply shut my eyes to, a plot against my cousin? I didn't consider Stefano perfect by any means. But the thought of doing away with him was repugnant. I felt nauseous. When Maranzano prodded for a response, I said,

—Thank you for taking me into your confidence, don Turridru, but I can't say I liked what I just heard.

—It's just words, Maranzano said. Nothing will ever happen probably.

Shortly after this incident, Gaspar DiGregorio invited me to his house on Avenue K. Stefano Magaddino was there and wanted to talk to me.

—That Maranzano, Stefano grumbled. The last time I was here and I went to see him I had to wait outside his office for over an hour. Can you imagine that? Who does he think he is?

From Stefano's keynote remark it quickly became apparent what was on his mind. He went on to express various vague grievances against Maranzano. Stefano peered at me, for the same reason as Maranzano had, to see my reaction. Stefano was purposely speaking against Maranzano to see if I agreed with his views. He was sounding me out, just as Maranzano had.

—Many people are upset with him, Stefano said.

I remained expressionless and said nothing.

—Will someone please tell me what's going on? Gaspar demanded.

—The three of us, Stefano said, can't betray each other.

—It's understood, I said.

—We can't betray each other, Stefano repeated.

—I'm in the dark, Gaspar said. What's all this talk about?

If things worsened between him and Maranzano, Stefano wanted to make sure that Gaspar and I wouldn't betray him. Also, just as Maranzano had tried to include me in his intrigues against Stefano, so now Stefano was trying to include me in his own intrigues against Maranzano. I had the same sickening feeling as before.

From my continued silence, Stefano gathered that I was not receptive to him. He eventually turned the conversation to another subject. Then we parted.

I was disgusted both with Maranzano and Stefano. What grisly games these older men played! Didn't they ever stop maneuvering? What compelled them to such dark purposes? That I should ask myself such questions shows how idealistic I was at the time. Going off to war had been a noble enterprise; we had fought the evil enemy to make our world safe and peaceful. But no sooner did the war end than I saw enmity again among my own friends. It looked like the cycle was beginning anew, the cycle that would lead to more fighting. This spectacle grossly disillusioned me.

I was a twenty-six-year-old war veteran, in love and about to be married. I was fed up with fighting. I was fed up with war. I was fed up with Stefano even though he was my relative. I was fed up with Maranzano even though he was my hero. I just wanted to be alone with Fanny.

11

IT WAS EARLY SEPTEMBER AND I HADN'T BEEN TO MARAN-
zano's office in weeks. I had been looking for furniture that
day for the residence Fay and I would occupy when we got
married. After I returned home I received a telephone call from
Buster.

—Get out of the apartment, Buster said. Maranzano's been
killed in his office.

Buster could provide me with no other details. He didn't
know any more. A quick and frantic series of phone calls
revealed that none of us on Maranzano's wartime staff knew
anything about the slaying. But we didn't have time to mull
the situation over. Whoever was responsible for Maranzano's
death might also want to harm us. All six of Maranzano's
musketeers went into hiding. We set up communications among
ourselves and coordinated contingency plans. We waited for
information of Maranzano's slaying to dribble in; another war
seemed imminent.

Maranzano's slaying thrust me into a position of responsibility that I had not sought. As I contacted more and more
people within our Family, they seemed to expect me to tell
them what to do, especially the war veterans with whom I had
worked during the war.

I told them to wait, to be on standby, until I found out more
about Maranzano's death. I think I was calmer during this
period than I would have been if I hadn't had all these people
demanding guidance. It forced me to be sober-minded. I didn't
have time to dwell on personal grief.

Maranzano had been stabbed and shot to death at his Park

Avenue office by men posing as IRS agents. When I read that in the newspapers I recalled how Maranzano had been expecting IRS agents to inspect his business records. In fact, after the war, Maranzano had forbidden us to wear guns in his office to avoid antagonizing any federal agents who might visit unexpectedly. Since Maranzano's assassins had posed as law agents, I had grounds to believe that whoever plotted Maranzano's death must have known something about Maranzano's impending IRS visit.

Because none of us on Maranzano's wartime staff was at his office when it happened, our information about the slaying was as sketchy as the newspaper reports. We had to remain in hiding. Even when Maranzano's funeral was held, none of us felt it was safe to show up. But I did ask others who attended the funeral to gather information concerning Maranzano's death. At the funeral it was learned that Stefano Magaddino wanted to talk to me. Stefano and I then arranged a meeting.

When I first heard of Maranzano's death it crossed my mind that Stefano might have been behind it. But in our subsequent talk it became obvious that my fears were unfounded. Stefano may well have been pleased by Maranzano's sudden departure, but he had not been the instigator of it. Stefano himself told me that Charlie Luciano had taken responsibility for Maranzano's death and was prepared to offer an explanation.

—Something like this was bound to happen to Maranzano, Stefano gloated. Power went to his head.

That was to become the common epitaph for Maranzano. People said that power had gone to his head. I agree with it in part. However, I wish I knew what was on Maranzano's mind in those last few days before his fall so I could provide a fuller explanation for his demise. Three months after he had been proclaimed the top man in my world, Maranzano was a corpse. Obviously, something had gone terribly wrong. Perhaps he did become intoxicated with power. Perhaps he did succumb to the temptation of trying to arrange everything to his liking all at once. But I also think that after the war Maranzano became somewhat of a misfit. He was a misfit in that he made a better warrior leader than he made a politician. He was a misfit in a cultural sense as well. Maranzano was old-world Sicilian in temperament and style. But he didn't live in Sicily anymore. In New York he was adviser not only to Sicilians but to American-Italians. Maranzano represented a style that often clashed with that of the Americanized men who surrounded him after the war. It was difficult, for example, for Maranzano even to communicate effectively with many of these men, for they only understood American street cant.

These reflections came later. At the time, after Maranzano's funeral, my principal thought was simply to find out what Charlie Lucky had to say.

The news that Luciano was behind Maranzano's death took me by complete surprise. I wasn't even aware that Maranzano and Luciano were at odds. The word from Luciano's camp was that he had acted in self-defense. That implied that Maranzano had wanted to strike against Luciano. Maranzano had never confided in me about a plot against Charlie Lucky. But then again, there must have been many things I didn't know about during Maranzano's last days.

For the men in my Family the months of September and October were tense and gloomy. We all dreaded the thought of taking up arms again. When war once again loomed as a possibility it was only natural that many of the men looked to me for leadership. Within the Family hierarchy, Angelo Caruso, the second, showed no inclination to lead us after Maranzano's death. Caruso was a mild conciliatory man and wasn't cut out for heroics.

The crisis had once again taken me away from Fay. My best man had died. I was in hiding. Our wedding couldn't go on as scheduled. I had to postpone it, not knowing when I could set another date. I was beginning to wonder if I would ever have a normal love life.

What sustained me during these nervous months was a Family of friends for whom I had become the nucleus. In their hearts the men of my Family had already given me their vote of confidence to lead them. Officially, however, we were without a Father. Who was going to replace Maranzano? We had to choose soon because we were in a crisis. I did not initially relish accepting the burdens of Fatherhood. After all, I was only twenty-six years old, without wife and without fortune. I didn't even have my own business. My friends, however, urged me to take the big step. My cousin Stefano Magaddino also wanted it. He gave me his support, and this carried a lot of weight both within my Family and among other Family leaders.

For his personal advantage, it no doubt suited Stefano to have what he perceived as his tractable younger cousin as head of the Castellammarese clan in Brooklyn.

The day came when the Family met to choose a new Father. I had overcome my reluctance and now looked forward to the challenge of being Father. The first motion of the meeting called for me to be named Father by acclamation. I objected. Although it was obvious I was the favorite, I didn't want to be drafted into office, as it were, without finding out who was actually against me or for me. A voice vote by acclamation would allow my opponents to retain anonymity. I called for a hand vote. And to make it a true election, I nominated a man to run against me. I nominated Frank Italiano, the Family member who probably liked me the least. Each man in our Family now had a clear choice, and he had to express his preference openly, by raising his hand in front of the others.

I think Italiano got about seven votes to about three hundred for me. Bonanno was Father. Henceforth, what I said and what I decided would affect many people. I always had to keep in mind that my personal sentiments did not matter as much as the interests of the Family. I had lost the privilege of selfishness.

My on-the-job training began with my meeting with Charlie Luciano. I could talk to him now as his peer. Luciano told me he was forced to strike against Maranzano after learning that Maranzano had hired Vincent Coll to kill Luciano. Vincent "Mad Dog" Coll was an American hoodlum, a hired gun. I detested his type and couldn't imagine why Maranzano should need such a man. He must have been desperate, or maybe he didn't want to involve anyone from our Family.

Others had already confirmed what Luciano had told me. Maranzano had hired Coll. Indeed, Coll was making his way up to Maranzano's office at the same time that Maranzano was killed. Also, I learned later, the informant who had channeled information to Luciano about Maranzano's office habits and his preoccupations with the IRS was Tommy Lucchese.

Be that as it may, Luciano had given me a credible explanation for his actions. After his clarification, Luciano said he wanted no fighting between us.

On the personal level, I always got along with Charlie. There never existed between us that undersurface tension that was present between the democratic Luciano and the autocratic Maranzano. I understood Luciano better than Maranzano did because I was younger and more flexible, whereas Maranzano was less tolerant of modern trends.

On the other hand, a good case could be made for the opposite: that Maranzano really understood Luciano better than I did. When I had time to put all the pieces together, it became obvious that Luciano hadn't simply struck at Maranzano out of self-defense. The truth wasn't that one-sided. The truth is that in August of 1931, Maranzano and Luciano simultaneously were plotting to kill each other. If Luciano had waited one more day to send his disguised IRS agents to Maranzano's office, Maranzano might have emerged victorious.

The immediate cause of their falling out was not known to me. A likely bone of contention was New York's garment district. Maranzano and Luciano vied for influence over jobs and for lucrative contracts in the cloth trade—at that time probably the largest single industry in the city. Tommy Lucchese also was known to have existing interests and further ambitions in the garment district. Somehow these men failed to contain their power struggle and they sought remedy through force.

I had the choice of rejecting Luciano's olive branch or of accepting it in good faith. If told to fight, the men in my Family would have fought. Outside my Family, leaders such as Frank Scalise, the Father of a Family and a pro-Maranzano man, were prepared to follow me into war. Despite Luciano's affluence and his ability to bankroll a war, we Castellammarese prided ourselves on being better fighters, more willing to sacrifice and to endure a long battle than the Americanized men under Luciano.

But what good would it have done to fight Luciano? He had claimed self-defense in the killing of Maranzano. Now he mainly wanted to be left alone to run his enterprises. He was not trying to impose himself on us as had Masseria. Lucky demanded nothing from us.

If I did have to muster my Family to war again it was bound to be a less popular war and the soldiers were bound to be less enthusiastic than before. Our lives had already been disrupted enough. Moreover, if war did come, I could not count on Stefano Magaddino to assume the same role as he had during the Castellammarese War, when he provided money and supplies. The death of Maranzano had worked to Stefano's advantage. With the charismatic Maranzano absent, Stefano could once more play the role of the "grand old man" of the Castellammarese and have no one to overshadow him. Lastly, although I rued the death of Maranzano, I had no personal animosity toward Charlie Lucky. Whatever animosity had developed between Maranzano and Luciano, that didn't change the fact that Luciano and I had nothing against each other individually.

For all these reasons, I chose the path of peace. At my baptism in Castellammare, I had been the symbol of peace between two warring factions in town. Now, in what probably was my first Fatherly pronouncement, I told Lucky,

—I have no quarrel with you.

Once again, the leaders of my world realigned and repositioned themselves according to the new political reality. Charlie Lucky's star was on the rise. Stefano's star seemed undiminished, and perhaps even enhanced. Scalise's star fell. Scalise had been too close a supporter of Maranzano. With Lucky's rise to power, Scalise became a liability to his Family, which didn't want to antagonize the powerful Luciano and his cohorts. Scalise was replaced as Father by Vincent Mangano. Therefore, the five New York Fathers were Luciano, Gagliano, Profaci, Mangano and me. I was a newborn star.

The most consequential aspect of this post-Maranzano era was our adoption of a new form of leadership consensus. We revised the old custom of looking toward one man, one supreme leader for advice and for the settling of disputes. We replaced leadership by one man with leadership by committee. We opted for a parliamentary arrangement whereby a group of the most important men in our world would assume the function formerly performed by one man. This group became known as the Commission. It originally consisted of the five New York Fathers and the Fathers from Chicago and Buffalo. One can see the influence that Stefano Magaddino enjoyed at the time. Buffalo is but a small town compared with Chicago and New York. And yet, Stefano had a seat on the Commission.

* * *

By November 1931, without having plotted or schemed, without any deadly connivance or treacherous contrivance, without even seeking it at first, I was leader of a Family of friends who called me Padre.

I told myself I was going to be a good Father: I was going to do things right, according to the old Tradition, as much as possible. And I was going to be my own man. I was not going to be dependent on anyone, not on Luciano and not on Magaddino. I was going to be me, Joseph Bonanno. . . .

And then, in the middle of my ruminations, I would startle myself with this thought:

—If I'm going to make a good Father, I'd better hurry up and become a husband.

I had postponed my marriage long enough. First the war had intervened, and then Maranzano's death. I don't know how Fay managed, but she had waited and loved me throughout all the disruptions, loving a man part of whose life would always remain secret, loving a man of whom she could not ask certain questions, loving a man who was often away from her, but loving him utterly, with unbounded affection and loyalty.

We were married on November 15, 1931, in St. Joseph's Church in Brooklyn. The reception was held at the Knights of Columbus Hall on Grand Army Plaza. Fay, dressed all in white, wore a delicate lace veil that covered her hair but not her face. The veil fell down her back and trailed to the floor. A string of pearls adorned her neck, and in her arms she cradled lilies. I wore a black tux with a white bow tie.

My best man was Gaspar DiGregorio. By no means could he replace Maranzano, but Gaspar was one of my oldest friends in America. We had been bootleggers together and we had fought a war together. He also was Stefano Magaddino's brother-in-law.

My ushers were Bastiano Domingo, Vincent Danna, Charlie DiBenedetto (boys of the first day), Natale Evola, Marty Bruno and Salvatore Profaci. The last was Joe Profaci's brother. Despite the understanding between Luciano and me, the times were still uncertain. Buster, Vincent and Charlie all wore pistols under their tuxedos.

Everything went smoothly, however. My marriage broke the ice. It indicated that peace had been restored and that everyone in our Family could resume a normal existence. The reception was a great success. Many people brought or sent envelopes of cash. Al Capone, I remember, sent me $5,000. That was pretty generous considering that during the Depression a lot of people would have considered $5,000 an adequate annual income.

Off we dashed to our honeymoon. Fanny and I could hardly believe it. We were actually man and wife. Nothing had interfered this time—Long Island hadn't sunk, icebergs hadn't beached on Coney Island, a tidal wave hadn't wiped out Brooklyn. What great good fortune! The world was whole and open to us. We went to Niagara Falls.

A year to the month after we were married, Fay gave birth to a boy. I named him Salvatore after my father.

BOOK III

The Commission

12

IN THE BEGINNING WAS THE FATHER. WITHOUT HIM NOTHING can be done. A Family of friends coalesces around the Father, from whom flows all authority.

The Family which a Father holds together embodies an ancient way of life, a mode of cooperation which precedes the formation of city-states and later of nations. It is a way of life that gives primary allegiance to the Family state, to the tribe, to the clan.

The Family should be viewed as an organism, a living tissue of binding personal relationships. The code of conduct prescribed by the Family is not written in any book. Our Tradition is mightier than any book. We pass down the knowledge personally from generation to generation.

As we traveled to new lands, we adapted our customs to our surroundings. Each Father ran his Family according to his understanding of our Tradition. Especially in America, some novel variations on the same basic unit crept into being. This is how I presided over my Family:

I became a Father, first of all, through the approval of the rest of the clan. Although each Family member votes for a Father, the election is not really intended to count votes so much as it is to establish consensus. It is unthinkable to elect a leader if he gets only one more vote than his opponent, as is done in the normal democratic process. Under such conditions the leader would rule over a divided house. The method of election of a Father is more akin to the election of the Pope. Each bishop votes his choice for Pope, but until there is a consensus no Pope is named.

The Father has the right to choose his own second, an assistant Father if you will, an underleader. The second is a figurehead who represents the Father on various Family matters. The second has no independent power of his own. He does all things in the name of the Father.

Because Americans liken the Family to a corporation, an institution run along bureaucratic lines, they often mistakenly compare the relationship between a Father and his second to that of a chairman of the board and the chief executive officer of the corporation.

This corporate analogy is misapplied, as are all comparisons between a Family and a business bureaucracy. The second mainly acts as the most visible and most accessible conduit to the Father himself. The Father prefers to remain in the background. He uses the second as his eyes and ears. Ideally, the Father is everywhere present but nowhere to be seen.

If the Father has to leave his home base for some reason, or if he goes to prison, his second doesn't automatically take charge of the Family. The Father may delegate that power to his second on a temporary basis, but he may choose not to. The second serves entirely at the discretion of the Father.

Directly accountable to the Father are the various group leaders within the Family. In American jargon these group leaders were often referred to as captains. This word in itself gives the erroneous impression that the relationship between a Father and his group leaders is a militaristic one. This is true perhaps only during emergency state of war against another Family. During normal times, however, the relationship between a Father and his group leaders is based on mutual sympathy, capacity and personal allegiance.

The group leader is the main intermediary between the Father and the rest of the Family members. The size of the group varies depending on the group leader's following.

When the Father makes a decision the responsibility for carrying it out often goes to a group leader, who then is free to assign the undertaking to people in his group.

At the foundation of this social unit are the "boys," the Father's "sons." In police cant, these are known as soldiers.

Once again, this gives the false impression that Family members all are on ready alert, waiting for the order to march.

It must be stressed that the Family members represented a cross section of society. We were a true microcosm of society at large in that our Family included shoemakers, tailors, barbers, bakers, doctors, lawyers, factory workers, fishermen, priests and politicians. I would say that the vast majority were private businessmen of one kind or another. Some Family members had illicit businesses such as bookmaking or numbers. In our world, such enterprises are not considered wrong.

In my Family, some activities were clearly considered out-of-bounds. I did not tolerate any dealings in prostitution or narcotics. I was against extortion as an arbitrary instrument of collecting money from people. Perhaps other Families didn't adhere to my strict guidelines, but this was my way.

Nonetheless, even within these restrictions, only a minority of my Family members were engaged in full-time illicit activity. Those who ran a lottery game or were bookmakers, by the very nature of their business, were in it full-time. These men in turn employed others for their business, not necessarily other Family members. Some Fathers may have had a lottery game or a bookmaking operation as their own private business. I did not.

In either case, it is wrong to conclude that the profits from these illicit enterprises automatically reverted to the Father or that the profits were distributed among all the Family members. The Family is *not* the same as a criminal gang. Each Family member is free to make his own living, within the restrictions I've mentioned.

Family membership does not entitle one to a monetary stipend; it simply places the Family member in a society of friends who can help each other through a network of connections.

My principles on how to run a Family according to my old Tradition were quickly put to a test. Although the Castellammarese War had brought me in contact with many important men of my world, it was not until I became a Father that I began to realize the new variations that some other Fathers brought to their role.

Among my peers in New York City, Charlie Luciano was the most interesting in many respects. He was one of us, and yet he was not. Although I was the youngest of the Fathers, I had old-fashioned views concerning our Tradition, while Lucky, in some ways, seemed avant-garde.

In his dealings with me, Luciano comported himself as a "man of respect." After Maranzano's slaying, Luciano and I had agreed on peace, and Lucky kept his word. Maranzano's death was accompanied by a series of other slayings in the New York area and in other parts of the country. In the popular press these slayings were fancifully referred to as the second Sicilian Vespers and were interpreted as Luciano's attempt to impose his rule on the "underworld" through a purge.

To view these slayings in a true light one must keep in mind that Lucky lived in two worlds. He lived among us, the men of the old Tradition; but he also lived in a world apart from us, among a largely Jewish coterie whose views of life and of moneymaking were alien to ours. The slayings that accompanied Maranzano's death bore little if any connection with our Sicilian world. As far as I can tell, they represented Lucky's desire to settle matters largely with people outside the pale of our Tradition.

This was none of my business, nor that of any other Father in New York. What I know for a fact is that after Maranzano's death no member of my Family suffered reprisals. The peace between Luciano and me held.

In time we grew more at ease with each other, and during one of our private meetings Lucky felt comfortable enough to make me an offer which he probably thought I would gladly accept.

—I was told Maranzano never paid his boys, Luciano began provocatively.

He spoke a mixture of Sicilian and English when addressing me, a combination that did not lend itself to great subtlety. Nonetheless, I realized that Lucky was sounding me out to see if I bore any secret resentment toward Maranzano.

—Maranzano took his time about those things, I answered. He was a true Sicilian about that, but I have no doubt that he would have taken care of us.

Luciano eyed me for a moment. Then he leaned forward and shook my hand. My answer had indicated to Lucky that I would not renege on my past friendship with Maranzano. By shaking my hand Luciano acknowledged my fidelity to the man and approved of my loyalty, although he and Maranzano had fought to the death. Luciano was the paramount figure in my world in the early 1930s, and another man would have joined him in condemning Maranzano simply to ingratiate himself with Lucky.

In light of this rebuff, the offer that Luciano proceeded to make caught me entirely off guard.

—Would you like a piece of the action in the garment district?

The offer was most tempting, considering that I was young and exactly at the point of seeking opportunities to make my fortune. The garment district, at that time, was one of the most lucrative areas in New York's economic life. Luciano had extensive interests in the clothing industry, especially in the Amalgamated Clothing Union, the union for men's clothing factories. Luciano said he could arrange for one of my men to assume an important position in the union, thus giving me an opening for influence over some jobs and some work contracts.

On reflection, however, Luciano's proposal had many drawbacks. If I accepted his offer, I would forever become obligated to Lucky. I would owe him a favor, and this would curtail my independence as a Father. At the beginning of my career as a Father, and as I continued to practice throughout my tenure, I did not want to place myself or my Family in a dependent relationship. An intuition, more than a well-developed rationale, told me to keep away from entangling alliances.

Lucky's offer also didn't appeal to me because I did not feel comfortable with the arrangement he had in mind. As I understood it, Luciano and his men received regular payoffs from the Amalgamated Clothing Union under the table. I had no objections to having a contact in the union, but the idea of graft was antipathetic. Furthermore, it would involve me in a practice with a high risk of discovery. Unlike Charlie Lucky, I wanted to keep my name clean and out of the public eye.

I thus rejected Lucky's offer and told him I merely wanted a sincere friendship with him in matters concerning our Tradition. Lucky showed a pleasant smile on his face and the subject never came up again.

I had overcome my first temptation—that of making money easily but heedlessly. I too wanted to make money, but it would be in my own fashion. This episode with Lucky impressed upon me the need to steer my own course. How he ran his affairs was his own business. I wanted to be free to pursue mine.

Although I became a Father after the Castellammarese War, that title alone did not exempt me from earning my own living. After my marriage, I used what money I had saved to invest in legitimate businesses. I formed partnerships or became a stockholder in various companies. In the main, then, I was a venture capitalist. This is how I made my money; this is how I earned my living.

In time I became a partner or stockholder in such businesses as the B&D (Bonanno and DiPasquale) Coat Co., the Morgan Coat Co., the Anello and Bonanno Funeral Home, the Brunswick Laundry, and the Grande Cheese Co. I paid income tax based on my holdings in such companies.

I didn't intimidate these people into becoming my partners. On the contrary, they sought me out. Aside from the fact that I invested in their companies, these people came to me because they knew that with me as a partner their business would grow. There was nothing mysterious in how I accomplished this: I developed connections.

A description of my connections and interests in the ladies' clothing industry will illustrate the point. In the clothing industry, a "jobber" is a manufacturer responsible for cutting the patterns and distributing them to factory outlets where the patterns can be sewn together. The operator of the factory is called a "contractor." The B&D Clothing Co. was a contractor operation. I also had a partnership with a friend, who happened to be a Family member, who operated the Miss Youth Clothing Co. in Manhattan; this was a jobber operation.

I also had a friend, a non-Family member, who was a director of the merchants' association (the jobber's trade group) in New York's garment district.

In addition, I had connections in the Ladies Garment Workers Union and connections with trucking companies.

Thus, by putting all my connections in touch with one another, I could harmonize our activities in a mutually advantageous way. By knowing me, an affiliated contractor could always count on contracts for his company; the jobber could count on reliable factory outlets; the trucking company could count on delivery orders between jobber and contractor; the union could count on a closed shop; the worker could count on getting work even during recessionary periods.

It was a matter of playing favorites among ourselves, but to keep the ball rolling required me, in this instance, not to use brute force, but to use tact and diplomacy.

Another of my main business interests was the Grande Cheese Co. of Fond du Lac, Wisconsin. The cheese plant had been the source of contention between rival groups in Chicago. These people played rough, and fighting broke out. In the meantime, because of these disruptions, the cheese company almost went out of business. The owners wanted to sell out. Word of this reached the DiBella brothers of Brooklyn, who were successful wholesale food distributors. The DiBella family had a long-standing friendship with the Labruzzo family, my wife's family. Before committing himself to buy the company, John DiBella came to me to explain his predicament.

He told me he was hesitating on the deal because of the company's violent history. He was worried that the same Chicago people would try to encroach on the business and cause more trouble. This was not the sort of problem that the authorities could solve, even if Mr. DiBella was inclined to ask them for help. What could the police do? Post a twenty-four-hour guard around the plant? Neither was it the sort of problem that could be settled by negotiations with the contending parties. Some men, just as some nations, respect only power, and to deal with them you have to be just as strong, or stronger. Mr. DiBella was an honest businessman and a gentleman, but he didn't have the means to take on these people. So he turned to me.

As much as I assured him that I would let it be known that I was his protector, Mr. DiBella desired a firmer alliance. He said it would give him great peace of mind if I became a stockholder in the company. That way there would be no misunderstanding; everyone would know then that I was his ally. It wasn't really necessary and I wasn't really looking for investment opportunities at the time. But to please him and honor the friendship between the DiBellas and the Labruzzos, I bought stock in the company and put the stock in Fay's name. After that, the company enjoyed peaceful relations. It was understood by the Chicago people that Grande was to be left alone. Grande prospered.

As Father, I also inherited the "rights" to the neighborhood lottery, or numbers game, operated within my Family. I appointed the people who actually ran this numbers-game business. I also acted as the "bank"—that is, if the game lost money, I had to cover all the bets. In turn, if the people who operated this game wanted to make me a gift now and then, I couldn't very well stop them. I certainly never had any pangs of conscience because of my indirect involvement in this illicit business.

All societies, whether the unit of cooperation be that of the family, the tribe, the city or the nation, use force, at some level, to enforce the rules of that society. No well-ordered society tolerates indiscriminate and arbitrary violence. My world was no exception.

In discussing the role of violence in my world I don't expect outsiders to condone or approve of the rules by which we lived. I would only ask the outsider to appreciate the context of our lives. The first step is to recognize that traditionally a Sicilian has a personal sense of justice. If a "man of honor" is wronged it is up to him to redress that wrong personally. He does not go to the judicial machinery of the state. For this to work, everyone clearly must understand what is wrong and what is right.

One of the inviolate rules of our old Tradition was that no Family member should fool around with another Family member's wife, or female relative. If a Family member discovered that his wife had gone to bed with another Family member, he was justified in killing him. No one had to tell the cuckolded Family member what to do and he didn't have to tell anyone else. He simply did what was necessary.

However, if this Family member used violence in this fashion he had to make absolutely sure the man he was after was indeed guilty. If the slayer made an intentional mistake, and if it was discovered that he got the wrong man, then the slayer himself must die.

A man of our world was held strictly accountable for his actions. If he did something of a violent nature against another Family member he had to be sure he was doing the right thing.

Another one of our rules was that no Family member should slap another on the face. This was an intolerable insult, and it was understood that the wronged party was free to take action. The object of many of these rules was to help a man contain his emotions. If a man slapped another in a moment of passion it clearly indicated he had lost his self-control.

Contrary to popular belief, business disputes rarely rose to the level of violence. If two Family members disagreed over a business arrangement between them, the matter was usually resolved at a hearing by their group leaders, whose decisions were binding.

Economic disagreements were less important in themselves than they were in the clues they gave to the characters of the men involved. Our entire system of cooperation and connections depended on trust. A handshake often closed a deal; a nod of the head indicated assent. Under such conditions, therefore, a business disagreement became an important issue not because one partner might be cheating another but because one partner might not be keeping his word to another. A strict money matter could be resolved by a hearing, but a breach of faith was a point of honor. It was in the latter case that economic disputes sometimes led to violent confrontation.

A Family member's behavior toward outsiders was his own responsibility. Within the Family we protected or punished our own, but outside the Family a man was on his own. If he felt strongly enough to commit violence against a non-Family member, then he had to assume the risks himself.

On the other hand, if outsiders tampered with a Family member the outsiders became the enemies of us all. I remember an instance when robbers broke into the house of Joe Profaci's nephew and stole a safe containing jewelry and money. Profaci's men found out that the thieves, although Italian, were not associated in any way with the Families. An attempt was made to negotiate with the thieves for the return of the valuables. However, intermediaries reported that the robbers scoffed at the gesture and held themselves independent from the sanctions of our world. Thereafter, the identity of the thieves was passed on to all the Families in New York. It was each member's responsibility to take action if he spotted any of them. No incentive, monetary or otherwise, was offered to bring the thieves to justice. Justice was done.

Another occasion of mafioso justice, with a much happier ending, presented itself in a church in the Bay Ridge section of Brooklyn. To celebrate the opening of Regina Pacis Church in the late 1940s, the parishioners were asked by the priests to bring donations to the church and to lay them before the statue of the Madonna. The call brought forth necklaces, wedding rings, jewels and other precious ornaments. From these offerings the monsignor commissioned the making of a crown. The bejeweled Madonna then was displayed in church, but shortly after the crowning, thieves stripped the statue of its adornments.

The taking of such sacrilegious booty offended Joe Profaci as much as anyone else. He was a prominent church member and had helped raise money for the new church. When the monsignor asked for his personal help to recover the jewels, Profaci, along with his many friends, went into action.

One Sunday the Madonna once again presided over mass in full regalia—crown and jewels restored to their rightful owner. Those old enough to remember still talk about the jewels' recovery when they reminisce about Joe Profaci, who had one brother who was a priest and two sisters who were nuns.

One of the strictest rules we had toward outsiders was the injunction against killing a policeman or a reporter. My Tradition recognized that a cop was merely the servant of the government and thus was not to be held fully responsible for his actions. He merely had a job to do. We understood that, and very often ways could be found so that he would not interfere with us and we wouldn't interfere with him.

Nonetheless, in America, I was shocked to discover that not all of us understood the wisdom of this rule. I remember a Commission meeting in the early 1930s in which was discussed the advent of Thomas E. Dewey as a special prosecutor in New York City. Dewey had made it very plain that he was out to jail Charlie Luciano, whom he called the vice overlord of the city.

At one point in the meeting, Albert Anastasia, the second in Vincent Mangano's Family, suggested that Dewey be eradicated. Anastasia was a hot-tempered man and a close friend of Lucky Luciano's. The audacity of his suggestion made the Fathers pause in disbelief. The rest of us turned to Luciano to see how he reacted.

Lucky hesitated to give his view. Since Albert and Lucky were such close friends it could have been the case that Lucky had let Albert make his suggestion to see how the rest of us felt about it. In any case, both Albert and Lucky seemed at least willing to entertain such a stupid notion, whereas the rest of us were totally against it. Seeing us recoil at the suggestion of killing a law-enforcement agent, Luciano deferred the matter to the other Fathers present, all of whom rejected it outright.

—If we all lose our heads, I recall Vincent Mangano saying forcefully, we'll wind up burning our own foundation.

To describe a typical day for me is impossible because I kept no set schedule. During normal peaceful times, being a Father was a most pleasant occupation. If everything was running smoothly, internal disagreements between Family members were solved at the grass-roots level either by group leaders or by the *consigliere*. A Family member's personal or business problems were usually handled in this manner, and the problem rarely had to be brought to my attention.

On the other hand, if a Family member wanted to go into business with a member of another Family, such an association would need the approval of the Fathers of the respective Families. A Family member's relations with non-Family members was his own affair.

For nearly a thirty-year period after the Castellammarese War no internal squabbles marred the unity of our Family and no outside interference threatened the Family or me.

During normal times, therefore, other than meeting with other Fathers and meeting with group leaders within my Family on an ad hoc basis, being a Father took up relatively little of my time. Family matters were largely handled by the group leaders under me. Indeed, there were many Family members I never met.

If I convened a Family meeting, I met only with the group leaders, who in turn passed the information to people in their groups. Once a year at Christmas I liked to hold a feast, a purely social function, with my group leaders. Of course, since these men were my friends we often saw each other at other functions, such as a wedding or a funeral or a baptism.

When there was peace—and peace-keeping, I reiterate, was the Father's main responsibility—I was free to devote most of my time to my private business concerns. When there was no emergency in the Family, I spent my time earning a living.

Usually, at my various businesses, my partner would make

an office available for me, where I could make phone calls or accept visitors or discuss business matters.

Early in my career as a Father I had an office on Metropolitan Avenue in the Williamsburg neighborhood. This office was a small private room in back of a political club which I had set up for the benefit of my friends. It was called the Abraham Lincoln Independent Political Club. The Brooklyn borough president attended the club's grand opening. Throughout the existence of the club, we would be visited by multitudes of politicians seeking our endorsement.

The club consisted of one long room with chairs and card tables, and a little kitchen. People, especially the older crowd, came there to while away the time, playing cards, drinking espresso or discussing soccer matches. My office was in the back. A tag on the door said "Private."

My visitors at the club might include a group leader or any of a number of people outside the Family. I was an important "man of respect," and in my immigrant world, at least, I was a crucial man to know, regardless of the visitor's background. Some old-timers would greet me. People might come by to chat about our hometowns, or to ask me to be the godfather at their baby's baptism, or to invite me to a wedding, or to ask me for a small favor concerning their business. The topics were random.

One of the side benefits of being connected with so many different people was that I rarely had to pay money (although I often did anyway) for many of my mundane needs. I had friends and associates in most every trade. Restaurant owners were available to dine me, barbers to clip me, tailors to suit me, doctors to cure me, mechanics to tune engines for me, and so on.

For nearly thirty years after I became Father my Family enjoyed balmy days, right through the Depression of the 1930s, the war years of the 1940s and the heydays of the 1950s.

Until the mid-1950s, my name was hardly known to the press, and the other members of my Family likewise stirred no publicity.

13

THE COMMISSION WAS NOT AN INTEGRAL PART OF MY TRA-
dition. No such agency existed in Sicily. The Commission was
an American adaptation.

First of all, we had to establish procedures. For example,
who would open our meetings? Who would call us to order?
Who would be in charge of contacting everyone else for a
meeting? If an out-of-town Father visited New York, who would
he contact in order to get in touch with the Commission?

We selected Vincent Mangano to chair our meetings. Joe
Profaci became a sort of secretary for the Commission. I don't
know what you would call Mangano. Maybe "chairman" or
"speaker of the house." He continued in this role until the early
1950s, when he disappeared and was presumed dead. Then I
replaced him.

On substantive issues, we agreed that no Family and no
Father should interfere with the affairs of another Family, but
that the Commission, as an agent of harmony, could arbitrate
disputes brought before it.

The Commission would have influence but no direct executive power. It had respect only insofar as its individual
members had respect. More than anything else, the Commission was a forum.

Modes of power are everywhere the same. In my world,
there were some Fathers I liked and some I detested. But I had
to try to work with all of them. Also, some of these Fathers
were more powerful than others, and these men, like myself
leaders of powerful Families, were entitled to sit on the Commission. By participating in these diplomatic conventions,

Families did not give up their independence; they were free to do what they wanted. The Commission could only exert influence.

As the Father of a Family I was like a head of state. I did the same sort of things that heads of state do on an international level. I too had to maintain internal order. I too had to conduct foreign affairs with other Families. And if my Family and other Families had similar interests, we tended to associate in the same political faction.

We agreed to hold national conventions once every five years. Our first national meeting was in 1931, when the Commission was formed. Subsequent meetings were held in 1936, 1941, 1946, 1951 and 1956. Among other things, these conventions served to confirm the membership of the Commission for another five-year term.

As a rule, the representatives from Chicago remained aloof from Commission business except when it affected them directly. Chicago enjoyed a quasi-independent status in the politics of our world. Unlike New York City, which had five Families, Chicago had only one. That created less tension and gave the Chicago people greater scope to solve their own problems. Also, it wasn't in Chicago's interest to get mixed up in the perpetual discord in New York City, which took up much of the Commission's attention.

New York City dominated the Commission, and the history of the Commission is largely the history of the rise and fall of the various leaders there. The Volcano, because of its intense energy and contested wealth, was not a safe place for Fathers. In other cities with only one Family, Fathers, with rare exceptions, enjoyed long careers and died of natural causes. In New York City, however, where strife was almost routine, Fathers led precarious lives.

Let's briefly trace the succession of Fathers in New York City up to 1957. Luciano remained Father of his Family until the mid-1930s. He was replaced by Frank Costello, who in turn was replaced by Vito Genovese in 1955.

Mangano remained Father of his Family until 1951. That's when Anastasia replaced him. After Anastasia, the Father of this Family became Carlo Gambino.

Gagliano was a Father until 1953, when Tommy Lucchese took his place.

Joe Profaci and I retained leadership of our Families without interruption throughout this period. Among Commission representatives, we shared this longevity with Stefano Magaddino of Buffalo.

The Families represented on the Commission that showed the most stability were those of Magaddino, Profaci and Bonanno. We composed the conservative faction on the Commission. Mangano and Gagliano too were considered conservatives. We were the Tories of the Commission, and for almost thirty years our views prevailed.

We were the most tradition-bound, and our philosophy reflected our Sicilian roots. For example, we steadfastly opposed such immoral enterprises as prostitution and narcotics trafficking. For nearly thirty years, we on the conservative faction presented a common front. In the early days, Mangano often was our spokesman; later, it fell on me to represent our faction.

If the Commission had its conservative, or Sicilian, wing, it also had its liberal, or American, wing. As a general rule, although they didn't always side together, men such as Luciano, Lucchese, Genovese, Anastasia and Gambino represented new tendencies in our Tradition. All of these men, to a greater or lesser extent, reflected and embodied American trends which we of the old school found distasteful and potentially ruinous.

The prime example of this new breed of "Americanized" men entering our world was Charlie "Lucky" Luciano. Although he didn't last long as a Father, Luciano was the forerunner of things to come. Because of his success and fame, Luciano left a legacy that eventually changed the face of my Tradition. For this reason, it is worthwhile to take a closer look at Charlie Lucky.

Although a Sicilian by birth, Luciano was brought to America at an early age. Consequently, he had more American traits than Sicilian traits. Luciano was the product of American ideas.

After Luciano became a Father of one of the New York City Families, he went on to become one of the most publicized figures in our world. In terms of recognition by the American public, Luciano's name probably ranked second only to that of Al Capone. Luciano, who didn't seem to shun the limelight, became a celebrity.

When I first met Charlie Lucky toward the end of the Castellammarese War, he was slightly older than me. Even then he was a very successful man with a wide range of contacts. Many parts of his character I personally liked. Although illiterate, he possessed a shrewd intelligence and level-mindedness that made him a good leader and superb organizer. Charlie Lucky and I treated each other as equals while we knew each other. Our personal relationship was marked by politeness and respect.

When I first got to know him, however, I was still in my twenties and I could not fully realize the implications of Luciano's ideas on my Tradition. Charlie Lucky paid lip service to our Tradition, largely because he had to deal with Sicilians in the course of his affairs; but he thought the Tradition was antiquated. Although he wouldn't say it to our faces, Charlie Lucky was contemptuous of the old-style Sicilian "dons," or "Mustache Petes," as they were derisively called.

Unlike most of the Family patriarchs of that era, Luciano had never "lived" the Tradition; he therefore never truly understood it instinctively. To him, when the old-style Sicilians talked of "honor" and "respect," it was all so much cant and blather.

Charlie Lucky was a true American in that he was free of tradition. He had grown up in lower Manhattan and had seen, perhaps better than those of us who immigrated to America later in our lives, the new conditions prevalent in this country. Charlie Lucky believed in business. Without a tradition to guide him, Charlie Lucky fell back for his system of values on the most primitive consideration: making money. His conversation was not laced with idealistic words such as "honor" and "trust" but with mundane ones such as "outfit" and "syndicate."

Men of my Tradition have always considered wealth a by-product of power. Men of the old Tradition were mainly in the people business. They derived their satisfaction from being responsible for a Family of men, who in turn were beholden to them. Cooperation of this kind almost always led to the mutual monetary satisfaction of all parties. But making money was not the uppermost consideration. The main purpose of banding into a Family was to establish a network of relationships that would at once establish order within the Family and give members of that Family an advantage in dealings outside the Family.

Americanized men such as Charlie Lucky marched to a different drummer. Luciano never imbibed the true spirit of our Tradition. In his personal life, for example, he was not a family man. He was a bachelor who conducted his business out of a suite in the Waldorf-Astoria under the name Charles Ross. Men of my Tradition, in addition to their prowess in fighting, are noted for their domestic natures. Luciano was essentially a loner, an "individual" as opposed to a family man.

Consequently, the relationship between Luciano and the men who congregated around him was less that of father to sons than that of board chairman to corporation officers. Luciano was most interested in monetary results; all of that other stuff about Sicilian ideals was phony baloney to him. When Charlie Lucky was coming up in the world during the 1920s, the President of the United States was Calvin Coolidge. If nothing else, both men had this in common: They both believed the business of America was business.

Luciano was iconoclastic also in that he had no qualms about working with non-Sicilians. He had in his coterie Jews such as Meyer Lansky, Louis Lepke and Bugsy Siegel, and non-Sicilian Italians such as Frank Costello, Vito Genovese and Albert Anastasia.

Men of my Tradition were always loath to associate with non-Sicilians. The reason for this was not bigotry but common sense. They knew that it is very difficult, if not impossible, to pass on a tradition unless one is exposed to it almost from the cradle. As we have already seen in this book, a lot of background has to be absorbed before the drama becomes sensible. A tradition is not something that one learns overnight. It is the work of a lifetime.

Even southern Italians, from the Naples region or from Calabria, who otherwise have much in common with Sicilians, cannot fully appreciate the old Tradition of Sicily.

For example, southern Italy has in the past given rise to such groups as the Camorra and the Black Hand. These non-Sicilian groups were orders formed to accommodate the interests of thugs, highwaymen and extortionists. It is a grave mistake to identify these groups as being the same as the "Families" of my Sicilian Tradition. Americans, as well as southern Italians, have often made this mistake. Camorra and the Black Hand never existed in Sicily. They have nothing to do with what Americans refer to as "the Mafia."

Because of the melting-pot effect in America and the need

for recruits during the Castellammarese War, we Sicilians found ourselves accepting into our confidence many non-Sicilians. Men joined our ranks who didn't fully appreciate our Tradition, or only understood it in a very rudimentary and superficial way.

It is in this context that one should evaluate the pronouncements of Joe Valachi. In the early 1960s, Valachi, a petty thief given protection by the FBI, went before the McClellan Committee of the U.S. Senate and before a national television audience revealed the so-called workings of what he called *la cosa nostra*.

I often used to hear this expression from Vincent Mangano. He used it idiomatically, as I use the phrase "in my world."

My Tradition goes by many names in this country: Some prefer the term "Mafia," others like *cosa nostra*. In his posthumous biography, Luciano refers to something called the *union Siciliano*. These are all metaphors. Presumably, we are all talking about the same thing. But notice how our different perspectives inspire us to adopt different terms to describe it. And, of course, the reason there is no formal term to describe it is that there never was a formal organization to describe. We're talking about a tradition, a way of life, a process.

There is no point in going over Valachi's testimony in detail. Often he described historical events in which he never participated but nonetheless inserted himself to make himself seem important to his gullible audience.

Valachi gave an interpretation to my Tradition that made it look cheap and totally criminal in operation. Because he never rose very high himself, Valachi mainly came in contact with the dregs of our society, our lowlife. In his unsophisticated mind, he probably thought everyone in our Tradition was like that.

In the same manner, one can have a simpleminded or an enlightened view of Catholicism, let's say. The simpleminded man will be attracted to the church's ceremonies, saints, miracles and all the outer show of religion. The more sophisticated man will go beyond these trappings to the ideas they stand for, to the elevated level of love, charity and grace.

Valachi is just a special instance of a broad trend of Americanization that began to transform my Tradition in this country as more non-Sicilians and Americanized Sicilians joined us.

Valachi represents an example of this trend on a low level as Luciano represented it on a high level. To return to Luciano, then, the crucial observation is that he didn't do things strictly in the Sicilian manner. He was much too American for that. Charlie Lucky was more businesslike and also more democratic than the old-style Sicilian leaders. This later tendency, in fact, probably was his undoing.

In the mid-1930s, New York special prosecutor Thomas Dewey successfully pinned a prostitution racket charge on Luciano. I don't know how Charlie Lucky made money when he was a young street hustler, but in the 1930s when he was a Father I personally doubt very much whether Lucky was the prostitution overlord of Manhattan, as was charged. At that time, Luciano already was a millionaire, and he undoubtedly had money-making interests of a more sophisticated and lucrative nature than prostitution.

Also, prostitution is one of the activities outlawed by my Tradition. It is unseemly and immoral for a man to make money off women. As head of one of the New York Families, I think Luciano respected the rest of us enough not to risk incurring our ill will over prostitution. Even Al Capone, who they say began his Chicago career in brothels, later gave up his prostitution interests as a gesture of respectability when he became part of our Tradition.

Lastly, Dewey built up a case not so much against Luciano as against Luciano's name. Prostitutes, madams, pimps, brothel owners and money collectors testified in court that they heard Luciano was *supposed* to be in control of prostitution in the city. Indeed, what probably happened was that men trying to organize the prostitution trade in Manhattan used Luciano's name as a way to intimidate recalcitrant brothel owners.

Also, former or present friends of Luciano's might have been involved in prostitution without Luciano's knowing about it. If this was true, Luciano should have been more careful about the activities of those in his Family. Luciano's men tended to be merely businesslike, and many of them liked to free-lance—thus undermining the authority of the Father. One can see how this way of thinking might have encouraged men within our Tradition, especially the young, the desperate or the disenchanted, to nurture private, egotistic ambitions instead of blending themselves into Family-oriented ambitions.

* * *

I never saw Luciano after he was convicted and sent to prison. His position as Father of one of the New York City Families was taken over by Frank Costello. Vito Genovese, a member of the same Family and the only other man who could have challenged Costello for the top spot, was not around to complicate Costello's life. Vito had fled to Italy after being charged with murder in the U.S.

Costello was a suave and diplomatic man. His skill at cultivating friendships among politicians and public officials was such that it earned him the nickname "the Prime Minister." He preferred to settle arguments at the conference table rather than in the streets.

Despite his moderate ways, Costello knew that to survive in our world a man had to be versatile, and thus Costello was not without his "muscle." In the 1940s, Costello's strong-arm was Willie Moretti—the man who had bailed me out of a detention center when I came to this country in 1924. In the 1920s, Willie was under the influence of my cousin Stefano Magaddino. Later, he moved to New Jersey and joined Luciano's Family. Willie was an exuberant man, colorful, quick to act and not afraid to speak his mind.

One of the reasons Costello relied on Moretti was to foil any lingering ambition Vito Genovese might have to become Father. Vito resurfaced in the mid-1940s when murder charges against him were dropped, clearing the way for him to leave Italy and return to the Volcano.

For a while, Genovese acted dutifully toward Costello, but trouble was brewing. If Costello was often seen in the company of Moretti, Genovese was now seen in the company of Tommy Lucchese, who belonged to a different Family. Meanwhile, Albert Anastasia, from yet a different Family, was known to like Costello; but Carlo Gambino, in the same Family as Anastasia, was very close to Lucchese. These inter-Family alliances were common in New York as no place else, and complicated all our lives.

By the late 1940s, New York City was like a firecracker that could go off anytime. We conservatives on the Commission viewed these developments with dismay. The Commission was supposed to alleviate such discord, but things seemed to be getting increasingly out of control. Although I knew all the men just mentioned, I didn't associate with them as closely as I did with such Fathers as Vincent Mangano, Joe Profaci and Stefano Magaddino, with all of whom I had either kinship, social or philosophic ties.

Vincent Mangano felt the pressure more than the rest of us, because he was older and younger men in his Family coveted his position. He had to be especially wary of Anastasia, who probably had the most fearsome reputation in our world. I used to call Albert *il terremoto*—the earthquake. Albert's ambition did not sit well with Mangano.

On many occasions, I would go to Mangano's city home or to his farm for a feast. Often Joe Profaci would be there, as would Profaci's right-hand man, Joe Magliocco, a prodigious eater. We'd have a fine time. Not only was there good talk, but the meals that Mangano and Magliocco cooked were often better, and certainly more elaborate, than those served at fancy restaurants.

These home meals were endless. We'd start dinner with fresh fish, which fishermen from Sheepshead Bay in Brooklyn would provide Mangano daily. At one meal we might sample halibut, snapper, shrimp, clams and lobster. Then Vincent would bring out platters of meat—veal and filet mignon. Each plate and each course appealed to a different taste bud. We would eat the pasta last. Magliocco always insisted on eating pasta last, almost as an afterthought.

By the time we reached the pasta, we'd have drunk many bottles of wine and it would usually be early in the morning.

—How can you think of leaving now? Vincent would say as the rest of us made ready to depart his home. It's two A.M. and it's snowing outside. Why don't we rest a bit, and then we'll start cooking all over again?

Meals such as these, prepared and presided over by us men only, were fraternal occasions that ranked among the finest pleasures of life. We'd drink, eat, sing, recite poems, tell jokes and swap stories. Every five minutes it seemed someone or other would be raising his glass to propose a toast.

The time-honored Sicilian manner of proposing a toast requires the recitation of a rhyming couplet. Each man at the table would take turns proposing a toast, displaying as much wit and ingenuity as he could.

148

—Lucky are we sitting at this table
—For if we stand up, we may not be able.

We'd all chink our glasses (which had to be full) and then, in a little while, another spontaneous toast would ring out. As the evening wore on and we emptied more wine bottles, our verses usually lapsed into doggerel.

—Friends, if after this meal I die in Brookulino,
—I ask to be buried with my mandolino.

Since we spoke in Italian, it's difficult to capture in English the exact spirit of our poetic attempts. But I think the idea is clear. Vincent was very good at this toasting ritual. On other occasions, my right-hand man, Frank Garofalo, also displayed talent in this game. They used to say, however, that I was the toasting champion of the dinner table.

Vincent was constantly alarmed at the new direction our Tradition was taking in America. He believed that as a Father it was his responsibility to guide his "sons."

—These boys nowadays, he would complain, they all think they're thoroughbreds. They don't listen.

—Aiii-iiaai! Joe Profaci would exclaim. These Americans are going to dirty us with their new ways.

Many times, I heard Vincent say:

—Peppino, we're going to lose our Tradition.

Once we were sitting on the porch of Magliocco's farmhouse in Long Island when Vincent pointed to a nearby tree.

—See that tree? Vincent said.

It was an old tree with no leaves. I sensed that Vincent wanted to make some comparison to himself, but I didn't want to encourage his pessimism.

—Come on, I said, they're waiting for us inside.

—See that tree?

—What are you talking about?

I also sensed, as can only a Sicilian who has been used to it all his life, that in trying to make the tree analogy Vincent wanted to test me. He was trying to judge how open he could be with me and he was trying to decide whether I wanted to hear everything that was on his mind.

—That tree, Vincent persisted. There, in front of us.

—What about it?

I was being noncommittal. It does no good to hear certain information. If you don't know certain things, you can remain neutral. Once you find out certain vital information, you have to take sides. The general rule in my world is that unless you're prepared to take sides, it's better not to know certain information.

Vincent was feeling me out to see if he could reveal certain information about his situation and his enemies, but from my evasive replies he realized that I was not prepared to get involved. Therefore, he used the allusion to the tree merely to make an obvious point about our respective ages, rather than as the starting point for the disclosure of privileged information.

—That's me, Vincent said of the old tree.

Then he pointed to another tree, a straight, young tree.

—See that tree?

—Are we going through this again? I said in mock resentment.

—That tree is you.

That was Vincent's way of telling me he understood my position and would not pursue the matter.

—I think you see what I see, Vincent said with great delicacy.

Don Vicenzu, as Mangano was known in Sicilian, was in his sixties then. No man his age relishes a knockout fight. Vincent had probably seen enough fighting from his days on the waterfront. After leaving Palermo for Brooklyn, Vincent made a name for himself along the wharves and docks. Out of this Brooklyn waterfront also emerged Albert Anastasia. If I had let him, Vincent would have talked about Anastasia.

Among other things, Mangano didn't like Anastasia's closeness to Costello. In 1950 or so, when Costello spent a short time in prison, it was said that Costello had asked Anastasia (whom he knew from their days with Luciano) to help Moretti look after his interests while Costello was in jail. Costello feared that while he was in prison Vito Genovese might make a move to seize power in that Family.

What bothered Mangano was that Costello, by asking for Anastasia's help, had never consulted Mangano and therefore had, in effect, snubbed the head of a Family by going directly to a subordinate. In my world, such a breach of decorum is a sign, a signal of new alliances and possible intrigues.

Fear is when you think ahead about what may happen to you. Fear is anticipating the future and assuming the worst possible scenario. Mangano and Anastasia were at a stage where they feared one another. Each man feared the other would act first; each wanted to be the first to act.

I read about it in the newspaper at my winter residence in Tucson, Arizona. Vincent Mangano disappeared. To this day, they haven't found his body.

14

Upon my return to the volcano in 1951, I wanted to observe the faces of the men to whom the disappearance of Vincent Mangano was of importance. In touchy situations such as these, you have to learn what you can by reading faces, by deciphering facial masks. You can't just go around to your peers, demanding confessions. That's looking for trouble.

On Anastasia's face I saw no emotion.

On the face of Costello, who had just been released from prison, I saw indifference.

Tommy Lucchese's face seemed to say, So what?

On Genovese's face, I saw a crease of concern.

The face of Willie Moretti showed agitation.

Joe Profaci and I had glum faces. Vincent's death was a personal loss. Otherwise, it didn't directly affect our positions. We had no immediate reason to feel threatened. Our only choice was to carry on. As a Father, my priority was to keep my Family out of intrigues that were fragmenting the other Families.

After Mangano's death, his Family recognized Anastasia as the new Father, and Albert took his place on the Commission. No one seemed to resent Albert's elevation more than Moretti. Anastasia now was head of his own Family and closer to Costello than ever. Up to then, it had been Moretti who was the closest to Costello. Moretti had prided himself on being the "iron" behind Costello's influence.

Neither Willie nor Albert was Sicilian. Their parents were from the Calabria region of southern Italy. However, they both admired the Sicilian Tradition, and I think what rubbed off on

152

them made them better men. An aspect of manly behavior, according to my Tradition, is strict control over one's emotions. This appealed to Willie and Albert because they themselves realized it was a failing of theirs. They were wild men inside.

Before they became antagonists, Willie and Albert were amusing to watch together. Since they both were *paesani* from Calabria and since both were hotheads, they never seemed at a loss for words when with each other. They would go to a corner or to an adjoining room and pretty soon you'd hear them squalling. They'd grow red in the face and get all agitated, barraging each other with profanities. You'd think something terrible would happen. Then, after the bawling, Willie and Albert would emerge smiling, with their arms around each other. Anger was their way of calming down.

When Anastasia talked in front of the Commission after Mangano's death, he neither denied nor admitted rumors that he was behind Vincent's disappearance. He didn't admit any-thing. However, he said he had proof that Mangano had been plotting to kill him. Anastasia wanted to impress on us that if someone was out to kill him, then he had the right to protect himself. Strictly speaking, Albert was correct. It was common knowledge that he and Mangano were heading for a showdown. Either man, once the other was out of the way, could claim self-protection. It just so happened Albert was the victor.

Costello also spoke before the Commission and vouched for Anastasia. Frank said Albert's story was correct. With such impressive backing from Costello, Anastasia's position on the Commission was assured.

Costello's corroboration of Anastasia's story must have up-set Moretti. The Costello-Anastasia nexus had been openly acknowledged. Where did this leave Moretti? It undermined him. Willie, who did not like to keep his feelings to himself, spread the word that he didn't know anything about Mangano's plot against Anastasia. If Anastasia had told Costello, Willie wondered, why hadn't Costello told his right-hand man? Moretti felt betrayed and diminished by Costello's new "love."

Moretti was a garrulous fellow to begin with, but this time he was being more talkative than usual. Some thought he had lost his mind brazenly to challenge Costello and Anastasia at once. Unfortunately for Willie, he did have something wrong with him at this time, a physical ailment. He was in the later stages of syphilis. Regardless of whether his grievance was right or wrong, Willie's mind was rapidly disintegrating. He was an embarrassment.

Moretti was shot to death inside a New Jersey restaurant. At our Commission meeting, we treated the news diplomatically. Costello and Anastasia said Moretti was a sick man. We could not disagree. Poor Willie.

Moretti's death, regardless of who was behind it, rid Costello of a fractious and disaffected ally. At the same time, Willie's demise provided Vito Genovese an opening for his machinations.

After Genovese returned from his self-imposed exile in Italy, he rejoined Costello's Family. After Moretti's death, Vito became the second most important man in that Family, a position that couldn't be denied him considering his long service in the Family and the support he had among many of its members.

Costello wanted a strong man next to him—first Moretti and then Anastasia—in order to thwart Genovese. To counter this, Vito made an alliance of his own with Tommy Lucchese, who at that time was the second in Gagliano's Family. It was common knowledge that Tommy and Vito were close. The expression I like to use is "They were making love."

In the early 1950s, after Gagliano died of natural causes, Lucchese became Father of that Family. Lucchese had his own reasons for allying himself with Genovese in a cold war against Costello. Lucchese and Costello more or less competed for the same sphere of influence in New York City. Both were good talkers, and this enabled them to cultivate valuable political connections. Lucchese wanted the same clout as Costello. This could only come at Costello's expense.

We had a cold war on our hands. On one side there was Costello-Anastasia, and on the other there was Lucchese-Genovese. It was a war of nerves, of strategy, of scheming. The rest of us, who were not involved, could only watch and wait.

At about this time (we're still in the early 1950s), Costello seized the initiative. He came before the Commission and declared that two individuals had told him that Tommy Lucchese was plotting against Anastasia. Costello demanded the Commission review his allegations and pronounce judgment.

Costello's startling accusation put Profaci, Magaddino and

myself in a sensitive position. By coming before us with such a seemingly strong case, Costello hoped to obtain the full backing of the Commission in censuring Lucchese. Such a censure carried a great deal of weight in my world. It could possibly give Lucchese's enemies a signal to move against him. Anything might happen, even the ultimate solution. In a sense, the Commission was being asked to decide Lucchese's fate.

Those of us who had been trying to remain aloof from the cold war, like nonaligned nations, were now being presented information that would make it impossible for us to remain neutral. Costello's diplomatic initiative was brilliant. If successful, he could ruin Lucchese and enlist the support of the conservatives all in one stroke.

We had no choice but to listen to Costello. He brought before us two men from Lucchese's Family who told us they had heard Lucchese plotting against Anastasia. They seemed to be telling the truth. Costello then said Lucchese's belligerent intentions were known to Anastasia, who did not intend to remain idle if the situation was not remedied. Costello added that if the Commission wanted to maintain peace it had to get to the truth and make a decision on Lucchese. As for himself, Costello said he would abide by whatever ruling the Commission made.

The "Prime Minister" had made his move. He did so in such a smooth, ingratiating manner that you'd think he was asking us merely to listen to a record or to look at a painting.

Profaci, Magaddino and I felt uncomfortable and reluctant to assume the role of judges over another Father.

My cousin Stefano Magaddino, when he thought is disadvantageous to participate in Commission politics in New York City, had a standard excuse:

—I live five hundred miles away in Buffalo, Stefano would say. I live far away. They can settle their arguments without me.

When it was advantageous, however, Stefano wanted to be the first to know everything that happened in New York City.

On this particular occasion, Stefano probably wished he was home in bed with a severe cold. But he couldn't wriggle out of it. Profaci also was of the same hesitant frame of mind. My mood was similar to theirs, but since there seemed no alternative but to get involved, it seemed a waste of time to continue grousing about it. Instead, I concentrated.

The day came for Lucchese to appear before the Commission. We were in session as a fact-finding tribunal. We had a right, as heads of the major Families, to arrive at a clarification of the charges brought before us. A proclamation by us was necessary.

We met in a private house which had a spacious basement and a large table. The atmosphere was cordial but restrained. There was none of the bonhomie that marked our less extraordinary meetings.

As always, Costello looked dapper. He was fond of well-tailored suits and manicured fingernails. He was an intelligent, fluent man who was as conscious of everything going on around him as he was of his appearance. Frank was a man of stature, with contacts at every level of society. In his lifetime, he dealt with such people as New York Mayor Fiorello La Guardia and Louisiana Senator Huey Long. Frank maintained, and I have no reason to doubt it, that during Prohibition he and Joe Kennedy of Boston were partners in the liquor business.

Frank lived to be eighty-two years old. He died of natural causes in 1973. Shortly before he died, so I read in the *New York Times*, Frank decided to tell the story of his life and he contacted a biographer. Too bad Frank didn't have time to carry out his project. Considering all the rich and mighty people he knew, it would have made fascinating reading.

For this special Commission meeting, Costello brought along Vito Genovese, his second. Of course, Genovese could not vote. By bringing him along, however, Costello once more showed his astuteness. Costello, as well as the rest of us, knew that Genovese had been "flirting" with Lucchese. By observing them in the same room, Costello could read their faces and try to determine how this latest development had affected their relationship. Perhaps Vito or Tommy would break down or make a slip of the tongue. Costello sought to scotch Lucchese and embarrass Genovese at the same time, thereby neutralizing his main opposition.

Genovese had dark hair and rugged good looks. He also dressed well but on the flashy side. Probably the most sensitive subject with Vito was his wife, who had a temperamental nature. You just didn't talk to Vito about his wife.

Also sitting at the meeting table was Anastasia, a tall, handsome man with wavy hair. He was a modest dresser. Albert was not interested in making a good impression. He was plainspoken and artless. To me, these qualities were more important than his pugnacity.

During World War II, I remember seeing Albert when he'd come home on leave. He reached the rank of sergeant in the army. And he was just as proud of his uniform and his stripes as any farm boy from Kansas.

Men who know their own strength, who know their mind and are secure, don't have to brag or make a show of their strength. Such men are not neurotic. There's no facade to their personality. That's how Albert was.

Next to me sat Joe Profaci and Stefano Magaddino. Joe and I had been Fathers since the era of the Castellammarese War. We were both based in Brooklyn. Joe's brother, Salvatore, was one of my best friends. Joe was of middle height, and although he wasn't fat, he had a paunch. Joe certainly never lost any sleep worrying about what to wear the following day. He dressed simply, if not carelessly. More than anything else, Joe liked to run his oil import business and be with his family. A most successful businessman, Joe's interest in Family politics and intra-fighting had been on the wane for some time.

Stefano was on the short side. His stoutness made him appear shorter than he was. My cousin was hardheaded and cantankerous. If you didn't know him well, you'd think he was obtuse. He affected a rustic simplicity. But he was far from dumb. His instinct for self-preservation was uncanny. Since he was my cousin and since we both came from Castellammare, people tended to think of us as inseparable.

Despite our closeness, however, Stefano and I had fundamentally different characters. I was debonair, articulate and, if I may say so, prepossessing. I don't think Stefano ever resigned himself to our differences. You see, I was younger than he, and yet in our world I had surpassed Stefano in prestige among other Fathers.

It's difficult to talk of oneself without prejudice. In general, people considered me an attractive man. They generally praised my charm and intelligence. I liked to dress well, but I preferred to evince an air of subdued good taste rather than gaudiness.

My one touch of flamboyance was my pinky rings. I had rings displaying ruby, sapphire, jade and onyx.

I had my faults, too. And I guess there's no better way to show them than to write a book about myself. It becomes obvious then what you're like and how you think. But setting aside these subjective remarks about myself, there are some objective remarks I can make that place me in the proper context in relation to the other Fathers. I had not trod on anyone else's feet. I had not meddled in the affairs of others. My Family was unbesmirched by scandal. My name was clean, my reputation solid.

Once we arranged ourselves around the table, in no particular order, we called on Tommy Lucchese to enter. We greeted him with forced politeness. Lucchese handled himself well, not showing any signs of nervousness. He was a short, fair-haired man. He had a clean-cut face and dressed with care. His appearance, however, was a little too slick, too studied. He always looked as if he had just been varnished. Finesse and opportunism were his trademarks. He also always seemed in control of himself, and when he walked into the room he didn't disappoint us. Not one of his mannerisms betrayed the fact that he was in a dire predicament.

On one of his hands he had only three fingers; hence his nickname, Three Fingers. No one called him that to his face. He was very sensitive about this slight deformity—the only dent in his otherwise spruce appearance.

Lucchese, as I well remembered, was instrumental in Maranzano's downfall.

It was an uncomfortable time for us all, but it was not the Amateur Hour. Despite the repugnance of our task, we were none of us novices in the game of power. We were all qualified.

Costello reviewed the case against Lucchese, including the damaging testimony from two of Lucchese's own men. This was Costello's big moment. With his eyes shifting from Lucchese to Genovese, Costello said the evidence spoke for itself. He had nothing to add. He disclaimed any bias. He said he was interested only in justice.

Lucchese remained expressionless. A man with less fortitude would have melted. We expected him to defend himself.

—I have nothing to say, Lucchese said calmly.

Lucchese rather gave the impression of a snobbish English gentleman who did not want to dignify the slanders against him with a reply. As for Costello, he seemed slightly frustrated but still confident of victory. In the meantime, not a peep out of Vito.

If by his accusations Costello intended to undercut Lucchese and Vito, so far his plan was not working. Lucchese had shown, by his willingness to appear before the Commission, that he was not afraid. He could have refused to come. He could have run away or barricaded himself. But then his chance of retaining power would have been nil. Lucchese was smart, as smart as Costello. Tommy had something on his mind.

Profaci and Magaddino took Lucchese's silence to be an admission of guilt. They didn't want, and were not inclined, to probe deeper. Neither of them particularly liked Lucchese. For that matter, neither did I. He was too sneaky for my taste. And he had betrayed Maranzano. Whatever my personal feelings, however, I had to transcend them. I had a higher responsibility than to myself.

I looked at Tommy from across our table and said:
—Look at my face. You know me well.
—Yes, Peppino, Lucchese answered with a wan smile.
—Say something.
—What can I say?

If this had been a standard court, Lucchese could be said to have pleaded nolo contendere. He didn't deny the charges. But he didn't admit guilt either.

During the subsequent lull, as we considered what to do next, I tried to interpret what had transpired. There had to be more than what appeared on the surface. I knew Costello and Lucchese were engaged in a deadly chess game.

Costello had made several deft moves. It was he who had called and had insisted on having Stefano attend this Commission meeting. Strictly speaking, the Lucchese matter was of concern mainly to the New York City Fathers. We could have held a Commission meeting without Stefano, because the Fathers in New York City alone composed a quorum. The Chicago representative was not there.

Nonetheless, Costello knew that Stefano, a member of the conservative wing, was valuable to him for other reasons. By insisting that all of us on the conservative wing be there, it seemed that Costello was making a concerted effort either to force us to take his side or maybe to splinter us.

Costello's strategy became clearer. By maneuvering the conservative faction to his side, he hoped to augment his position on the Commission. Also, by putting Lucchese in an untenable position, Costello hoped to break up an alliance between Lucchese and Genovese that threatened him. In short, Costello had devised a daring and imaginative plan.

Profaci and Magaddino seemed oblivious to these considerations. They would just as soon have voted and gotten the whole wretched business out of the way. In a sense, I had to think for both of them. The drama before the Commission went beyond Lucchese's innocence or guilt. The viability of the conservative faction was also at stake.

For all his cunning, Costello had not counted on Lucchese's strange silence. When a man is accused of plotting to kill another man he is usually eager to speak up, to own up to it or deny it. This Lucchese had a grip on himself. The evidence went wholly against him. Costello had a strong case, or he wouldn't have made it. Why had Lucchese chosen to remain silent? It baffled me, although I knew he was up to something.

What was Tommy trying to tell me?

It must be remembered that I did not have a great deal of time to pursue my deliberations. We were hardly in a position to table the matter and adjourn. I had to make decisions on the spur of the moment, relying on all my experience and instincts.

I tried to put myself in Lucchese's place. Since he had not denied it, it seemed to be true that Lucchese had plotted to kill Anastasia. In that case, Lucchese's only legitimate defense could be that he was trying to protect himself against Albert. There could be no other rationalization. If Lucchese admitted anything else, he would damn himself. So why hadn't Lucchese come right out and said this? Why didn't Lucchese say something along the lines of "I was trying to get Albert because I knew he was trying to get me"?

Well, if Lucchese had asserted this it would have placed him in a difficult spot. Anastasia, for one, would have immediately protested and demanded that Lucchese prove his assertion. Apparently, Lucchese didn't have clear-cut proof against Anastasia. If he did, Lucchese might have been the first one before the Commission instead of Costello. Also, the moment Lucchese admitted plotting against Anastasia, Costello would have jumped on this to force Lucchese to implicate Genovese in the plot as well. Costello would have averred that in plotting against such a powerful man as Anastasia, Lucchese would have had to have the tacit or active support of someone else. And all eyes in the room would have glanced at Genovese.

I concluded that Costello wanted Lucchese to talk in order to implicate Genovese with him. This had not happened. Lucchese and Genovese were acting like mutes. Although he had not ensnared Genovese, Costello was nonetheless confident that the Commission would at least remove the pestiferous Lucchese. Costello therefore called for a quick vote on Lucchese's alleged treachery.

I did not want to move so fast. My only chance of discovering the full truth was to talk to Lucchese alone. He might tell me something which he wouldn't in front of the entire group.

How could I propose such a private conversation at the eleventh hour? Costello was getting impatient for a vote. He wanted us to go into the next room to make our decision immediately.

How would it have looked in front of the others if I had suddenly objected and asked to talk to Lucchese in private? The others would have wondered why I was sticking up for this weasel Lucchese. I would have needlessly opened myself to reproof or suspicion. Most assuredly, Costello would have objected. I would have put myself in a position of defending a louse.

—I was just thinking, Frank, I said. Perhaps if we let Joe Profaci talk to Tommy, he'll open up. Let's give Tommy the full benefit of the doubt.

Costello had already presented himself as being only interested in justice. Now that I had appealed to his sense of fairness in front of the other men, if Costello refused to go along with my suggestion it would have put him in a bad light. It would have made him seem to be out only for vengeance.

Costello also knew that he wouldn't be risking much by agreeing to allow Profaci to talk to Lucchese. Costello realized, as I did, that Profaci and Magaddino hadn't penetrated behind the screen of his well-orchestrated scenario. He agreed to my suggestion, not suspecting that I had ulterior motives and was matching wits against him.

Profaci and Lucchese stepped into the next room, with Profaci mumbling,

—Why do I have to do this?

A few minutes later they returned to the main room.

—Tommy won't open up to me, Profaci declared. Perhaps he'll open up to Peppino.

That's exactly what I wanted to hear. But that's not what Costello wanted to hear. Frank was beginning to catch on. He knew that Lucchese had always spoken highly of me and always tried to ingratiate himself with me. He also knew that among Profaci, Magaddino and me, I was the only one alert enough to outmaneuver him.

—All right, Costello said, but let Stefano go with Peppino.

A good parry on Costello's part. Frank knew that Stefano didn't like Lucchese and that Lucchese was aware of this. In all probability, therefore, Lucchese wouldn't talk freely with Stefano in the room. Costello knew that Profaci and Magaddino had made up their minds against Lucchese. However, he knew that I had a supple mind and he wanted to avoid, if possible, my talking to Lucchese individually.

Stefano grumbled and hemmed at Costello's suggestion. Talking to Lucchese was a waste of time as far as Stefano was concerned. But to be magnanimous, Stefano agreed. He and I went into the next room to talk to Lucchese.

Lucchese remained silent.

—Don't you understand, Stefano said futilely, we *want* to hear what you have to say.

Stefano and I left Tommy in the side room and joined the others. Stefano's opinion of Lucchese hadn't changed. Since the Castellammarese War, Stefano had considered Tommy to be but an opportunist who survived by spying. Nevertheless, Stefano now became intrigued at my persistence in trying to get Tommy to talk. Stefano was probably asking himself, What's that cousin of mine up to? Does he know something I don't know? If he does, I want to know too. Let's see where Peppino's going.

In front of the others, Stefano suggested that since everything else had failed I should be allowed to confer with Lucchese alone. Stefano's curiosity had gotten the best of him.

And that's what I wanted all along. But I wanted someone else to suggest that I have a private tête-à-tête with Lucchese. I didn't want to make it appear that I was taking sides or trying to defend Tommy. I wanted to retain my neutrality so that whatever I might propose after my talk with Tommy would be considered impartial advice. Since Stefano was the disinterested out-of-town representative whom Costello had expressly wanted at the meeting, Frank could hardly reject Stefano's recommendation.

Lucchese and I, once alone in the side room, briefly studied each other's faces.

—Let's forget the past. We must start as if today was the first day of our lives. We must make a fresh start. Don't you agree?

—Peppino, you always understood me, Lucchese said in a cloying tone.

His silence had puzzled me at first. Gradually, I began to recognize it as a crafty ploy. Coming into the Commission meeting, Lucchese had but one trump card: information. Information is only valuable if it gets to the right person. In this case, the right person was me. I was the only person on the Commission who was adroit enough to use that information as leverage to save Lucchese. Lucchese had but one slim hope at the Commission tribunal—he had to interest me in his information. His silence was like a bait to me. It was as if he was counting on me, and me alone, to rescue him.

This delicate and dangerous game of brinkmanship was Lucchese's only hope of saving himself. But his strategy would have failed if he and I hadn't had a thorough understanding of each other's character. Lucchese knew that I had the type of character that wasn't satisfied with superficial explanation; he was counting on me to doggedly pursue the entire truth. I, on the other hand, understood Lucchese's character well enough to know that Tommy wasn't being silent out of principle. If he was being silent, he had something up his sleeve. That was Tommy—resourceful but furtive, always sly.

Alone with me, Lucchese admitted he had taken preparations to defend himself against Anastasia. His use of the word "defend" meant that in Lucchese's mind he was doing nothing wrong. He was but defending himself and his interests against a belligerent. I had suspected this, but now I had the confirmation.

Lucchese, then, by implication, had accused Anastasia of starting hostilities.

—Who gave you such an idea? I asked Tommy.

—Vito.

Lucchese didn't say any more, and I didn't urge him to say more. You have to be discreet in such delicate conversations. You don't want to know more than you have to know. One word was enough. I understood the situation.

Lucchese felt threatened by Anastasia. The information that made him feel this way came from Genovese. When men share information of this nature, as did Genovese and Lucchese, it means they are very close. If something happens to one of them, the other one feels it also. What was Vito's message to Tommy? It could only have been one thing, that Anastasia had tried or was trying to eliminate Genovese, and that if Genovese expired, Lucchese would probably be next. Lucchese, therefore, had made preparations to defend himself by striking first against Anastasia.

Neither side was right or wrong. They were both right and they were both wrong. But since each side was plotting against the other, it was a clear indication that the cold war between the Costello-Anastasia faction and the Genovese-Lucchese faction had heated up. Once combat begins, it's almost impossible to determine who started what and who's at fault. I was not interested in assigning blame. I wanted to preserve the status quo in the interest of peace.

If he succeeded in his maneuvers, Costello would tip the balance of power on the Commission in his favor. He would thwart Lucchese and check Genovese. He would succeed in his parliamentary wooing of Magaddino. If he gained Stefano's confidence and drew Stefano closer to him, Costello would splinter the conservative faction.

I wanted the political situation on the Commission to remain stable. Regardless of Lucchese's innocence or guilt, and despite his betrayal of Maranzano, I had to devise a way to rescue him. His presence on the Commission was necessary to preserve the balance of power. Although Lucchese wasn't a member of the conservative faction, I could count on his antagonism with Costello to keep the liberal wing fragmented. Also, saving

Lucchese could turn into an added advantage in that he would know where the favor came from and might help me one day—or so I vainly thought.

As I considered my next move, I had to keep in mind that whatever recommendation I made, it had to be one that would allow everyone to save face. I couldn't very well save Lucchese only to embarrass Costello and risk making him my enemy.

I advised Lucchese to place himself at the mercy of Anastasia.

Lucchese looked at me as if he had just been told to wave a flag in front of a bull.

—It's your only chance, I said. Do what I say. Your only chance is to be a true man of honor.

For the first time that evening, Lucchese's face showed signs of worry. My proposed cure to his malady seemed worse than the disease. I assured him it was for the best and that I knew what I was doing. Even if he wanted to back out, Tommy had no choice but to comply with my wishes. Without me he was defenseless and at the mercy of his enemies. I advised him on how to comport himself before the Commission. We walked out.

Before the others, I said that Lucchese had remained silent on the charges brought against him.

—But I understand Tommy wants to say something to us all, I added.

Lucchese glanced at everyone in the room. Of all the times I've seen this man, this was perhaps his finest moment. He had to convince everyone in the room that he was sincere or we'd dismiss his words. He'd actually have to be a "man of honor," perhaps for the first time in his life.

Lucchese rose to the occasion.

—I appear before you as a man of honor, he said. If I have made a mistake, I know I have to pay the penalty, no matter what it is. Albert is in the right. Albert has the right to decide my fate.

Then, turning to face Anastasia directly, Lucchese said,

—You, Albert, only you have the right to say if I should die.

For a moment, no one knew what to say. By making his appeal directly to Anastasia, as I had urged him to do, Lucchese had neutralized Costello. Anastasia couldn't very well call a time out to huddle with Costello for advice. It was a matter of pride. Anastasia had to say something on his own, make up his own mind. It was no longer up to the Commission to decide Lucchese's fate. Lucchese had put himself at Anastasia's mercy. Who better to make the judgment than the man whom Lucchese was accused of plotting against? We were all off the hook. It was up to Anastasia to decide.

The reason I thought this strategy would work was that I understood something about Anastasia's character. In the wild, when wolves fight, one wolf will indicate he is ready to yield to the other by offering his throat; then the fighting stops. In effect, Lucchese had bared his throat to Anastasia. Just as in the wild among wolves, once Lucchese yielded to Anastasia, this diffused Anastasia's ferocity.

Albert had to be in a state of rage when fighting. He was incapable of pursuing an opponent in the cool intellectual way of Costello. Albert had to feel excited about a fight. Once you calmed him, you in fact disarmed him. He wasn't a bully at heart. Once calmed, he acted generous.

—Albert Anastasia does not kill people who beg for his mercy, Albert said.

That was it.

Tommy Lucchese got off with his life, thanks to me and Albert. As for Albert, he proved he could be noble. Most important, the balance of power on the Commission was maintained.

After the meeting, my cousin Stefano was still shaking his head. He couldn't understand how Albert could have spared the life of a man who wanted to kill him.

—I have to admire Albert, he said. He's got balls.

You need much more than your masculinity, however, to survive in the Volcano. You need friends. A few years after the Lucchese tribunal, Anastasia lost his best friend on the Commission. One evening in 1955, while he was returning to his apartment, Frank Costello was sniped at. The bullet only grazed Costello's scalp but it served its purpose. It was a warning and a signal. After he recovered from his wound, Costello went into permanent retirement and lived to a ripe old age.

If someone felt confident enough to make an attempt on Costello's life, it could only mean that the tide of power in

Costello's Family had shifted from Costello to Genovese. Indeed, after the Costello shooting, his Family rallied around Genovese. The Commission couldn't interfere. For better or for worse, Costello was out, Genovese was in. Vito had been waiting a long time for this moment and he had worked diligently for it. He became a Father and took his place on the Commission.

Costello's shooting enraged Anastasia. Albert's antagonists, Vito and Tommy Lucchese, were both Fathers now. Their power was on the rise. Albert was stranded. His response was typical. He wanted to make war on Vito Genovese, possibly restoring Costello to power. Before taking to the warpath, however, Albert tested the reactions of Profaci, Magaddino and myself. Would we try to stop such a war from breaking out?

At a meeting of just us four, Albert pleaded his case. He maintained that he had a right to declare war. He asked us not to interfere or take sides. Albert wanted to wipe out Vito and anyone else with Vito. Caution was not in Anastasia's repertoire.

If we had remained neutral, Anastasia undoubtedly would have jousted with Genovese. Furthermore, during such a conflict it would have been difficult to maintain neutrality. Wars have a way of sucking everyone in. We strongly urged Albert, therefore, to desist from putting on his armor.

I stepped in vigorously to dissuade Anastasia. This was no time for subtle statecraft.

—If war breaks out, I told Albert, there'll be no winners. We're all going to lose.

In the next moment, I saw a man grow up a little. Without our promise of neutrality, Anastasia's hopes to prosecute a war were dashed. He was so impetuous, however, that he could have rushed out and initiated a war in any case. It took a new level of maturity for him to relent, as he did. Albert yielded to reason. He was making great strides as a man.

—But you three are now responsible for me, Albert said sternly after he acquiesced to our advice.

Albert was right. We had talked him into not declaring war. It was now our responsibility to guarantee the peace.

Subsequently, Anastasia and Genovese met at a select dinner

gathering attended by the other New York City Fathers. Albert and Vito exchanged accusations and made countercharges. They clarified and rationalized their positions. But at last, though reluctantly, they renounced going to war against each other. The rest of us raised our glasses in a toast for peace.

Albert and Vito kissed each other on the cheek.

15

WHAT BRINGS MOST JOY TO A FATHER'S HEART IS PEACE.

In 1956 there was peace in my world. That year, as if to celebrate this peace, my older son, Salvatore, decided to marry.

—Leave everything to me, I told him. It will be a wedding no one will ever forget.

I wanted to give my son the greatest wedding in the greatest city in the greatest country in the world.

The marriage of the eldest son is a milestone in any father's life. It marks a turning point and gives him pause to look back on his life and to look forward. When I reached that landmark in my life, I was most thankful for what I had. Fortune had been good to me. Indeed, in my most complacent moods, I imagined that the rest of my life would be placid, even dull.

I was a man of substance. I was fifty-one years old, husband to Fay and father to Salvatore, Catherine and Joseph. I owned a house on Long Island, a second house in upstate New York and a third house in Tucson, Arizona.

My fourteen-room colonial house in New York near Middletown was surrounded by 280 acres of pastures and hills. The benign atmosphere of the place inspired me to name it the Sunshine Dairy Farm. We had several steers, chickens galore and about seventy-five dairy cows, in addition to our riding horses and a menagerie of dogs. We also rotated crops of corn, barley, alfalfa and timothy.

The job of running the farm belonged to my Uncle John Bonventre, an expert dairyman. I will often choose as a business partner a man who's either related to me or is a close friend. I like to do business as if it's all in the family. And if to you this smacks of nepotism or patronage, it is. But whereas many attach negative meanings to those words, I give them positive connotations.

Aside from its business aspect, the Sunshine Dairy Farm served as a rural retreat. The pressure and stress of daily life in the Volcano can be terrific. Men have been known to keel over for good without so much as saying adieu.

It amused me to learn that in colonial times my farm was owned by an aristocratic family from England. You'd have to be an immigrant yourself to appreciate fully my pride in owning such an estate. I remember how proud my friend Joe Profaci was when he bought his estate in rural New Jersey. His spacious house was once owned by Teddy Roosevelt, and years after he bought it Joe would say the house was so large that there were rooms he hadn't discovered yet.

If my business interests were doing well by the mid-1950s, so was my personal family. Our younger son, Joseph, who was born in 1945, lived with Fay and me. Catherine, born in 1934, had recently completed high school at Mt. St. Mary's on the Hudson, a boarding school run by Dominican sisters. My older son, Salvatore, was attending the University of Arizona in Tucson. Ever since he was about nine years old, Salvatore had been living and attending schools in Arizona. He suffered from a mastoid ear infection and doctors had advised us to take him to a dry climate where his ailment wouldn't bother him as much. It was on Salvatore's account that I bought a house in Tucson.

Although he lived in Tucson most of the year, Salvatore would visit us in the summer or on holidays. He was taking pre-law courses at the University of Arizona in Tucson. Salvatore was tall and handsome, articulate and well-mannered. On one of his trips to the East, Salvatore met Rosalie Profaci, a schoolmate of Catherine's at Mt. St. Mary's and the daughter of Salvatore Profaci, a close personal friend of mine and the brother of Joe Profaci. Salvatore and Rosalie fell in love.

I was very pleased with the romance. Their marriage would bring together two eminent families. But it would be unfair to infer that I forced the marriage on Salvatore, regardless of his personal feelings. No doubt, especially when they were young, my own children saw me as an authoritarian and, at times, even a forbidding father. Nonetheless, though I desired the match between Salvatore and Rosalie, I would not have stood in his way if Salvatore had openly protested.

I was on top.

Men called me Padre and I was recognized as the leader of a *casa*—a house. I had a Family of men I was responsible for.

Being a Father was not a job in the ordinary sense of the word. Rather, I fulfilled a social function within my Tradition.

It is an injustice to the fragile network of relationships in a Family to refer to it blithely, as is done in the mass media, as an "organization." The two terms describe different levels of cooperation.

Strictly speaking, an organization is a creature of bureaucracy. It is a legal entity. Its life is really on paper. It has a charter (actual or implied), a chain of command, division of labor. It has a purpose. It is there to do a specific task, whether to manufacture widgets or to sell insurance or to rob banks.

It bears repeating how different a Family is from an organization. A Family, as an association of persons, doesn't have a specific economic task. In an organization you get paid according to your job title. But in a Family you don't receive a salary simply because you're someone's brother or cousin; you have to earn your own money. An organization is judged by such factors as profit and productivity. But a Family is judged by such factors as unity and harmony.

I did not get paid for being a Father. My recompense was in terms of influence and respect—which in turn made many other things possible. It was this prestige, not any forced servitude, that enabled me to command men.

Picture, then, an assortment of relatives and friends who share a common Tradition and who, although pursuing different activities (most legal and some illicit), do so within the framework of a Family because this enhances their chances of success. The Family members can be from all walks of life. Some of them have a high character and some of them have a low character. Some are rich and some are poor. Some are bad and some are good. To make this form of cooperation work they have to give allegiance to one man, the Father. He's the symbol that holds them together. He's the coordinator and the conciliator. He's the mediator and the fixer. He makes connections. He puts things in order when life gets complicated.

The Father has to be somewhat of a universal man. He has to deal with a variety of people, both within the Family and outside it. He has to deal with men of reason and with men who only understand force. Like a head of state, a Father has to be adept in the use of diplomacy as well as in the use of force. This is a fundamental condition of mankind.

As Machiavelli said in *The Prince:*

"For a man who, in all respects, will carry out only his profession of good, will be apt to be ruined among so many who are evil. A prince, therefore, who desires to maintain himself must learn to be not always good, but to be so or not as necessity may require. . . .

"You must know that there are two ways to carry out a contest; the one by law, and the other by force. The first is practiced by men and the other by brutes; and as the first is often insufficient, it becomes necessary to resort to the second."

By 1956, among the other Fathers in my world, both in New York and nationwide, I was highly respected. My Family was not the largest nor the wealthiest, but of the highest quality. Other Fathers often turned to me for counsel. Of all the Fathers, I was the most successful in bridging the gap between how our Tradition worked in Sicily and how we tried to make it work in America. Indeed, I was one of the few Fathers in the United States who knew how to approach Fathers of our Tradition in Sicily. I was one of the youngest Fathers, but since I had become a Father at such an early age I was also one of the most experienced Fathers. I was educated, a rarity. I knew the history of our Tradition better than most. I enjoyed a reputation for fairness and tact. Not everyone might have agreed with me but they always knew where I stood.

That which speaks more effectively for my prestige than anything else is that when my son Salvatore was married in 1956 no one had ever seen a wedding reception attended by so many important men from my world.

The festivities, that August day in 1956, began in the shrine church of St. Bernadette, a modest church in the Bay Ridge section of Brooklyn, the neighborhood of the bride's uncle, Joseph Profaci. Salvatore and Rosalie were married by a friend, Father Sylvio Ross of Casa Grande, Arizona. People jammed the church, overflowing into the street. But this crowd of several hundred was but a fraction of the number of people invited to the wedding reception afterward.

We held it in the grand ballroom of the Hotel Astor in Manhattan. About three thousand guests attended. The wedding cake was seven feet tall and had six tiers on it; you could have skied on it. A band entertained us, as well as the singing group The Four Lads. Tony Bennett crooned until very late. One or two opera singers whose names I can't remember also sang. Choruses of Sicilian folksongs wafted from the balcony. People tinkled their glasses to indicate they wanted to see Rosalie and Salvatore kiss or take to the dance floor.

As I go on now to identify some of the guests, it should not be assumed that they were limited to men of my Tradition. The majority of the guests were simply friends, a representative mixture of businessmen, working people, politicians, clergymen, doctors, lawyers and sundry others. One of the guests was Congressman Victor Anfuso of Brooklyn. Another was Fortune Pope, publisher of the Italian-language newspaper in New York called *Il Progresso Italo-Americano*.

It behooves me for the purposes of this book, however, to concentrate on the men of my Tradition. Within my own Family, my second was Frank Garofalo. Don Ciccio, as he was known to his close friends, was born in my hometown of Castellammare, the son of a leatherworker. After immigrating to the United States, he went into the export-import business and did well. Although he was about a dozen years older than I, Mr. Garofalo and I were very compatible. He was a self-educated man and could talk about literature and history. We were both cultured; we respected etiquette and decorum. He dressed as well as Cary Grant. His manners were impeccable. What I especially admired about him was his self-taught facility in English, which made him valuable as an intermediary between me and some people with whom I couldn't readily converse. He was an urbane and sophisticated man with a fondness for good opera, good food and good conversation.

Mr. Garofalo also had the good sense to know when to retire. In fact, not long after Salvatore's wedding, Mr. Garofalo went to Sicily, and he spent the rest of his life there. Not many men would have walked away from what he had. He was in his mid-sixties when he retired, and his graceful, level-headed removal made a deep impression on me.

Also at the wedding were three others in my Family who figure in our story. They were Johnny Morales, John Tartamella and Gaspar DiGregorio. Morales, who started out as my driver and bodyguard, had a quick mind and readily accepted even the most dangerous assignments. Tartamella was the *consigliere;* he was the president of a barber's local in Brooklyn and had connections in the hierarchy of the CIO. DiGregorio was my oldest friend of the three, and was a group leader within the Family. He was the brother-in-law of my cousin Stefano Magaddino of Buffalo and the godfather of my son Salvatore. Of the three men, Gaspar was the most deficient in leadership qualities.

In making the seating arrangements, I allotted separate tables to each of the Families. A prominent place was given to Joe Profaci, leader of his own Family. With Profaci was his right-hand man, Joe Magliocco, who was also related to my son's wife, Rosalie, on her mother's side.

The other three New York City Families were represented by their respective leaders: Tommy Lucchese, Vito Genovese and Albert Anastasia.

Of the out-of-town Fathers who attended the wedding, I want to single out Joe Zerilli of Detroit and Stefano Magaddino of Buffalo.

Zerilli was born in a village about ten miles away from Castellammare; his son was married to Joe Profaci's daughter. Of all the Fathers, Stefano and I, of course, knew each other the longest and had the deepest kinship ties.

The guest list didn't stop there. New Orleans was there, Pittsburgh was there, Los Angeles was there, St. Louis and Kansas City were there, Milwaukee was there, Chicago was there, Boston was there, Philadelphia was there . . . I think all the United States was there.

The wedding symbolized unity, although to be sure there were sour notes here and there. Among the guests, Vito Genovese and Albert Anastasia still had their long-standing animosity. I made sure to seat them at opposite sides of the hall. But at least they came. They were making an effort to be nice.

I was very proud of the truce I had arranged between them, not only because it showed the respect both Genovese and Anastasia had for me but also because it avoided yet another of those internecine rampages that give my Tradition a bad name.

Little could I guess at my son's wedding how fragile was the architecture of peace. At the time, I rather complimented myself for having been responsible for a sort of Pax Bonanno.

What can I say? . . . I don't want to appear to be casting stones to make myself seem immaculate. Some of us might have been better or worse than our peers, but we were not any of us saints. We lived in a rough world.

Another errant note, which was to grow louder and more discordant, came from my cousin Stefano Magaddino. Through others at his table I learned that Stefano seemed rather disconcerted by the lavishness of the reception and the number of important people who attended. At the wedding he was heard to remark:

—Look at all these people! It's going to go to Peppino's head.

Since the marriage of Stefano's son had not attracted nearly as many luminaries, I saw in Stefano's words the unmistakable tincture of envy.

The wedding was a milestone in my life at a time when I was perhaps at the apex of my prestige. As I gazed over the assembly, I felt a profound sense of harmony. For the moment, everyone was happy; no strife troubled us. We were all related through bonds of friendship. We were all connected to one another, each of us a piece of a beautiful mosaic, each of us in his place, each of us indispensable to the design—or so it seemed.

16

MY SON AND HIS WIFE HONEYMOONED IN ITALY.

Fay and I wanted to trade places with the lucky couple. I had not been in Italy since leaving there in 1924. Fay was born in Tunis; she had never been to Sicily. We were all set to take an Italian holiday in 1955, but had to cancel the trip when Fay became ill.

In my heart I still considered Sicily my home. My good friend Frank Garofalo had wisely quit the United States to retire in Sicily. Perhaps I too might retire there one day. It was all tentative, and retirement seemed a long way off. Still, I often pined for my homeland.

Fay and I spent the winter of 1956–1957 in Tucson. All our children were close to us. Joseph was going to parochial school in Tucson, and Catherine was enrolled in a business college there. Meanwhile, Salvatore and Rosalie, upon their return from Europe, decided to settle in Flagstaff, Arizona.

We had a wonderful Christmas that year. We decorated the exterior of the house with gay lights and we displayed a nativity scene on the front lawn. This was somewhat of a curiosity in Tucson; people drove by just to look at our Christmas decorations. As if to crown our celebrations, early in 1957, my children surprised Fay and me with a twenty-fifth wedding anniversary party at the Santa Rita Hotel in Tucson. It was well attended by most of the prominent members of the Italian community, as well as others. I gave Fay a diamond necklace.

After all the hoopla subsided, my daughter began hinting

Bonanno in the style of the day.

2

JOE MASSERIA

3

MEYER LANSKY

4

CHARLES "LUCY"
LUCIANO

AL CAPONE

6

"BUGS" MORAN

Circa 1931: The beginning
of the end of my Sicilian
Tradition in America and
the birth of the Syndicate
with its questionable values

The body of Salvatore Maranzano, "wartime" leader during the Castellammarese War in America, 1930-31. Upon his death, I assumed his mantle.

The Five Families of New York City

MARANZANO FAMILY	REINA FAMILY	MINEO FAMILY

BONANNO

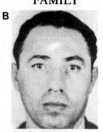

GAGLIANO

SCALISE

LUCCHESE

MANGANO

ANASTASIA

GAMBINO

From the end of the Castellammarese War to 1968

8

MASSERIA FAMILY

H

LUCIANO

I

COSTELLO

J

GENOVESE

PROFACI FAMILY

K

PROFACI

L

MAGLIOCCO

M

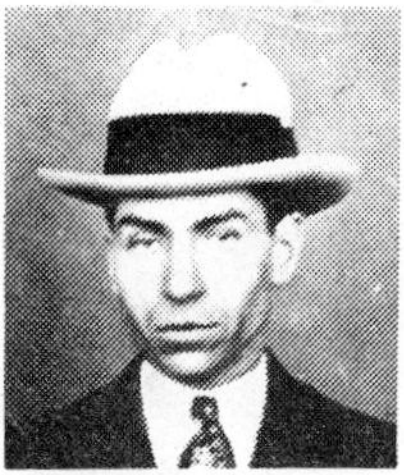

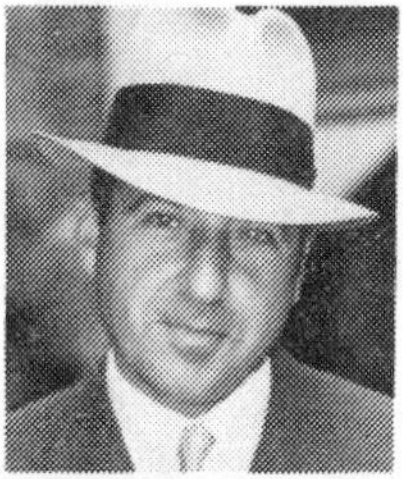

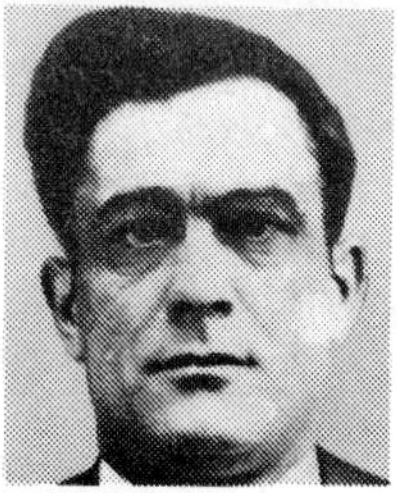

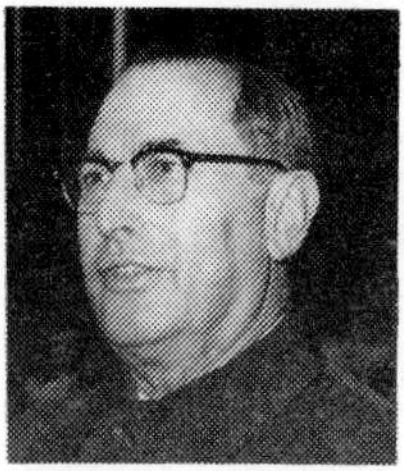

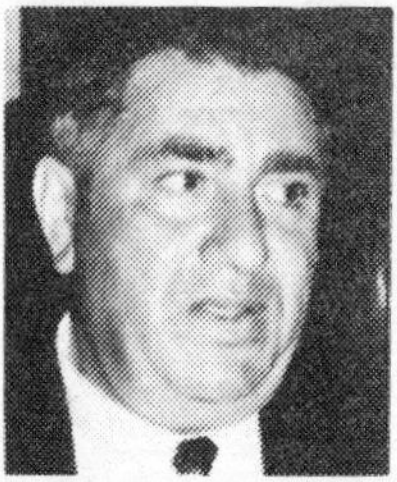

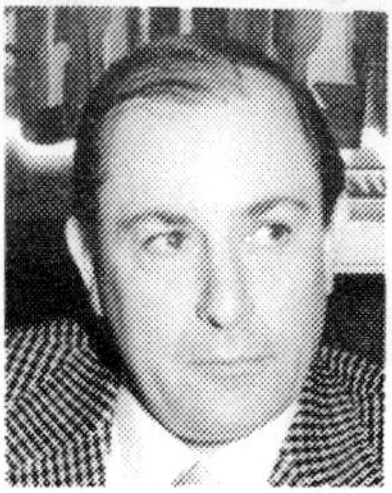

COLOMBO

My special Cadillac, built to specifications in Detroit for the Castellammarese War. Bulletproof, it was equipped with submachine guns. Fay, third from the right, with her sisters in Smithtown, Long Island. Natale De Pasquale is behind the wheel.

Men of my Tradition at my home in Hempstead, 1946.
Left to right: Myself, Joe Evola, John Tartamella, Sr.,
Frank Garafalo, Gaspar Di Gregorio.

Toasting the coming of a new year in my Tucson home, 1953. Left to right: Bishop Gercke, me, Father Radtke, Salvatore, and Father Rosetti.

Introducing Salvatore's bride-to-be Rosalie Profaci (fifth from the left) to intimate friends and family at the Paulos Restaurant, Tucson, April 1956. On my right are Rosalie's mother, Rose, next to Judge Evo De Concini, and Fay. On my left are Mrs. Ora De Concini and Judge and Mrs. Paul Cella.

Salvatore and Rosalie's wedding reception at the Hotel Astor, New York City, August 18, 1956.

2886 people came to dinner, and over a hundred more
joined us later for dancing.

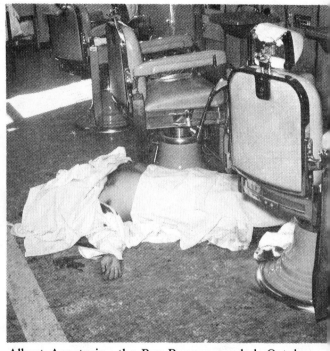

Albert Anastasia—the Pax Bonanno ended, October
1957.

Frank Costello, "The Prime Minister," testifying before a Senate subcommittee, 1950.

Senator John L. McClellan listening to Vito Genovese, 1958.

Host Joseph Barbara and view of his home which was the site of the Apalachin meeting, November 1957.

21

22

23

THE DISAPPEARING TRIO. They couldn't get it together to deliver the Commission's message to me. 1964. Top left: Angelo Bruno (Philadelphia); top right: Joe Zerilli (Detroit); center: Sam "The Plumber" De Cavalcante.

that she too wanted to travel. After all, she reasoned, up to then she had spent all her time in a Catholic school, and she felt like a nun. She wanted to see a little bit of the world. I couldn't permit my vivacious twenty-two-year-old daughter to keep thinking she was a nun, could I?

Off we went to Miami Beach. It was just as much a holiday for Fay and me as it was for Catherine. Although I wasn't ready for retirement yet, I did feel I had at least earned a rest. Salvatore's wedding seemed to have ushered in a period of relaxation. In Florida, we were joined by personal friends and their wives. It was suggested we take a quick excursion to Havana, and we did so on the spur of the moment.

Cuba in those days was a mecca for Americans and their dollars. We stayed at the Hotel Nacional in Havana. Meyer Lansky owned or had an interest in the hotel casino. When Lansky found out I was at the hotel, he came to say hello. I had become acquainted with Lansky through his association with Charlie Luciano, but Lansky and I had no ties to each other. The benefit of my knowing Lansky was visited on the wives—they got some of their gambling chips on the house.

I took advantage of this sojourn to revisit the dingy streets and the cheap Havana hotel where I had stayed in 1924. A tide of nostalgia flooded my heart. Like a homesick sailor, I longed for that port where the journey had begun. I felt like Homer's Ulysses, who had experienced enough adventures and enterprises to satisfy a normal man for a lifetime, but who was less lucky than others in that he was a wanderer away from home.

In August 1957, Fortune Pope, the publisher, invited me to join him on a trip to Italy. He was going to Sicily to take part in a dedication ceremony for an orphanage to which he contributed. Mr. Pope said I could come along as part of the dedication committee he was organizing.

As much as I wanted to go to Italy I was not initially enthusiastic about the trip. For one thing, I was feeling slightly sick that summer. Also, I had tentatively planned on taking my wife to Italy the following year; going there by myself in 1957 seemed pointless.

Nonetheless, I didn't want to offend Mr. Pope. Instead of

bluntly refusing, I vacillated and told him I would apply for a passport. Since the trip was about two weeks away, I was sure I wouldn't obtain a passport in time, thereby giving me an excuse to remain behind. To this day I don't know if it was Mr. Pope who had connections in Washington or if it was my lawyer who pulled the strings. But much to my surprise the passport arrived on time. Destiny seemed to be my travel agent.

I had to make preparations to avoid confusion and to ensure continuity in my absence. Within my Family, I lacked a deputy because Frank Garofalo had already returned to Sicily; I therefore appointed Johnny Morales and John Tartamella, with Gaspar DiGregorio as an alternate, as my representatives while I was gone.

I also informed the other Fathers on the Commission. I personally told Stefano Magaddino of my travel plans, and my cousin seemed overjoyed at the news. He seemed almost too glad to see me off.

Joe Magliocco invited me to a little bon voyage dinner at his house, attended by Joe Profaci and Albert Anastasia. Magliocco, in addition to being Profaci's right-hand man, was also Profaci's brother-in-law; they made a great team. Magliocco was a close personal friend of Anastasia's. They all wished me well on my trip. As always, Magliocco cooked a great meal.

All that was left to do was to touch bases with Vito Genovese and Tommy Lucchese. We arranged to meet over lunch at an uptown Manhattan restaurant. Several times during the lunch, Vito stood up to hug me and wish me a bon voyage. My trip, which was going to keep me away for several months, seemed to please everyone.

Toward the end of the meal, Tommy Lucchese, in that smooth and polished way of his, asked me:

—What should we do if something comes up?

He meant, who should the Commission members turn to for advice in case of a crisis? Vito looked up at me. Both he and Tommy acted utterly nonchalant but nonetheless intent on my answer.

Until Lucchese had asked me, I hadn't even thought about designating anyone. I didn't see any need for it. But now that he had asked me, I saw a chance to make my cousin Stefano Magaddino happy. I had already noticed how Stefano at various times resented my rise to prominence in the politics of my world. Here was a handy opportunity to appease his pride and possibly prevent a potential rift between us.

—If something comes up, I replied, talk to my cousin.

With such simple instructions born out of fraternal considerations did I lay the groundwork for my own downfall.

17

My traveling companion, Mr. Pope, seemed to have thought of everything. He had booked us first-class passage, which, in those days, included sleeping compartments. If we wanted to we could stretch out like pashas.

Before leaving New York, many of my friends, knowing how much I appreciated a fine smoke, had given me cigars as bon voyage gifts. I received so many cigars—perhaps a thousand, of all lengths and thicknesses—that they entirely filled a valise, which I carried aboard. To Mr. Pope I expressed my fears about getting the cigars past customs in Italy. An arch smile spread across his face. Without explaining why, he said I shouldn't fret.

At Rome's Fiumicino Airport, while taxiing to a stop, I noticed a cluster of official-looking people standing near the deplaning spot. A red carpet was being rolled to the airplane ramp.

I thought the reception committee was for some dignitary aboard, and I wanted to wait until the rest of the passengers got off before stepping out. The red carpet was for us. Wouldn't my friends in the FBI have been astonished at this princely welcome?

Among those who greeted us was an Italian government minister. I recognized him immediately. He was Bernardo Mattarella, who had grown up with me in Castellammare and had pursued a career in politics, having been named to several cabinet posts with the ruling Christian Democrats. In 1957 I believe he was minister of foreign trade.

Pleased as I was at the reception, the matter of the cigars

still vexed me. I held the valise firmly in my hand. Once the introductions were complete, a spiffy, obliging man with a little mustache came up to me and said,

—May I have the pleasure of carrying your valise?

I relaxed my grip. In a jiffy, before I could respond, he grabbed the valise and walked smartly away. Nonplussed, I turned to Mr. Pope.

—Is he one of your boys?

—No, Mr. Pope said, trying to keep a straight face, he's a customs inspector.

Needless to say, with such a porter, the valise of cigars got past customs without my having to pay a lira. How gracious life can be when one has friends in the right places!

From the moment I landed in Rome, I felt myself unwinding—like a watch with no more time to keep. The Volcano, that furious stronghold, seemed very remote. By crossing the ocean not only had I traversed thousands of miles, but I also had seemingly gone through a time warp. I had come back to a different culture with remnants of a bygone era.

From my suite in the Hotel Excelsior I could see, at an angle, the woodline of the Villa Borghese. Below me was Via Veneto. In the evenings, thousands of people milled and sauntered on this boulevard flanked by sidewalk cafés. In New York people seemed to glumly bump or ram into you. In Rome, as crowded as it was, everyone seemed more sociable. People waved, they hugged, they kissed, they strolled hand in hand, women and men alike.

I don't mean to degrade the United States. I'm an American citizen and it's a great country. But when I revisited Italy I felt as if I had returned to high civilization. As a modern industrial nation, Italy has its disabilities. Its government machinery, everyone agrees, is appalling. And yet, in the Italians themselves, in their every gesture and in the very *bel canto* of their language, one finds redemption. Italians have a refined sense of what Luigi Barzini calls "the art of living"—a sociability, a geniality, an exuberance of warmth that surpasses all their other works of art.

Something else that I immediately liked about being in Italy was that no one thought my name sounded odd. Bonanno is a lovely-sounding name; in Italian, it literally means "good year."

English-speakers, however, seem to have difficulty with it. Rather than mispronounce my name, many of my American friends refer to me as J. B. or Mr. B. Rather terse, but still better than that abomination Joe Bananas. I don't know who invented this moniker for me; I'd like to throttle him.

In Italy, not only did they know how to pronounce my name, but they also sprinkled honorary titles before it. You really have to be a nobody to escape being addressed by one title or other in Italy. Even if the title is meaningless, it makes you feel important.

When the floor captain at the Hotel Excelsior wanted a word with me, he knocked on the door and said:

—Your excellency, with your permission, your excellency.

—Yes?

He said he hoped my suite met with my approval and that he was glad I had chosen to stay at the hotel again.

—Again?

I told him this was my initial stay at the hotel.

He remonstrated with me. He was sure a Mr. Bonanno had occupied the very same suite the previous year. Although he couldn't remember my face, he did remember the name.

—Your excellency, how could I forget such a lovely name?

The mystery was solved when the floor captain checked the hotel register. He rushed back to tell me that in 1956 my rooms were occupied by a Mr. and Mrs. Salvatore Bonanno, who were on their honeymoon.

My spacious suite had elegant appointments; it was an apartment fit for a prince. That son of mine, I thought, he likes to travel in style. I wonder where he gets it from?

I thanked the floor captain and tipped him.

—You're welcome, your excellency. And thank you kindly, your excellency.

He was walking out the door when he added,

—Good evening, your excellency.

From the capital of Italy, we next went to the capital of Sicily. I was met in Palermo by my former deputy, Frank Garofalo, and by my former dairy manager, Uncle John Bonventre, who also had returned to the island.

One day, I left this group to join some other friends, natives of Palermo and some of them "men of honor." There had been

182

much construction in Palermo after World War II and my friends wanted to show me all the new boulevards and office buildings.

—But we have those in America, I protested.

I wanted to see the old places that I remembered from my youth. It was in Palermo, for instance, that I had seen L'Opera dei Puppi, the puppet theater. I remember being enthralled by the near-life-sized marionettes dressed as armored knights and engaged in furious battles for the honor of their king, Charlemagne.

One of the places we visited was the Teatro Massimo, one of the largest theaters in Europe. Two bronze lions guard the stairs outside the opera house. The inscription over the entrance of the Teatro Massimo is one I know by heart:

L'ARTE RINNOVA I POPOLI E NE RIVELA LA VITA. VANO DELLE SCENE IL DILETTO OVE NON MIRI A PREPARAR L'AVVENIRE.

(Art renews the people and reveals their lives. Vain the pleasure from these scenes if you don't contemplate them to prepare for the future.)

We eventually made our way to a fine restaurant on the Piazza Politeama. It was a favorite restaurant of my escorts. Since they were men of my Tradition, they had taken me to a restaurant in which they knew they would be welcomed and treated with respect. Indeed, the restaurant owner greeted us as if we were lords. He kissed his patron's hand and asked for his blessing.

—*Vossia mi benerica.*

After the ceremonial greeting, I momentarily found myself alone at the table. I asked for water from a waiter. He brought back a pitcher of icewater. I happen to have an aversion to icewater because it constricts my throat. Speaking in standard Italian, as opposed to a Sicilian dialect, I told the waiter to bring me some water without ice.

My request irritated him. Assuming that I wouldn't be able to understand, the waiter muttered words in his native dialect.

—They go to America, the waiter mumbled, and when they

183

come back they think they can show off. They put on all sorts of airs!

His remarks enraged me. I was only asking him to do his job. What difference should it make to him if I liked my water without ice? This waiter had picked the wrong time to act peevish, for I was very thirsty. And he had picked the wrong man to trifle with. I was more Sicilian than he was. My temper snapped. I reached for the pitcher of icewater and flung it at him.

The pitcher struck his skull. The glass cracked. Blood trickled down his head. Then I began reprimanding him in his own dialect.

—How could I know? the dazed waiter answered back. Forgive me, your excellency. I didn't know.

The fellow cowered before me. In a way, I had taught him a lesson. The next time he would be more careful around whom to let his tongue run wild. As far as I was concerned, no more needed to be said or done.

However, when my friends saw our little tilt, they returned to the table looking very grim indeed. If the waiter had offended me, they were prepared to punish him.

At this point, the restaurant owner came to the rescue. Judging from the frowns and beetling brows of my important friends, the owner probably genuinely thought that the waiter's life was in danger. He therefore sought to take upon himself the responsibility for punishing the waiter to spare him more dire consequences.

—If it was up to me, the owner scolded the waiter, I would give you a good kicking and a hard whipping. And then I'd fire you, you wretch.

The owner looked at us next. As if pleading for the waiter's life, he said,

—I'm sure the gentlemen would be satisfied.

The incident had gone too far. It had become farcical. I declared that I didn't want to see the waiter lose his limbs or his job on account of icewater. I forgave him. No sooner did I say this than everyone went back to his normal business, and none of us said another word about it. But that's the Sicilian temper for you: easily angered, easily soothed, if you know how to handle it. At the end of the meal, the waiter received a generous tip and the restaurant owner invited us to come back soon.

The next day, for our drive to Ribera to dedicate the orphanage, a city official close to the mayor of Palermo insisted that Mr. Pope and I have a police escort. We were important men from America, and the official didn't want to take any chances on any hill bandits kidnapping us. And so our party drove out of Palermo accompanied by an impressive but utterly superfluous police escort. In New York, they would never believe this.

The dedication ceremony was as it should be: short on speeches and full of flowers and children. Seeing the orphans reminded me of my youth and made me think of my parents. I had known them for but a short time. Perhaps for this reason I have always idealized them.

I wanted to be with them in spirit, as soon as possible. Already, Mr. Pope and I had decided to follow separate itineraries once the dedication ceremony was completed. Therefore, when it was over, I entreated Frank Garofalo to drive me to the cemetery in Castellammare.

My parents' grave marker is one of the tallest and most prominent in the town cemetery. I bought fresh flowers to lay on the marble tombstone.

For the next couple of weeks I remained in Castellammare, visiting my childhood haunts and reliving memories. I rented an entire small motel to accommodate the many friends and relatives who came to see me, often bringing gifts of fresh food and delicacies.

18

THE VACATION HAD SUCCEEDED IN TAKING MY MIND OFF MY
affairs in New York City. It was exhilarating to chat with old
friends and remember the past; but, as a consequence, I got
little rest. About five weeks into my vacation, I began tiring
of the pace. I was run down, perhaps emotionally as well as
physically.

Heedlessly, I accepted an invitation to accompany a friend
on a side trip to India, where he was involved in some construction projects. I returned from India with a few mementos
and also the flu. Back in Sicily, I couldn't shake off the bug.
It would die down, only to flare up again. No one expected
me to return to America so soon, but I made arrangements to
leave.

My Italian vacation forced me to realize how different I had
become. For better or worse, living in America had changed
me. No matter how deeply I treasured memories of Sicily, I
was Joseph Bonanno of America. I was from Sicily but not of
that world anymore. When I became sick, my first thought was
to go home to America.

On my return flight to America I recalled my 1924 odyssey,
but I was glad I didn't have to sneak into the country this time.
I was a naturalized citizen of the United States. I was returning
home to family and friends. I had established myself. I owned
three homes and even a motel near Newark Airport. My position as Father of a Family was secure. My oldest son had
been married the previous year, and, with any luck, he would

become a lawyer, a professional man. I was on top of my world.

The men I had left in charge of my affairs met me at the airport. They greeted me warmly, expressing their surprise at my premature return. During my absence I had not been in touch with anyone in my Family. I asked them if anything important had happened while I was away.

—Don Peppino, haven't you heard?

—Heard what?

—Albert Anastasia was shot to death. Didn't you read about it in the papers?

The news shocked me deeply, to the extent that I could only peevishly think of saying:

—What papers? Do you think that in Paris or Bombay they know who Albert Anastasia is?

It was an ominous turn of events that my own men couldn't fully appreciate. But the next bit of news was just as startling and even more upsetting.

—Surely you've come back for the big meeting.

—What meeting?

—The big meeting, the national meeting. Everyone's going to be there.

—Where?

—Upstate, at Apalachin.

—When?

—In a couple of weeks from now.

Although I knew none of the details, my instincts told me the peace, the Pax Bonanno, that I was so proud of having forged was on the verge of disintegration.

My men, unaware of the behind-the-scenes implications of Anastasia's death and the Apalachin meeting, were vying among themselves for the privilege of accompanying me to the big meeting.

—Don't be foolish, I said, can't you see what's going on?

In the Volcano, men of my world were in a tizzy over the upcoming national convention at Apalachin, New York. All the people who mattered from the whole country had been invited. Everyone was talking about the Big Barbecue at Apalachin.

Those privileged enough to attend such a national meeting anticipated it with the same glee as do Republicans or Democrats when they meet every four years for their national conventions. As with the Republicans and the Democrats, our conventions served more than political purposes. These national meetings were also great social occasions for men of my world to mingle, to renew friendships and to exchange views. National meetings were both pageants of power and ceremonies that reminded us of our common way of life.

Given the importance of such a convention, you can imagine the bewilderment of my friends at my negative reaction to Apalachin.

—Who are you going to take with you, don Peppino? several of my closest men asked.

It utterly floored them when I said I didn't intend to participate in the Apalachin meeting.

My seemingly inscrutable decision was based on my assessment of what had happened during my absence in Italy. Anastasia's death was particularly upsetting to me because it violated the peace that had been arranged through my leadership.

BOOK IV

Between Hammer and Anvil

19

ALBERT ANASTASIA HAD GIVEN HIS WORD ON PEACE. DESPITE a violent streak, Anastasia was an open and bluff man. I had no reason to believe that Albert had broken his word. He was shot to death while having a shave in the barber shop of the Park Sheraton Hotel. He obviously thought the peace was in effect or he wouldn't have ventured into such a public place unguarded. Apparently, then, Albert hadn't thought his life was in danger and he hadn't taken any precautions.

Whoever killed Anastasia—and the indications were that it was men within his own Family—was not really my concern, but the concern of his Family. The identity of Albert's slayers was of interest to those who wanted to avenge his death.

My main preoccupation was with the effects of Albert's death. On the Commission, Anastasia's demise benefited both Genovese and Lucchese, whose animosity toward Albert was well known. The man being mentioned to replace Albert as Father of his Family was Carlo Gambino. Lucchese and Gambino were very close; they were related because their children had intermarried. If Gambino was confirmed as Father, that would mean that on the Commission the liberal wing of Genovese-Lucchese-Gambino would form a united faction of equal voting strength with the conservative faction of Bonanno-Profaci-Magaddino.

Just because Genovese and Lucchese benefited from Anastasia's death didn't necessarily mean that they had initiated it. However, the timing of Albert's death indicated that at the very least either Genovese or Lucchese condoned or did nothing to try to prevent it. The timing of Albert's slaying was crucial. If I had been around when Albert died, I would not have tolerated facile explanations for his killing. Anastasia was the linchpin to the Pax Bonanno. In fact, if I had not gone off to Italy I doubt whether anyone would have felt bold enough to make an attempt on Albert's life. The other Fathers knew that I, in particular, felt responsible for guaranteeing the peace and Albert's safety.

With me out of the way, however, Anastasia's enemies had room to maneuver. Now I realized why Genovese and Lucchese bubbled with cheerfulness as they wished me bon voyage to Italy. The smiles on their faces hid the knavery in their hearts.

The elimination of Anastasia, regardless of who was responsible, was merely the first phase of a twofold strategy. The second phase involved the quick recognition of Carlo Gambino as Anastasia's successor so that no one else in that Family, perhaps someone friendlier to the conservatives on the Commission, could seize power. Obviously, Lucchese and Genovese favored the immediate installation of Gambino.

I did not suspect Stefano Magaddino of having anything to do with Anastasia's death. But once Albert was killed, Stefano was seduced by vanity.

If I had been in the United States when Anastasia was killed, I would have moved very slowly. I would have given the people in Anastasia's Family time to resolve their leadership crisis. Perhaps someone other than Gambino might have emerged as Father if things had been left alone without outside interference.

If I had been around I would have definitely lobbied against a national meeting. Such a conference would have the effect of giving official sanction to Gambino, pulling the rug out from under any dissidents within his Family. Of course, that's exactly what Lucchese and Genovese wanted.

Before I left for Italy, those two had expressly asked me whom I recommended that they consult in case of a crisis. I recommended Stefano. Now I realized what a blunder that was.

Lucchese and Genovese could not have called a national convention on their own. A national meeting had to have bilateral sponsorship. If I had been around, as leader of the conservative faction, I would have balked at calling such a meeting. But with me in Italy, Stefano was the spokesman for the conservative wing. He, too, could have discouraged a national meeting, realizing what a coup that would be for the liberal wing. Instead, Stefano did the opposite. Not only did he support the meeting, he was its main sponsor. Stefano was going to host the affair. He had selected the site.

I had arrived at some sad conclusions. Stefano was willing to overlook the broader implications of holding a national meeting under such hasty circumstances because he wanted the chance to play the big shot in front of a national audience. It was an act of vanity. At previous national meetings, I was the one who had taken a leading role. I was not around to overshadow Stefano this time. Since he expected me to remain in Italy, Stefano thought the show would be all his. He, not Peppino, would be the man of the hour, the center of attention. In other words, to satisfy his vanity, Stefano was willing to ignore or go along with the maneuverings of Lucchese and Genovese.

There was another reason I opposed this national meeting at Apalachin. Up to 1957, we had been holding our national meetings every five years. Our last one had been in 1956. There was no precedent for another national convention a year later. We could have handled the Anastasia matter among ourselves in New York City. Holding a national meeting a year after our previous one smacked of hasty decision-making and hurried connivance.

This out-of-season national meeting reinforced my suspicion that Stefano somehow was playing ball with Lucchese and Genovese. Each would get what he wanted. Lucchese and Genovese would get confirmation of their man Gambino. Stefano would get his chance to play the big man.

Aside from introducing Gambino to the important men in our world, another item on the Apalachin agenda was supposed to be the narcotics issue. My Tradition outlaws narcotics. It had always been understood that "men of honor" don't deal in narcotics. However, the lure of high profits had tempted some underlings to free-lance in the narcotics trade. This growing problem had been discussed at our 1956 national meeting. If the 1957 meeting had gone according to plan there no doubt would have been a reaffirmation of our Tradition's opposition to narcotics. It was sad, nonetheless, that people had to be reminded of this. It reflected how much ground our Traditional values had lost.

I was so disgusted with the turn of events, particularly Stefano's part in them, that upon my return to the Volcano, I didn't want to talk to Stefano or any of the other Fathers. Stefano and the others could hold their big barbecue in Apalachin without me. I didn't want to attend.

My first week back from Italy I simply nursed my flu and attended to private business affairs. The only people who saw me were my own men. In a short time, however, my early return from Italy became known. I was told Lucchese wanted to talk to me. I avoided him. Since Lucchese was on the Commission, if he formally informed me of a national meeting and I refused to attend, it would put me in a bad light. Lucchese would report to the other Fathers that I was being uncooperative for mysterious reasons. He would play my refusal to his advantage so that I would appear contrary or inexplicably opposed to such a meeting. If I remained elusive, he couldn't exploit the situation. All he could say was that he wasn't able to reach me. If the Apalachin meeting turned out to be a fiasco, I didn't want to share in the blame. My best alternative was to dissociate myself from it.

Intermediaries told me that my cousin Stefano knew I opposed the meeting. Stefano sent a message saying it was too late to stop the meeting. People had already made plans, everything was set up. Since I didn't want to attend, Stefano suggested I should at least send representatives.

Stefano had the advantageous position here. If I didn't send representatives to the national meeting, people would think I was being arrogant. To protect myself from such insinuations, I was going to send two of my top men, Johnny Morales and Gaspar DiGregorio, to Apalachin. I chose Johnny because I could rely on him to bring back an accurate account of the meeting; I selected Gaspar to go along with him because Gaspar was Stefano's brother-in-law and thus, because of their closeness, Gaspar might pick up additional information.

I was going to Arizona. Then, at the last moment, I decided to talk to Stefano personally. I still was not going to attend the meeting, but a private talk was in order. I had to act fast, for the convention was but a few days away. Gaspar contacted his brother-in-law and arranged a private talk between Stefano and me in Endicott, a larger town just east of Apalachin.

Earlier in the century, when Sicilian immigrants flooded into America, the town of Endicott attracted many Castellammarese. Endicott was a manufacturing town, and its shoe factory, especially, provided work for the immigrants. This region of upstate New York is about midway between Buffalo and Middletown, where I had a dairy farm. I knew the area fairly well and had friends there.

Apalachin is a very small town about six or seven miles west of Endicott in forested, rolling countryside. The leading citizen of Apalachin, its most substantial resident, was Joe Barbara. It was at his sprawling estate that the national conference was to be held.

Joe Barbara was from Castellammare. He was only a year older than I; we grew up together. Joe made his fortune in the soda-pop distributing business. He held a franchise for the entire upstate region, and he owned a bottling plant outside Endicott. I was a visitor to his house many times. His estate occupied a knoll overlooking the town. To reach it, you had to pull off the main road and follow a private drive, severed at one point by stone posts on either side of the road and a big chain stretching between the posts. Joe had a large ranch-style home with exterior walls of gray-and-dun stone. He often hosted meetings in connection with his soda-distributing business. Therefore, his house included several large meeting rooms and a large parking lot.

In 1956, when we were considering a site for our national convention, we chose Joe Barbara's place. Besides being scenic and capable of accommodating a large number of people, it was a safe site where we would not be bothered by police. Joe Barbara had many connections with law-enforcement agents who, Barbara told me, were paid off for leaving Joe Barbara and his friends alone.

The 1956 national meeting at Apalachin went very well. The Pax Bonanno was in effect and I chaired the meeting. Those were among the most satisfying moments of my life. The Apalachin site pleased everyone. The police didn't bother us, although they must have known something was going on at Barbara's estate. Apalachin is tiny, and the main road into town has a state trooper station sitting on it; the police would have had to be blind not to notice the large gathering of out-of-town people. The police looked the other way.

Months after the 1956 national meeting, Joe Barbara was recovering from a heart attack, and he complained of his health. Joe mentioned to me that he was having a little trouble with some of the law agents around Apalachin. Some of them were getting greedy and were making exorbitant demands on Barbara in exchange for their cooperation. There had been a falling-out. Joe wanted to warn me, therefore, that his estate was not the safe meeting place that it had been. Joe asked me to reiterate his misgivings to Stefano Magaddino, whom he had already told.

Here was another reason that I opposed the 1957 national meeting. Not only was it not the time to hold another national convention, only one year after our previous one, but Apalachin was a lousy place to hold it. Stefano, however, in his eagerness to make a big splash, had completely discarded Barbara's cautions.

My second, Johnny Morales, drove me to Endicott from New York City. Already at Endicott were Gaspar DiGregorio and my Uncle John Bonventre. My Uncle John had been in Sicily that summer, too, and Stefano wanted to see him to hear news from Castellammare.

Stefano and I met at a private house owned by a mutual friend. We talked late into the night, and we remained at the house overnight. We got very little sleep, however, because of our rambling and persistent conversation.

Basically, Stefano maintained that there was nothing more to consider concerning Anastasia's death. Albert was gone and that was that. Every time I wanted to explore the ramifications and implications of his death, Stefano would scoff. He would say I was imagining things, that I was splitting hairs. When I mentioned that I thought the national meeting was ill advised, Stefano would ruffle, saying,

—What's the matter, are you too good to come to the meeting?

He intimated that I opposed the national meeting because I wasn't in charge of it. On other matters, he played dumb, claiming that he was only doing what he thought was best for all.

This night-long session with Stefano convinced me that my relationship with my cousin was indeed in peril, although for the time being we still kept our resentments submerged.

Outsiders would have been incredulous if I told them that Stefano and I had differences. On the outside, we were loving cousins. Our families in Sicily were the staunchest of allies. In America, Stefano and I were the leaders of our own Families. We were the backbone of the conservative faction on the Commission. No one would have believed that Stefano and I had begun to wrench apart.

When I came to America in 1924, it was Stefano who had sent two of his men to bail me out of trouble in Florida. Stefano had offered me a place in his Family in Buffalo. It was a generous offer, but I refused. I had not yet decided what to do with my life. Other than that, however, I instinctively did not fancy myself being under Stefano Magaddino.

Within ten years of my arrival in this country, after I had distinguished myself in the Castellammarese War, I became Father of a Family. I was only twenty-six years old. Instead of being Stefano's ward, I was now his peer. I was educated and bright; I must have seemed like the "golden boy." I don't say this to sing my own praises. I just want to describe how I must have appeared to Stefano, the older man who slowly would become jealous of me.

It took some thirty years for these latent hostilities to make themselves visible. But the conflict between Stefano and me was never over money, domain or territory. Our quarrel was grounded in differences in character.

Stefano was the son of the "black sheep" of the Magaddino family in Castellammare. The other Magaddinos, such as Uncle Stefano, never liked the young Stefano. There was no future for the young Stefano in Castellammare, and he came to America. After becoming an important man in Buffalo, Stefano visited Sicily in the 1930s. The story goes that Uncle Stefano went to meet his nephew hoping that he had changed while in America.

When Stefano strutted down the gangplank he shouted to his uncle,

—Hello there, Rusty.

Uncle Stefano had reddish hair, but for his nephew to call him Rusty was definitely improper and boorish. It embarrassed

Uncle Stefano in front of the other men. As if this insult wasn't enough, Stefano, while embracing his uncle, squashed Uncle Stefano's straw hat.

Uncle Stefano couldn't stand to be humiliated by his show-off nephew any longer, and, in front of the others who had come to greet Stefano, he shouted:

—You were no good when you left. You're no good in America. And you'll always be no good.

It was now my turn to see what Uncle Stefano had detected in Stefano's character a long time ago.

Our night-long discussion in Endicott was an exercise in futility. Neither one of us wanted to launch into forthright character attacks. Our suspicions of each other's motives remained covert.

—Why, of all places, I asked Stefano, did you want to hold a meeting at Joe Barbara's farm? You know he's sick and has been having trouble with the law around here.

—Ah, sick, go on, Stefano sneered. I'm not asking him to do cartwheels on his lawn. I just thought we might use his place for a get-together. And what's wrong with that, heh? I never ask him for a favor. When I do, he tries to get out of it. Joe feels all right. Everything's going to be all right. You'll see.

—Whose idea was this in the first place? I said.

—Well, after Albert was shot, Tommy Lucchese came to me and said several boys in Anastasia's Family were out for revenge. We had to do something, he said, or there would be fighting. It was up to us on the Commission to keep the peace.

—He came to you?

—He came to me, that's right. You're the one who told him to see me if anything came up while you were gone. If you didn't want him to come to me, you should have told him so. I got my own problems. Why are you blaming me?

—I'm not blaming you, cousin.

—What's the fuss, then? Stefano grumbled. We've been here all night. You know, it's going to be daylight pretty soon. It's too late to change anything. Everyone's going to be here in the morning.

—Stefano, please, I implore you. It will be the greatest disaster of our lives if we—two cousins—fail to understand each other.

—Isn't everything obvious?

—What is obvious? When Tommy came to see you, you didn't have to call for a national meeting. You could have . . .

—It wasn't my idea, it was Tommy's, Stefano interrupted.

—You could have waited. You could have considered other possibilities.

—He made it sound urgent.

—Sure it was urgent, urgent to Tommy. But others were looking for time, others in Albert's Family. And with time, perhaps the situation could have resolved itself. Don't you understand?

—You get me all confused with your logic, Stefano stammered. What could I have done? Tommy came to me with his information. And I said, "But I don't know what we should do, Tommy."

—That's exactly what he wanted to hear from you.

—And when I told him I didn't know what to do, Stefano continued, Tommy suggested that we should hold a meeting. It was all Lucchese's idea.

—Yes, but you practically invited him to make the suggestion.

—Bah, you're impossible, Stefano grumped. Always splitting hairs . . . so meticulous. Just don't worry, will you?

By about noon of November 14, 1957, Stefano and I were too weary to dance around each other any longer. Our private session had been inconclusive. Stefano left for Apalachin, saying he had a ravenous appetite.

Not long after his departure from Endicott, I learned of the calamitous developments on Barbara's farm that very morning. Police and state troopers had posted roadblocks around the farm. Since no crime had been committed, all the policemen could do was to ask for driver's licenses, make cursory searches of the cars and take down names. That was enough. It was horrendous: all those men caught in the same place, a ton of publicity, a public-relations coup for law enforcement, a field day for journalists.

I didn't have time to ponder all the implications of the Apalachin fiasco. I had to get out of Endicott before I was discovered. Johnny Morales drove me away.

The next day, a safe distance from Endicott, I read the

newspaper accounts of the Apalachin debacle. Identified as having been at the meeting were Vito Genovese, Carlo Gambino, Joe Profaci, Joe Magliocco and some sixty or seventy others. Tommy Lucchese, I later learned from my own sources, had avoided police detection by simply walking through the woods alone and later grabbing a ride with a soda delivery truck. Another man *not* identified as being at the meeting was Stefano Magaddino. By detaining Stefano with me in Endicott, I had inadvertently kept him out of trouble. After leaving me and finding out about the police roadblocks, Stefano avoided Apalachin and made his way back to Buffalo.

The newspapers identified Joe Bonanno as being caught by police at Apalachin. I didn't want to believe it at first. I had done everything possible to avoid the meeting, and yet I had been wrongly implicated in the whole mess. I was dumbstruck by the perverted whimsy of life.

I found out how my name surfaced through a phone call to my brother-in-law. While Stefano and I were still talking in Endicott, Gaspar DiGregorio and my Uncle John Bonventre had gone hunting. They drove back on a side road that curved across the border of Barbara's property. Police had one of their roadblocks there, and, assuming Gaspar and Uncle John were guests at Barbara's farm, they stopped and examined the two.

Gaspar was a likable, simple fellow not noted for his brilliance. He lacked power of concentration and often lapsed into carelessness. Before leaving for my Italian vacation in 1957, I had given my driver's license to my brother-in-law Frank Labruzzo so he could renew it. In those days, you didn't have to renew a driver's license in person in New York. When I returned from Italy, Frank didn't get a chance to hand me my new driver's license. He gave it to Gaspar, knowing that he would see me in Endicott. But in Endicott, Gaspar forgot to give me my license.

If Gaspar had to drive from his house to mine at night, it was not uncommon for him to call me up for directions after having made a wrong turn. That was Gaspar, a bit of a bumbler.

When police stopped Gaspar and Uncle John at Apalachin, they found my driver's license on Gaspar. That's how my name entered the public record as having been one of the men at the Apalàchin meeting. Gaspar's name was never implicated. As usual, he was not carrying his own driver's license. He had forgotten it at home.

I was caught in the flux of life: a messy haphazard juxtaposition of people and events—a human comedy.

20

THE SENSATIONAL PUBLICITY CREATED BY APALACHIN AF-
fected me tremendously, because up to then I had been relatively inconspicuous. Publicity can maim and destroy. Apalachin
destroyed Joe Barbara. His business license was revoked. His
fine estate went up for sale. Joe's son had to drop out of college
because of the harassment and bad publicity. Joe suffered a
fatal heart attack.

To understand me and others of my Tradition, one must
have an open mind and an open heart. One must learn to think
in terms of another culture, whose values are different from
standard American culture. The bad publicity generated by
Apalachin helped destroy any hope for an intelligent examination of my Tradition. Instead, the publicity perpetuated a
myth . . . the myth of the "Mafia."

In 1950–1951, U.S. Senator Estes Kefauver held his celebrated committee hearings on organized crime in gambling.
The Kefauver Committee made the not-so-startling discovery
that illicit gambling outlets existed in just about every major
city in the United States. These bookie operations or numbers
games, to take but two examples, were run by private businessmen. Because these forms of gambling were illegal,
Kefauver, and police in general, referred to these private
businessmen as "crime syndicates" and referred to their gambling enterprises as "organized crime."

Gambling, like moneylending, is one of those human
activities that defy government intervention, no matter how
well-meaning. That should have been obvious during Prohi-

bition when the government tried to ban the selling of liquor. People didn't put up with it. They found a way to buy their liquor. It wasn't the bootleggers' fault that people wanted liquor. Bootleggers simply filled a demand. The government finally gave in. It allowed private businessmen to sell liquor, taxing their profits. The same can be done with gambling.

It is not my place to denounce or defend these activities. I merely wish to point out that if people, ordinary people, didn't demand such services as gambling and moneylending, no one would bother to supply these services. If you truly wanted to crack down on gambling, for example, you would have to eradicate the wish to gamble in the hearts of ordinary people.

It is difficult for me, therefore, to take seriously government attempts to dislodge the entrepreneurs who provide such services. Such attempts are misplaced and self-defeating in the long run. If you remove the current private individuals who provide illicit gambling services, for example, other individuals will take their place, because there will always be customers.

Men of my Tradition (Family members), some of whom were involved in illicit gambling operations, understood the human condition and provided these services, which society demanded. The naive view is to believe that a certain group of people, such as Sicilians, somehow force these activities on society, thereby infecting it and corrupting it.

In the book he wrote after the committee hearings, Kefauver stated that behind the "crime syndicates" in this country was a sinister, secret criminal society called "the Mafia." If Kefauver had merely said that some of the men who ran illicit gambling operations were Sicilian, he would have been partly correct; if he had added that many non-Sicilians also ran gambling operations, he would have been wholly correct.

In conjuring a central, all-powerful, directing body which he called "the Mafia," Kefauver was totally wrong. In doing so, he perpetuated a myth. Originally, Kefauver's conclusions applied only to illicit gambling, as one form of organized crime. By extension, however, his pronouncements were applied to any and all forms of illegal activity. *Thus, to this day, most Americans still believe that "the Mafia" controls all organized crime in America. This is a fantasy.*

202

There is no *institution* called "the Mafia." The term refers to a process, to a special set of relationships among men. I stay away from the word because it creates more confusion than it is worth. The confusion is compounded by the fact that because of its currency, the word "Mafia" by itself has become a buzzword for mobsters in general. One reads in the newspapers of the Italian Mafia, the Mexican Mafia, the Jewish Mafia, and so on. This is a figurative use of the word, quite apart from the descriptive use of the word by Kefauver and the police. As a rule of thumb, however, it is better to use an English word for what you are trying to say.

One may rightly speak of a mafioso way of life, a Tradition if you will, a set of ideals and customs, a mode of thinking, that is peculiar to Sicilians. This Tradition provides a code of conduct for a Sicilian to follow, regardless of the enterprise he's engaged in. A mafioso way of life may be exemplified by a doctor or a barber, as well as by a numbers runner. Such a way of life, such cultural expressions, are the proper study of sociologists and anthropologists, not just criminologists.

The Kefauver Committee assumed "the Mafia" was a monolithic organization that controlled organized crime in America. Such a body, as defined by the committee, doesn't exist. Organized crime embraces a lot of people—not just Sicilians, but Jews, Irish, Puerto Ricans, Cubans, Blacks, Anglos, you name it—and to posit that these various groups are controlled by one agency is preposterous.

My Tradition may be likened to the stars in the firmament by which a mariner plots his course. The stars enable the mariner to determine his direction, but they do not control where the mariner decides to go. That's up to the individual.

Out of misplaced zeal, then, the Kefauver Committee contributed to the myth that "the Mafia" is the bogeyman of American society. Anyone connected with or related to this bogeyman was automatically denounced and branded by society as being undesirable.

After the Apalachin *cause célèbre*, the government intensified its pressure on me. To law officials, I must have seemed like the big one who had always slipped their grasp. I know this must have gnawed at them, quite apart from my actual or imagined offenses against society. In their eyes, I was an elusive rascal.

To avoid their snares, I found myself spending more and more time in Tucson rather than in the Volcano. The Apalachin notoriety made me extremely aware that I might be a liability or pose an embarrassment to some of my Tucson friends. I spoke of this to my Tucson friend Evo DeConcini, a retired Arizona state judge. I told him I didn't want to jeopardize his career and suggested tactfully that perhaps it would be better for him if we didn't see each other in public.

—Apalachin was something that shouldn't have happened, I observed, hoping that Evo would grasp more than what I actually said.

Evo replied that Apalachin was not going to break up our friendship, that our friendship was open for all to see. He even quipped that if while making my way to his house a policeman should ask me where I was going, I should say I was going to visit my friend Evo DeConcini.

The loyalty of my Tucson friends encouraged me while I awaited developments after Apalachin. The town's sunny, dry climate was very good for my bones. But I couldn't altogether regain that excellent health that I enjoyed as a younger man. Friends had been telling me to slow down ever since my first heart attack in 1951.

That stroke occurred while I was leaving the Rialto movie house in Tucson. I was with my son Salvatore and a friend. When we reached the sidewalk, I felt dizzy and grabbed the wall. Salvatore and my friend propped me up. They took me to St. Mary's Hospital, where I remained for almost a month.

After several weeks, friends began sneaking me bottles of cognac. I had accumulated five or six bottles when my doctor, Harold Kohl, Sr., discovered my cache.

—Too much cognac is no good for you, he said drolly. I'll have to take two of these bottles from you. That way, we'll each have a little. A little cognac will do you good, and will do me good, too.

I had survived my first heart attack, and I felt euphoric. I promised myself to take it easy. But how calm can one remain in the Volcano? Less than a decade after that first heart attack, the stress and pressure on me seemed as great as ever. Going off to Tucson for the winter had provided me some relief from this constant strain.

In the newspapers I read about the formation of the New York State Investigation Commission, which was issuing subpoenas in connection with the Apalachin meeting. Since it was a state commission, it had no jurisdiction outside New York. In 1958, therefore, Arizona was where I wanted to be.

Late that year, my Tucson lawyer, Lawrence D'Antonio, told me an FBI agent wanted to see me. The FBI agent had approached D'Antonio's law partner, Ray Hayes, because the two knew each other. According to Hayes, the FBI agent wanted to arrange a discreet meeting with me, perhaps to talk about Apalachin. Hayes assured me his FBI friend just wanted to talk and could be trusted to keep his word.

It smelled fishy, but I wanted to avoid more publicity. Perhaps if I talked to this FBI agent, the FBI wouldn't make a big public flap over me in Arizona. I agreed to see him at my house. Initially, I had wanted my lawyers to be present, but the FBI agent told Hayes he wanted to see me alone. The FBI agent promised I wouldn't be arrested.

At the appointed hour, when I went to answer the front doorbell, I saw that about six FBI agents had surrounded my house. One of them handed me a federal warrant demanding my appearance in federal court in New York City, and they arrested me.

The timing of the arrest, as well as the whole operation, had been planned meticulously. They arrested me late on a Friday afternoon, knowing that if I had any trouble raising my bail I would be stuck in jail the entire weekend. Bond was set at $75,000—one of the highest bonds ever set in Arizona up to then.

Luckily, my bank was on the same block as the federal courthouse in Tucson. I signed a personal check, and my lawyer had just enough time to rush to the bank and cash it.

I was free on bail, but I still had to appear in New York City. Through my New York lawyer I found out that the federal warrant that I had been handed was improper. The FBI had obtained the warrant based on a list of prospective witnesses that might be called before a federal grand jury in New York City. But since the grand jury had not yet called for me, the warrant was premature.

I was apprehensive about returning to New York to clear up the matter. When I got there, my lawyer quickly corrected the warrant impropriety, but there was more in store for me.

While my lawyer, Harry Oshrin, went to the court clerk's office, I waited for him in a coffee shop across the street. At the counter, I noticed a man sneaking looks at me. Then another man came up to me and handed me a subpoena from the New York State Investigation Commission. The subpoena said I had to appear before the New York Crime Commission that very day.

The fog lifted. Everything became clear. The federal warrant handed to me by the FBI in Tucson was but a ruse to lure me to New York so I could be handed another warrant to appear before the state commission.

As the state troopers prepared for the court case stemming from Apalachin, they realized that although they had found my driver's license at Apalachin, none of them could testify in court that he had actually seen me there. They had some old photographs of me, but none of them could personally identify me. The two men at the coffee shop were state police agents. They wanted a good look at me so they could positively identify me as having seen me in Apalachin.

The following year, in 1959, a federal grand jury indicted me along with the Apalachin visitors on a charge of conspiracy to obstruct justice. The government based its tenuous case on the fact that no one would answer questions as to the purpose of the Apalachin meeting.

All the defendants were found guilty, but the verdict was later overturned in appeals court. It's not a crime to visit with your friends.

I never stood trial, however. My case was severed before the trial even began. While waiting to go on trial, I had my second heart attack. A court-appointed doctor examined me to make sure I was indeed sick.

This second heart attack stunned me far more than my first heart attack. I could trace its derivation almost directly to the turmoil in the Volcano and to Apalachin.

Often in my life, I've had people tell me they wish they were Joe Bonanno, that they had Joe Bonanno's power, his influence, his wealth. Such people don't know what they're talking about. If they want to be like me, they also have to assume the pressures, the anxiety, the tension inherent in my life-style. None of the people who say they want to be Joe Bonanno has ever told me he'd like to have Joe Bonanno's blood pressure.

21

THROUGHOUT THE 1930s, 1940s AND 1950s, MY FAMILY OF friends prospered. No small measure of our success was due to our unity. Many of us were Castellammarese, or somehow related to a Castellammarese. We were never the largest Family in New York City, but we were the most tightly knit. As Father, I kept my Family out of the business of other Families more notorious than mine and constantly racked by bloody battles of succession.

The Bonanno Family was not only the most cohesive but also the most conservative. I hewed to the old ways, the ways of my Tradition. The way of life I and my friends had chosen was but a means to attain social advancement and respectability. We didn't consider ourselves criminals. In fact, we considered our code of ethics stricter and fairer than any we encountered in America.

But in America, I had seen my Tradition corroded by social forces at work in this new country and by fellow Italian-Americans who adopted the terms and concepts of my Tradition without living up to its ideals.

When I first committed myself to the "mafioso" way of life, I thought that men like me were merely transplanting our Tradition to another setting. Little by little, however, our Tradition deteriorated until it lost its connotation of honor and became instead a byword for gangsterism.

For nearly three decades I had observed the unwholesome changes decaying my Tradition, but since I wasn't in a position to pull out (and probably wouldn't have, because I thought myself smarter than I do now), I applied my energies toward trying to keep my Family untainted by these corrosive forces.

Apalachin changed all that.

In the aftermath of Apalachin, I saw my Tradition die away completely and a distantly related mutation take its place.

After I recuperated in Tucson from my second heart attack, I resolved more than ever to avoid publicity. The Apalachin affair had taught me how dramatic was the power of the mass media. It was publicity, above all else, that had transformed the Apalachin meeting into a conclave that supposedly threatened national security. The Sicilian Families were likened to a conspiratorial group, similar to the Communists in that they were intent on overthrowing the American system. The mass media equated the Sicilian Families with a national crime syndicate. Journalists took the word "Mafia" and went on a verbal rampage with it.

Most Americans undoubtedly considered "Mafia" some sort of foreign germ. The word brought to mind gangland slayings and seamy rackets. That's the only context in which they heard the word. It's not surprising, therefore, that Americans concluded that's all there was to it.

There was another side, however, to American interest in "Mafia." All good Americans wanted to destroy it, but they were also enthralled by it. They read gory accounts of it in paperbacks and flocked to the movies to watch men wearing dark glasses and carrying violin cases.

The more the government battled a bogeyman which wasn't there, the more vivid and outrageous this bogeyman appeared in works of fiction.

That's why I so ardently wanted to keep out of the limelight. Any publicity was bad publicity. Every disclosure concerning "Mafia" was subjected to muddled thinking and sensationalism.

I can't say that men of my world helped matters any. At a time when we should have been seeking obscurity, we found ourselves involved in a sorry and visible series of battles among ourselves. At the same time that the public thirsted for lurid accounts of our world, we fought among ourselves and, as if in response, provided the public its thrills.

We were falling, falling, falling apart.

No sooner did the federal appeals court dismiss the charges

against the Apalachin visitors than fresh trouble erupted in my world.

In 1961 or so, a group within the Profaci Family rebelled against their Father. This dissident group was led by the Gallo brothers, Albert, Larry and Joey. In an internal revolt such as this, the matter is normally resolved within the Family. To bolster their position, however, the Gallos sought the support of another Family head, Carlo Gambino. Gambino could have refused to listen to the Gallos, because, according to the old Tradition, one Father is not supposed to take the side of another Father's children. But Gambino granted an audience to the Gallos themselves and heard their complaints. When Profaci found out about this, he was incensed that Gambino hadn't shunned the Gallos.

In the aftermath of Apalachin—what with investigators, commissions, committees, prosecutors, grand juries and reporters breathing down our necks—the heads of the New York Families largely avoided one another for some four years. In addition to not having seen each other, there were also some new faces. Gambino was one of them. After a probationary period of some three years, his Family confirmed him as their Father. Also, Vito Genovese was now in jail on a narcotics conviction. In Vito's absence, Tommy Eboli became the temporary representative for his Family.

The Commission, in the hiatus forced on us by Apalachin, had been dormant. When we began to meet again, we all had much "face-reading" to do. The Apalachin fiasco had estranged us somewhat. After our long separation, we all wanted to know what new alliances would develop.

On my part, I knew that the relationship between Stefano Magaddino and me would never be the same. On the surface we were still friendly, but we harbored subterranean animosities toward each other. He suspected me of arrogance and I suspected him of jealousy. Our differences, I must emphasize again, centered on our different personalities. I had differences with other Fathers—Lucchese, for example—but these differences were over policy issues. With Stefano, it was a much more intimate matter.

Because of the uneasiness between us, the conservative wing of the Commission suffered. Profaci was having trouble with the Gallos. The Gallos were close to Gambino. Gambino was very close to Lucchese. Lucchese was flirting with Magaddino. The center was not holding.

In early 1962, at Gambino's request, the Commission met. We took up the Profaci matter. In his presentation, Gambino made it seem as if he had only the welfare of all of us at heart. He said the troubles between Profaci and the Gallo brothers were getting out of hand.

—Joe Profaci has been the Father of his Family for many glorious years, Gambino said. But it is my duty to tell the Commission that for the sake of peace, and to avoid more trouble, perhaps it would be best if he retires.

Profaci had to employ all his self-restraint to keep from telling Gambino what he really thought of him. I sympathized with Joe. He was one of my oldest friends on the Commission. We were proud of the fact that up to then only our Families, of the five New York clans, had avoided turmoil and bloodshed.

And this Gambino, where did he get the nerve to challenge Profaci? I knew Carlo's character. He was not a warrior. Given a choice, he avoided violence. He was a squirrel of a man, a servile and cringing individual. When Anastasia was alive, Albert used to use Gambino as his gopher, to go on errands for him. I once saw Albert get so angry at Carlo for bungling a simple assignment that Albert raised his hand and almost slapped him. In my Tradition, a slap on the face is tantamount to a mortal offense. Another man would not have tolerated such public humiliation. Carlo responded with a fawning grin. No, I couldn't believe that Gambino was man enough to challenge Profaci. There had to be someone behind him.

After Gambino's speech, Profaci was asked to leave the room while the rest of us deliberated. I invited comments from the others.

—Would you like to talk first, Tommy? I said.

It was his face and his words I wanted to study the most. The Volcano had taken its toll on Lucchese. His face was beginning to sag. His hair had thinned. Age had drooped his varnished features.

Lucchese lauded Profaci for his many years as a "man of respect." Lately, however, there had been trouble in his Family, Lucchese continued with unctuous smoothness. Disunity brings a Family down. It takes a strong and vigorous leader to restore peace. Don Piddru had distinguished himself in the past. Why should the serenity of don Piddru be disturbed? He should be resting, leaving the work to the others, to the young.

Lucchese made it sound as if Profaci would be doing himself a favor if he retired. The Commission could not force Profaci to retire, but by withholding a vote of confidence, the Commission would be sending signals to the rest of our world, thereby encouraging others to challenge Profaci in his own Family.

If only in a practical sense, Profaci perhaps would have been more sensible if he had left the field to retire to sunny Florida, where he often went. But a man doesn't easily walk away from what he has spent a lifetime creating. A Father has his pride. It would have been unseemly for Profaci to abandon his Family during its difficulties. A Father doesn't like to leave until he has bequeathed peace to his Family.

No one else in the room wanted to speak after Lucchese.

—Don Piddru should stay, I said loudly and emphatically.

I said that the real issue was not old age. We were all getting older. The real issue was trust. Should we trust each other to settle our own affairs? Or should we distrust each other? If we distrusted each other, we would invite malcontents from every Family to foment turmoil.

By my vigorous defense, everyone understood that I was ready to back up my words with force if need be. It was clear that I would not stand idly by while Profaci was sacrificed on the altar of youth.

My views prevailed. Profaci was saved. By dinnertime, we were all acting like friends again.

—Here, Peppino, try some of this. It's very good, Lucchese said, handing me the blue cheese.

Two new members had been added to the Commission by the early 1960s, increasing the number of representatives to nine. This had been favored by all and had been ratified at our 1956 national convention. Additional representatives would bring fresh views to the Commission. We hoped to distribute responsibilities among the Fathers.

The two new representatives were Joe Zerilli of Detroit and Angelo Bruno of Philadelphia. Zerilli was known to lean closer to the conservatives, especially Profaci. Bruno, through his friend and go-between Sam DeCavalcante of New Jersey, leaned closer to the liberals. Nevertheless, being novices in their positions, neither Bruno nor Zerilli played a critical role in Commission business. The old hands dominated, and the roiling situation in New York continued to receive most of the attention.

The Commission's vote of confidence for Profaci secured only a temporary truce. Later that same year, in 1962, Profaci died of cancer, and his right-hand man, Joe Magliocco, assumed his place. Once again, hostilities broke out with the Gallo brothers. Magliocco's position was the same as Profaci's: that the Gallos were an internal problem that he should handle alone. Magliocco resented the meddling of Gambino and Lucchese.

In the high parliamentary games at the Commission, however, Magliocco was at a disadvantage. Profaci could always have counted on my support and that of Magaddino. Also, Profaci could rely on the backing of Zerilli; they had extensive kinship ties. After Profaci's death, Magliocco could not count on such support, other than myself. Zerilli was cool toward Magliocco. Magaddino had become an unknown factor.

On the whole, then, I felt uneasy both with how things were going in my world in general and with the makeup of the Commission. Although no one had threatened me directly, I sensed that no one would be terribly put out if I quietly left. An air of suspicion pervaded all our conversations on the Commission. I was being outflanked and placed in the role of recalcitrant.

During one of our discussions during this period, it was casually suggested that the Commission representatives extend their terms without being ratified at a national meeting. Lucchese and Magaddino were in favor of voting ourselves in for another five-year term without calling a national meeting. Since we all wanted to avoid another Apalachin, their suggestion seemed motivated solely by caution. I suspected there was more to it than that.

I too recognized that it would have been an inopportune time to call a national meeting. Nonetheless, I was not eager to install ourselves for another term so cavalierly. I reminded my peers that since our last uninterrupted national meeting had been in 1956, our terms had formally expired in 1961. Strictly speaking, we were an unauthorized Commission.

Because Lucchese, Gambino and Magaddino now held the upper hand in Commission politics, it served their purpose to continue business as usual and brush over the issue of illegality I had brought up. Furthermore, they did not want me to take the stage at a national meeting. Before a national audience, because of my experience and popularity, I still had more influence than any of them individually. Also, a national meeting would have to include Magliocco; and he, by now, was plainly not their favorite.

None of us was prepared to force the issue over our expired terms. We let the matter rest for discussion at another time. Still, having voiced my objections, I was greeted by many grave faces. I had given my opponents a clear indication that I was not satisfied with the present situation. In doing so, I piqued some and deeply worried others. I was wondering what their next move might be, and they were wondering what my next move might be, all of us playing it close to the vest.

The Magliocco issue brought out the new coalitions of interests on the Commission. I favored Magliocco and his fight to keep leadership of his Family. And yet, other than speaking on his behalf, there was little I could do. Because of the forces against us on the Commission, any open move to assist Magliocco would have been suicide. In any case, to intervene directly in his fight against the Gallos as much as Magliocco would probably have wanted me to would have violated my very preachings to the Commission.

Lucchese and his ally Gambino now held majority power on the Commission. With Vito Genovese in prison, his stand-ins more or less followed the majority. The representative from Chicago, at this time, was Sam Giancana, who tended to side against me. Zerilli of Detroit played it cagey and noncommittal. Bruno of Philadelphia was a neophyte and could be led by the nose by Gambino or Stefano Magaddino.

Stefano's two-faced conduct bothered and hurt me the most That we were drifting apart filled me with shame—two cousins and yet we couldn't hold it together. Stefano had not openly broken with me, but his increasingly apparent efforts to dissociate himself from me gave my opponents on the Commission encouragement to challenge me.

About this time, my aversion to the top men in my own

world was cresting. I, who had been on the Commission since it was founded, now felt myself becoming isolated, almost an outcast. My views had been running increasingly counter to the rest of the Commission. It was as if I didn't belong.

My worries did not end with the Commission. Outside my world, I was a marked man among law-enforcement agents. So far, they had failed to put me out of action, but with each failed attempt, they were goaded all the more to pursue me anew. As head of one of the New York Families, I was a prize catch. They all wanted my head on their trophy shelf.

This unceasing police pressure began drastically to affect my domestic life and the lives of those nearest to me. It affected my son Salvatore the worst. Over my vehement protest, Salvatore had abandoned his dream of becoming a lawyer. When he told me about it, I challenged my son to continue his studies, saying that if he remained in school I would enroll in law school as well. We would graduate together. Levity was as useless as anger in changing Salvatore's predicament. Being the son of Joe Bonanno had deprived him of his privacy. Because of his name, it was impossible, unless he became a recluse, for him to lead a normal life. His name was Bonanno; he lived in a glass house. On top of this, Salvatore and his wife, Rosalie, were having personal problems that jeopardized their marriage.

My younger son, Joseph, although still in high school, also had been affected by my notoriety, which forced me to keep away from home for long stretches. Joseph had spent most of his life either with his mother or in military boarding school. He hardly knew me.

As for my wife, loving and loyal Fay, she too, of course, wanted to see more of me at home. She would ask me about that trip to Italy I had been promising her for a long time. She asked me about retirement, a gentle reminder that I was approaching that age; and as far as she was concerned, the sooner I retired the better.

Lately, I had given the subject much thought. In the mid-1950s, after Salvatore's wedding and my trip to Italy, I thought it was too early to retire. After my 1959 heart attack and the wedding of my daughter, Catherine, in 1960, retirement seemed feasible. Catherine's marriage and her leaving the house meant that Fay and I, along with Joseph, were free to do what we liked.

Our comparative freedom from encumbrances afforded Fay and me the luxury of daydreaming. We chatted blithely about possibly retiring to a villa in Italy. I definitely wanted at least to visit Italy with my wife. I also wanted to take her to Australia. I had a childhood friend there who was trying to interest me in a 55,000-acre ranch. He had told me in a letter that Australia was the place to start a new life. Another possibility was simply to retire in Tucson, where we had many friends and no chill winds blew.

Developments in the Volcano now convinced me the time was ripe for a gradual and tactful divestment of my interests there.

If I hoped to retire from my world, I had to be careful not to antagonize anyone. My main concern was Stefano. I decided that despite our recent spats, Stefano Magaddino, and he only among the Fathers, should know ahead of time of my intentions to retire. I wanted him to know so that my absences and movements away from the Volcano wouldn't alarm him. Stefano envied me, but I didn't want him to begin fearing me, for that would make him nervous and reckless. Since from then on I didn't intend to spend much time in the Volcano, I wanted to reassure Stefano that my absence did not mean I was maneuvering against him or the Commission.

I paid a social visit to Stefano at his new home in Lewiston, near Niagara Falls. I told him nothing should come between us and that whatever differences we had, we should keep them to ourselves. I had the utmost respect for the Magaddino family in Sicily; after my father's death, Stefano's uncles, Giuseppe and Stefano, had been like foster fathers to me. I hated to see the two of us, two cousins, feuding.

Family feuds, whether in America or in Sicily, had always disgusted me. Such feuds and vendettas represent the degeneration of society. As an orphan, I was extremely sensitive, preternaturally so, to the waste, stupidity and stridency of quarrels among relatives.

—Friendship is what counts in life, I said.

Stefano seconded my remarks, but on his face I detected a tremor of uncertainty. My remarks had been straightforward. But by this time Stefano distrusted me, and I didn't quite trust him. He may have wondered whether or not to take my words at face value.

When I said I intended to retire soon, his eyes opened wide and seemed to twinkle.

I made sure the announcement was also heard by Stefano's son-in-law, who was in the house with us. I had done this on purpose so that someone else in Stefano's Family would know my intentions. If I had informed only Stefano, he might have withheld this information from the rest of his Family if it suited his purpose. I didn't want any misunderstandings. This frequently happened in my world, because other than the top men, no one knew what was going on in the highest circle of power. Because of this grapevine system of passing information, rumor and innuendo often traded places with truth. When a Father reported to his men about Commission business, the Father had it in his power, if he wanted to, to shape the minds of his subordinates, by withholding information or slanting it. For example, the men in Stefano's Family, like the men in my Family, knew little, if anything, about the disenchantment between Stefano and me. Very few people under us knew about Stefano's dalliance with Lucchese and Gambino.

—Beware of Lucchese, that viper, I said to Stefano in front of his son-in-law.

Stefano responded with an uncomfortable smile. He was miffed that I should make such a statement in front of his son-in-law. It seemed like a breach of decorum among Fathers.

On the whole, however, Stefano reacted favorably to my visit. He was glad I would soon retire, and I wanted to put him at ease while I tried to extricate myself, deliberately, and in a dignified manner, from the top of my world.

By 1963, I was largely leading a remote existence, as much to avoid complications on the Commission and to avoid Magliocco's family turmoil as to avoid ruinous publicity. A federal witch hunt was under way. With the advent of Robert F. Kennedy as U.S. Attorney General, the U.S. Justice Department made organized crime its chief target. New federal laws had been passed that gave the FBI jurisdiction over interstate gambling and racketeering. Political pressure was on FBI Director J. Edgar Hoover to stop chasing Communists and start chasing men of my Tradition. Regardless of our backgrounds, whether we were benign or malevolent, good or bad, productive or destructive, the FBI lumped us all together. Hunting us became one of the FBI's most glamorous assignments.

I kept on the go, never remaining in one place for long, hopscotching here and there, spending much of my time on the road remaining out of reach of summonses and subpoenas.

I was fifty-eight years old, and such a mobile life-style, away from my family much of the time, was not what I preferred. I accepted my wandering as an enforced holiday. It was a respite from the burden of responsibility. Despite my home-sickness and my worries about the future, I also relaxed during those days in the 1960s that I spent on the road.

In the Volcano, I had delegated responsibilities to subordinates, including the responsibility of representing me on the Commission. Sooner or later, someone in my Family would have to replace me. By dispersing my authority, I wanted to see who had the essential leadership qualities to rise above the others. I remained in the background, however, watching events.

Joe Magliocco's fight was not only against the Gallo brothers but also against the Gallo supporters on the Commission: Lucchese and Gambino. As I had foreseen, Joe Zerilli of Detroit had just about abandoned Magliocco after Profaci died. In addition, Profaci's son and Profaci's nephew had both remained aloof from Magliocco. I was still Magliocco's friend, but my hands were tied. It was not in the best interest of my Family to aid Magliocco openly or to conspire with him against the other Fathers.

That was the situation in the summer of 1963 when fate decided to play a trick on me. At that time, the marital problems between my son Salvatore and his wife, Rosalie, intensified. This precipitated a visit from Rosalie's mother, Mrs. Salvatore Profaci (Salvatore Profaci was dead), to Phoenix, where my son made his home. After he left college, I had helped Salvatore set up a wholesale food business. Rosalie decided to return with her mother to New York and to take the children with her. Salvatore followed his wife there, not wanting to break up his marriage. Then the two reconciled, and even though Salvatore didn't like New York, he agreed to set up house on Long Island so that Rosalie would be close to her relatives. While their new house was being fixed up, Salvatore and Rosalie temporarily stayed with Rosalie's uncle, Joe Magliocco, who had an estate on Long Island.

Magliocco welcomed Salvatore's presence. Joe would be a steadying influence on Rosalie, whose marriage with Salvatore he wanted to save. Also, having Salvatore at his side made Magliocco feel closer to me. Magliocco figured Salvatore was the link through which to keep me informed of his situation. Magliocco's situation was becoming desperate, more so than Salvatore knew. Joe grasped for whatever friends remained.

Since I was on the move, I did not find out about Salvatore's move to New York until after it happened. I never wanted him to be in New York because of the possibility he might be drawn into the intrigue there. Because he was my son, people tended to regard Salvatore as my standard-bearer as well, even though Salvatore was not involved in the in-house politics in the Volcano.

Nevertheless, I couldn't prevent Salvatore from remaining in New York if he wanted to. He was fighting to keep his marriage intact; I could hardly expect him to stay away from Rosalie and their children.

One day, while Salvatore was still living at Magliocco's home, Joe asked Salvatore to drive him to the railroad station, since Magliocco's regular driver was unavailable. Magliocco didn't tell Salvatore the purpose of their drive, but he asked Salvatore to take a gun. Salvatore felt strongly that you don't abandon friends and relatives in need. They drove to the terminal, where they met a train passenger from Brooklyn. The man greeted Magliocco and said hello to Salvatore. The man seemed to know my son, but Salvatore didn't recognize him. Magliocco and the man briefly exchanged a few words. On the way home, Magliocco didn't explain what it was all about.

As I later learned, Magliocco apparently was receiving some sort of progress report from someone within his Family. I don't know specifically what Magliocco had in mind, but it was no secret that Magliocco blamed Gambino and Lucchese for his troubles with the Gallo brothers. There was a man in Magliocco's Family who had access to and had the confidence of Gambino and Lucchese. Magliocco apparently used this man to keep tabs on his enemies and to let him know what Gambino and Lucchese were saying about him. This man was close to Joseph Colombo.

Not long after the incident at the railroad terminal, Colombo apparently decided he would have more to gain if he betrayed Magliocco and switched sides. He therefore went to Gambino and Lucchese to tell them what he knew about Magliocco as proof of his new allegiance.

The reader must keep in mind that throughout this period I was not in New York. I depended for my information on others and I was not in a position to participate in the unfolding drama.

By the fall of 1963, Magliocco was in deep trouble. His man Colombo, a group leader within his Family, had defected. Gambino and Lucchese accused Magliocco of plotting to depose them. They declared they didn't recognize Magliocco as head of his Family anymore. And they encouraged others to follow Colombo's example and defect.

Now for the hook that snagged me.

Gambino and Lucchese passed on Colombo's disclosures to their new "sweetheart," Stefano Magaddino. Stefano's ears must have pricked up when he heard that my son was in Magliocco's car during the railroad-terminal meeting. A more prudent man would first have troubled himself to find out the particulars instead of jumping to conclusions. But Stefano's reasoning must have gone something life this: If the son of Joe Bonanno was driving Magliocco to such a sensitive meeting, then Joe Bonanno must be behind Magliocco.

Stefano began disseminating the story that Joe Bonanno wanted to kill Gambino and Lucchese, and that I was so power-hungry I wanted to kill my own cousin Stefano as well.

In his state of semi-hysteria, Stefano now wanted to believe the very worst about me. He chose to believe that my travels were but a ruse to buy me time while I planned some sort of coup that would topple him and the others on the Commission. Stefano saw darkness in the middle of the day.

What I had wanted to avoid had happened. In addition to being envious of me, Stefano was now also fearful. After hearing what Stefano was saying about me, I tried to get in touch with my cousin. I was willing to go see him in Buffalo, or for him to come see me in New York. Stefano refused to do either. He refused even to come to the telephone when I called him at his home. By this time, Stefano had become so jittery that he interpreted my attempts to contact him as yet another trick.

Soon he began spreading another rumor: that I was going to send my men to Buffalo to get him.

The death of Joe Magliocco late in 1963 alleviated the tension in the Volcano somewhat. Magliocco died of a heart attack. If he had died of gunfire, it probably would have sparked retaliation and general battle. Since he died of natural causes, however, Magliocco's death cleared the way for Joseph Colombo to seize power in that Family. He did so at the expense of the Gallos, who had lost favor with Gambino and Lucchese once Colombo became their darling. Colombo put down the Gallo insurrection. Then the Commission, with me absent, accepted Colombo as the new leader of his Family on a temporary basis.

For the moment, the fighting had ceased. Lucchese and Gambino, with Magaddino and Colombo as allies, were in clear control of the Commission. Stefano was riding high. By spreading lies about me, he came out looking like the champion of justice; he made me out to be the ungrateful prodigal son. With Stefano at their side, Gambino and Lucchese had destroyed the conservative faction. To keep him at their side, Gambino and Lucchese propitiated and flattered Stefano. Short-lived as it would turn out to be, this was Stefano's moment of glory.

Although I no longer personally involved myself in Commission business, as I have explained, I too benefited, in a sense, from Magliocco's death. As long as either Profaci or Magliocco was alive, I was bound to them as an ally and as a friend. Magliocco's death relieved me of my obligations toward his successor. I had no ties with Colombo or the Gallos.

I was free, then, to continue to pursue my plans of gradually stepping out of the picture in New York.

The slackening of tension produced in me an almost airy feeling. I felt light and footloose. Even during the bad times, it wasn't all tedium and pain. There were breaks, and this was one of them. When such breaks come along, it's best to take advantage of them even though the rest of your world is coming apart. You never know when you're going to get another holiday or if you'll ever get one at all. So, I always try to live in the present.

It was spring.

—Let's go around the world, I said to my wife.

Fay thought I was kidding.

—Bermuda, Italy, Australia, Hawaii, I drawled enticingly.

—Are you serious?

—Let's get away from it all, I said. We might never get another chance.

Pack and leave your worries behind! Hurrah! That's the spirit in which Fay and I undertook our trip in the spring of 1964.

22

WHEN MY BUSINESS ASSOCIATE JOHN DIBELLA OF THE GRANDE Cheese Co. found out about my upcoming travels, he asked me to make Montreal my first stop. Mr. DiBella had a close friend from his hometown in Sicily, Joseph Saputo, who was also in the cheese business. Because of immigration quotas, Mr. Saputo and his family hadn't been able to enter the United States. As the next best thing, Mr. Saputo immigrated to Montreal, Canada, where he established the Saputo Cheese Co. He was now looking for investors to expand operations.

Fay and I went to Canada, expecting to be there but a short time.

At the cheese plant, Mr. Saputo and I agreed to a deal. Mr. Saputo signed a letter of intent, stating that once I made payment, I would own twenty percent of the business. To effect the transaction, I opened an account at the Bank of Commerce in Montreal, which would take care of transferring the necessary funds from my bank in the United States. The bank manager extended me limited credit. It was suggested that I take advantage of Canada's friendly policy toward investments from abroad. He said that if I applied for a special Canadian immigration card, it would make it easier for me to get more credit in the future, and it also would allow me to travel freely in and out of Canada.

My lawyer in Canada said American businessmen frequently applied for such cards. An immigration card entitled its holder eventually to settle in Canada if he wished. Its main value for me, the lawyer explained, was convenience. I certainly had no intention of settling in Montreal.

223

I applied for the card. The application form asked, among other things, if I was a fugitive and if I had ever been convicted of a crime. I answered no.

Several weeks went by. My wife and I were merely waiting for my application to clear, then we would be on our way. Then my lawyer informed me that the Canadian immigration authorities wanted to see me. They wanted to ask me some questions. Would I kindly go to their office?

From experience I had learned that you always take a risk when government officials ask to talk to you, even when everything seems proper. Fay, who normally didn't offer opinions about business matters, advised me not to go and to forget about the immigration card.

—Oh, what do you understand! I said petulantly.

Although I really agreed with her, I guess I didn't want to admit to myself that I had anything to fear. My retort to Fay wasn't really directed at her, but at that part of myself that was cautioning me to not take any chances. I should have relied on instinct. Instead, I listened to reason.

On the way to the immigration office, my lawyer and I stopped at a coffee shop. I was growing more and more pessimistic the closer we got to the authorities. He said it would just be a routine matter.

All my lawyers have advised me to remain calm. But I'm still waiting for a lawyer to volunteer to change places with me so I might have the satisfaction of telling him:

—You be Joe Bonanno. You stay calm.

In any case, this Montreal lawyer wasn't thinking ahead. He was satisfied everything we had done was legal. He had good intentions, of course, but little insight. He led me to the authorities.

At the immigration office, I repeated my intentions of investing in a Canadian business for the purpose of expanding a cheese plant and hiring more people. I was helping Canada reduce its unemployment. To back up my statement I had brought the letter of intent signed by Joseph Saputo.

—Are you in Canada for something else, Mr. Bonanno?

—I just told you why I'm in Canada.

It was obvious from the start that the Canadian authorities had already made up their minds about me. They arrested me.

When I found out the charges against me, I had to laugh.

The Canadian government claimed that I had lied on my immigration-card application by not mentioning that I had been convicted of a wage-and-hour violation in the 1940s in the United States. To make such a charge, the Canadian authorities had to have been in contact with the U.S. authorities. Only from Washington could Canada have received this erroneous information. This was the same charge lodged against me by federal authorities in the United States. I was vindicated on that same charge in U.S. District Court in Tucson. Everything concerning this wage-and-hour violation had been cleared up, or so I thought. If I didn't think the matter had been settled, why would I intentionally perjure myself on the immigration-card application? I wouldn't have made such an application in the first place.

At a hearing after my arrest, a Canadian judge refused to grant me bail. I had no history of wrongdoing in Canada, and yet he would not set bond. That told me that Ottawa, at Washington's behest, was exerting pressure to hamper me.

My befuddled lawyer told me I could choose between going to jail and being deported.

I didn't want to be deported. If Canada deported me as a persona non grata, I would lose my rights to invest in the Saputo Cheese Co. Also, now that it was obvious the United States was behind my predicament, I knew that once I was deported back to the United States, the FBI would be waiting for me.

I refused to accept deportation. Pending further litigation, I would have to go to jail. I was released from the custody of the immigration authorities and taken to Bordeaux Prison in Montreal.

My arrest in Canada, as I later learned, created headlines. Publicity of this sort was just what I had wanted to avoid. The newspapers in Canada called me the big boss from America who had come to Canada to organize "the Mafia."

I was taken to a prison which contained hardened criminals, some eighteen hundred inmates of every stripe and hue. I was no longer in a detention center; this was the slammer. Although I had been arrested before, I never had spent time in prison. The experience was new to me. At the check-in station, prison officials took my watch, my pinky ring and $2,000 I had in my pocket. I had a couple of cigars on me, and I gave them to the guards.

They transferred me to this prison late on a Friday. That meant that I couldn't be processed until after the weekend. During this weekend, I couldn't communicate with anyone outside the prison. Until my processing was complete, I couldn't join the general prison population either.

The prison guards escorted me through gleaming hallways. They pushed buttons on the wall; barred doors slid open. We walked through more corridors and went down a flight of stairs, then entered a dimmer place, dank and grubby. A row of single cells with metal doors on the inside and bars on the outside came into view. The guards opened one of them. The cell was about four by six feet. There was a toilet, a sink and a cot. Cockroaches scurried about. The dim light on the ceiling gave everything a sickly, yellowish appearance. The dirt and the dust made you cough and sneeze.

Then came the terrible sound of the heavy door being locked behind me . . . and I was alone in a bleak cubicle; six paces and I ran into a wall. The universe had shrunk. My stomach was queasy, my head pounded, my heart palpitated.

I sat on the cot.

—I don't belong here.

I was talking *out loud* . . . to myself, or to the cockroaches.

—I don't belong in this hole.

Later that evening, they slid a tray under the door. It contained a glob of meat, some crusty beans and a chunk of hard bread. The meat tasted as if it had come off a sick caribou. I spat it out. I wanted to rinse my mouth. I had no glass and had to gather water in my cupped hands.

I felt lousy.

Lights out.

The darkness crawled on my flesh.

I tried to concentrate, but my mind flitted uncontrollably. My mind would not hold still. It went from thoughts of Fay to the FBI to the Volcano to lawyers to how cold I was. I did this until my mind simply tired itself and refused to entertain ideas altogether. The rage in my heart eventually sputtered out. I was left with silence and emptiness.

—Monsieur Bonanno. *Le boss.*

It was a low voice. It wasn't my voice. Someone was calling me. But was I imagining it? Or did I actually hear it?

—Monsieur Bonanno. *Le boss.*

I was sure of it now. A prisoner in one of the cells down the corridor was calling my name. He must have heard it from the guards. Hearing my name restored my vitality. It jolted me back to my senses. I didn't know who was calling me or why. I just know that on hearing my name I became self-possessed again. It was as if that low, anonymous voice had affirmed my identity.

Yes, I'm Joe Bonanno, I said to myself. I've always been able to take care of myself, and I can take care of myself in this inferno. I'm Joe Bonanno.

Nothing tangible had changed, but, oh, what a spiritual transformation in me. I was in possession of myself once again. A manly attitude animated me once more, and I became alert, contained, keenly aware, poised for action.

I grabbed the dinner tray and rattled it on the door.

A guard came to my cell door.

—*Qu'est-ce que c'est?*

—*J'ai froid,* I said.

—*N'avez-vous pas couverture?*

—*Non.*

—*Un moment.*

I had told the guard I was cold, and he went to fetch me a blanket. He was not the same guard who had been on duty before. He was younger and had a friendlier voice. The guard returned with a blanket.

—Thank you.

—Welcome, the guard said.

I led him further in conversation, as well as I could manage in French. He told me that the rest of the prisoners in this section of the jail were hard-core criminals, many of whom would spend the remainder of their lives in prison. He agreed I didn't belong with them. The decision to put me in solitary confinement—which was the section I occupied—must have been made on the outside, meaning outside the prison, the guard said. He added that after the weekend I would undoubtedly be moved to different quarters.

—*C'est seulement pour le weekend,* he reassured me.

I told the guard I figured as much, that it was all harassment. He didn't seem the least bit antagonistic toward me, and this encouraged me to continue drawing him out. He told me his name was Tony, saying it in English. I asked him where he lived. He said St. Michel. What a coincidence! That was the same section of Montreal where the Saputo cheese plant was located and the same section of town where my wife was staying with friends.

—Tony, *je vous demande une faveur.*

I told him my wife was in St. Michel and that she must be very worried about me. Perhaps, after his shift on duty, he could go to her and tell her I was fine. Could he do that? Before he could answer, I added,

—*Les femmes italiennes sont émotives, n'est-ce pas?*

Tony pumped his head up and down. He knew from experience that Italian women were very emotional.

—*C'est bon alors?* I said.

—*Bien*, he agreed. *D'accord.*

Then I said that after he delivered my message to my wife, he should tell her that I wanted her to give him some cheese. The guard made a gesture of refusal.

—*Je t'en prie*, I said. *Ce fromage est délicieux. Je ne puis pas le manger en prison, mais tu peux.*

Since I couldn't eat the delicious cheese, he might as well take it.

—*Comme vous voudrez*, the guard said, granting me my wish.

—*Une autre chose*, I added.

There was something else I wanted to tell him.

—*Dites-moi*, he said.

We were getting along famously by now.

—*Mon coeur*, I said, fluttering my hand over my chest. *J'ai malade de coeur.*

I told him I had a heart condition.

—*Ah, votre coeur*, the guard said, concerned.

He asked me how bad it was.

—*Je souffre.*

I told him I was suffering. The guard and I exchanged glances. We had established a tacit sympathy, Tony and I, and I trusted him to know what to do.

Tony left without saying a word and returned in a short time with another guard. They took me to the infirmary. I wasn't about to argue with that. It would at least take me out of my squalid pit.

On Monday a doctor examined me. My blood pressure was

228

high. The doctor reassigned me to the prison hospital. By then I think the entire prison population knew I was in their midst. When I arrived at the hospital, one of the prisoners immediately approached me. He saw what bed I had been assigned. He said he was the inmate "in charge" of this particular ward. He told me I could have his bed, which had the best position in the ward. I didn't know the guy, and yet he was looking out for me. He showed me to his bed. He said he would take the bed next to it. Another man was lying on that bed. My protector told him to find another bed. The invalid got up and walked away.

That afternoon, the prison's chief of guards came to my ward. He introduced himself and said he wanted to talk to me in private in his office. But first things first, he added. This official wanted to give me yet another bed, better than the one I already occupied. He pointed to the trustee's room at the end of the ward and said I could have it. He told the trustee to look after me, to give me all I wanted to eat, to let me walk about.

Needless to say, I was impressed with this unexpected prison hospitality. My prospects had brightened indeed. I almost felt I was in a hotel. More surprises awaited me when I went to see the chief of guards in his office. After I entered, he locked the door. He then sat behind his desk, smiling. He maintained a toothsome expression as he reached in his drawer and pulled out a bottle of Cordon Bleu cognac and a box of cigars.

—Mr. Bonanno, may I have the pleasure? he said, handing me one of the cigars and asking my permission to light it.

I accepted. He lit a cigar for himself. He had an appealing smile. We alternated speaking English and French.

—Cognac? he said, holding up the drank green bottle.

—*Versez*, I said. *Servez-vous*.

He poured the precious amber liquid into two ordinary glasses.

—*A la santé.*

—*Santé.*

As I sipped the cognac, I noticed how carefully he was observing me. He was always smiling, as if he knew something I didn't know. The cognac and the cigars were my favorite brands. How could he possibly have known?

—May I call you Joe?

He had already told me his name, and I answered with another question.

—May I call you Albert?

We smiled.

The chief of guards couldn't keep it to himself any longer.

—This is you cognac and these are your cigars, he said. A friend of yours is now a friend of mine. This friend of yours told me you can't live without your cognac and cigars . . . so here we are.

This time we laughed out loud.

When you have friends, all things are possible.

The chief of guards and I shared cognac and cigars for the rest of the time I spent in prison, which was a month or so. I had to go to his office to enjoy these treats, and the chief of guards always took his tariff for allowing me to do so. He was helpful in other ways. He let me make private calls from his office. That way I was sure no one was tapping the line. I called Fay. I called Tucson and New York.

During my imprisonment, my Tucson lawyer, Lawrence D'Antonio, brought to Montreal the court papers pertaining to my acquittal on the wage-and-hour case. This was proof that I had not lied on my immigration-card application. The perjury charges against me were dismissed. Nonetheless, Canada didn't want to release me from prison. The U.S. authorities wanted me, and Canada still desired to deport me back to the U.S.

I had no choice but to compromise, or I would remain in prison for who knew how long. I had to promise to abandon my investment in the cheese plant. I could not return to Canada unless I first notified the authorities. For its part, Canada would release me from prison and wouldn't deport me. However, once released from prison I had to leave Canada voluntarily and return to the United States.

Before leaving prison, I had an experience that echoes hauntingly in my mind. It seems that the prisoners were restless. They had heard that Joe Bonanno was in their midst, but I still had not been allowed among the general prison population.

One day the prisoners in the main jail block began a minor disturbance. They yelled and rattled things. They told the guards they wanted to see me before I left the prison. They clamored to see me.

Having never been to prison, I was somewhat dumbfounded

230

at this outcry. Everyone wanted to see me, as if I were a movie star.

The chief of guards told me it would be a shame to have mutiny break out in prison over a matter that could easily be rectified.

—What can I do? I said.

He took me to the main prison block and told me to simply walk down the hall.

I sauntered down the prison block glancing at the cells on either side. None of the frustrated and rowdy prisoners inside the cells knew me. And yet, on seeing me pass, they cheered. Some clapped or waved their hands. Others made a victory sign with their fingers. A few shouted their names and begged me not to forget them, for they were getting out soon. A few volunteered on the spot to serve me.

Who did these men think I was?

What made them accord me such adulation and praise? They knew as little about me as the Canadian authorities. They were treating me like a potentate. I had no power over them.

—*Le boss*, they shouted. *Le grand boss!*

23

THE FBI SERVED ME WITH A SUBPOENA WHEN I STEPPED OFF
the airplane at O'Hare Airport in Chicago. My Tucson lawyer,
Lawrence D'Antonio, who had traveled with me from Montreal, accepted the subpoena on my behalf. The document required me to appear before a federal grand jury in New York
investigating organized crime.

To the questions put to me before the grand jury, I took the
Fifth Amendment. That's not being dodgy, that's being sensible. If the government prosecutors had had a concrete case
against me, they could have simply lodged charges. Since they
really had nothing, however, they went to the grand jury in
order to ask me a lot of random questions in the hope that my
answers might give them an opening or an excuse for an indictment. Taking the Fifth was my way of telling the U.S.
attorney to put up or shut up.

I forget the name of the government attorney who questioned
me before this particular grand jury, but he grilled me for three
days in a row. He plowed on, asking me question after question,
although it was obvious I was going to take the Fifth. He
interrogated me in a lackluster, smug fashion. If he had any
substantial grounds on which to prosecute, he could have asked
me all the necessary questions in three minutes. After three
days before the grand jury, the government told me to appear
again in another week. It was obvious the government had
nothing on me. What sudden enlightenment would they attain
after another week?

When I returned before the grand jury, the assistant U.S.
attorney questioning me now spoke in a caustic tone of voice

even though his questions were quite mundane. He asked me my name. He asked me my wife's name. He asked me my children's names. Evidently, he was trying to unnerve me, to rattle me, to make me lose my temper.

After each question, I droned my Fifth Amendment homily.

—I respectfully decline to answer the question on the grounds that . . .

It had become a game between the U.S. attorney and me to see who could shatter the other's poise first.

Since I wanted to be letter-perfect in my response, before going to court that day I had my New York lawyer, William Maloney, type the Fifth Amendment statement on an index card. It gave me something to read while the attorney battered me with his questions.

The U.S. attorney curtly demanded to know what I was reading. I was holding the index card on my knee. Instead of satisfying his rude curiosity, I ripped the index card in small pieces.

The miffed government attorney, assuming that I was trying to hide something, told a U.S. marshal to gather the torn pieces and tape the card together again. When that was done, the index card was delivered to the grand jury foreman, who read the innocuous Fifth Amendment statement aloud. The reading induced the other grand jury members to guffaw. After that, the government attorney's voice lost its zip.

At the end of this inconclusive session, the grand jury returned my index card inside a paper bag.

The grand jury appearance behind me, I could concentrate on finding out what was going on in my world. I quickly ascertained that my Canadian escapade had disturbed my cousin Stefano Magaddino and had given him fresh ammunition to use against me.

Stefano chose to interpret my Montreal trip as an imperialistic venture. Let me explain. It had long been acknowledged in my world that certain Families and their Fathers had spheres of influence outside their own resident cities. For example, Toronto had long been recognized as being within Magaddino's sphere of influence. Montreal, on the other hand, was considered within the domain of the Bonanno Family.

In my world, we often arrived at such arrangements so as

not to step on each other's toes and thus avoid territorial disputes. Terms such as "sphere of influence," "territory" and "domain," however, give an overblown impression of the actual state of affairs. If Toronto was considered within Stefano's province, all that meant was that Stefano, as opposed to another Father, had the right to establish contacts within the Sicilian community in Toronto. We're talking about a relatively small world, the world of the immigrants. But even among ourselves, we were apt to become bombastic when referring to such spheres of influence. We might say something like "Don Stefano controls Toronto." The word "control" merely meant that Stefano had business contacts and friends in Toronto; it didn't mean that Stefano controlled the entire city, as if he could make Lake Ontario rise and flood Toronto.

What bothered Stefano about my Canadian trip was not that I went to Montreal but that I might use Montreal as a jumping-off point to encroach on his cherished Toronto. There was no truth to this. I was looking to extricate myself from my world, not to entangle myself in territorial disputes. I wouldn't even have gone to Montreal in 1964 if the Saputo investment opportunity hadn't come up. I went there without ulterior designs on Stefano's turf.

I realized now that it had been a waste of time to tell Stefano of my retirement plans. It had been meant as a gesture of goodwill, as a reassurance. All it had really accomplished, as I learned upon my return to New York, was to give Stefano foreknowledge he could use to his advantage. As much as I wanted to deny it, my cousin had become my enemy.

During my absence, I had left Johnny Morales in charge. On my return, I established contact with Johnny immediately, but I couldn't get hold of Gaspar DiGregorio. After such a long absence, I wanted to see all my top men in person. I called Gaspar at home. His wife answered and said he was out. When I call one of my men at home, he is very prompt in returning my call. I waited two days for Gaspar's call; then I called his house again, a highly unusual consideration on the part of a Father and one I probably wouldn't have shown if Gaspar hadn't been such a longtime friend. Again his wife answered and said Gaspar was out of town. I told her he should call me when he returned.

Gaspar's stature in my Family was based on his closeness

to me, his length of service and, to an extent, his being a pipeline to Stefano, his brother-in-law. But Gasparino didn't possess sterling leadership qualities. He was too slow of thought, and he was lax.

Once Gaspar and Johnny were traveling by car from New York City to Buffalo. Gaspar, who was driving, made a wrong turn at an interchange, and when he got back on the road it was in the wrong direction. When Johnny discovered they were backtracking, he told Gaspar. But Gaspar insisted he knew the route, having made the trip countless times.

—Don't you understand? Johnny protested. We're going in the wrong direction. Look at the sun, it's in back of us. At this time of day, if we were heading west to Buffalo the sun would be in front of us.

—What's the sun got to do with it? Gaspar snapped.

When irritable, Gaspar would rather deny the obvious than admit to a fault. He was weak, and that's why Johnny, rather than Gaspar, was my favorite to take command during my absence.

The reader will recall that this period of my life coincided with the return of my son Salvatore to New York. Salvatore's presence pleased Johnny, because in him Johnny had a direct pipeline to me.

In 1964, while I was being detained in Canada, John Tartamella, my Family's *consigliere*, suffered from an ailment which made him an invalid. Johnny Morales sent word to me in Canada that the various group leaders favored naming another *consigliere*, and he wanted to know if I wanted to nominate anyone.

I always preferred that Salvatore not get directly involved with the hierarchy of the Family. I therefore instructed Johnny, and later my group leaders, that I wished to nominate no one for *consigliere* and that they were free to choose whom they wanted.

A Family vote was held and Salvatore was elected *consigliere*. The group leaders probably voted for Salvatore as much for his individual talents as for his closeness to me, as my son.

After Salvatore's election, Gaspar began to sulk. Although he lacked the abilities needed for the position of *consigliere*, Gaspar perhaps thought that after his many years in the Family he should be rewarded with this important position. Although

Gaspar had nominated Salvatore, Gaspar secretly coveted the position himself.

Sometime during my Canadian detainment, Gaspar took his peevish complaints to his brother-in-law, Stefano Magaddino, who exploited Gaspar's wounded pride and encouraged Gaspar to work against me.

By indulging Gaspar's puerile resentment, Stefano was also laying the groundwork for setting up Gaspar as a successor to me once I left the scene. Stefano already knew from me personally that I intended to retire; only a few other people knew this. Stefano, therefore, was looking forward to the day when he might exercise indirect control over my Family, through Gaspar, as he had done in the 1920s through his puppet Cola Schiro. When I was arrested in Canada, Stefano assumed that I would remain in prison a long time.

This was his opportunity, then, to persuade Gaspar to defect from me and to set him up as my successor. This also was Stefano's opportunity to talk against me before the Commission and thus steer the other Fathers in New York to favor Gaspar.

Before the Commission (I have to keep referring to it as that, even though to my mind it had lost its legitimacy), Stefano maintained a truculent attitude toward me. He charged that I was trying to install my young and inexperienced son over the older man, Gaspar. Stefano claimed that Salvatore's elevation confirmed Stefano's earlier accusations that Magliocco had plotted against Gambino and Lucchese, with the blessing of the Bonannos.

As a grandstand play, Stefano demanded that I appear before the Commission to give an account of myself.

I felt that since I had done nothing wrong, I shouldn't have to justify myself to the Commission and certainly not in matters concerning only my Family.

A parliamentary showdown with Stefano before the Commission was undersirable for other reasons as well. The odds were stacked against me. No matter how well I could explain myself, I knew that Magaddino, Lucchese and Gambino were in league against me. I could not count on the other Commission members for support. My relations with Sam Giancana of Chicago were cool at best. Colombo was against me. Zerilli of Detroit preferred to sit on the fence. Bruno of Philadelphia was a greenhorn.

By demanding that I appear before the Commission, Stefano was trying to set me up. He was trying to put me on the defensive. If Stefano could persuade the Commission to make some unfavorable ruling toward me and if I refused to accept the decision, then Stefano would have a perfect excuse for branding me a scofflaw and renegade.

It was Stefano who pressed the issue against me. Although the other Commission members would have appreciated a clarification of my situation, they nonetheless wanted to avoid an all-out confrontation with me. Gambino and Lucchese, as much as they opposed me, did not relish a fight against me; they did not personally hate me, they just wanted me out of their way.

By this time, I think Gambino and Lucchese realized that Stefano's vituperations against me did not have substantial foundation but rather stemmed from a personality clash between cousins. But since they needed Stefano as an ally, they went along with him, as far as they could without injury to themselves. They probably would have preferred to see Stefano and me settle matters between ourselves, rather than involve the whole Commission.

To appease Stefano, therefore, the Commission sent a three-man delegation to see me and formally request that I appear before the Commission. On the delegation were two Commission members—Zerilli of Detroit and Bruno of Philadelphia—and a Commission envoy, Sammy DeCavalcante of New Jersey.

When I found out this committee was looking for me, I was in Wisconsin on business concerning the Grande Cheese Co. The committee, however, did talk to Johnny Morales and my son Salvatore, who relayed the message to me. I had no objections to talking with the Commission delegation. But when I returned to New York, I discovered that the senior of the three, Zerilli, had gone back to Detroit and was not expected to come back to New York soon.

Zerilli's hasty departure was an important signal, if you knew how to interpret it. Of the three-man committee, I wanted to talk to Zerilli the most. He had been a close friend of Joe Profaci and had been an ally during the Castellammarese War. Of the three, I had known him the longest. I wanted to see him face to face, to study his expressions. Depending on how he reacted, I could better judge the attitude toward me on the

Commission—to decide if it was safe to appear before the Commission or if conspiracy was afoot.

Zerilli knew the tide in parliament was running against me and that if I appeared before the Commission, I would be walking into a trap. Therefore, when he couldn't find me right away, this was a perfect excuse for him to repair to Detroit and absent himself from the messy situation. In that manner, he could save face before the Commission, simply saying to them he couldn't complete his mission because I was unavailable. At the same time, if he never saw me, he wouldn't have to place himself in the awkward position of having to choose between me and the Commission. Zerilli's paramount policy was to remain disentangled.

Zerilli's withdrawal from the committee—for that's how I interpreted it—discredited its entire objective. Nonetheless, I had to take care not to make it seem that I was pursuing a stubbornly independent policy beyond all measure and restraint; that was the rhetoric Stefano Magaddino was using against me in the hope of sowing dissent within my Family. I had already lost Gaspar, and I didn't want other malcontents to follow him.

Consequently, I arranged a meeting of my top men so they could hear Bruno and DeCavalcante for themselves. We met at the motel I owned near Newark Airport. Bruno and De-Cavalcante were somewhat amazed both at my readiness to discuss the issues and at the loyalty of my top men. To Bruno and DeCavalcante, I had been depicted as a fugitive and artful dodger. And yet there I was, with my group leaders, calmly listening.

The two told us the Commission wanted to see me. I answered that I would be more receptive to such a request if all three members of the Commission's delegation gave me notice of it. Bruno and DeCavalcante said they would get in touch with Zerilli and then return to me.

Having already figured out Zerilli's motive in leaving New York, I doubted whether Bruno and DeCavalcante could carry out their promise. In the meantime, by demanding that all three men contact me, I was indirectly telling the ruling faction on the Commission that I had penetrated their tactic, and that unless it was to a fair request I was not going to be duped into appearing before them.

When Bruno and DeCavalcante reported back to the Commission, this must have, at the very least, partly discredited Magaddino's line that I was being purposely evasive and inaccessible. It was only because of Stefano's hysterical alarm that the Commission had tried to contact me to appear before them.

It seems pretty fair to assume that at this point Lucchese and Gambino began to reconsider how far to back Stefano in his obsessive intent to scuttle me. Lucchese and Gambino had gone along with Stefano as long as it was convenient to them; my adamant stance, however, persuaded them to hold back a little. They realized that if they gave Stefano full rein, he might suck them into an open conflict with me, which both Gambino and Lucchese wanted to avoid. It's fair to assume this because after the Newark motel meeting Bruno and DeCavalcante never tried to get hold of Zerilli. The three-man committee was dropped. Apparently, the Commission didn't want to press the issue.

Since I was not in direct contact with the Commission, I waited for some news from Bruno or DeCavalcante. When I didn't hear from them, I decided to pay Sammy DeCavalcante a visit in New Jersey. I found him at one of his business offices.

I ordered one of my men—who had been frequently decorated in World War II—to stand guard at the door. Sam was nervous. I invited him to a private chat.

Sammy was not a Commission member. He was used by some Commission members as a courier or intermediary. What he knew of my situation was secondhand, through other Commission members, principally Carlo Gambino and Stefano Magaddino. DeCavalcante did not have a well-informed viewpoint of his own; he merely parroted what he heard from Carlo or Stefano, seeing events through their point of view.

I feel it necessary to describe Sammy's position a bit because, inadvertently, it was through Sammy that the police and the public got a glimpse of my world. The FBI bugged one of Sammy's offices between 1964 and 1965; these taped conversations were later made public. On these tapes, DeCavalcante is heard discussing, among other things, my situation and his efforts to fulfill his mission for the Commission. Books were written based on these tapes. And since these books repeated without critical insight the partial and confused views of DeCavalcante, these so-called historical accounts portray me as some sort of power-hungry schemer who challenged the Commission in order to destroy it and seize nationwide control.

The opposite was true. It was the principal members of the deteriorated Commission who took the offensive against me. I was not seeking more power; I merely wanted them to leave me and my Family alone. It was my enemies—mainly Stefano Magaddino—who cast me as a renegade and usurper to further their own objectives. I did not wish ill on the Commission. I was one of its founding fathers; the concept of a Commission was sound. But by 1964, the Commission was a travesty of itself. It was a Commission in name only.

One of the biggest misconceptions created by the De-Cavalcante tapes was that the Commission was a viable body. Sammy may have thought it was, but what did he know? He had no experience on the Commission, and had no knowledge of what happened behind the scenes. Also, Sammy was an impressionable soul. When some Commission members decided to use him as a courier, this made Sammy feel very important and close to the seat of power in my world. Sammy thought he was being taken into the confidence of some of the most important men in my world. The truth was that these important men were using Sammy for their own ends.

In my conversation with Sam in a New Jersey business office (not the one bugged by the FBI), I first of all assured him that I hadn't come to hurt him. That relieved the tension somewhat. When I first entered his office, Sammy had looked very scared.

The tone I used with him was paternal and stern. I told him what he had heard about me was not based on fact but on intrigue by some Commission members.

—But Stefano told me . . . Sammy started to say.

—Stefano? Stefano? I interrupted angrily. You talk to me about Stefano? He's my cousin. You're going to talk to me about my cousin? Sammy, please, you think I don't know Stefano better than you?

—But the Commission told me . . .

—What Commission, Sammy?

—The Commission.

—Sammy, you can't be expected to know, but there is no Commission. You understand? What Commission?

DeCavalcante never did understand. He looked at me the same way a Catholic priest would if I had told him the Vatican didn't exist. To Sammy, the Commission was inviolate and anyone who disobeyed it was breaking the law. Be that as it may, Sammy's enlightenment was not my uppermost consideration. I knew that whatever I told him, Sammy would repeat it to Magaddino and Gambino. In a sense, I now was using Sammy as my messenger.

By mentioning my skepticism of the Commission, I wanted the ruling faction—Lucchese, Gambino and Magaddino—to know that if they wanted to pursue an unfriendly policy toward me, then I was prepared to make an issue of the fact that the present Commission membership had never been ratified by a national meeting, thus making the present Commission an illegitimate agency.

As I have mentioned before, if a national meeting was held, I would have the upper hand because of my contacts and my respect nationwide. People from across the country knew me and trusted me because for nearly forty years I was one of the few constant factors in the Volcano.

By telling DeCavalcante that the Commission didn't exist, I knew that Gambino, Magaddino and Lucchese would get the message that I was prepared to take them on in a national forum, if need be.

Having promulgated this strategy toward the Commission, I then devoted myself again to internal Family matters. It was now September 1964. Gaspar DiGregorio had not talked to me since I had returned from Canada in August. Some of my men, however, had been in touch with Gaspar, who told them he was under instructions from Stefano Magaddino not to talk, not to move, not to make contact with me.

When my top men and I held a Family meeting to discuss the matter, Gaspar refused to attend. Attendance at such meetings was mandatory. It looked very bad for Gaspar when he refused to answer the call. I asked my top men what they thought should be done about Gaspar. They said he deserved a traitor's punishment.

I had wanted to see how my top men stood on the matter of Gaspar's defection. Once I reassured myself, however, that they considered Gaspar a traitor, I let them know I wanted no bloodshed. I told my men I would try to contact Gaspar again in an effort to talk sense into him. My men, not accustomed to such leniency for those who betrayed our Family, looked at me in dismay, wondering why I should want to spare Gaspar's life.

There were several reasons. First of all, I knew that Gaspar was but a puppet of Stefano. Left to himself, Gaspar was ineffectual. It would have been an empty triumph to get rid of Gaspar when it was Stefano who was the true source of my problems. If I could isolate Gaspar from Stefano, however, I could probably bring Gaspar back into the fold, on a different footing perhaps but still as a member of my Family. If I could accomplish this I would probably eliminate once and forever Stefano's threat to my Family. If I could bring back Stefano's own brother-in-law, Stefano's prestige would suffer permanent damage.

But most of all, I spared Gaspar's life because I could not bring myself to execute a man who had been with me for so long and whose strengths and failings I understood only too well.

As a leader, the more politic thing to do would have been to go along with my Family's wish to eliminate Gaspar. There are times when a man must use force. This was one of those times. And yet, I hesitated. Under these conditions, mercy was a luxury. My willingness to spare Gaspar's life was a sign of weakness. I admit it. As a leader, I should have been ruthless. I was too sensitive, too scrupulous, too reflective concerning Gaspar. If self-restraint is the hallmark of a civilized man, then on this matter I was too civilized for my own world.

My scruples led me once again to call Gaspar at his home. Gasparino answered the phone. If anyone else had answered, I'm sure Gaspar would have refused to come to the phone.

—You are the godfather of my son, I told Gaspar. Stefano is my relative as well as yours. Why can't we solve our problems peacefully among ourselves?

Gaspar didn't answer right away. Although Gaspar's tall good looks gave him the appearance of a man, he was a boy in many ways. He didn't have the courage to stand up to me, as he didn't have the courage to stand up to Stefano. Both of us tugged at his allegiance, creating a sort of split personality in Gaspar. Tugged this way and that, stuck between two more powerful characters, Gasparino didn't know exactly where he stood.

—You and Stefano, Gaspar whined at last, as if lamenting his being stuck in the middle, you and Stefano patch it up.

In Gaspar's fragmented state more talk would have been futile. I simply told him I was willing to meet Stefano, if need be in Gaspar's house and in Gaspar's presence.

I didn't hear from Gaspar. But since I still hoped for a peaceful resolution, I again asked my Family to defer any action against Gasparino.

Toward the end of 1964, Stefano Magaddino stepped up his propaganda campaign.

Foiled in his attempt to maneuver me into appearing before the illegitimate Commission, Stefano bellowed that I was in defiance of the Commission and no longer should be recognized as head of my Family.

Stefano's calumnies knew no end. He spread the false rumor that I was snubbing Gaspar DiGregorio in order to make way for my son Salvatore, who would take over for me after my retirement. Salvatore, as Stefano well knew, disliked New York; he did not covet the top spot in my Family. Circumstances, however, had thrown Salvatore into the caldron, and out of loyalty to me and respect for himself, Salvatore hadn't shirked from taking his place at my side.

If anyone had designs on my Family, it was Stefano. He gave himself away, at least to those who had insight into the situation, when he openly urged that Gaspar DiGregorio should be recognized as head of my Family. This was pure folly. Gaspar was barely in control of his own faculties. How could he hope to control a whole Family? Anyone who knew Gaspar realized he wasn't leadership timber. Outside my Family, however, Gaspar was not well known. This worked to Stefano's advantage. When Stefano Magaddino championed Gaspar, such was the prestige of the old man from Buffalo that many outsiders were fooled into thinking that Gaspar had indeed been mistreated and that he did indeed deserve to be Father of my Family.

Although that was Stefano's individual position, the Commission itself took no formal stand on the matter. The information I received was that Lucchese and Gambino were content to see Stefano engage me on his own without their direct participation. They were more than willing to let Stefano carry the fight, because that would shield them from possible future reprisals.

One thing is for certain: If the Commission had actually voted to depose me, there would have been, as Sam De-Cavalcante put it, "World War III." Such a war never materialized.

Stefano had sent his cousin, Gaspar Magaddino, to the Volcano to inform Gaspar DiGregorio personally that he was to consider himself head of the Bonanno Family. Although Gaspar DiGregorio had influence over a subgroup within my Family, this business of taking over the entire Family must have shocked Gaspar as much as anyone else. DiGregorio admitted as much when he told Gaspar Magaddino that trying to be Father of my Family had never been his idea but Stefano's.

I know about this conversation because after it took place, Gaspar Magaddino, who was supposed to stay in New York to help DiGregorio in his new role, instead came to me and told me everything. Gaspar Magaddino was not about to play Stefano's fool. Before coming to New York, Gaspar Magaddino probably believed what his cousin Stefano was saying about me. But when he learned the true situation from Di-Gregorio himself and when he saw what a reluctant Father DiGregorio made, Gaspar Magaddino decided he would have no part of Stefano's intrigue. Gaspar Magaddino never went back to Stefano. He turned his back on his Buffalo cousin and remained with me.

Thus, without even trying, I had a defector from Stefano Magaddino's Family. Gaspar Magaddino was even willing to speak openly about Stefano's treachery in front of my Family.

Stefano was finding out that trying to be a big shot in the Volcano was a most difficult job. Taking care of business in Buffalo was one thing, but the Volcano was quite another. The Volcano was the big time, the big leagues, the big crusher. Vincent Mangano used to tell me how out-of-towners envied the power and glamour of Fathers in New York City, but that none of them could survive more than a month in such an intense environment. I didn't think Stefano could stand the pressure. He was getting in over his head. Now that his own man, and first cousin, had defected, what would Stefano do next?

Would he do something crazy?

* * *

In October 1964, as if out of a whirlwind, the government ordered me to appear yet again before a federal grand jury.

The unexpected call to appear before a grand jury made me suspect the government might be working on a conspiracy case against me. They hadn't been able to get at me directly. Now they might be trying to prosecute me by connecting me with men whom I had nothing to do with, or with men who were in trouble. Numerous possibilities came to mind of how the government might use the judicial machinery to grind me down.

Meanwhile, developments in my world continued at their furious pace. While waiting for my grand jury appearance, another Magaddino relative deserted Buffalo for New York City. This time it was my old sidekick and childhood chum Peter Magaddino.

After Peter and I came to America in 1924, Peter had settled in Buffalo with the Family of Stefano Magaddino, Pete's first cousin. Recently, however, because of the friction between Stefano and me, Peter had been ostracized. Stefano isolated Pete because he feared that if Pete shared Family confidences he might divulge the information to me, his longtime friend. After Gaspar Magaddino, Pete's brother, defected to me, Pete was completely cut off from his Family. Nonetheless, Pete remained loyal to me; in his heart, Pete knew that Stefano had disgraced himself in his behavior toward me.

Despite the unhappy circumstances under which we were reunited, I was glad to see Pete when he came to New York City. Seeing him reminded me of the whole Magaddino clan in Castellammare. In Sicily, the Magaddinos were my second family. I never tired of contemplating the variety of characters dispersed among that single family. Uncle Stefano Magaddino of Castellammare was one of the most forceful and most convincing examples of manhood I ever knew. At the other end of the spectrum, Stefano Magaddino of Buffalo was one of the most puerile of men.

Through Gaspar and Pete, I now became aware that the quarrel between Stefano and me was causing a great many misgivings among Stefano's closest relatives.

On October 20, 1964, the day before my grand jury appearance, I conferred with my lawyer, William Maloney, who offered to let me stay overnight at his apartment so I wouldn't have to commute to my Long Island home. Maloney, along with his law partner, Joe Allen, and my Tucson lawyer, Lawrence D'Antonio, had dinner with me that night at an uptown restaurant. D'Antonio departed after dinner, while the others and I left for Maloney's apartment house on Park Avenue and 36th Street in Manhattan. It was close to midnight and drizzling.

My grand jury date the following morning had been widely publicized by the news media. I was one of the main targets of U.S. Attorney Robert Morgenthau, who was leading a crackdown on organized crime. This campaign reminded me a lot of the one staged by special prosecutor Thomas Dewey in the days of Charlie Luciano. Morgenthau's assault, however, was on a grander scale.

Dewey was a state official, backed up by state laws and state law-enforcement officials. Morgenthau was backed up by the federal government and by the FBI. Morgenthau was following the lead of U.S. Attorney General Robert F. Kennedy, who was then riding the Mafia hobbyhorse. Kennedy, in turn, had enlisted the formidable aid of J. Edgar Hoover and his FBI.

Joe Bonanno's presence was in high demand in those days. From the Commission to the U.S. government, everyone, it seemed, wanted to see me, to talk to me, to press against me. My head felt like red-hot, glowing metal being flattened between hammer and anvil.

Although I was apprehensive about what the government might do with me, I possessed a clear conscience, a profound consolation if only to myself. Let the questions come, I thought, let them ask questions until they tire of asking questions.

Also, although I was disturbed with the situation in my world, I was not in fear of my life. I moved about in New York without bodyguards. If I had thought I was in danger, I would have protected myself or moved about stealthily.

When the taxi stopped in front of Maloney's apartment building, Joe Allen got out and made his way to the entrance while Maloney and I bickered over who was going to pay the cab driver. I prevailed and took care of the fare. In the meantime, Maloney scurried out and sought protection from the rain under the front canopy of the apartment house.

As soon as I stepped out on the curb, two men grabbed me

from behind by each arm and immediately forced me forward toward the nearby street corner.

When they first snatched me, one of my captors said something to the effect of:

—Come on, Joe, my boss wants you.

I couldn't get a good look at my captors. They had appeared suddenly out of the mist, like specters. They were tall, had long coats and brimmed hats; their coat collars were turned up. They squeezed me between them and pushed me forward.

I was not then as interested in identifying my captors as I was in fighting down my fright and trying to keep my wits. I kept thinking, Is this going to be the end of me?

As they rushed me toward the corner, I heard Maloney shouting after us. He was saying something about my being his client and they couldn't take me away like that. A pistol bullet pinged on the sidewalk. Maloney retreated.

At the corner, my captors pushed me inside a car, its motor running. They told me to crouch on the floor with my head down. The car sped off. I could tell we were making many turns, as if deliberately taking a circuitous route in case of pursuers.

I still had no clue as to their intentions. Did these men want to kill me? Were they going to wait until we arrived at a safe destination? But that didn't make sense. If these men had been assassins, they could have dispatched me on the sidewalk and driven away. They wanted me alive.

After a while, I heard different kinds of traffic noise. It sounded more like highway traffic. We were moving straight and fast.

That's when my abductors apologized.

They said they were sorry for the manner in which they had been forced to handle me.

—You can get up now. Sit between us.

Two sad faces peered at me. One was that of Nino, Stefano's only living brother. The other was that of Peter, Stefano's only son. Familiar faces with strange, awkward and somber expressions.

—*Cosa si puo dire?* Nino said.

What's there to say?

For the moment, there was nothing to say.

I sat between them, and when I looked outside I beheld a canopy of swooping and rising lights—the night lights of the George Washington Bridge.

Our car drove through the night and rain, across the somnolent Hudson River.

24

On the innumerable times I have gone over this phantasmagoric scene, I have never ceased to marvel at the dark magic of it, at the hocus-pocus of circumstances which took me out of the real world and into the invisible world of the missing person.

I was being taken for a long night's journey.

We swished into the night, gaining elevation, the temperature getting colder. We were driving through rolling hills, somewhere in upstate New York. Through the wet windows the countryside appeared spectral, as if in a ghostly dream. We swooshed ahead. My abductors remained taciturn. The only accompaniment to my thoughts was the steady hiss of the tires on the slick roads.

I tried to relax. The most difficult thing to do when you're stuck in a knot of adversity is to stay loose. If you try to resist, the knot gets tighter. I told myself that, captive though I was, I still retained one liberty—I still had the freedom to think.

And I thought. So much of life is beyond individual control. Events fall on us haphazardly, taking us this way and that without asking our permission. When we find ourselves in such dire circumstances, we realize that the only power we ever truly had in life was not power over events nor power over other men, but power over ourselves. True power is the talent for self-control.

At daybreak, the dreary mist that shrouded us during the night continued to swirl about us. The morning was dismal and gray. Thick clouds smudged the feeble sun.

Sometime in midmorning we arrived at a farmhouse in the

woods. My captors showed me inside and told me to make myself comfortable. They said I had to wait.

Strict security precautions were unnecessary, because even if I had wanted to escape, there was no place to run to in the remote region where I found myself.

In the afternoon, I heard a car pull up to the farmhouse. This was it. My nemesis had arrived. I was summoned to the main room of the house.

Stefano Magaddino tromped in—an old, spry and portly man with ruddy cheeks and an amiable smile.

—Hello, cousin Stefano said sardonically.

I unclenched my jaw and tried to keep calm so as to loosen the knot in back of my neck.

—What brings you here? Stefano added in that same snide tone of voice which belied his actual words.

—I'm here, that's all.

Control, control, I told myself, keep your control.

—I find you here, like this, so unexpectedly, Stefano said, cracking his knuckles, which he often did out of habit. Have you nothing to say?

Stefano sounded as if he had stumbled upon me in the woods, but I knew that behind his sarcasm Stefano was testing me, observing my reactions, reading my face.

—I'm being treated very nicely, I replied.

Stefano sighed. Then, as if he had run out of pleasantries, he paced the room and briefly looked out the window.

—Excellent country, isn't it? Stefano observed.

—A little cold for me.

—Oh, it gets much colder in Montreal.

—Yes, I answered dryly. But all in all, I prefer Arizona.

—Nice place to retire, Stefano drawled.

—One cannot always be where one likes.

—Regrettable.

—Sad.

—But sometimes unavoidable, heh?

—If you say so.

—What do you mean, if I say so? Stefano grumbled in the first manifestation of any real emotion. Do you think I wanted it this way?

—I certainly didn't.

Stefano squinted into my eyes, pitched his voice low and said,

—You could have made yourself more available.

—You could have come to the phone when I called you, I retorted.

—Peppino, sometimes I think your mind is too big for your own good.

—Sometimes I think your mind is too little for your own good, I told Stefano.

—What? Stefano huffed. Is that how you talk to your older cousin?

—We could not be talking at all.

—But we have to talk, cousin. We must talk.

—I'm here. I might as well listen, then.

And talk we did, for weeks and weeks. Stefano came and went to the farmhouse as it suited him. I was his captive audience.

Our conversations seemed to cover everything under the sun. We'd hit upon a subject randomly. Then we'd go off on a tangent. Or we would wander away in separate directions. Or we'd circle each other with barbed comments or probing observations. We watched each other keenly—the eyes, the mouth, the hands—for signs of what the other was truly feeling.

What we actually said was not in the nature of a true dialogue, but more like a melodramatic opera. We engaged in arias of discontent, duets of woe, choruses of dissatisfaction. We didn't so much resolve anything as simply get things off our chest.

After arriving at the farmhouse unexpectedly, Stefano would stomp into the room, his head bent slightly down and cocked to the left. His face would have a determined yet slightly roguish expression. Usually he wore a suit, tie and hat. He was seventy-three years old at the time, graying at the temples. Although stout, he had vigorous movements. His hands, especially, were very ebullient.

When flustered or overwrought, Stefano would intertwine his fingers and wave his cradled hands over his head; at the same time he would stoop his shoulders and mumble that the whole world was going crazy.

251

—Everything's going click, click, click, Stefano would say when nervous.

Once he became too agitated, Stefano would open the door, call someone else into the room and call for a drink. Then he'd go away to return at an undesignated time.

During those intervals while I waited for Stefano to show up, my most frequent company at the farmhouse was Nino Magaddino. My old friend Nino was in an awkward spot. He liked me, but he couldn't completely open himself to me because he had his brother Stefano to protect. He gave me enough hints, however, for me to realize that my kidnapping was something he had participated in most reluctantly and did so only because he considered it a last chance for a reconciliation between Stefano and me—if not a rapprochement, then at least an understanding that would avoid disaster. I did not hold anything against Nino.

Since he was not at liberty to discuss my abduction, Nino and I whiled away much of our time with reminiscences of Sicily. Naturally, we mentioned Uncle Stefano Magaddino of Castellammare, whom we both admired. Nino had fought alongside Uncle Stefano in the war against the Buccellatos. Whereas we revered Uncle Stefano, Nino's brother, Stefano, often clashed with his uncle, the patriarch of the Magaddino family.

When I had Nino to talk to during the day, he would sometimes make me forget my troubles. But when he wasn't around, scattered thoughts assailed me. I thought about my wife, Fay, who was surely worried sick over my disappearance. I thought of my son Salvatore, who, alone, would have to contend against the sinister forces in the Volcano. I thought of my immediate family and my greater Family. Who would step in to prevent my Family from disintegrating now that I wasn't there to lead them?

Also, I thought about the government. The FBI would be looking for me, but, unlike most kidnapping victims, I did not desire their help. In fact, I felt safer where I was than in the clutches of the FBI.

At nights, a disjointed collage of images imprinted itself on my imagination. I dreamed about marionettes. A company of knights, in shiny panoply, hopped jerkily across the theater of my mind. There was the valiant Rinaldo, along with his companions in arms, vassals all to King Charlemagne in his war against the infidels.

The adventures of these paladins make up the stories of the Sicilian puppet opera, which I used to love to watch as a youth. These stirring tales included a cast of sorcerers, giants, dragons, witches and ogres.

In the end, Rinaldo dies. He must die. That is his story. This splendid knight falls because of the treachery of a fellow knight, the baleful Gano de Magonza. To Magonza goes the infamy, and yet Magonza never dies in these tales. Magonza always skirts destruction. Rinaldo is noble, but he dies. Magonza is ignoble, but he gets away.

I would wake up with the name Magonza on my lips and my cousin Stefano Magaddino on my mind.

—You've always been independent, Stefano said during one of our sessions.

—After all, I answered quickly, I am an orphan.

—When you came to America, didn't I offer to take you into my Family?

—And I thank you. I've been thanking you always for everything you and your relatives have done for me.

—Fine thanks, fine thanks, Stefano complained. Why don't you admit it? You thought you were too good for my Family.

—I wanted to be on my own, that's all.

—Oh, yes, Stefano whined, you went to New York and became a big shot. My cousin Peppino, the big shot.

—If other people think I'm a big shot, it's in their mind, not mine.

—In the old days, Stefano said wistfully, people from all over used to call me. They wanted to know how I was, and they asked to speak to me for advice. Then you in New York with all your big friends . . . I never got calls anymore.

—I always gave you respect, I said.

—Oh, why don't you admit it? You like it. You like people to consider you a big shot. You want it.

—I've never let power go to my head, I said indignantly. If I had let power go to my head, it would have destroyed me a long time ago. But, as you see, I'm still here . . . thanks to you.

—You're welcome, you're welcome, cousin.

—Where do all your suspicions of me come from? I said.

—I'm older than you, and I have long practice in the world.

—Yes, I continued, but where do you get your ideas about me?

—What? is this one of your riddles? Stefano said. You think I'm a dumb peasant because I'm not educated like you.

—Look at you, I went on. The minute I say something, right away you think I'm making fun of you. I just want to make you understand.

—I understand all right. I understand.

—Then you must understand that it is the nature of a distrustful man to be the first to accuse everyone else of mistrust.

—Bah, Stefano scoffed. You think you can trick me with your words?

Stefano began pacing about the room, his hands flailing in the air.

—Let's drop the masks, shall we? I said. Do you remember how after Apalachin I told you I wanted to retire? Why didn't you believe me? You know, I still want to retire.

—Oh? Oh?

His exclamations expressed an attitude somewhere between disbelief and belief. It seemed he wanted to believe what I was saying but his fears made him stop short. At the same time, he didn't want to let on that he was ambivalent. He wanted to pretend he knew his mind.

—Ah? So, you still want to retire, do you?

—I still want that, but only when the time is ripe and my Family is at peace.. All you had to do was trust me.

—There you go turning things all around again, Stefano bellowed. I want to trust you . . .

—What prevents you then? Jealousy?

—Ingratitude, Stefano shouted, what ingratitude!

—But this is a farce.

Stefano crocheted his fingers and pumped his fretted hands in front of him.

—I want to be taken seriously . . . yes . . . seriously, Stefano rattled on, gesticulating wildly. But the whole world is going crazy. . . . It's too much . . . too much . . . click, click, click.

—You don't fool me, I said softly, having seen these theatrics before.

—And you don't fool me, Stefano insisted nervously.
Then he flung open the door and called for a stiff drink.

For the six weeks or so I was in captivity, I had much time to reflect on Stefano's character.

He had many good traits, among them a good sense of humor and a practical, down-to-earth solidity. Although he was illiterate, he was not stupid by any means. He was mainly a family man; the sporting life, the night life, the libertine life did not interest Stefano.

My cousin was at his most docile and contented after a big meal among friends. After eating, he liked to smoke a big cigar and lounge in praise. Stefano craved attention. In the old days, when he came to visit me in New York City, he expected to be treated with deference; if I didn't send one of my high-ranking men to pick him up at the airport, Stefano would get insulted. As his host in New York City, I would go out of my way to humor Stefano, especially at the dinner table. I would invite people who I knew would pay homage to my cousin. At the table, I would subordinate my opinions to Stefano's in order to let him sparkle. Stefano beamed. It made him feel good to act the important man before my friends in the big city.

In addition to emotional bonds, Stefano and I also had pragmatic reasons for being close. When I became a Father in 1931, my rise to power was facilitated by Stefano, who was already established. My position, in turn, solidified Stefano's place in Buffalo. My strength in the Volcano helped Stefano maintain a position of influence in my world that Stefano, although he was one of the original oldtimers, perhaps would not have been able to retain if he had had no allies such as I.

Stefano had come up in life the hard and rough way, forging a place for himself through sheer doggedness. He possessed a mulish determination, one of the attributes needed for success. Once enthroned in the seat of power, Stefano had no need to feel insecure among subordinates and men of lower status; in fact, these men often praised Stefano for his equanimity. Stefano's weakness came to the fore only when in confrontation with a forceful personality of equal status, such as I, who outshone him. That's when Stefano became uncomfortable with himself.

We all possess a measure of envy, but we try to keep it in

check. We try to control the meanness and baseness in us. With Stefano, I think it got to the point where he simply lost control. I had touched off something in him that hid underneath his genial exterior—a shameful sense of inferiority.

To me, Stefano's envy represented an old man's last wicked passion, a last gasp of perverse self-assertion to try to vanquish not only me but the insecurity within him. This attitude led Stefano, whether subconsciously or consciously, to constantly misinterpret me. Stefano mistook my sense of confidence for arrogance, my self-reliance for ingratitude. He deprecated my education because it made him feel inadequate. My achievements stung him, so he called me ostentatious. The more I implored him to trust me, the more he suspected trickery. At last, he convinced himself that everything I did was to spite him.

Until our talks at the farmhouse, I had always thought I could talk some sense into Stefano. As strained as relations got between us, I had always thought I could mend our friendship by simply presenting my clear, logical and sane analysis. I think I put too much faith in rationality. In my final confrontation with Stefano, all my reasoning might as well have fallen on deaf ears. Stefano didn't want rationality. My cousin wanted emotional satisfaction.

In the end, we accomplished little during our rural tryst. We played out our scenes unrepentantly and we remained adamantly true to ourselves.

Understanding the psychology of a man does not excuse his conduct.

Magonza had behaved most foully.

In 1957, when I was abroad, Magonza seized the opportunity to set up the abortive Apalachin meeting as a way to undercut me and at the same time flaunt himself.

Then Magonza made a marriage of convenience with Lucchese and Gambino. With them at his side, Magonza tried to isolate me and humiliate me.

When Magliocco tried to restore order to the Profaci Family, Magonza maligned me by spreading the false story that Magliocco and I were planning to eliminate all our opponents.

When I was detained in Canada, Magonza thought I would be in prison and out of action for a good long time. He therefore treacherously used this as a pretext to slander my name before the so-called Commission. He bruited all sorts of lies and innuendos, claiming I had gone to Montreal to "plant flags all over the world." He also contended I was evasive and contrary.

And when Gaspar DiGregorio, a sulking, scatterbrained man, estranged himself from my Family, Magonza fed Gaspar's resentment and encouraged him to claim leadership of the Bonanno Family, so as to have a vassal in the Volcano.

Magonza had disgraced himself.

He had fallen into the roiling Volcano and had become tainted by the same forces that were destroying our Tradition.

Although Stefano, in the years that followed, would be treated with contempt and derision by his own relatives for his conduct toward me, for the moment he had the upper hand.

I had been kidnapped, but I was not sure at the time whether Stefano had acted alone or in concert with others. It was in Stefano's interest to keep me unenlightened.

For one thing, kidnapping is not something a man of my Tradition likes to brag about. My Tradition, in its pure form, shuns prostitution, narcotics peddling, extortion and kidnapping. These are considered unmanly activities.

For Stefano to have taken such an extreme measure, I knew that he must have been under great pressure both from inside and outside his Family to square away his dispute with me.

From all sides, Stefano was being urged to do something decisive to settle our accounts once and for all.

But as for the abduction itself, was it Stefano's doing alone? Was it Stefano with the assent of Lucchese and Gambino? Was it Stefano with the support of the entire Commission? Was it Stefano in agreement with his Family? Was it Stefano with the cooperation of only a few very close relatives within his Family? Was it none of these, or a combination of these?

Stefano wanted to keep me in the dark so as to keep me off balance. The kidnapping was a scare tactic in that Stefano perhaps hoped it would induce me to abandon the Volcano without his having to resort to deadly force. That would have been disastrous for Stefano's Family, and, in any case, Stefano didn't want my blood on his conscience. But even if the kidnapping failed to scare me off, Stefano would still have to guard against retaliation; therefore, he kept me guessing as to who was responsible for my kidnapping. For lack of a culprit, my supporters wouldn't know who to strike against. They would also have to think twice about revenge if Stefano had the backing of strong allies on the Commission.

If nothing else, Stefano had succeeded in maintaining an air of mystery about the kidnapping.

But now that it's in my past, when I reflect on this incident, I am not so interested in assigning blame, as I was at the time, as I am in capturing the specialness of the situation. I am fascinated still by what happened between Stefano and me.

Until now, when I can describe this incident in my own way, I have kept it to myself. I let the public think what it liked, even in the face of speculations that I had staged my own kidnapping to frustrate and confound the government. It didn't really matter what others thought. I considered my explanation for what happened too precious to waste on cursory accusations and flippant disclosures. What happened between Stefano and me was very special. I needed a book to tell about it properly.

Now that the danger is gone, the kidnapping lives as an enchanted affair. I remember the sharp, crystalline day I last saw Stefano. Winter was approaching, and it was time to release me. Stefano and I did not talk. A friendship of forty years was ending in cold, agonizing silence. We said goodbye with our eyes.

And yet, even though I never saw Stefano again after this "farewell," that's not all there was to it. In a sense, we never parted. The kidnapping incident and our weeks and weeks of discussions had been a most private and intense experience, a catharsis for both of us. We would never forget it for as long as we both lived. Ironically enough, this incident which ruptured relations between us really bound us together forever.

Our silent stares expressed what we could not in words. We knew we would never be friends again, but we were past the stage of reproach and denial. We were beyond that. We were in the occult stage of final affirmation. With our eyes only, we said to each other:

You know what you know. I know what I know. And no one else will really know as we know.

25

— GO WEST, I WOULD SAY.

The same men who had whisked me off Park Avenue a month and a half before became my chauffeurs after my release from the farmhouse. They—Stefano's brother and son—had been instructed to drive me anywhere I desired. I therefore had my own taxi cab and I wanted it to take me west.

Returning to New York City immediately would have been foolhardy. For all I knew there might be people there who, emboldened by my kidnapping, might make an attempt on my life. I needed a little time to scout the situation and determine who was with Stefano and who was not.

Also, if I returned to the Volcano right away, I would be arrested. The government would surely try to exploit my disappearance in its campaign against me. A hasty return would place me at the government's mercy while the firebrand of publicity was hot. I could hardly hope to defend myself against the enemies in my world if I was bogged down by court appearances and hearings.

And so when Stefano's son would turn around in the driver's seat to ask for directions, I would say,

— Go west, young man. I'll tell you when to stop.

Our direction, to be precise, was southwesterly. From upstate New York, we traversed the Ohio Valley, crossed the Mississippi River, cut through the prairie, plunged down into Texas and bowled over great expanses of scrubby flats.

By going West, away from the Volcano, I figured I would placate my abductors, at least temporarily. Even though they had released me, I didn't want to rile them unnecessarily. At

259

first, I couldn't absolutely rule out the possibility that despite their assurances, my captors were taking me for a ride into oblivion. But the longer we rode, the less apprehensive I became. I even reached the point where I allowed myself a little cheer. I wasn't exactly happy, just glad to be alive.

A change was coming over me. I was beginning to feel different, to think differently, as if I were a different person. An unseen force had begun to take control of me. This peculiar sensation mystified me, because, obviously, I was the same person. And yet, I felt myself passing into another world.

At El Paso, I told my escorts to let me off.

We had been driving steady for two days and nights, with a brief layover at a motel during one night. Nino and his nephew gave me a quizzical look when I told them to stop at El Paso. They hadn't expected this to be my destination. Since they would report back to Stefano, I wanted Nino and Peter to be surprised and confused. Perhaps they would think I had chosen El Paso in order to cross the border and hide out in Mexico. That would be just fine. From now on, until I decided what to do, my whereabouts would be my secret. I had been plucked off Park Avenue and could have easily been shot on the spot. I was not going to expose myself again.

After we exchanged grim adieux, Peter and Nino let me off and their car sped off. Although I was free, I still felt emotionally groggy after my ordeal. To try to shake myself out of it, I roamed aimlessly through the streets of El Paso. It occurred to me that no one around me knew I was Joe Bonanno.

In a way, I liked the feeling. It reminded me of the sensations I had had when as a young man I had visited my cousin Salvatore in Paris; we hadn't seen each other since we were youngsters, and instead of immediately identifying myself I pretended I was someone else. I had gone into a whimsical disguise so that I could observe but not be observed. Come to think of it, I had played the same joke on my cousin Peppino in Tunis.

All at once, I realized what had come over me—the change. It was quite simple. I had become invisible. I could see everyone, but no one could really see me. I was nobody, and there was power in this.

From El Paso, I called a trusted friend in Tucson. He was a loyal family friend who often visited my house in Tucson and whose presence there wouldn't unduly arouse the suspicion of the police. I told him to telephone my wife in Long Island and assure her of my safety. I gave instructions for Fay to leave the city and stay with relatives in New Jersey. This was a precaution in case the Volcano blew up.

I would decide when to reappear, when to become visible again. In the meantime, I could reconnoiter the situation quietly, traveling in shadow, unobserved. My status as a missing person had given me an advantage over my enemies: that of surprise.

My friend picked me up in El Paso and drove me to Tucson. He, like everyone else I revealed myself to during my disappearance, wanted to know what had happened. I didn't tell him or anyone at the time. That information was of no use to anyone but me.

It was already dark when we arrived in Tucson. My friend dropped me off at a park while he went to check out my house. We had to be careful not to tip off police or inquisitive neighbors. My friend wouldn't arouse attention, because when Fay and I weren't in Tucson he had the keys to our place and would go there to inspect it. My friend visited my house that night, and before leaving he left open a backyard gate. Later, using a service road behind my house, I snuck into my own home.

For the moment, I was safe. People weren't likely to look for me here because they assumed I was dead. My friend had bought some provisions which he had hidden in the trunk of his car and then stashed in the refrigerator when he came in the house. I ate by flashlight, not wanting any room lights to show from outside the house. I slept in my own bed, but if someone should come into the house looking for me, I had a secret room to hide in.

With Fay safely in New Jersey with relatives, I then wanted to get some sort of message to Salvatore, my son. I wanted to tell him I was all right, that he should remain calm and that neither he nor others should cause trouble. I didn't want anyone to start shooting and set off a war.

For Salvatore's own protection, I didn't want him to know my whereabouts, or any other details for that matter. I simply wanted to reassure him. The less he knew about me, the safer he would be from the government.

Salvatore and I had an understanding that if anything should happen to one of us, we would call a certain public booth at a certain time and day of the week. One Thursday in mid-December of 1964, I had my friend call Salvatore at this phone booth. The kernel of the message was:

—Your father's safe. Don't worry, don't make any waves. He'll be back soon.

When Salvatore asked for more information, my friend hung up.

I couldn't guess what confusion would result from my contacting Salvatore. As I later learned, Salvatore surmised from the telephone call that I would be reappearing soon, maybe in a couple of days. He thought it best to inform my lawyer, William Maloney, so the attorney could make whatever legal preparations were necessary. Maloney, however, with good intentions but little foresight, went further than this. Maloney informed the whole world. He called a press conference to announce that Joe Bonanno was safe and would appear in federal court the following Monday.

If I had been in a position to communicate with my son directly, all this would have been avoided. I certainly had no intention of going back to the Volcano amid a cackle of waiting newsmen and police officers and—who knows?—a befuddled crackpot or a clear-eyed assassin, lurking around Foley Square outside the courthouse.

Maloney's ill-advised announcement had stirred up a furor. I didn't show up as he had predicted. This incensed the government all the more, for it reminded them of their inability to find me. No one believed Salvatore when he said he didn't know where I was.

The mixup was all the more frustrating because I couldn't do anything to help. For the moment, I had to keep undercover. I had to resign myself to being a spectator. My friend told me the news or brought me newspaper clips to read. The mass media were indulging in an orgy of speculation. They reported I was hiding in Canada, in Haiti, in Tunisia, in Sicily, in South America. They reported me alive one day and dead the next. The FBI kept insisting they were very close to apprehending me. On hearing these reports, I would laugh to myself or sigh heavily.

I lived like a recluse. In my bedroom, I had a secret little room. It was concealed behind one of the walls. To open the door, you had to press a secret button three times. The hidden cubicle, about six feet by six feet, contained a small bunk, a television, a portable heater, a beverage cooler and reading matter.

I kept the door of that poky room open in case I had to jump inside to avoid detection. The emergency never arose. But sometimes I'd get the urge, a snifter of cognac in hand, to enter the cubicle, quiet as the inside of a tomb, and sit on the bunk. I would think and plan.

26

WHILE HIDING IN TUCSON, I GREW A BEARD.

As much as I might have wanted to remain in Tucson, I couldn't remain in my desert haunt for long—my responsibilities were in the Volcano. But after my kidnapping, New York City wasn't safe. Outside my world, I was being hunted by the government; inside my world, some men were interested in toppling me, if not disposing of me altogether. I therefore had to move unnoticed.

Hence the need for a beard and a disguise: a sixty-year-old man with a straggly, silver-flecked beard, dressed in a dark, coarse overcoat, carrying a walking cane, wearing a black astrakhan cap of curled lamb's wool and a black eyepatch.

When I looked at myself in the mirror, I thought of how proud of me my old drama professor would have been. I doubt whether my own wife would have recognized me if I had walked by her on the street. I could have passed for a devout Hasidic Jew, or an over-the-hill hippie, or a lame pirate. I looked as if I belonged on a Salvation Army soup line—a bent old man lurching down the street.

Dressed in this fashion, I ventured back to Brooklyn.

I felt a little bit like Ulysses returning to the island of Ithaca. After his odyssey, Ulysses returns home disguised as an old beggar. He adopts a disguise in order to have the freedom to move around the island undetected, safe from his enemies. But he also does it to see who in his kingdom has remained loyal to him. My strategy was the same.

No one in the Volcano knew I was back except for some friends I had to take into my confidence. Most people conjectured I was hiding out overseas, perhaps in the Caribbean or even in Sicily. Some people speculated that I had staged my own kidnapping. Some thought I had fled to Montreal. None thought I was anywhere near the Volcano.

For his own protection, I had to leave my son Salvatore in the dark as to my whereabouts. At the end of 1964 Salvatore went to Arizona for income tax purposes. The FBI arrested Salvatore in Tucson on a material witness warrant. He was subpoenaed before a grand jury in New York investigating organized crime and my disappearance.

Salvatore had to appear in court repeatedly. (My other son, Joseph, was also briefly questioned in court in New York.) The government thought Salvatore was keeping something from them. Salvatore refused to answer any questions. A judge cited him for contempt, and Salvatore was sent to jail, where he remained for three months.

The first person I revealed myself to was Johnny Morales, my second, who had led my Family as best he could during my absence. I telephoned him and told him and another friend to meet me inside a store owned by someone we knew. When I walked into the store, Johnny was talking to his friend. On noticing me, Johnny nudged the man and told him in Sicilian,

—Wait until the old man passes and talk low until don Peppino arrives.

In none of my encounters with my loyal friends did any of them recognize me ahead of time. They all had been used to seeing me elegantly dressed and immaculately groomed. Their expectations, more than my beard, kept them from identifying me.

The sweetest moments came when I revealed myself to my friends and they, often in tears, embraced me, laughing through their sobs at my preposterous disguise and at the weird circumstances of our lives. To no one did I divulge details of my kidnapping, although everyone was curious. They had to trust me. They knew that if I kept things from them, it was for their own good.

After I made my initial contacts, I always kept on the go, sometimes traveling alone and sometimes with a personal escort, but always in the general area of the Volcano. There were several houses at my disposal for sleep and shelter, some in

Long Island, some in New Jersey and some in the Catskill Mountains of upstate New York.

Although I was on the go, there were moments of relaxation. I would go hunting upstate, or go swimming in Long Island Sound. Sometimes my men and I would play golf at a private country club on Long Island. In case of an emergency, my driver would always be parked nearby behind some tree. Most of the time, however, this sort of life was dull.

I was invisible to the police. Throughout my nineteen-month disappearance, the police never suspected I was right under their noses, and for this I have my friends to thank. There was a risk each and every time I revealed myself to anyone. Someone could have informed on me to the police. Or someone could have passed information of my whereabouts to Di-Gregorio's dissidents.

One of my most loyal friends was Joe Notaro, who was another group leader in my Family. Notaro was subpoenaed many times as the government attempted to squeeze him for information about me. And yet, throughout this turmoil, he remained steadfast.

I was literally under the protection of my friends, who fed, sheltered and comforted me. Without them I wouldn't be alive today. In many ways, their trust and loyalty was my greatest reward for all my years as their Father.

The Bonanno Family had an insurrection in progress.

In normal times, when I could move about freely, it would have been relatively easy to deal with Gaspar DiGregorio and his defectors. But I was restricted by extraordinary circumstances: my cool relations with the Commission, my open break with Stefano Magaddino, my problems with the law, my need to keep on the go and in disguise.

I felt like some huge beast mired in mud. Whereas usually no animal would even come near to disturb me, now, stuck in the mud, little birds could land on my head and peck out my eyes. All I could do was try to keep from sinking deeper.

The delay in my reappearance had apparently put my cousin Stefano Magaddino on edge again, and this destroyed whatever meager meeting of the minds we had worked out during our talks at the farmhouse in upstate New York. I had intended to reappear soon after my release, but I was forced to postpone that after my lawyer, William Maloney, blundered by prematurely announcing when I would return. Since Stefano didn't know the reason for my continued disappearance, he became very nervous. Reverting to his customary form, Stefano suspected me of deliberately remaining away in order to plot and maneuver against him and his puppet, Gaspar.

Around this time, Gaspar's ineptitude as a leader become evident to those who didn't know him. I think even Stefano became disgusted with Gaspar, but he couldn't simply drop him. That would have involved an insufferable loss of face before both the Commission and Stefano's own Family, many members of which already had reservations about Stefano's handling of the affair.

To bolster Gaspar, Stefano encouraged Joseph Colombo to incite people to defect from the Bonanno Family. Colombo, now the Father of the Family that had been headed by Joe Profaci and Joe Magliocco, had been instrumental in destroying Magliocco before the Commission. Stefano encouraged Colombo to undermine my leadership. This suited Colombo, because by weakening me, he could strengthen himself and his Family, which like mine was centered in Brooklyn.

The subversive actions of both DiGregorio and Colombo resulted in a great deal of confusion and some bloodshed. The shootings of this period, however, cannot rightly be said to have constituted a war—the Bananas War, as it was dubbed in the press. A war would have resulted in mayhem, in total destruction. What we had was more in the nature of a civil disturbance. We experienced a series of inconclusive skirmishes that dragged on and on.

To describe each individual incident, even if I could, would be tedious. Some people were killed and some were wounded. For the most part, they were men of inconsequential position, men on the fringes of the Family, dissidents looking for any excuse to rebel and advance themselves. What violence there was came as a result of the general confusion rather than as the outcome of a master plan.

Gaspar DiGregorio, the nominal leader of the insurgents, escaped death. I had favored trying to bring back Gaspar into the Family, no matter how much he had disgraced himself. However, the general consensus in the Family was that Gaspar should die.

One day in 1965, after my son had been released from jail on his contempt citation, Salvatore and Johnny Morales and another went to a Brooklyn tavern often frequented by men of my Tradition. At the bar the startled trio saw Gasparino. As the story was later told to me, Johnny and the other were ready to grab their pistols and dispatch Gaspar on the spot, but Salvatore stopped them. At the same time, the tavern owner intervened, and this gave Gaspar the chance to escape unharmed.

When the incident became known to the top members of my Family, they voted to censure Salvatore. They had a valid viewpoint. As long as Gaspar remained alive and continued to rally defectors around him, the well-being of the entire Family was in jeopardy. My Family had tolerated forbearance toward Gaspar from me, their Father, but as the situation become more tense and their own positions more precarious, they couldn't understand such kindness toward Gaspar from my son, who was a relative newcomer among them.

And yet, I cannot blame Salvatore. If anything, I am proud of his temperance. Gasparino was his godfather and the best man at my wedding. Salvatore had known Gaspar from childhood. Perhaps it would have been better for everyone if Gaspar had been killed. But what a price in conscience Salvatore would have had to pay! He would have had to reject his upbringing.

In this fitful manner, 1965 slowly passed—an engagement here, a bout there, commotion followed by tedium. I had remained undetected, but who knew if a gunman was waiting in ambush around the next corner? I was always conscious that someone out there, some lonely hunter, might have me in his sights.

27

I WAS IN ONE OF MY FARM HIDEAWAYS IN UPSTATE NEW YORK, shortly after my sixty-first birthday in January 1966, when I heard that an attempt had been made on my son's life.

Salvatore, as well as my brother-in-law Frank Labruzzo and my friend Joe Notaro, had been ambushed on their way to a meeting with Gaspar DiGregorio. All of them escaped unhurt.

Gaspar had sent word to Johnny Morales and to Salvatore that he wanted to talk with them about lessening hostilities. To put Johnny and Salvatore at ease as to their safety, Gaspar agreed to hold the meeting at the house of Vito Bonventre on Troutman Street in the Bushwick section of Brooklyn. This was the same Vito Bonventre, my uncle, with whom I briefly worked as a baker in the 1920s. Uncle Vito was the father-in-law of Johnny Morales.

On the night of the conference, Johnny was sick in bed with flu. Salvatore therefore went to the meeting accompanied by Frank Labruzzo, Joe Notaro and another trusted man. They parked their car and were walking toward the house on Troutman Street when shots rang out. Salvatore and the rest of the men ducked for cover between parked cars, then scattered into the night. None of them had been hit by the ambushers.

The police found abandoned weapons in a house across the street from Uncle Vito's house.

The news of this sad spectacle infuriated me. For the moment, it didn't matter who was on the ambush team; it was obvious that Gaspar DiGregorio was behind it. Befittingly, Gaspar had bungled the job. He had chosen gunmen who couldn't shoot straight. The feckless Gaspar wouldn't have dared attempt such a double cross, however, if he hadn't first consulted with Stefano Magaddino.

Had both of them gone crazy? What was my world coming to? Sanity and reason had been forsaken. If it weren't for sheer luck, my son would have been killed.

As angry as I was, I had to assert control over my emotions. Rage is the luxury of an idle man. I thanked God for my son's safety, and I planned my next move.

Remaining in hiding after the Troutman Street ambush was out of the question. My seclusion was beginning to work against me. Some people in my Family I had taken into my confidence—on those I could rely. But others in my Family, further removed from me, some of whom I had never even met, found themselves sitting on the fence during my disappearance. They waited for my return, but they also had to think about whose side to take in case I didn't return. Therefore, they temporized and gave lip service to each of the contending sides. Above all, these people wanted things to return to normal again.

My invisibility had safeguarded me; it was now beginning to plunge my Family into more turmoil. My own son had nearly lost his life. My kidnapping had suddenly thrust Salvatore into the lava pit of the Volcano; and out of loyalty to me, Salvatore had endured the heat. It was not supposed to have happened that way. I had other dreams for Salvatore. I had other dreams for my world and my Family. But my world was changing—had changed already—into something that I had stopped loving. My way of life had become transformed into a mutant of itself.

It was time for me to show myself and put an end to a bygone attachment.

On May 17, 1966, a friend of mine dropped me off at a street corner in lower Manhattan. I calmly walked toward the U.S. Courthouse.

I looked like myself again: clean-shaven, slightly tanned and dressed in a conservative gray suit—the same suit I had worn the night of my kidnapping. I was also wearing the same shirt, the same tie, the same hat and the same shoes and socks.

My attire was but one of the matters I had carefully planned before showing up at the courthouse. I had to arrange for an attorney to meet me there. William Maloney no longer represented me. To replace him, I chose Albert Krieger, a young Jewish lawyer who had previously represented my son Salvatore and Joe Notaro. Bail was another consideration. I arranged for proper collateral for my bail and for a bondsman to service it. I anticipated that the bail might be set as high as half a million dollars.

I walked into the U.S. Courthouse through a side door, because I didn't want to take any chance of being detected by FBI agents. I did not want to be taken into custody by the FBI. For one thing, I didn't want to give the FBI the satisfaction of arresting me. This agency had harassed me and my children, had pestered my friends, had invaded my privacy and had generally made life miserable for me. And yet, despite its vaunted reputation and its tremendous resources, when it came down to doing some actual police work, the FBI had flunked. They couldn't find me for nineteen months, and I was right there in New York most of the time.

I also did not want the FBI to arrest me because I knew what would happen if they had me all to themselves before I got a chance to see a judge. If I was in their custody, the FBI would shuttle me here and there, question me relentlessly, try to make me trip on my words, try to trap me, try to make a deal. I wanted to avoid being at their mercy.

My plan was to turn myself in directly to a judge in a courtroom. If I did that, I would be under the jurisdiction of the judge and his U.S. marshals instead of the FBI.

When I reached the lobby of the courthouse on Foley Square, I tried as best I could to act nonchalant. As I entered the elevator, someone recognized me. He was a man in the Lucchese Family. He was about to greet me when I scowled at him severely. This stopped him flat. He sensed I didn't want to be greeted, and he retreated into the lobby. The elevator door closed. I let out a deep breath.

At the third floor, the elevator doors opened into a nearly empty corridor, and I marched directly toward Room 318. With my hand on the courtroom door, I paused to glance at both ends of the hallway. Then I sallied inside.

The judge paid me no attention at first. At the railing, I said something to this effect:

—Your Honor, excuse me for imposing on you, but I don't

know what to do. I understand the government is looking for me. I'm Joe Bonanno.

The people in front of me all seemed to do a double take. The judge asked me if I was really Joe Bonanno. I reconfirmed my identity. He asked me please to sit down in the spectators' section. By previous arrangement, I was soon joined in the courtroom by my lawyer, Krieger, and one of his associates. Before coming to the courtroom, Krieger had gone upstairs to the U.S. attorney's office to inform them of my surrender. While I sat in the courtroom awaiting some instructions from the judge, a couple of U.S. marshals sat behind me and told me I was under arrest. The U.S. marshals took me to be fingerprinted and processed. Then we returned to the courtroom.

I pleaded not guilty to a charge of willfully failing to appear before a grand jury. Before setting bail, Judge Marvin Frankel heard from U.S. attorney Robert Morgenthau, who read a description of my past which was full of misinformation.

Morgenthau recommended that bail be set at half a million dollars. Krieger pointed out that this was tantamount to no bail at all. Preposterous as it was, I was prepared to pay it. The judge, however, set bail at $150,000.

It was late afternoon by the time my arraignment was concluded and I posted bail. When my lawyer and I walked out of the courthouse, reporters and photographers flocked around us. I told them I had nothing to say except that, under the circumstances, I felt well.

Until a trial date could be set, I had to appear in court every month to check in with the authorities. I also had to remain in New York, or, with prior notification, I could travel to Tucson. During this period, I lived at my son's house in East Meadow, Long Island. Police kept a constant watch on me. I was not as free as I wanted to be, but free enough.

My dramatic and well-publicized reappearance had served notice in my world that I was as hale and unshakable as ever. I was back and I had to be reckoned with.

After the abortive attempt on my son's life, Gaspar DiGregorio sort of melted away. Even before my reappearance, the so-called Commission, which once had recognized Gaspar as temporary Father of my Family, abandoned him. The clumsy ambush on Troutman Street had convinced everyone that Gaspar was a bungler and unfit leader.

Even as Gaspar was losing favor, however, my cousin Stefano, looking now for other support, solidified an alliance with Joseph Colombo. Stefano continued to encourage Colombo to work against me by drawing defectors from my Family.

A few years after the Troutman Street ambush, Gaspar DiGregorio had a heart attack. He was through, a broken man, and spent the rest of his life ailing and isolated.

A nobody by the name of Paul Sciacca replaced Gaspar as leader of the defectors. Sciacca was an example of what I call a *mezza-figura*—a half-figure. These are people who only show part of themselves. When the climate changes, they show another part of themselves. You never know where they stand.

Except for a score or so of these half-figures and malcontents, the rest of my Family promptly renewed their allegiance to me. Among my group leaders, I chose Angelo Caruso and two other men to deliver a message to the so-called Commission.

At one time the Commission had truly reflected a consensus in my world. But after 1961, the Commission reflected only who was the most powerful. The former was a legitimate regulatory body; the latter was self-appointed and self-imposed. I considered the Commission an unauthorized body and one of the prime examples of the deterioration in my world.

Nonetheless, as much as I scoffed at their pretensions, I did have to deal with the Commission members, because they were powerful.

The message I told my three men to bring before the Commission went something like this:

—Don Peppino is in good health. He sends his best regards and affection to everyone. Don Peppino says he is still the Father of his Family. Nothing has changed. If there has been trouble in his Family, he didn't create it. However, someone dear to him has been under a false impression. The problem is only between don Peppino and his cousin don Stefano. Don Peppino still loves his cousin don Stefano. Don Peppino still loves his cousin and his cousin loves him. No one should interfere in don Peppino's Family. He wishes to forget the past. When his Family is united, don Peppino will know what to do.

I had to use diplomatic language so as not to antagonize anyone needlessly. The message, however, was abundantly clear. I was telling the Commission that if they didn't bother me, I wouldn't bother any of them. My reference to my cousin Stefano left no doubt whom I considered the culprit. In my last sentence, I was letting everyone know indirectly that I intended to retire.

My men delivered the message to an assemblage that included Carlo Gambino, who was acting as ad hoc chairman; Tommy Eboli, a representative for Vito Genovese, who was in prison; a delegate for Tommy Lucchese, who by this time was bedridden with a terminal disease; Joe Colombo; Joe Zerilli of Detroit; and Stefano Magaddino of Buffalo.

Later, through my men and through Zerilli, I was told how various men on the Commission had reacted to my message.

Gambino had clearly looked relieved. It was no longer in his interest to take Stefano's side against me. Now that Luchese was sickly and inactive, Gambino had to be more cautious. His greatest fear after my reappearance was that I had returned in order to go on the warpath. Carlo didn't want that kind of trouble.

As for Colombo, he squirmed in his seat. To save face, Colombo said his inexperience (he was the youngest father there) disqualified him from making a pertinent remark. Colombo was the most discomfited by my message. Whereas earlier both Gambino and Magaddino had used Colombo to stir dissension in my Family, Gambino's attitude of appeasement toward me had left Colombo in the lurch, with only the teetering Magaddino as his cohort.

My cousin Stefano was a sight to behold at the Commission meeting, I was told. After my message was delivered, Stefano pursed his lips, creased his forehead, knitted his eyebrows, crossed his arms and through this sulky countenance tried to show that he, not I, was the injured party. But other than sighing and snorting, he said little.

When the representatives briefly discussed the clear implication in my message—that Stefano was to blame—Tommy Eboli was reported as saying to Stefano,

—If the shoe fits, wear it.

For Eboli to say something like that indicated that Stefano had been soundly embarrassed before his peers. In fact, from this moment on Stefano Magaddino never again enjoyed the prestige he once had.

At the end of the Commission meeting, the representatives passed a resolution declaring their amicable intentions toward me. I did not delude myself that this resolution would end my troubles. Magaddino and Colombo might remain tactful in front of the others, but behind the scenes I knew they would continue to scheme against my Family.

Be that as it may, I had succeeded in diffusing any concerted attempt to overthrow me. In turn, I had assured the other Fathers I would not wage war against them. The problems within my Family were by no means settled, but the issues, at long last, were clear.

Matters dragged on and on. Nothing came to a head. There was no conclusive resolution of affairs, no climax. The government, which had been champing at the bit to get its hands on me, was at a loss what to do with me once I surrendered. At first I was required to report to court once a month. Then I had to show up in court once every three months. Still later, I had to report only once every six months. I had reappeared in 1966, but I was not brought to trial that year . . . nor in 1967 . . . nor in 1968 . . . nor in 1969 . . . nor in 1970 . . . nor in 1971.

In 1971, my lawyer, Albert Krieger, reported to U.S. District Court Judge E. Palmieri, who had been assigned my case in New York. The judge asked him if I was ready to go to trial. Krieger answered that unless my health intervened, I was ready.

Everyone warned me that Palmieri was a tough judge, but I have always preferred a tough judge to a weak one. A tough judge may hand down a severe sentence, but a tough judge will also be the first to protect your legal rights. A tough judge won't cave in to prosecutorial pressure or to public opinion.

After Krieger reported to Palmieri about my condition, I think the government asked for a three-month delay. That was absurd. The government had had more than four years to prepare a case. The government's procrastination annoyed the judge, and because of the delays and also probably because of my heart condition, Judge Palmieri ruled nolle prosequi—"we will proceed no longer."

Thus came to an undramatic end the government's celebrated but specious case against me concerning my disappearance. By its inability to prepare a case, the government showed that it never had had anything substantial against me in the first place. In 1964, before my kidnapping, when the government prosecutors kept calling me in front of a grand jury, they were just on a fishing expedition. They were simply scrounging around in the hope that they might find something.

As for myself, I have a clear conscience. If I didn't, I would have wilted a long time ago. Where judgment of my conduct is concerned, I'll take my chances with God. I hear he's a tough judge.

When men such as myself, men from western Sicily, came to the new world, we had the same aspirations as other immigrants. We came here looking for a better life. Most of us didn't have much, if any, money. We didn't speak English. The country needed our cheap labor, but other than that we didn't feel especially welcomed here. People tended to make fun of us, or to revile our customs, even the food we ate. We had only each other.

We carried our Tradition in our hearts.

We didn't constitute a corporate entity. We didn't have a charter. Our Tradition was not a criminal conspiracy. It was not a master plan to undermine civilization. It was a Tradition. Our fathers handed it down to us so we would know how to survive in an inhospitable world.

For us these old ways were perfectly natural. Sicilian immigrants wanted the same things for their children as all the other immigrants did. We wanted our children to become doctors and lawyers and engineers.

Slowly, but irreversibly, our Tradition deteriorated. The ideals for which it stood became corrupted. These changes occurred as a result of pressures from both inside and outside our world.

In America we found ourselves allowing people into our Families who didn't really understand our old Tradition. These newcomers were of a different world. The newcomers saw only the outward form of our Tradition; they never penetrated the mystery within.

The supremacy of the clan is the very foundation of my

Tradition. In America, however, the clan, or the family, is not the basic unit of society. Americans think of themselves primarily as independent individuals, and they act accordingly.

American values, therefore, conflicted with our Traditional values. And pretty soon, people in our own world began to think of themselves as "individuals." Instead of subordinating their individual desires to the welfare of the clan, they tended to break away from these binding ties. The whole beauty of the clan or Family grouping was that it nurtured harmony and responsibility. The Family restrained individual desire, while at the same time it provided a broader base for a Family member's activity. In America, everyone was out for himself. There was nothing holding back the individual. There was no use for a Father.

In my world, this individualistic orientation encouraged license, wantonness, disrespect and unsanctioned activities. It sapped the authority of the Father. It destroyed the Father as the symbol of moral order. American values tended to displace kinship relationships with economic relationships.

American words reflected this new orientation. In Sicily we referred to our leader as our Father. In America, Father became boss, Family became organization, friend became business associate, "man of respect" became gangster.

The lack of respect for Family-based virtues—such as loyalty, trust and honor—created the general conditions under which my Tradition deteriorated. But the specific catalyst of change was money. There was too much money in America, and in many cases it was all too easy to make. People worshiped money in this country. Money turned people's heads completely around, to the exclusion of every other value.

Everyone likes to have money, but in the absence of a higher moral code the making of money becomes an unwholesome goal. Consider a man who has persuaded himself that there's nothing wrong with selling narcotics. He rationalizes the activity as a mere business proposition. After all, he tells himself, bottling companies don't have any qualms about selling soda pop even though it gives you rotten teeth. Tobacco companies keep on selling cigarettes even though they give you cancer. So why can't he sell narcotics? He's not forcing anyone to buy his product. It's just business.

My old Tradition represented a moral outlook on the world,

although some of our values differed from those of society at large. In its pure form, my Tradition is against narcotics. We consider narcotics morally wrong. It's not a point of debate. A man wanting to trade in narcotics will be discouraged from doing so. But let's say the old Tradition is in a state of decline and cannot enforce its code. Or let's say people start believing that making money off narcotics is really no different from making money off bottling sugar water. That's when things fall apart.

By the 1960s, and certainly by the 1970s, my Tradition in America had become a grotesque parody of itself.

I had cherished the thought that when the time came for me to retire, my Family and I would hold a banquet, at which time I would thank them, give them my blessing and make way for the new Father. That day never came.

In February 1968, with my court case still unsettled and the situation in my world still partly in turmoil, I suffered my third heart attack.

I was in Tucson when I had my stroke, and Tucson, with its dry, balmy climate, is where I wanted to remain, far away from the belching Volcano. I was sixty-three years old.

After my recuperation at St. Joseph's Hospital in Tucson, two or three government-appointed doctors visited me and examined me. The government wanted to make sure I wasn't faking. They must have thought I was a medical marvel, able to induce heart attacks at will. They hardly thought I was human.

I wasn't the only one to have heart problems about that time. Stefano Magaddino had a heart attack just before my reappearance in 1966. Tommy Lucchese died in 1967 of a cerebral hemorrhage. Carlo Gambino had a heart attack that year also. High blood pressure was having a field day.

Before leaving New York for good, I appointed a three-man committee to fill the leadership vacuum temporarily until a new Father could be chosen. The committee included Angelo Caruso, a steady and peaceful man of the old Tradition. This was but a caretaker arrangement.

As I faded away from power, the situation in the Family became desultory. The insurgent group, although much diminished, still fomented trouble with the continued support of

Joseph Colombo. But by 1970 or so, Colombo began his decline. Gambino, so I was told, no longer considered himself to be Colombo's ally. Magaddino, Colombo's other ally, had by now begun to lose control of his own Family in Buffalo and thus stopped being a source of strength for Colombo.

In the 1970s, leadership of the Family in Buffalo passed away from Stefano Magaddino. Stefano's conduct toward me in the 1960s had shamed his own Family, the leading members of which realized Stefano was no longer fit to lead. Stefano was allowed to step down unhurt, but he was a virtual prisoner in his own house for the rest of his life. He died of natural causes in 1977. Before dying he had made several overtures to see me, but it was too late.

My removal to Arizona left the question open as to who would succeed me as Father. If everything is going right, succession is not as problematic as one would think. If there is unity, the Family members easily recognize who among them has the necessary qualities to make a good Father. Such a man will have proved himself by example over the years and will have undertaken duties to test his mettle. It is only in chaotic times that succession becomes a chore.

It might be supposed that since Johnny Morales was my second, he would be the logical choice to succeed me. This was not the case. Johnny was fine as long as I was behind him, but he couldn't function by himself. We're now talking about a period when I ceased to be in control of the Family. I still had friends, but I wasn't in charge anymore. I daresay that after my departure, the fragmentation of the Family was such that you probably can't say it had a Father at all. The situation was similar to a country in which three or four political parties vie for power but none of them has a majority control.

Be that as it may, it is not up to me to discuss the affairs of the Family after I left. And it is improper for people still to refer to this Family as the Bonanno Family. It stopped being the Bonanno Family when I retired. In Sicily, a Family is sometimes likened to a *cosca*—an artichoke. The Family members are like the artichoke leaves and the Father is like the central stem on which they all hang. Remove the central stem and all you have is a lot of separate leaves. When I left New York to retire, all the separate leaves had to find themselves another stem.

I'm not a Father anymore, and there is no *Bonanno* Family anymore.

I would like to close this era of my life with a story about a teacher of mine in Sicily. His name was Professor Nunnari, an imposing man who taught history. If you didn't know your lesson, you could expect Professor Nunnari to call you a dolt or a blockhead.

One day he had asked a question of a student who couldn't answer correctly. The professor berated the student,

—You're a fool.

The professor then asked the same question of another student, who also gave the wrong answer.

—You're a fool, the professor scolded.

Extremely annoyed by the wrong answers, Professor Nunnari went down the same row, asking each student the same question. No one answered correctly.

—You're a row of fools!

After that, Professor Nunnari began calling on students in the next row. As he approached me, I prepared myself for what was to come. I didn't know the correct answer either, but I wasn't going to let the professor get away with calling me a fool.

When he called me, I said,

—Sir, if I can't answer your question, what does that make me?

The professor regarded me skeptically and said,

—What do you think?

—Does it make me a fool too?

If I could get the professor to call me a fool, I was going to respond with some such silly response as "It takes one to know one."

However, the professor, accustomed to juvenile repartee, answered,

—It makes you like all the others.

He had outfoxed me. But in order to rescue my faltering position, I said,

—Sir, if everyone's a fool, who are you?

Instead of getting angry and calling me an impertinent dunce, Professor Nunnari gave out a loud and hearty laugh.

—Why, I'm the biggest fool of all.

BOOK V

My
Golden
Years

28

ALL MEN HAVE EYES, MACHIAVELLI SAYS, BUT FEW HAVE THE gift of penetration.

I fully realize that for an outsider the gift of penetration is a difficult one to attain when considering my world, because we of that world are normally silent, and when we do speak we use the terms of an alien culture.

This book has tried to bridge that gap.

We now come to the part of my life after my retirement from the Volcano. Mine might not have been the most elegant nor the most dramatic exit from power, but I had accomplished what I had set out to do. I retired while I was still on top, with life and limb, with my wife and children and with my worldly goods.

I would have been content, after 1968, to lead a quiet, uneventful life, in which case I would have nothing to report and my story would end here. My retirement to Tucson, however, turned out to be a retreat into an inferno. I repaired to Tucson thinking that perhaps I might leave my reputation behind. I voluntarily came to Arizona to get away from my world and not to establish a branch of it in Tucson. There has never been what Americans call a "crime family" in Arizona. From the time I first came to Tucson, in 1942, I had always rejected any attempt to include Tucson in my world. Tucson was a place to get away from it all.

The early 1940s were a fruitful, happy time for me. I had

been blessed with a loving wife, two children and many, many friends. I had just acquired the Sunshine Dairy Farm in upstate New York. My affairs in the Volcano were running smoothly and peacefully. I was in the process of becoming an American citizen. My health was good.

My wife, Fay, and I were concerned about our son's health, however. Salvatore suffered from an ear infection. An operation in 1940 had failed to stem the discharge from his ear, and the doctor had recommended a dry climate. So in the spring of 1941, Fay and I, accompanied by eight-year-old Salvatore and six-year-old Catherine, climbed into the family Cadillac, with Johnny Morales at the wheel, and took off to discover the American frontier and find a dry climate.

The trip west was my first cross-country trip, for which I was glad I owned a Cadillac—a great car in those days. We traveled through Colorado, New Mexico and Utah, states which to us Easterners seemed to have otherworldly landscapes. At Taos, Johnny and I had our picture taken with a real American Indian who had braided pigtails down to his waist. I bought Salvatore and the tomboyish Catherine a pair of cowboy boots. In contrast to the kids, we grown-ups looked incongruous in the West. Fay wore a black jump suit with a turbanlike sash over her hair. Johnny liked to go around in his white socks and sandals. I wore a pair of two-toned oxfords, white at the instep and brown at the toe cap and heel.

Our motley crew made its way to Los Angeles. Back then Los Angeles was a gracious city with clean air, with actors and cowboys and also with men of my Tradition. As Father of one of the New York Families, I was greeted and treated like a visiting dignitary by the leaders of my world on the West Coast. I dined, for example, with Jack Dragna, who hailed from Corleone, Sicily, and was the top man of my Tradition in the Los Angeles area. A leader from San Diego, Tony Mirabile, who was born in the Sicilian town of Alcamo, some five miles from Castellammare, came to pay his respects. But the man I enjoyed seeing most was Jimmy Costa, who was about my age and who also came from Castellammare.

Jimmy took me to a Hollywood eatery where many of the movie actors dined. Among the actors there at the time were Errol Flynn and Jean Harlow. Jimmy introduced me to Flynn, who suggested we all go to Catalina Island on his yacht. My dinner companion for the evening was a famous actress, whose name I won't mention. She was a sweet and lovely woman. Flynn, on the other hand, was no gentleman, contrary to his swashbuckling screen image. He was foul and rough with women. And as for Jean Harlow, she seemed a slatternly sort. As movie stars, I enjoyed both Flynn and Harlow, but as human beings I disliked them. They were just living it up, nothing else.

For our return trip to the East, we took a southerly route through Arizona. Here was the dry climate we were looking for, but summertime in Phoenix, which we passed through, was so hot that Fay didn't understand how people could live in such a climate. They didn't have air conditioning then. We returned to New York, thankful for its ocean breezes. Later that year, Salvatore's ear was operated on again for mastoiditis, and once again, the doctor advised us that the only thing the boy could do for his ear was to sit in the sun and allow his ear to drain. This second operation hastened my decision to take Salvatore to live outside New York. So we shoved off for Arizona again. Fay and I chose Tucson over Phoenix because we wanted a small town where no one knew me and where we could enjoy an existence far apart from that which we knew in New York.

I didn't know a soul in Tucson. All I had was a letter of introduction from Bishop Francis Spellman in New York to Bishop Daniel Gercke in Tucson.

In the winter of 1942–1943, my family and I left Brooklyn during a terrific blizzard. Our second trip to the West was less leisurely than the first, because the United States was now at war. Certain foods and sundry other products were scarce. The government rationed gasoline. The whole country was under wartime restrictions and immersed in war-related activities. I registered for the draft, but I was never drafted because I owned a dairy, a vital wartime industry. You could say I contributed milk to the Allied cause.

In my world, according to the old Tradition, a man fights for personal honor and he feels patriotism for his family. Our fighting is personal, direct, man-to-man. You call this a feudal notion. In your world, in wars between nations, a pilot pushes a button and releases a bomb that will kill thousands of human beings. The pilot never hears a single scream. Today, war among nations is indiscriminate, impersonal, remote . . . less manly, as it were. War has become a sort of video game.

One of the proudest moments of my life was the day I became a naturalized U.S. citizen in 1945. At my naturalization ceremony in Brooklyn, the federal commissioner asked me,

—If you become a citizen and have to fight against Italians, what will you do?

Another Italian, also seeking citizenship, had been asked the same question and had replied that if sent to war he would kill every Italian without compunction. This man wanted to show how patriotic he was to his new country in order to impress the commissioner.

When I was asked the same question, I didn't want to take a chance on offending the commissioner or having him doubt my patriotism, but I didn't want to be untruthful either.

—My duty is to fight for my country, I answered.

—But what if you are sent to fight in Italy? the commissioner persisted.

I was beginning to think the commissioner was trying to taunt me.

—I would do my duty, I answered. But in my heart I would feel bad about killing Italians.

Instead of reproving me, the commissioner approved:

—You will make a good American, he said.

On the way to Tucson, we stopped in Dallas to visit with a friend, a lieutenant commander in the Navy. The next day, about seventy-five miles west of Dallas, my wife realized she had left something behind.

—Whatever's the matter?

—I forgot my coffee pot in Dallas, Fay said, looking out the window like a mournful spaniel.

It was not your ordinary coffee pot. It was an Italian coffee pot, the kind used to make espresso coffee. In those days, I doubt whether there was such a coffee pot for sale in all of the Southwest.

To many Italians, a meal that does not conclude with a tiny cup of espresso is no meal at all. Italians become addicted to this very dark and very strong coffee at an early age. Although most Italian-Americans get used to drinking regular coffee, usually rather contemptuously referred to as "brown coffee," nothing can quite replace the taste of "black coffee" to an Italian's palate. Black coffee is a symbol of culture and heritage: it represents home and the dinner table. Fay carried along her coffee pot and her "black coffee" the way a farmer moving to a foreign country might take along a pot of his native soil.

—Stop the car, Fay demanded abruptly. Let's go back for the coffee pot.

Fay and I began bickering about the advisability of wasting a couple of hours to retrieve the coffee pot. It was a comical scene now that I look back on it, but at the time it was an exchange full of bluster and indignation, as most domestic tiffs are. I wound up telling everyone to keep quiet.

Once we reached Tucson, our Dallas friend sent us the coffee pot by mail. Even so, for the couple of weeks before it arrived, Fay was inconsolable.

In Tucson we resided in a motel for about a month while we searched for a house and a school that Salvatore and Catherine could attend. When I took my letter of introduction to Bishop Daniel Gercke of Tucson, he recommended I enroll my children at SS. Peter and Paul Church, which had a school. Eventually, Fay and I rented a house near the church. The pastor of the church was Father Francis Green, who had come to Tucson from the Ithaca-Cornell area of upstate New York, with which I was acquainted. We became friends. After Bishop Gercke died, Francis Green succeeded him as bishop of the archdiocese of Tucson.

In May of 1943, Fay and I went back to New York, taking Catherine with us. We enrolled Salvatore in a boarding school for the summer. The Arizona climate was good for Salvatore's ear, but Salvatore would have to remain away from the rest of his family most of the year. These were melancholy years for him, but there were compensations.

Salvatore (as well as Catherine, a regular Annie Oakley in those days) had taken an immediate liking to Western life. I bought him a horse, a saddle, tack, boots, a complete western outfit. Salvatore already was a good horse rider, but in Arizona riding horses became a passion.

* * *

That first winter in Tucson, a couple of policemen came to the house. On spotting them, Fay shook her head in dismay. I thought, Oh no, here we go again.

Instead of handing me a subpoena, the policemen asked me if I wanted to buy a ticket to the policemen's annual ball. They said they had not sold many tickets. I was so happy that the policemen had not come to harass me that I reached into my pocket and gave them all the money I found, about $450.

Shortly after we rented our house, a fruit basket, containing fresh oranges, grapefruits, dates and bananas, would appear just about every morning at our back door. Since we didn't know anyone in town, we couldn't imagine who was delivering the basket. One morning I was driving around town when I noticed a car following me. I stopped suddenly. The pursuing driver also stopped and came rushing out of his car. He was a middle-aged man, short, slightly chubby, with graying hair and deep-set eyes. He came up to my door and said in Italian:

—My name is Andrea Cracchiolo. I've been bringing you fruit every morning.

Don Andrea, as I was to call him out of courtesy, was to become one of my best friends in Tucson. Cracchiolo was born in Cinisi, which is at the eastern tip of the Gulf of Castellammare. Although he himself did not participate in the affairs of my world, Cracchiolo understood the old Tradition and had relatives and friends in my world. One of these friends was Joe Zerilli, the Father of the Detroit Family.

—He told me to put myself at your disposal, Cracchiolo told me during our initial encounter. He told me to put myself at your disposal from A to Z.

Through motel and real estate investments, Cracchiolo made a fortune. He's in his nineties today. Two of his sons are lawyers, one is a doctor. One of his daughters married a lawyer who became a superior court judge in Tucson.

It pleased me to have met another Sicilian in Tucson. Cracchiolo was glad to do me favors. When I wasn't in town, he would visit Salvatore at school, take him for rides and bring him Italian delicacies. My second winter in Tucson, rather than rent a house again, Fay and I lived with the Cracchiolos at their house.

It certainly didn't hurt Cracchiolo in those days to have me as a friend. Later on in his career, there were times when the fact that he was my friend saved Cracchiolo from possible harm from others. To some degree, at least, I was instrumental in helping Cracchiolo come up in the world. His sons and daughters might be loath to admit this today. Nevertheless, I was one of many steppingstones in their father's success. It takes many steppingstones, you know, for a man to rise. None can do it unaided.

Cracchiolo, the first Italian I met in Tucson, was to lead me to the second. One day Cracchiolo invited me to an Italian restaurant in town. He wanted us to go without our wives. He took me to a restaurant called Caruso's because he wanted to introduce me to its owner, Nino Zagona.

—This Zagona is an enigma, Cracchiolo told me. He works, he cooks, he sleeps near his kitchen and talks to no one.

I asked to talk to the chef.

—Tell him there's an Italian in his restaurant who wants to eat a true Italian meal and who desires to speak to him.

The waitress left and quickly returned, saying the chef was too busy.

—See, Cracchiolo said, what'd I tell you?

—Tell the chef, I said, there's a gentleman from out of town who wants only the chef to take care of him.

We had to wait a bit, but at last Zagona came to our table. He looked at me warily at first. Then, in a flash, we recognized each other. But the apprehension didn't leave Zagona's face, as if he was trying to determine what I wanted.

—Excuse me, don Peppino, excuse me, Zagona said.

Cracchiolo, of course, was stupefied that Zagona knew me. Zagona offered to cook anything I wanted. He and I gave each other a knowing glance, and he went back to his kitchen. Zagona had good reason to be worried on first seeing me. I knew about Zagona when he lived in New York. In New York, Zagona used to be associated with the Mineo Family, which after the Castellammarese War became the Mangano Family. Zagona also got himself in some sort of trouble in New York with people in our world. My coincidental meeting with him worried Zagona, because he thought I would tell his enemies in New York his whereabouts.

When we had a chance to talk in private, away from Cracchiolo, Zagona told me that my cousin Stefano Magaddino had once saved his life. He said he had always sympathized with the Castellammarese. Basically, he put himself at my mercy.

—Either you trust me or you don't, I told Zagona. If you don't trust me, you might as well get out of town right now. But if you do trust me, I'll see what I can do for you.

That spring, upon my return to New York, I talked to Vincent Mangano about the Zagona matter. Although there were people in Mangano's Family who felt they still had a score to settle with Zagona, Vincent and I agreed that as long as Zagona remained in Tucson and as long as I took responsibility for him, then no harm would come to Zagona. I relayed the good tidings to Zagona; he could now build his new life in Tucson without dread. After I did him this favor, Zagona was a generous host whenever my family went to his restaurant. On many occasions, Zagona brought Italian food to my son at his boarding school.

During my third winter excursion to Tucson, Zagona told me he wanted me to meet one of the frequent visitors to his restaurant, a county judge. This was Evo DeConcini, whom I have mentioned before. Since the judge knew the establishment in town and the legal system, Zagona told me, he had been useful to him. Zagona said he would often give the judge free meals or take food to his house on feast days. It was a cozy relationship in the Italian manner.

Evo DeConcini was by far the most prominent Italian in Tucson. His roots were northern Italian. In Italy, there exists a schism between northerners and southerners. The northerners think the southerners, the Sicilians in particular, are savages. In northern Italy they derogatorily refer to the south of Italy as *la terra bruciata*—the scorched land. The southerners think the northerners are cold and smug.

It was about 1944 that Zagona introduced me to Evo DeConcini at Caruso's restaurant. Thereafter, we began to see each other again at the restaurant. Then Cracchiolo, ever eager to make new contacts himself, began inviting Fay, me and Evo for dinner. Thus, Evo became the friend of both Cracchiolo and me.

I began to feel even more comfortable around Evo after I learned that he and his family had been befriended by Tony Mirabile, the leader of a Sicilian clan in San Diego. When Mirabile, Papa Tony as he was sometimes called, visited Tucson, in the mid-1940s, he, Evo and I went out to dinner many times.

The earlier days of our friendship were the most enjoyable. When I was in town, we would visit each other's homes. The DeConcinis were never reluctant to accept my generosity. I would take them out to restaurants and I would pick up the tab. Evo and I played golf together with club pro Wes Conrad at the Randolph Park golf course. I can still see Wes instructing the stiff judge:

—Hey, judge, look at me. You have to be loose as a goose.

Later on, Evo liked to take me to the exclusive Old Pueblo Club, a private club in downtown Tucson where Evo was well known; he would introduce me to his friends. I joined the Italian-American Club, a social-political club whose guiding force was Evo DeConcini. Sometimes we had dinners at Cracchiolo's house. It was there that I have my first recollection of Evo's son, Dennis DeConcini, currently the junior U.S. Senator from Arizona. This must have been in 1949 or 1950. Dennis, barely a teenager, would play with Cracchiolo's youngest son, Andrew, who was about the same age. I used to smoke long, thick cigars back then, and when I threw away the butt, Dennis and Andrew would scamper to scoop it up and puff on it, out of view of their parents.

Evo was a tall, thin, pallid man. He was in his forties when I first met him. He already was losing his hair and wore spectacles. Evo was rarely loud or demonstrative, around me anyway. He was a reserved chap, soft-spoken, discreet, low-key. In contrast, his wife, Ora, was a robust and vivacious woman. She seemed to be more "natural" around people than her husband. With me, Evo hardly ever talked about his youth or his background. He was polite and genial, but very guarded. I could never imagine Evo standing up to another man and saying, "I hate your guts." Evo was very politic.

The DeConcinis are often referred to as a political dynasty in Arizona. Evo, the father, has been Democratic Party chairman, a member of the University of Arizona Board of Regents, a state attorney general, a superior court judge and a state supreme court judge.

After retiring from the state supreme court in the early 1950s, Evo devoted his time to business. It is no secret that his family is well off. It is one of the richest and most influential families in the state.

Throughout the 1940s and the early 1950s, I made many friends in town, over the entire spectrum of society, just as I did in New York. For example, I was the friend of Gus Battaglia, a rancher and cotton farmer in nearby Eloy (Gus was no relation to Charlie Battaglia). I knew Sam Nannini, a land developer; and Paul Cella, a lawyer who went on to become a city magistrate. I met a young, struggling lawyer by the name of Larry D'Antonio, who went on to become my civil attorney. I became friends with Victor Tronolone, an accountant who was to handle my income tax returns and who also handled Evo DeConcini's business taxes until 1980. I knew Pete Licavoli, a man of my Tradition from Detroit who also had retired in Tucson. I knew Dr. Salvatore Megna, a retired doctor from Milwaukee who became a successful real estate investor when he came to Tucson; Dr. Megna was also a man of my Tradition. I knew Tucson Police Chief Bernard Garmire and U.S. Congressman Harold Patten, who was my neighbor. I knew businessmen by the score. A good friend of mine was Dick Drachman, a member of one of Tucson's pioneer families. Dick's brother, Roy, handled the sale of the Five Bar B Ranch, an exclusive piece of property I owned on Tucson's east side. Through Dr. Megna, I became friends with Dr. Francis Roy, Dean of the Liberal Arts College at the University of Arizona. I became friends with several priests. Probably the closest to me was Father Theodore Radtke, who was a priest in Phoenix and later on in Payson, Arizona. When Father Radtke died of a heart attack, the caretaker of his church called me before anyone else. Father Radtke had told her that if anything happened to him, she should call me first.

All this namedropping has a purpose.

I have mentioned enough names to show that I had friends in Tucson from all walks of life, as I did in New York. In Tucson, some of my friends knew who I was in New York, some suspected, and some had no idea. It didn't matter. The fact is, we all got along. I hadn't come to Tucson to subvert the town. The businesses I had were legitimate. I had many real estate holdings. One of them was the Cortaro Cotton Farm in Marana, Arizona. One of the numerous parcels of land I owned (and still own) was a parking lot in downtown Tucson.

I used to be a partner in the Sciortino Italian-American bakery in Tucson.

Politics also drew my attention, albeit as an interested spectator and little else. In the mid 1950s, I attended a political meeting of Democratic Party supporters of Ernest McFarland, who was later elected state governor. Evo DeConcini was there, as was Stewart Udall, the Arizona Congressman who went on to become U.S. Secretary of the Interior in the John Kennedy administration. Udall, Evo DeConcini and I, as well as others, all sat together in the first row.

In 1959–1960, before the Democratic Party National Convention, I met John Kennedy, who was the guest of honor at a reception at the Eloy ranch of my friend Gus Battaglia.

The only other President I have ever met was Franklin Roosevelt, and that was in 1933, the first year of Roosevelt's presidency. In those days, the Tammany Hall political machine still ruled New York City. My contact with Tammany Hall was a politico named Albert Madinelli. He wanted me to pass the word among my people that Roosevelt was the man to vote for in 1932.

After the election, Madinelli said he wanted me to attend a private party for Roosevelt. I hesitated to accept his invitation. Although I was the Father of a Family, I was brand-new at it and but twenty-eight years of age. I felt somewhat bashful.

—I have to meet the President? I asked Madinelli. Aren't you enough?

—Nonsense, Madinelli said. It will be good for you.

—But why should I meet the President?

—Because you and your friends contributed many votes.

I attended the private reception, which, if I recall correctly, was held at a restaurant on Lafayette Avenue in Manhattan. The wait to see Roosevelt was excruciating for me. I could see Roosevelt at one end of the room, a vibrant, charismatic man, posturing, gesticulating, cocking his head sideways, fingering his cigarette holder. I could hear what a glib and clever speaker he was.

I felt self-conscious about my poor English, and when I was introduced to him I really didn't know what to say. Madinelli spoke a few words to Roosevelt, and from then on Roosevelt took charge:

—So, you're the handsome guy they told me about.

Then he pointed to a photographer across the room and shouted,

—Hey, you, take a picture of us.

Turning to me once again, the President said,

—If you ever come to Washington don't forget to come see me. Glad to see you. Thanks for your help.

He was all blarney, but I liked him.

I can't say I liked Kennedy, however. My opinion of John Kennedy is tainted by the low opinion I had of his brother Robert, whom I considered a demagogue when he was U.S. Attorney General. When I shook hands with John Kennedy, I thought of his dad, Joe Kennedy. When I lived in New York, I would sometimes go to Sag Harbor, Long Island, in the summer. This was one of the coves, so I was told, that the Kennedy people used to transport whiskey during Prohibition. How different have been the fortunes of our two families since then!

In 1953, in Tucson, the federal government charged me with concealing information on my naturalization papers. If the government could prove its charge, I faced possible loss of citizenship and deportment.

I had become a U.S. citizen in 1945. On citizenship applications they ask you if you have ever been convicted of a crime. I answered no, which was the truth. The government contended I was convicted of a wage-and-hour violation in the early 1940s.

I consulted my Tucson friend Evo DeConcini, who had just resigned as an Arizona supreme court judge. He agreed that the government was trying to pull a fast one.

—They must like your name, Evo said.

Evo recommended several lawyers. Although these lawyers consulted Evo, Evo preferred to remain in the background.

At my trial in Tucson in 1954, the prosecution contended I had perjured myself on the citizenship application by not mentioning that two Brooklyn clothing factories in which I had an interest were fined a total of $450 for having violated the federal minimum-wage-and-hour law. My defense established, however, that I was only a stockholder in the companies. The companies, not I, were fined for the violation. The companies, not I, paid the fines.

In addition, several of my Tucson friends appeared in court as character witnesses: Evo DeConcini; Mundy Johnson, general manager of Valley National Bank in Tucson; Bishop Francis Green, bishop of Tucson's Roman Catholic diocese; and Harold Patten, U.S. Congressman from Tucson.

They all rated my character as good.

The case was dismissed.

After that, my relationship with Evo became more intimate. He and I did each other small favors. In addition to fresh fruit and fine cheese, I gave Evo ties, a ruby tiepin and a Patek Philippe gold watch.

In May of 1955 Evo was awarded the Star of Solidarity— a decoration by the Italian government in recognition of outstanding achievement. I was the program chairman of the banquet for the formal presentation. I wound up contributing a big share for the banquet through my lawyer, Larry D'Antonio, whom I instructed to work on the arrangements.

In the summer of 1955, Evo and his wife, Ora, visited Europe. I gave them bon voyage gifts of flowers, fruits and candy, and I saw them off at the ship. During this trip, the DeConcinis visited Sicily. Frank Garofalo, who had been the second in my Family, had retired to Sicily. Since Evo had already met Frank in Tucson, I asked Frank to be the guide and helper of the DeConcinis while they stayed on the island.

When the DeConcinis returned to New York in November 1955, I treated them, as well as their son Dino and Evo's secretary, Hassie Baker, to a swanky supper at the Latin Quarter.

In 1957, Evo and his wife attended the twenty-fifth anniversary celebration for my wife and me in Tucson. Later that year came the Apalachin debacle. I asked Evo if it would be better if we didn't see each other in public. I didn't want to embarrass him needlessly.

Evo asked me if I had anything to hide. I said no, that my conscience was clear. Evo then said he didn't care who knew about our friendship.

In 1966, after my well-publicized reappearance in New York following my kidnapping, I was in Tucson for the Christmas holidays. I was eager to see how many of my Tucson friends would remain true. Evo surprised me one morning by visiting my house. Evo wished me a Merry Christmas and asked me how I was.

—Well, I'm not dead.

I couldn't go into details with Evo, but I could see he was genuinely concerned about me. I thought this was the finest moment of our relationship. He wished me good luck in New York.

Several times after that I dropped in to see Evo at his office. Evo's son, Dennis, also a lawyer, had an office on the same floor. Once Dennis invited me into his office to meet some clients. In those days, whenever Dennis DeConcini saw me he acted respectful.

My past friendship with Evo has led to unfounded speculation that perhaps Evo had ties to organized crime. It should be abundantly clear, however, that Evo and I had a clean relationship.

What sticks in my craw is the family's hypocrisy.

The DeConcinis began to estrange themselves from me in the early 1970s. That was a low time for me. That's when my fair-weather friend Evo dropped me.

The break roughly coincided with the election of Evo's son Dennis as Pima County attorney in 1972. Since then Dennis DeConcini has tried to whitewash and disinfect Evo's friendship with me. As you would expect, Dennis DeConcini, now a U.S. Senator, continues to give the impression that his father and I had but a casual, fleeting friendship. Dennis says that although his father knew me, he didn't know who I really was.

It is true that I never leaned across the dinner table and told Evo DeConcini,

—Hey, judge, do you want to know who I am? I'm "duh boss."

Technically, then, Evo and his son could say the DeConcinis knew me only as a retired Wisconsin cheesemaker. But that hides more truth than it reveals. After all I've said about my contacts with Evo (and there were many more I haven't mentioned), it is an insult to Evo's intelligence to say he didn't really know who I was. Evo would have to be a dunderhead not to have a pretty good idea of who I was. Evo was no dummy. He wouldn't have gotten to be who he was if he were that naive.

29

IT MIGHT SURPRISE MY OWN CHILDREN TO HEAR ME ADMIT I haven't been the easiest man in the world to live with. I can be very difficult at times, I know. But Fay always put up with my defects, and, moreover, she knew how to bring out the best in me.

Fay's favorite room was the kitchen. She loved making a meal. It was fun, creative, love in action.

She loved company. She would say,

—Why don't we have some company over tonight?

And I would say,

—Who should I invite?

And she would say,

—Oh, make it ten or twelve people.

When I get up in the morning now, I shuffle to the kitchen to put some coffee on and maybe to cook some oatmeal or a soft-boiled egg. The kitchen is the same as when she was alive. Her homey plaque still hangs on the wall:

RECIPE OF LIFE

Ingredients
1 cupful of love
2 tbs of tenderness
1½ cups of complete inner peacefulness
1 cup of sifted patience mixed with
½ cup of mature understanding.

Tacked to the kitchen wall is a decorative slipper with Fay's eyeglasses in it. It might be the same room, but it can never be the same kitchen as when my Sicilian Rose was alive. Her kitchen always smelled good, even when she wasn't cooking. And it always looked colorful. She'd grow basil and parsley in pots. She'd hang up garlic baskets. She had clay pots the shape of doves. On the side cabinet she'd hang a good-luck witch. In her kitchen you would see saucers of red, yellow and white onions; clusters of red peppers; breadsticks in a glass jar; homemade cookies in a bowl. Fay would set fresh roses from her garden at the breakfast table.

Although as the wife of a "man of honor" Fay had to restrain herself, keep a stiff upper lip and bravely carry on, she was a wonderfully merry woman as well. During our honeymoon, Fay and I were invited for a couple of days to the house of my friend Angelo Palmieri in Buffalo. Don Angelo met us at the door wearing a tuxedo and a top hat. Don Angelo had a huge, bulbous red nose, which gave rise to many jokes about his drinking. At the door of his house, Don Angelo clamped his fingers on his nose, explaining that he had slept all night with a clothespin over his nostrils in order to shrink his nose and make himself more presentable to us. I still remember how hard Fay laughed.

Although respectful toward men, Fay also liked to puncture masculine pretensions. One of the things Fay and the children constantly had to put up with was the conferences at our house between me and other men. Since the conversations often were confidential, I would close the door or take my friends to another room where we could talk in private. When we were through, we'd join the rest of the company. My son Joseph would then wisecrack,

—Is confession over yet?

An especially long conversation occurred one day when my son Salvatore was four years old. The men in conference with me had all left their hats in the vestibule. During our lengthy conference, Salvatore became fascinated with the hats. He threw them on the floor and did a Mexican hat dance over them. When we saw the flattened hats, I scolded Salvatore. The men were infuriated. Salvatore was probably scared to death. But Fay was laughing. She got a kick out of these incidents when a babe could burst the bubble of the "big shots" in her husband's world.

—You big shots, she would scoff. All you do is talk, talk, talk.

Another incident that highly amused my wife involved our German shepherd, Rebel. This incident occurred when I returned to Tucson after a long absence. I had been gone for such a long time that I was practically a stranger in my own household. It was night and Fay was already asleep. The moment I entered the bedroom, I heard a ferocious growl. Then I saw Rebel springing over the bed (he usually slept on the floor next to Fay). He backed me against the wall, snarling and growling at me. For a while it was a standoff. Neither the dog nor I made a move. Fay clicked on her lamp just in time to catch me trying to reason with the animal.

—Look here boy, I said, I'm your master. See this room? It's my room. See this bed? It's my bed. See this woman? She's my wife.

If I stopped talking I thought for sure that Rebel would chew a chunk off my leg, which he almost did anyway. He suddenly snapped at me, snagging his teeth on my trousers. Then he shook his head vigorously, as if he were in a tug of war with my pants leg.

—Fay, why don't you do something?

Fay kept ordering Rebel to back off, but the dog wasn't paying attention. Rebel thought he was defending her from a burglar. He was proud of himself.

—I'm going to kill you, I shouted at Rebel. I'm going to grab my shotgun and kill you.

Fay was unable to stifle her laughter beyond this point.

—Oh yeah? she said. And how do you intend to get to your shotgun?

Finally, my son Joseph came into the room and pulled Rebel away. Fay never let me forget this incident, and she liked to repeat it, accompanied by gales of laughter, whenever she thought I was being too uppity.

It bothered Fay, as it did the children, that I should be away from home as often as I was. Despite my long absences, however, Fay never became a jealous woman. She never feared losing me to another woman. We knew what we had between us, and it was precious. She understood that in the course of a long marriage, a man (as well as a woman) has opportunities to go to bed with someone else. Fay knew the difference between sex and love. And we knew how to kid ourselves about it.

Once I said to her,

—What do you think about moments of attraction between a man and a woman?

She gave me the probing eye. Fay understood that I was alluding to extramarital sex, but she feigned ignorance.

—Moments of attraction? Hmmm.

—You know, between a man and a woman.

—I don't like them, she said in mock disapproval.

—But what if it's just a physical attraction?

—Oh Joe, she said. I trust you, if that's what you mean.

Fay was a practical, down-to-earth woman whose movements were like nature—regular and cyclical. Up at five every morning. Let the dog out. Off to church. Back from church. Make breakfast. House cleaning. Lunch. Afternoon "black coffee" break. Shopping. Dinner.

My schedule, in contrast, was random, like the weather.

She knew just how far she could push me or criticize me without offending me to the point that we would argue. My fastidiousness has been known to drive some people to nervous frustration. Instead of allowing my idiosyncrasies to unnerve her, however, Fay would circumnavigate them. When I grew tiresome, she would simply vacate the room, saying,

—Ah! You're so particular you'd think you were the Pope. I'm going to sleep.

Fay knew how to make her point without challenging me. She was more tolerant, more compliant, more forgiving than I ever was. Only once did I really see Fay take an unyielding position. That was the time my daughter Catherine wanted to marry a young man whom Fay disapproved of. Fay demanded that Catherine stop seeing the young man. Fay told me she had her reasons for being adamant. She didn't volunteer these reasons, and I didn't really want to know them. Her judgment was enough for me. I backed Fay in her row with Catherine, who thought both of us were being highhanded.

As it turned out, Fay's judgment was sound. The young man in question didn't defend himself, didn't stand up to Fay, didn't assert himself. If his ardor for my daughter was all that insipid, that alone convinced me he was unsuitable for Catherine. My girl was a strong, mettlesome woman.

* * *

Salvatore was born in 1932, when Fay was twenty-seven years old. Catherine came to us when Fay was twenty-nine years old. We wanted another child, but for a long time it seemed the odds were against it. Fay became pregnant again in 1941, when she was thirty-six years old. Four or five months into the pregnancy, she had a miscarriage. The doctors told us it would have been a boy. In 1943, when she was eight months into another pregnancy, Fay fell down some stairs and doctors had to induce her labor because both she and her unborn child were in danger. They saved the baby, another boy, but he lived only two and a half days. Perhaps it was for the best, because the baby had defects that would have remained with him for life. We had named this child Calogero (Charles) after Fay's father.

Fay gave birth to Joseph in 1945. She was forty-one years old and had an easy time of it in labor—a minor miracle.

Joseph's baptism party was held at the Canzoneri Hotel near Newburgh, New York. The hotel was near my dairy farm, and I knew the owners, the Canzoneri family. Since it was the off-season, the Canzoneris offered to cook for and accommodate my guests.

We had invited about a hundred people to the baptism party, but when word spread of Fay's long-awaited third child our friends flocked to the hotel. About two hundred people showed up at the baptism party. A friend, the leader of the band which played at the Waldorf-Astoria Hotel, brought the entire ensemble to play for us. Before long, my guests and well-wishers exhausted the meat supply at the Canzoneri Hotel, so I told one of my men to go to my farm and slaughter a steer.

The Canzoneri Hotel was the site of another memorable party, this one focused on Catherine. I wanted to give my daughter a sweet-sixteen party. Once again the Canzoneris offered the use of their hotel. Catherine, knowing the soft spot I have for her, cajoled me into inviting every one of the hundred or so girls who attended her school, Mount St. Mary's-on-the-Hudson. She left to me the formidable task of persuading the school's principal to go along with the idea.

I went to pay my respects to the principal, Sister Mary Vincent. I had already established amicable relations with the Dominican sisters at the school. Since my dairy farm was fairly close to the school, the sisters often accepted my standing invitation for them to visit the farm for outings. Whenever the schoolgirls came, I would provide baskets of fruits, cheese and other dairy products.

At the principal's office, we engaged in some small talk and then I delivered the bombshell about the schoolgirls coming over to the Canzoneri hotel.

—You mean *all* the girls? Sister Mary Vincent gasped.

—Yes, sister. They can stay overnight at the hotel.

Sister Mary Vincent pushed her wimple slightly back and fiddled with her hair.

—Mr. Bonanno, you know . . . you know, that is a very gracious invitation. But . . . ah . . . but every morning the girls must be in church. At six A.M.

I figured she had mentioned this obstacle as a polite way of showing me the impossibility of my request. Undaunted, I said,

—Thank you very much, sister. I'll have the girls in church. Don't worry about that. I'll pick them up in the afternoon. We'll have our party. The following morning they'll all be in church. Thank you once again.

As I left, I asked her to remember me in her prayers.

A fleet of Cadillacs picked up the girls at the school and brought them to the hotel. The bandleader of the Waldorf-Astoria band—a Castellammarese, by the way—again provided the music. The girls, all gaily attired in their flouncy party dresses, danced the evening away. They had a swell time, and so did I, watching them mince and cavort. However, they wanted to stay up too late.

—This is an order now, I said, addressing the entire gathering. Everyone to sleep. Church first thing in the morning.

At dawn the next morning, a parade of Cadillacs rolled in front of the church, in front of which stood Sister Mary Vincent, like a field marshal reviewing the troops. As the girls traipsed inside, I think the sister must have counted every one of them to make sure they were all there.

One of the greatest ironies of my life, for a man who has spent a lifetime being a Father, is that at childhood I was deprived of my own father and in adulthood, because of unavoidable absences, I couldn't always be the father I wanted to be to my own children. They missed me and I missed them.

Like other families, my children and I have had our share of misunderstandings and reconciliations. Our disagreements have never been tepid. The intensity of our disagreements, however, was proof of how much we really cared for each other. Afterward, we would have an increased measure of love and understanding.

My children were exposed to a rich and, at times, extravagant family life. But they also knew solitude, prejudice and exclusion. They bear a name which they cannot escape. They've always lived under the shadow of a famous father.

Catherine, being the girl, lived perhaps the least disrupted life, although that doesn't imply that she suffered less than her brothers. Her private school was near our dairy farm and only a few hours' drive from our Long Island home. We protected Catherine, sheltered her, doted on her. As a child, she was tomboyish—a vigorous, athletic girl who would attempt anything a boy would. Fay, noticing my admiration of Catherine's indomitable spirit, would say that if Catherine weren't a girl, she'd be the spitting image of me.

As she grew into a woman, Catherine sometimes chafed under the strict supervision that Sicilian parents traditionally provide their daughters. We thought it our responsibility to guide her. But at times, I'm sure, Catherine thought we were interfering and restricting her. Now that Catherine has children of her own, I hear her say,

—Dad, now I know what you were talking about.

Salvatore and Catherine were very close as children, and they have remained close in adulthood. I think Catherine understands Salvatore better than any other person. Salvatore, as the oldest son, always held a special place. It takes a special understanding to appreciate him.

Physically, Salvatore is tall and imposing. As a child and as a young man, he was always slim. In mid-life, especially while he was under tremendous stress, he became hefty. Now he's slender again.

Salvatore is the most introspective of my children. Although Salvatore makes his living in the business world, I venture to say that he has an artistic more than a business mind. He has a rare talent. He has the ability to contemplate, which involves fixing your mind on something, grasping it and then rising above it.

During the most important test of his life, Salvatore didn't let himself or me down. After my kidnapping in 1964, Salvatore remained steadfast to his principles. My disappearance sucked him into a world that was not really *his* world. He would probably have preferred to stay clear of my entanglements. But he stood by his father and he stood by his heritage, even though later it would cost him dearly. With me out of action, my son filled the void. It would have been more convenient for him to have shirked his moral responsibilities, but he did not run away from them. He displayed grace under pressure.

Salvatore has expressed his feelings about me—and about what it means to be a Bonanno—in a poem he wrote that means a great deal to me, and which I would like to share.

to dad . . .

let me travel the circle of time
each degree to challenge . . . one by one . . .
until each is conquered.

let me ride the winds to the wilds of nature
to the heights and depths of love
until I understand its passions

then will I commence to know your depth
then will I understand your strength
then will I grasp your wisdom
then will I know you truly . . .

your blood etches the labyrinth of my being
my life . . . my heart . . . my soul . . .
like grains of sand multiplying in time . . .

I stand stately in your shadow
bathed in the wisdom of your nearness
it is an honor I covet . . .

I accept the tumultuousness of life
I accept the sins heaped upon me
I accept the onus yoked around my neck
I accept the stigmas . . . I am a Bonanno . . .

in the bible of Bonanno . . . I stand
    proud . . . next to you . . .
though its pages be filled with live or blood
we are together . . . in love . . . in blood

in the merits of man . . . the good . . . the
    bad . . . the inbetween
we strive for the best . . . whether it be up or
    down or inbetween
a philosophy inscribed from the beginning

you have given me courage
you have given me tolerance
you have given me strength
you have given me honor

you have given me the name Bonanno . . .
the son of Joe Bonanno.

If, for a time, Salvatore was part of my world, my youngest
son, Joseph, never was. Joseph has a different character from
his older brother. Salvatore is the quieter and the more intellectual of the two. Joseph is brassy and more temperamental.
Whereas Salvatore was fond of dressage and the steeplechase,
Joseph liked bronco busting and car racing.

Joseph's formative years were almost devoid of my presence. Joseph grew up largely with his mother. Fay had a special
place in her heart for Joseph. He was her *picciotto*. You couldn't
touch Joseph when Fay was around.

From an early age, Joseph displayed impetuosity and a dare-
devil nature. He would walk on the ledges of hotel windows.
He once got himself locked up in an ice-cream truck and would
have frozen to death if he hadn't been discovered. Later on,
he drove in drag races and participated in demolition derbies.

When Joseph was about two and a half years old, Fay and
I took him to Miami with us. We stayed at the Fontainebleau
Hotel, where we also met the vacationing Vincent Mangano,
Joe Profaci, Albert Anastasia, Stefano Magaddino and Willie
Moretti. These men and I, all dressed in suits, were walking
toward a yacht. Our route took us past Joseph, who was playing

with a hose on the lawn. The little grinning tyke doused us. *Madonna!* we cried out, *Madonna!* When a Sicilian invokes the Virgin Mary, you know he's truly peeved. Joseph was only a child, however. What could we do? Throw him in the ocean? Moretti was the only one who seemed to retain his sense of humor.

—This boy can't fail, Willie said while shaking water from his pants. He's not afraid of nobody.

As he grew older, the problems attending his famous name got Joseph into more serious trouble. In the early 1970s, Joseph was charged as a co-conspirator in an alleged murder plot. It would make this book endless if I went into detail about this case, as well as others involving my sons. However, I do want to make a general observation about this case because it is indicative of the way the government has habitually gone after my sons.

When it comes to me and my sons, the government has been extremely gullible. The conspiracy case against Joseph, for example, was not based on the testimony of an unbiased, third-party witness. It was based on testimony from someone cooperating with the government in order to save his own skin. However, once the Bonanno name is mentioned by someone, the government will stand on its head.

Such was the foundation of the case against Joseph when he went to trial on the conspiracy charge in 1972. The jury trial was held in Phoenix before U.S. District Court Judge Walter Craig. It was a long and complicated case, originally involving ten co-defendants. I had wanted to attend the trial. However, I feared that if my presence in the courtroom became known, the publicity would probably hurt my son. Nonetheless, during the last days of the trial I couldn't refrain from entering the courtroom. I sat in the back row. No one recognized me.

I was there when the jury returned its guilty verdict against Joseph. My heart sank. My younger son was going to be sent to prison. My older son was already in prison at the time. The government had just barely failed sending me to jail in the William Reinke case described later. Unfavorable publicity about the Bonannos appeared in the mass media constantly.

Then something happened to restore my flagging faith in justice. Six weeks after Joseph's guilty verdict, Judge Walter Craig reversed the verdict against him, ruling that the evidence produced at the trial did not support the charges in the government's indictment.

What an extraordinary decision! On reviewing the case, the judge saw that the jury had become confused during the complex trial. The evidence presented by the government, the judge recognized, could not possibly support the murder-conspiracy charge.

As soon as he released my son, Judge Craig came under strong criticism in the press for being soft on criminals. Everyone thought of me and my family as the devil's first cousin. Judge Craig had made a courageous decision, and he stuck to it.

As I am proud of Salvatore, so I am proud of Joseph for not turning his back on his father and for not rejecting his roots. Joseph could have changed his name, left the country and started a new life. He has chosen to remain and be called Joseph Bonanno. Joseph is not junior to anyone. He is a man in his own right.

30

My dream of retiring peacefully in Tucson was a delusion. Such was my reputation as a "Mafia chieftain" that people became engrossed with their image of me and overlooked the man who actually lived in their midst. My reputation preyed on people's minds. I was more "real" to people in their imaginations than I was in the flesh.

Nowhere was the desire to paint me in lurid colors stronger than in the hearts and minds of law-enforcement agents, particularly the FBI. To this agency, as well as to the public and to public officials, I was a Bad Man. The fact that I had never been convicted of a crime they attributed to my cleverness. The government thought I had eluded them and made a laughingstock of them in New York. When I moved to the West, government agents there continued stalking me.

From 1968 to 1980, various law-enforcement agents would not rest until they got me. I had no enemies in my world anymore to worry about. We were finished with each other. What I had was the government constantly on my back.

In the summer of 1968—the same year I had my third heart attack—I was trying to get used to the idea that I was a senior citizen in my golden years. In previous years, I would stay in Tucson mainly in the winter when the weather is beautiful. From then on I would pretty much be staying there year-round, even in the summer when the weather is beastly.

My wife and children felt very much at home in the West. Salvatore had gone to boarding school, high school, and college in Arizona. My second-oldest, Catherine, came to live in Tuc-

307

son after she graduated from parochial school, Mount St. Mary's-on-the-Hudson in upstate New York. Joseph attended Catholic school in Tucson and a military school in California.

Fay loved Tucson, where she could garden the year round. We had friends in the community, we owned property and businesses, and we participated in the community life.

An indication of our commitment to Tucson—you might say our eternal commitment—is my ownership of a corner tomb in the mausoleum that dominates the center mound of Holy Hope Cemetery in Tucson. A sculpture of Christ, made entirely of Carrara marble from Italy, stands on the mausoleum altar. My contribution toward erection of the mausoleum entitled me to my family space in it. Fay's body is buried there. One day my body will lie there too.

In Tucson I looked forward to spending more time with my wife and children. After Apalachin, my life-style rarely permitted me lengthy stays at home, as much because of my duties to my greater Family as to avoid publicity and harassment by lawmen. By the end of the 1960s, my immediate family and I needed to spend more time with each other. I wanted to make my children understand me better so they themselves wouldn't become alienated from their own name and heritage. My retirement put me close to all my children.

We were Westerners now, living on the American frontier.

On July 22, 1968, Salvatore happened to be visiting me in Tucson. He had dinner at home that evening, and afterward he and Joseph left the house. Fay didn't feel well and she went to sleep early. I remained in the living room, watching television.

When Salvatore returned he went outside to smoke a cigar. My backyard patio was surrounded by a brick wall, along one side of which was a side road. Alongside the driveway wall was a brick barbecue pit and grill. On the side of the house facing the patio was a porch. In the corner of the porch, near the doorway to the patio, I kept a loaded shotgun.

At about nine-thirty that night, I heard the porch door open.

—Salvatore? I said.

—It's me, Salvatore responded. I came in to . . .

He didn't finish his sentence. Then I heard the porch door slam loudly. Salvatore, I was thinking, that's no way to close a door. I heard a shotgun blast. A split second later, I heard an explosion. And soon after that, another, more forceful explosion shook the house.

My wife came screaming into the living room, her hair full of glass slivers. The explosion had shattered the bedroom window, and the glass had showered over her as she lay sleeping. She was bleeding in several spots, but wasn't seriously hurt. I rushed to the porch to check on Salvatore. I met him coming into the house, shotgun in hand. He was bleeding from the face.

—In a second I'll explain, he said, looking at his mother in anguish.

Salvatore didn't want to talk in front of his mother.

—But I want to hear, Fay said, nearly hysterical.

—Go in the next room, I told her. Salvatore's all right. I'll tell you about this later. Go ahead and have a little cognac.

Soon, and predictably, the Tucson news media were speculating that the bombing of my house signaled the outbreak of gang warfare in their pristine town. In no time at all, Tucson's mayor, its U.S. Congressman and one of its U.S. Senators, all of whom didn't know any more about the incident than the police or I did, nonetheless spoke out against organized crime, spouted homilies and expounded whatever pet theory they held. FBI Director J. Edgar Hoover, no less, promised his full cooperation in solving the case.

My house had not been the only one bombed in 1968. Two bombs had exploded on the Tucson ranch of Peter Licavoli, damaging a carport and four vehicles. Pete, a man of my Tradition, was also in retirement. And before that, in the beginning of July, a shotgun blast had shattered the picture window in the Tucson home of the daughter of Sam Giancana, the Chicago bigwig. After my home was bombed, a bomb was tossed (but fizzled out) behind Pete Notaro's house while his wife and daughter were inside. Notaro, the cousin of my dear friend Joe Notaro, is a Tucson businessman.

One hasty conclusion, if you were observing this from the outside, was that the bombings represented, or gave the impression of, a quarrel between Licavoli and me. But that made no sense. Pete and I were both retired; my son Salvatore was the godfather of Pete's son. We had no reason to be angry with each other.

When we were alone Salvatore told me that he had come into the house for a drink of water, but no sooner did he enter the porch than he saw an object sailing over the patio wall. Salvatore ran outside, having picked up the shotgun from the corner of the porch. When he glanced over the patio wall, he saw a person's silhouette on the side road. Salvatore had time to pull off only one shot in that direction. Then the first of two explosions knocked him over and he banged his head. He was pretty sure he had hit the person running away on the side road.

We inspected the damage. One bundle of dynamite sticks had landed on the garage roof. The second bomb had been thrown down the chimney of the barbecue pit, blasting a huge hole in the patio wall as well as destroying the chimney and the outdoor stove. The explosions had roused our neighbors. They congregated around our house. Then the police department and the fire department arrived.

I couldn't satisfy the police when they asked me questions, even if I wanted to. I lapsed into sarcasm.

—Gentlemen, I said, do you want to know the truth? I had a beautiful barbecue here. Why did they do this to my beautiful barbecue? My barbecue never hurt anyone.

While the police kept asking me questions, I talked about the lovely view I had from my patio of the Catalina Mountains.

Another plausible but equally inaccurate inference was that the bombings represented a fight between Sam Giancana and me. Some of my own friends gave credence to this story, because, as was well known in my world, Sam Giancana and I did not admire one another.

However, I dismissed Giancana as being behind the bombings. By the late 1960s, Giancana was in trouble not only with the law but with people in our world. Giancana was on his way out of Chicago.

I had to conclude then that the bombings were the work of outsiders, men outside my Tradition. Probably the strongest point in favor of this conclusion, over and above what I've already mentioned, was that if someone from my world had wanted to kill me he would have gone after me and not have wasted time eliminating my barbecue pit.

A slight break in the mystery came later in the summer of 1968. In my household, we had decided to post a lookout to watch cars which passed by the house. One night, one of my lookouts detected a slow-moving car with its headlights off creeping down the street. Salvatore, who happened to be in Tucson again, grabbed my shotgun and hid in front of my house, awaiting the car.

The car was being driven by a man; a woman sat on the passenger side. As the car inched its way to the front of my house, the woman opened the door. The car stopped alongside a car parked by the curb directly in front of my house. I had instructed everyone not to shoot unless absolutely necessary. The lookout, who was hiding behind some bushes, made a noise with his foot. That alerted the driver and the car screeched away. Everyone ran for cover inside the house. We expected an explosion under the car parked by the curb.

We waited and waited, but there was no blast. After a while, a neighbor walked across the street from her house, squatted by the parked car, reached under it and grabbed the package there; then she knocked on my front door and handed the bundle of dynamite sticks to my wife. An unspent fuse dangled out one end of the bundle. Our terrorists apparently had sped off without having enough time to light the fuse properly.

Salvatore had had enough presence of mind to memorize the license number of the terrorist car. We traced the number and found it was registered to a fictitious company in Phoenix. When we tried to find the company's location, we discovered that the address given on the license registration did not exist. Someone had taken extraordinary precautions against being traced.

The presence of a woman in this strange affair was proof positive once again that the bombings had nothing to do with my world. In my Tradition, we don't involve women in men's affairs.

The mystery had become macabre. Who was after me? Pranksters? Vigilantes? A deranged feminist?

About a year after the spate of bombings, we heard on the radio that Tucson police had arrested two suspects in connection with the bombings.

The arrested pair were Paul Stevens, who worked for an aircraft company in Tucson; and William Dunbar, who was an auto mechanic and jack-of-all-trades. Both were in their mid-twenties. Stevens' right arm still bore evidence of a wound;

A MAN OF HONOR

this was the man who had been shot in the alley alongside my house on the night of the bombings.

At first, the men refused to say if they had any accomplices. But a friend of theirs materialized. She was a woman in her early twenties. She testified in court that she had been told the man behind the bombings was an FBI agent!

Less than a month after the arrests, a Tucson-based FBI agent by the name of David Hale resigned his post. He refused to comment on his resignation. The FBI refused to comment. The U.S. Justice Department refused to comment.

Stevens and Dunbar pleaded guilty to the bombings and eventually told the full story. The following background information is based on their testimony, the statements of other Tucson residents involved in the affair and my personal knowledge of what happened.

FBI agent Hale, who had been known to myself and my sons for years, was a particularly obnoxious man. On the several occasions that Hale questioned my son on official business, he was always crude and crass. He seemed to go out of his way to show his contempt for us when the situation didn't require it, when he could have been matter-of-fact. I considered him an extremely offensive man with a one-sided view of men in my world. Hale had once gone around town speaking at a series of seminars. He billed himself as a "Mafia expert." He went around town saying that the "Mafia" (read Joe Bonanno) was infiltrating Tucson.

In the summer of 1968, Hale recruited Tucson businessman Walter Prideaux in a bizarre plan to rid Tucson of its unsavory (read Sicilian) element. The plan called for a series of bombings that would confuse us and lead us to suspect one another. According to the plan, we then would go after each other, eliminating ourselves.

In addition to Prideaux, Hale also conscripted the aid of Dunbar, an employee at an auto-supply company of which Prideaux was sort of a general office manager. Next to join the team was Stevens, a friend of Dunbar's and a former marine with some knowledge of explosives.

FBI agent Hale, Prideaux, Dunbar and Stevens all participated in the bombing of the Licavoli ranch and of my home. In the latter incident, Hale and Prideaux remained in the car, while Dunbar and Stevens skulked outside my patio wall, lit

312

the dynamite, threw it over the wall and ran away. Stevens, however, was wounded by my son.

A thorough investigation of FBI agent Hale's part in this affair never took place. Dunbar and Stevens, after pleading guilty to their part in the bombings, were each fined a measly sum, less than $300 apiece. Prideaux and Hale were never charged.

After Dunbar and Stevens were fined and set free, I was shopping alone in a supermarket near my home when I saw Walter Prideaux coming toward me. Since it was known that I often frequented this supermarket, I figured Prideaux had come there on purpose to talk to me.

Prideaux and I were not strangers. He was a man in his fifties. He had some sort of teaching experience and had briefly tutored my son Joseph for his college entrance exams. Joseph, who liked to tinker with cars, often went to Prideaux's auto-parts store. Joseph invited Prideaux to my house once, and that's how I first met him.

Like many other businessmen I've known in Tucson, Prideaux acted cordial, even fawning, around me. Not only do these businessmen enjoy telling their friends they "know" Joe Bonanno, but they are most eager to discuss, when they can slip it into the conversation, possible business ventures.

At the supermarket, Prideaux said that Hale had approached him in the summer of 1968. Hale knew Prideaux had met me, and he wanted Prideaux to cooperate in Hale's investigation of me. Prideaux told Hale he had nothing against me. Then the FBI agent told Prideaux that if he didn't cooperate with the FBI, Hale would get Prideaux in trouble by releasing information on a business deal that Prideaux had been involved in.

Prideaux wasn't confessing to me out of the goodness of his heart. The man was both ashamed at what he had done and also fearful of what might happen to him. He wanted me to know the full story so I wouldn't get the wrong idea about him.

—He had me, Prideaux told me. Hale had me.

I wished no harm to Prideaux, and I told him so. He had been used by Hale. Before we departed, Prideaux said that Hale, in justifying the bombing mission to his accomplices, intimated that they were working under sanction of "the Department in Washington"—the FBI.

I now want to quote from an article about me that appeared

in the February 12, 1978, issue of *Parade* magazine. In that article, one of the few times I've allowed myself to be interviewed, I told reporter Michael Satchell about the bombing incident and he checked out what I said with Prideaux and Dunbar; Satchell was unable to trace the whereabouts of Hale. Prideaux and Dunbar told Satchell that an automatic rifle and a crossbow had been purchased to assassinate me and my friend Pete Notaro. I quote from the article:

"Hale wanted to kill Joe Bonanno with the rifle, but I told him that if he really wanted to hurt the old man, a better target would be his son, Bill," Prideaux said. "The crossbow was to be used to kill Notaro."

It doesn't take a genius to realize that the FBI threw a blanket of silence around this whole affair. *There was a cover-up.* That is irrefutable. FBI Agent Hale was a public servant. He almost got away with murder. How come there was no public outcry of indignation? Heaven forbid, what happened to me might someday happen to *you!*

31

WHEN MY SON JOSEPH ASKED ME IF HIS FRIEND COULD COME live with us, I was most reluctant about agreeing to the idea. I am wary of strangers. Fay, however, took Joseph's side. She had taken a liking to Joseph's friend. She chided me good-naturedly about my reluctance to have him come live with us temporarily.

—You only want to be around other Italians, she said.

—Sicilians, I corrected her. I only feel safe around other Sicilians.

When I thought it over, however, I decided my xenophobia was probably foolish. I relented and allowed Joseph's friend to live under our roof.

Blond-haired David Hill was a tall, lean Texan, about twenty-one years old, when Joseph introduced him to me in 1968, sometime after the bombing of my house. David had come to Tucson to visit a former girlfriend. Joseph, who was attending the University of Arizona at the time, knew the girl, and she introduced the two young men. David had no place to stay in Tucson, and that's why Joseph invited David to our house.

I grew to like David. He had delicate facial features and a perceptive mind. His background was interesting. David's grandfather was a Texas Ranger; David once showed me his grandfather's badge. David's other grandfather was a Presbyterian pastor. David's father, David L. Hill, had been a member of the Flying Tigers during World War II, and retired from military service with the rank of general.

David's parents, who lived in San Antonio, were well off financially. He seemed to have everything going for him: money, brains, looks and an impeccable background. Yet he was at a stage in life in which, as young people like to say, he was trying to find himself.

At the age of twenty, David rebelled against his father's discipline and left home. He went to Europe on the pretext of studying art. But in the evenings he would frequent private gambling clubs, dressed in white suits and cowboy boots imprinted with the map of Texas. Eventually, his money ran out and he returned to the United States.

David knew who I was and was curious about me. He undoubtedly considered it an adventure to be living with me. After staying with us awhile, his interest shifted from Joe Bonanno the public figure to Joe Bonanno the private man. David, it soon became obvious, was a young man in search of a family.

In return for our hospitality, David didn't mind helping out around the house. He would frequently drive me around town when I went out on errands. At home, he became very attached to Fay, and to her cooking. I could tell that the close home life he was experiencing with us was something he missed in his own home. We became surrogate parents for him.

David and I would have long meandering discussions on the patio about philosophy, poetry, religion, life in general. At night, looking up at the twinkling sky, we would talk about distance and the stars. These dialogues stimulated me. I didn't often run into people with whom I could talk on this elevated level. David was an intellectual, and a spiritual young man as well. It was as if I found in him the side of me that I've never been able to fulfill—my intellectual, artistic side.

I taught David that family was the cornerstone of the Sicilian way of life. David was a smart fellow; his mind contained abundant ideas, but his ideas were all scattered, like refuse in a landfill. I told him that in order to integrate his ideas, he had to adopt a system of values. This involves committing yourself to some ideas, making other ideas secondary and abandoning some ideas forever. Having values means making choices.

I grew so fond of David Hill that I introduced him to cognac. One day, looking extremely nervous, David told me:

—Throw me out if you want, do whatever you like with me, but I have to confess why I came to stay at your house.

David went on to explain that in the period between the day he first met my son and the day he became my house guest, the FBI had approached him. This wasn't surprising, I thought, since the FBI made it a practice of harassing just about anyone my sons or I associate with.

—They described you as one of the worst guys in the world, David said of his encounter with FBI agents. They made you out worse than they do in the newspapers.

At first, David related, the FBI had warned him to stay away from me and my son. Then the FBI persuaded David to wangle his way into my house, keep alert, gather information and relay the information to them. David agreed, partly out of a sense of public service but mainly out of caprice, so he could have an experience, an adventure. Therefore, when David Hill first came to sleep at my house, he was an FBI informant.

After a while, the FBI agents became vexed with David because he wasn't bringing them the kind of information they were looking for.

—They would ask me what we talked about, David said, and I would say we talked about literature and the stars. They didn't believe me.

Perhaps thinking that David was holding out on them or acting as a double agent, the FBI agents pressured David to produce information. They told him if his relationship with me became public, it would bring shame on his parents and would ruin his future career.

Then David began telling the FBI agents to leave him alone. He squarely told them he didn't want to be their informant and that he was going to remain at my house for as long as I would let him. The FBI agents told David that by associating with me he would become implicated in my affairs and would get in trouble with the law.

—I would never have believed that my own government would treat me this way, David told me.

After his confession, I simply told David:

—You stay here. There's your room.

He came up to me and kissed me.

David did not escape the FBI's resentment at his unwillingness to remain an informant. After he stopped cooperating, his name began to appear in the newspapers. In these articles he was described as my chauffeur or my bodyguard.

David remained in my house until the end of 1969, at which

time my son Joseph also left home to start a new life in California. David was uncertain of what he wanted to do. I had noticed in David a strong spiritual inclination. One of my favorite spiritual figures is Billy Graham, to whose evangelical work I've contributed for years, and I urged David to emulate him.

David didn't immediately follow my advice. After leaving Tucson, he roamed through Latin America, searching for enlightenment. But when he returned to Texas, he began studying the Bible, and eventually he joined Billy Graham.

After he took up his religious calling, David talked highly of me to Billy Graham. In 1974, while Dr. Graham had a speaking engagement in Phoenix, he kindly took time out to visit me in Tucson. David Hill was with Dr. Graham when they came to my home.

We ate and prayed together. We also chatted freely over a wide range of subjects. Billy Graham is a beautiful man, a man of peace. He impressed me as being alert and clear-minded. He asked me to call him Billy, and I told him to please call me Joe. I was very grateful for his visit.

Every year I receive a Christmas card from Ruth and Billy Graham. He once sent me an autographed Bible. He also sent me a book entitled *How to Be Born Again*. When my wife Fay died in 1980, Dr. Graham telephoned to express his condolences. He and his wife also sent a beautiful crystal vase filled with roses.

32

MY DOCTOR WOULD SNAP HIS FINGERS THREE TIMES.

—That's all it takes Joe. One, two, three. You could go just like that.

He made that dire observation in 1969, a year after my third heart attack. I was sixty-five years old. My doctor had already eliminated salt and sugar from my diet, and he had forbidden me to smoke cigars. He also wanted me to avoid intense excitement, but it always stumped him when I asked him,

—How?

One morning in November 1969, Fay went to early mass at SS. Peter and Paul Church, a few blocks from our home. My wife was a well-known parishioner. Not only did she go to mass daily, but she also involved herself in numerous charitable activities.

Both Fay and I have belonged to many charitable or civic organizations. I'm a life member of the Elks, as well as a perpetual member of the Society for the Propagation of the Faith. I'm a member of the Knights of Columbus. In Tucson, I was one of the stockholders of the El Rio Country Club and used to be a member of the Italian-American Club. I've contributed to St. Mary's Hospital. I can't begin to count the money I've donated to the Roman Catholic archdiocese in Tucson. Just west of Tucson, in Casa Grande, stands St. Anthony's Church, whose former pastor, the Reverend Sylvio Ross, was a friend of mine. A large metal crucifix adorns the top of the church—I paid for that crucifix.

When Fay returned from church, she didn't have a chance

to close the front door behind her before FBI agents charged through the entrance and told her they had a warrant for my arrest. An FBI agent barged into my bedroom before I could get out of bed. He said he was looking for letters. Throughout my house, law agents searched through drawers, desks, consoles, cabinets and cupboards.

I felt sick, and I told Fay to call my doctor. After he arrived, he examined me and gave the first of three injections to calm me. The doctor told the FBI that I was in no condition to be moved outside the house.

—But he has to be arraigned, the agent in charge protested.

—Look, the doctor said, my main obligation is to keep people alive, and I say he can't be moved under any circumstances.

The law agents continued scouring through the house. In the meantime, my criminal lawyer, Albert Krieger, had been alerted. Krieger arrived that afternoon from New York. He had obviously come to Tucson in a rush, for he was unshaven and he was wearing a sweatshirt and sneakers.

The law agents completed their search without finding any of the letters they were looking for. Although disappointed, they still looked forward to the thrill of arresting me and arraigning me. I felt weak and dizzy. All my worries seemed to converge on me. My kidnapping court case in New York was still pending. My son Salvatore was facing a court case in New York himself, and he had become a target of the IRS. The situation with the crazed FBI agent David Hale was still current. My wife's health was failing. And now this.

My bedroom became an ad hoc courtroom. Among those present at my bedside arraignment were my doctor and my lawyer, the FBI agents, two assistant U.S. attorneys, a court recorder and a federal magistrate.

I was groggy from the tranquilizer shots the doctor had administered. During the reading of the charges against me, I remained in bed, under the covers, wearing my comfortable pajamas and my silk bathrobe. The magistrate allowed me to remain free on $50,000 personal recognizance bond.

The government charged that I and my friend Pete Notaro (who was arrested the same day I was) conspired with Charlie

Battaglia, a Tucsonan, to obtain Battaglia's release from prison through illegal means.

Battaglia was a prisoner at Leavenworth Federal Penitentiary. He was serving a ten-year sentence on an extortion charge involving a Tucson vending-machine company. I knew of Charlie Battaglia, but I had never had any business with him.

While in prison, Battaglia came in contact with a "jailhouse lawyer"—another inmate who did rudimentary legal work for the other prisoners. Battaglia believed that his conviction had been based on information gathered by illegal wiretap, and he apparently instructed the jailhouse lawyer to pursue the matter and work on the necessary writs and motions.

Battaglia's jailhouse lawyer was a prisoner by the name of William Reinke, who had no formal legal training but had acquired some knowledge of the law in prison libraries. The government's case against me, Pete Notaro and Battaglia was based *entirely* on Reinke's testimony.

In the resulting trial in U.S. district court in Tucson, Reinke testified that while he was a prisoner at Leavenworth, Battaglia asked him to smuggle letters out of the institution. Reinke testified that he agreed to smuggle letters in order to learn about Battaglia's illegal activities. Reinke hoped that the information he gathered would be useful to the FBI and would put him in good standing with his parole board.

Many of the letters that Reinke said were dictated by Battaglia were read in court. The subject matter of the letters was vague, on the whole. The prosecutor therefore asked Reinke to interpret the letters. Reinke said he understood the letters because, so he contended, Battaglia would explain the content of each letter after dictating it. As Reinke explained them, the letters outlined various illegal maneuvers and the use of force to help Battaglia acquire information he sought for his appeal.

Some of the letters allegedly were addressed to Pete Notaro and some to me. According to Reinke, I was supposed to be helping Battaglia in all these maneuvers. In exchange, Battaglia was supposed to see to it that FBI agent David Hale would be killed.

Reinke testified that he was supposed to be a central figure in the plot to kill Hale. Reinke said that upon Reinke's release from prison, Battaglia wanted him to get in touch with Jimmy Fratianno, often described as a professional hit man. Fratianno was supposed to kill the FBI agent, Reinke claimed. After contacting Fratianno, Reinke said he was supposed to pick up nearly $1 million worth of jewels in Los Angeles, keep part of the money for himself and use most of it to purchase narcotics in Chicago. Then he was supposed to go to Phoenix and set up a research center which ostensibly would do legal work for lawyers. The legal center was supposed to be a front. Actually, Reinke said, it would be a distribution center for narcotics and other contraband in Arizona. Reinke added that Arizona was to be divided into spheres of influence, with Battaglia taking the northern part of the state and my son and I taking the south. William Reinke was supposed to be our go-between.

William Reinke was a shifty character with dirty-blond hair, a sallow complexion and darting, furtive eyes. His criminal record showed that he had been convicted for transporting stolen vehicles, burglary and passing phony checks. He was a specialist at forging documents and had been a con man all his life.

My defense lawyer was Albert Krieger. His strategy was to ask Reinke a barrage of minute and seemingly innocuous questions. The more Reinke talked the more he impeached his own testimony. The more he talked the more his testimony could be contradicted by others. It soon became obvious that Reinke's original testimony represented a severely modified version of the truth.

The full story was this:

In August 1969, Lieutenant John Brown, the Leavenworth security officer, had called Reinke to his office to ask Reinke why he had been receiving large money orders. Reinke told Brown he was receiving money orders from his parents. Brown was skeptical of Reinke's story. Reinke was a known jailhouse lawyer, and Brown suspected that Reinke might be receiving money orders for legal work done for prisoners. Brown told Reinke that if the money orders came from other inmates then Reinke could be punished.

Reinke was in a jam. Punishment could consist of loss of "good time." Every prisoner is allotted a certain number of days off his sentence for good behavior, as many as ninety-six days a year. Since Reinke was serving a five-year sentence, he faced the loss of 480 days of good time if he violated prison rules. Reinke's request for parole had recently been denied. The loss of good time would have been devastating to his hopes of getting out of prison early.

Reinke told the security officer that the money orders were coming from Charlie Battaglia. Reinke also said that Battaglia had asked him to smuggle letters out of the institution. Upon hearing this, Brown told Reinke to accept the letters from Battaglia.

Throughout August and September of 1969, Brown received copies of handwritten letters that Reinke said had been given to him the night before by Battaglia. Reinke also told Brown that Battaglia was receiving incoming mail surreptitiously. Reinke started giving Lieutenant Brown forged letters, incoming and outgoing, which detailed several illegal schemes. When FBI agents were called into the case, they must have been overjoyed—the letters seemed to give the government the means with which to prosecute that elusive, clever man Joe Bonanno.

In October 1969, the letter-smuggling apparatus suddenly stopped. Reinke, together with all his belongings, was taken from his cell and transported to another prison. Lieutenant Brown had discovered that Reinke had lied on several matters. The money orders that Reinke said were coming from Battaglia were discovered to be coming from other inmates at Leavenworth. The letters that Reinke had said were handwritten by Battaglia were discovered to be in the handwriting of two different persons, not Battaglia.

Once removed from Leavenworth, Reinke admitted he had lied to Brown about the money orders. Reinke also admitted the letters were not in Battaglia's handwriting but in the handwriting of cellmates who regularly did copy work for Reinke. But Reinke insisted that he had not lied about the authenticity of the letters themselves.

As the trial progressed, Reinke's testimony, shaky from the start, began to totter. For example, all the illegal schemes that Reinke said Battaglia had outlined to him—the research center, the killing of FBI agent Hale, the pickup of jewels—were to be put in effect after Reinke left prison. Reinke was supposed to make all the necessary contacts.

Reinke's parole, however, had been denied. The man had no prospect of leaving Leavenworth in the immediate future. Why would Battaglia have entrusted Reinke with a mission outside the prison if Reinke was going to be in prison for a long time?

Reinke had testified that he was to be the go-between for Battaglia and me when we carved up the state for distribution of narcotics. I had never met Reinke, had never seen him. And yet I was supposed practically to make him my partner upon his release from jail. That didn't sound very realistic.

Reinke had testified that Battaglia would dictate the letters in the prison yard. Reinke would take down Battaglia's words in shorthand, using a pad and pencil. The jailhouse lawyer testified that he would then return to his cell, write out the shorthand abbreviations in longhand and give the writing to his "copy men."

One of these "copy men" was Daniel Grindstaff, a cellmate of Reinke's. Grindstaff testified that the letters he copied for Reinke contained many cross-overs and corrections. Words and phrases had been scratched out, as if Reinke was composing the letters himself.

This if from Grindstaff's testimony under questioning by defense lawyers:

Q—Did you ever see Reinke writing letters during the month of September, writing letters as he sat in his bed?

A—This man wrote constantly, constantly.

Q—Did you ever see Reinke in the [prison] yard in August and September of 1969?

A—That was a rarity too. He very rarely went to the yard.

Q—Did you ever see Reinke walk around when you did see him in the yard with a pencil and pad?

A—That would be more or less against the rules.

Q—Did you ever see Reinke carry a pencil and pad when he walked around the prison?

A—No, because—say—

Q—Go ahead.

A—If you get caught with a pencil and pad walking around like this they will arrest you for booking baseball or football or something.

In light of this testimony, it is hard for me to believe that Reinke went to the prison yard with pencil and pad to copy letters allegedly dictated by Battaglia.

The letters that Reinke handed prison officials contained numerous names, addresses and personal references. The defense contended that those letters were forgeries. But if Battaglia had not dictated these letters and if he had not provided the names and references in them, where did Reinke get the information?

From the testimony I concluded that these letters, and all the details in them, were fabricated from information gathered from Battaglia's legal papers (which Reinke had in his cell) and from Arizona newspapers (which were delivered to Reinke's cell).

Considering the numerous discrepancies in Reinke's story, I find it amazing that the U.S. Justice Department brought this case to trial. The whole case was based on circumstantial evidence provided by only one man, Reinke. The prosecutors knew Reinke was a forger. They knew Reinke's medical file identified him as a "psychopathic liar." They knew Reinke had already lied to prison officials.

Why did the U.S. Justice Department prosecute this case? I believe that somewhere along the line, though they knew they had a flimsy case, the prosecutors nonetheless went through with it, hoping that the sensational contents of Reinke's letters, coupled with my bad reputation, would persuade a jury to find me guilty.

The jury acquitted me, as it also did Notaro and Battaglia, but I have no reason to gloat on that score. In a sense, what really saved me was not Judge Walsh's fairness nor the jury's common sense, although they both exhibited these qualities. Neither was I really saved by the defense lawyers, although they did a brilliant job. What really saved me was William Reinke's own words, which the jury didn't believe. Except for that the government might have won its case.

33

By the beginning of the 1970s, I found myself besieged by lurid publicity, tormented by overzealous lawmen, misunderstood and abandoned by friends, haunted by my reputation and, for a time, estranged from my own sons.

My relationship with Joseph had become strained. In the autumn of 1969, he dropped out of college and decided to leave Tucson. He wanted to be on his own. Joseph was the most Americanized of my children and the farthest from me in age. He had trouble understanding some of my principles and my philosophy. And I didn't approve of some of his ideas and his life-style. I also didn't like some of his friends. Joseph, then in his mid-twenties, was in an independent mood, eager to live outside the shadow of his name. Our separation was not warm.

I had some painful advice to give him before he left. I told Joseph to associate with Americans and to avoid Italians from my world. Once Joseph went to California, I knew that people from my world might seek him out and that he might get into trouble. Even if he did nothing wrong, his mere association with such men would lead to unfavorable complications with the law. I went so far as to tell him to stay away from his brother, Salvatore, who had settled in the San Jose area.

I had never thought I would say such words to a son of mine. Fay cried.

When Joseph left Tucson, Salvatore was serving time at the Terminal Island federal prison camp for first offenders. His conviction, which was in New York, stemmed from a credit-card-fraud case. Because he lived in San Jose, Salvatore was allowed to serve his prison sentence in California.

326

The credit-card case came about because someone double-crossed Salvatore. The fraud was on Salvatore, not by him. This trial was amply described in *Honor Thy Father* by Gay Talese.

The 1971 publication of this book, which dealt with Salvatore's life up to then, caused a rift between Salvatore and me. I didn't talk to him for about a year.

The book itself centers on Salvatore's relationship with me and on his involvement in my world in New York, mainly during the time of my disappearance. If the book had dealt only with this, I would have no objections to it. Whatever Salvatore wants to say about his life is up to him.

But the book goes much further. As Talese tells Salvatore's story, he interweaves a narrative about me and also a history of the "Mafia" in America. The narrative about Salvatore is fine. That's because Talese got this information from Salvatore himself. But since I didn't, and wouldn't, talk to him for purposes of the book, Talese had to get information on me from secondary sources. He turned to public records, district attorneys' files, newspaper clippings, etc. Consequently, in writing about me, he repeated information that was tainted and distorted to begin with.

The timing of the book's publication also riled me.

In the early 1970s, when the book came out, I had more than enough problems of my own, inside and outside my world, without having to contend with a blockbuster best-seller.

I had only a vague idea of what to expect in the book. I knew that Salvatore and Talese were cooperating on some sort of literary project. They talked about wanting to write a "classic." But I didn't know too much more. I had presumed the book was going to be mainly about Salvatore.

In August of 1971, someone handed me a copy of *Esquire* magazine with a full-page photograph of me on the front cover. I recognized the photograph—it had been in a family photo album which I had lost track of. The caption said:

"Honor Thy Father . . . The Story of Joe Bonanno and His Son by Gay Talese."

If this was a book about Salvatore, why was my picture on the cover? By emphasizing me over Salvatore, the magazine editors apparently revealed their impression that Talese wrote with equal validity about both me and my son. If they got that impression, so did a lot of other people.

When referring to *me, Honor Thy Father* has only the patina of authenticity. However, since my son is quoted in it, it gives the impression that the book had my tacit stamp of approval as well. People both in my world and outside assumed that the book did indeed represent my point of view, despite any disclaimers to the contrary.

The truth is that Salvatore had agreed to be interviewed on his own; he was almost afraid to tell me about it. As I later learned, he had decided to talk to Talese at a time in his life when he didn't know if the next day he might be dead. If he did become a fatality in the Volcano, he wanted to leave something behind so that posterity might understand him better. However, the book aggravated Salvatore's already precarious position with the law. More publicity was the last thing either one of us needed in the early 1970s. The book increased both Salvatore's visibility and mine. It made us even more desirable targets for speculation by newsmen and law officials.

In 1972, Joseph and Salvatore (who was already in jail on the credit-card case) were found guilty of extortion to collect a debt. Without knowing the facts of the case, you're apt to consider this conviction proof of some sort of heinous conduct. It was nothing of the sort. It was a case of someone who had borrowed private money but didn't repay it. When this person got in trouble with the law for something else, he made a deal with the government for leniency in exchange for squealing on those who had helped him.

Joseph and Salvatore were sentenced to five years in prison. Salvatore was allowed to serve his new sentence concurrently with his old one. Salvatore was released on parole in 1974. In the meantime, Joseph went to prison in 1973 and was released on parole in 1975.

On their release from prison both my sons had trouble making a living. They were free from prison but not free from government harassment. If Joseph went to apply for a job, the FBI would talk to the prospective employer; the mere presence of the FBI discouraged employers from having anything to do with Joseph. Salvatore had similar experiences. After prison, he had some speaking engagements on the college lecture circuit and he tried his hand in public relations. Salvatore's situation was aggravated by the fact that because of his tax-debt problems, the IRS could appropriate almost all his income.

Eventually, Salvatore became associated with a firm called U.S. Mattress Co. and Joseph with a company called Kachina Fashions. Neither of these companies did well, and they were struggling enterprises throughout their existence.

In 1976 Fay wanted to do something to help the children, and she talked me into lending $20,000 to U.S. Mattress. Fay signed the check and I had my lawyer, Albert Krieger, draw up the necessary papers. In 1978 I lent another $20,000 to Kachina Fashions.

In the summer of 1978, both my sons returned to prison for violating their probation. Without getting into details, I just want to say that the government used petty technicalities to get them back in jail. Salvatore remained in prison until the spring of 1980. Joseph stayed in jail until the very end of 1979. When he went to prison the first time in 1973, Joseph had just gotten married. Of the first seven years of his marriage, he spent almost six of them in prison.

The Christmas of 1976 was one of the few times my entire family was together during the 1970s. My sons were out of jail. Salvatore, Joseph, Catherine and their families all came to Tucson for the holidays.

Fay had been in poor health from a blood disease. At one point, she was taken to the intensive-care unit of a hospital. Her weight had dropped from about 140 pounds to under 100 pounds. Doctors gave her a week to live. Fay's sisters and our children came to Tucson expecting the worst. Thanks to the will of God, Fay recovered. Although she was a frail version of her former self, at least she was with us.

Fay and I were both seventy-one years old during that Christmas season. We were at an age when the end of all things becomes a tangible reality. Despite our troubles we had our three children and our seven grandchildren. The Bonannos still had each other.

The rest of society had largely abandoned us. Many so-called respectable people shunned us. The prime example of this estrangement was Evo DeConcini, but I merely use Evo as being emblematic of a whole assortment of people. When the tempest over me blew furious, even the Cracchiolos positioned themselves further from me. When the Catholic church officials in Tucson became embarrassed because I had been a major contributor to the mausoleum at Holy Hope Cemetery, they made overtures to find out if I would give up my family vault in the mausoleum.

34

Don Bolles, an investigative reporter for the *Arizona Republic* in Phoenix, was murdered in 1976 when a bomb planted under his car blew up.

Because of the method of execution, the slaying immediately gave rise to speculation among police and journalists that the killing had something to do with the "Mafia." The Bolles slaying led to the formation of a group, Investigative Reporters and Editors (IRE), which launched an open-ended "investigation" into Arizona's criminal element. Eventually, thirty-six journalists from twenty-seven news organizations throughout the country participated in the project. Spearheading the project were Bob Greene, a reporter for *Newsday,* and Tom Renner, a so-called organized crime expert, also of *Newsday*.

The IRE said its goal was to continue the investigative work begun by Bolles. Self-appointed an self-mandated, the IRE produced a series of lengthy articles published in newspapers nationwide. The articles were also compiled into a paperback book.

Not long after the Bolles murder, I received a letter from John Rawlinson, an *Arizona Daily Star* (Tucson) reporter on leave to work with the IRE group.

Rawlinson, a former city policeman, had previously written about me in his newspaper in an article of minor importance. But since he had succeeded in interviewing me where others had failed, he gained a reputation as one who had access to Joe Bonanno.

In his letter, he assured me that he didn't think I had anything to do with the Bolles murder. Then he asked for my help in identifying the culprits, the assumption being that I knew about every crime committed in the state anyway.

He also offered me his protection. If I cooperated with him, Rawlinson assured me anonymity.

The IRE series was published early in 1977. Here are some excerpts from the article about me:

Federal mob watchers estimate that 200 members of organized crime families are currently living in Arizona. And the biggest most important man of all is Joe Bonanno, today probably the most powerful Mafioso in America, the undisputed Boss West of the Rocky Mountains.

Today, the Bonanno organization moves kilo amounts of heroin through Pueblo, Colo., for shipment to St. Louis.

Now that Bonanno's two sons are established in San Jose in Northern California, the old man appears to be making a concerted effort to gain control of the rackets in the entire state.

Federal and local police officials who have plotted all these moves and traced all this action are convinced that Joe Bananas, from his home base in Arizona, is in the midst of bringing it all together under the mantle and protection of the Bonanno family.

None of these statements concerning me has ever been substantiated. The reporters were merely mimicking the unfounded speculations of lawmen, from whom they received this distorted information.

Here's another example of this yellow journalism:

There's a telephone booth outside the Lucky Wishbone, and after carefully closing himself in, the old man fishes a handful of quarters from his pocket, drops one into the slot and begins chatting quietly. In Sicilian.

Exactly what the old man says is known only to him and
whomever he calls. *But chances are* the conversation is
about narcotics, guns, girls, gambling, money, deliv-
eries, meetings, couriers, payoffs, discipline, punishment, and other elements of Arizona's biggest growth
industry, organized crime.

What kind of comic book were these reporters writing?
These reporters never overheard me talk in a public telephone
booth.

I want to say a few things about my making calls in public
telephone booths.

It's my right, of course, to talk in private with whomever
I want, whether in Sicilian or Swahili. However, since I'm Joe
Bonanno, I have to assume that my house phone is always
wiretapped, whether legally or illegally.

I also have to assume that whomever I call from my house
phone, law-enforcement agents will link that person, rightly or
wrongly, with some sort of clandestine and nefarious activity.
If I call my Aunt Tilly to ask her how everything is going,
police will interpret this as meaning, "Did the heroin get there
all right?" I don't care who you are. If you had to worry about
every single word that came out of your mouth, as I do, you'd
use a public phone too.

I wasn't the only one outraged by the IRE series. Several
people mentioned in the articles filed multimillion-dollar def-
amation suits. The *Arizona Republic,* Bolles' own newspaper,
refused to print the stories.

After the IRE series had done its damage to the reputation
of many innocent people, the perpetrators of the Bolles murder were eventually arrested, tried and convicted. None of
them was of Italian background. The murder had nothing to do
with the "Mafia." The culprits were not foreigners but Arizonans.

In addition to Bolles' murder, the summer of 1976 was
significant in my life also because Dennis DeConcini, the son
of my fair-weather friend Evo DeConcini, successfully ran for
the U.S. Senate.

Dennis' political career had moved at an astronomical rate.

He started out being a lawyer, with an office across from his dad's. He later became an administrative aide to Arizona Governor Sam Goddard, a friend of the DeConcinis. In 1972 Dennis was elected Pima County attorney.

The county attorney's job was only a steppingstone. While at that job, however, Dennis established the Narcotics Strike Force, which was supported by state and federal funds. Dennis was the strike force administrator. He appointed Terry Grimble, a lawyer in the county attorney's office, to be strike force director.

The Narcotics Strike Force was an attempt to combat the narcotics traffic along the Arizona-Mexico border. Since I've never had anything to do with narcotics in my life, I didn't pay too much attention to this new agency when it was established.

Dennis was running for the U.S. Senate when Bolles was murdered in June 1976. The very next month, while on the campaign trail, Dennis said (*Arizona Daily Star*, June 8, 1976):

"America has not only tolerated organized crime, we have utterly been romanced by it. The death of Phoenix reporter Don Bolles may be the end of that for Arizonans and other citizens throughout the country."

I hadn't heard Dennis speak so vehemently against organized crime before. I was very sensitive to his remarks, because whenever anyone in Arizona talks about organized crime the inference is that he's talking about Joe Bonanno. I ascribed Dennis' words to political rhetoric, however. After all, if you're a politician it's pretty safe to come out against Communism, government waste and organized crime.

My misgivings intensified when I read the following in the *Arizona Republic* on October 28, 1976:

> Dennis DeConcini, whose campaign for the U.S. Senate has emphasized his record against organized crime as Pima County Attorney, has received a number of campaign contributions from individuals identified as associates of organized crime.
>
> DeConcini told the *Arizona Republic* he has returned some of the money and that he intends to return more of it. . . .

334

DeConcini said he has returned $50 donated to him April 15 by Victor Tronolone, longtime accountant for Mafia chieftain Joseph Bonanno and Peter Licavoli.

Dennis had gone beyond normal campaign rhetoric here. Victor Tronolone is my accountant, but does that make him an "organized crime figure"? Did Dennis mean to imply that Tronolone's $50 contribution (to a campaign fund that was in the hundreds of thousands of dollars) was an attempt to influence him on behalf of organized crime? Tronolone was a friend and an accountant not only to me and Peter Licavoli but also to Dennis' father. At the same time that Dennis was rejecting Tronolone's harmless contribution, Tronolone was handling (and continued to do so until about 1980) some of Evo De-Concini's business tax returns. Does that make Evo DeConcini an "organized crime figure"?

The year after Dennis was elected U.S. Senator the subject of his father's friendship with me again came up. On June 5, 1977, Dennis appeared on a local televised news conference. A reporter named Leasa Conze asked him about Evo's friendship with me, and Dennis responded that his father had first met me in 1948. When asked how many times Evo and I had seen each other since 1948, Dennis replied that it had been only a couple of times, just a few. Dennis said his father knew me only as a cheese man from Wisconsin. Dennis also said that his father and I hadn't been that friendly.

About a month after this television appearance, I had a letter prepared and mailed to Dennis, and a copy of it also went to his father, Evo. The letter is dated July 13, 1977:

Dear Senator DeConcini,

As a person who has known you for many years and has followed your career with interest, I viewed your election to the United States Senate with pride. I believed that the youth I knew, and the man I know, would enter the Senate and bring with him, in his public appearances, the traits of character which we all have traditionally held dear.

Throughout history, many have breached their oath and principles in order to further political aims and ambitions. The truth has been distorted and warped in order

335

to justify immediate self-centered goals. If we are men of principle, then there can be no deviation from truth in its purest form. Thus, I was dismayed on seeing a report on Channel 13, here in Tucson, in which you had cast aside past relationships with cavalier disregard for your own integrity. In truth, there can be no wrong. A practiced deceit, however, flaws our character forever.

Mark Twain hid great wisdom behind a humorous facade, and it is with respect that I quote from *Advice to Youth:*

"An awkward, feeble, leaky lie is a thing which you ought to make it your unceasing study to avoid; such a lie as that has no more real permanence than an average truth. Why, you might as well tell the truth at once and be done with it. A feeble, stupid, preposterous lie will not live two years—except it be a slander upon somebody. It is indestructible, then, of course, but that is no merit of yours."

I hope that your disavowal of those whom you counted as friends was a careless gesture, unintended and one which will be corrected, if the opportunity were to rise in the future. I am not ashamed of having known you, and feel that you should not be ashamed of having known me.

I pray that your career will be marked with great achievement and benefit to our country. I also pray that you will always comport yourself with integrity.

Most respectfully,
Joseph Bonanno, Sr.

I never received an answer, not from Dennis nor from Evo.

BOOK VI

The Grand Inquisition

35

THE GRAND INQUISITION INTO MY LIFE—THE STORY LINE OF
the last chapters of this book—brings to a conclusion the un-
relenting government attempts to destroy me.

Up to now, the government had failed to get me. They tried
to deport me in 1954 by falsely contending that I had perjured
myself in my citizenship application. They tried to put me in
jail after the Apalachin debacle. They tried to jail me when I
went to Canada. They tried to pin something on me before and
after my kidnapping. All to no avail.

In Tucson, an FBI agent bombed my house and made plans
to have me murdered. The FBI made an informant for a while
out of my son's friend David Hill. The U.S. Justice Department
tried to imprison me on the word of the convict and con man
William Reinke. After the murder of reporter Don Bolles, law-
enforcement agents and their journalist conduits launched what
amounted to a propaganda campaign against me.

After each failed attempt, new individuals carried on the
campaign against me. Whatever I could say in my defense was
met with skepticism or mockery. On the other hand, all investigations of me were complacently and smugly praised, as
if I were a monster or the devil himself.

What follows is a description of a Byzantine investigation,
spanning five years, involving several law-enforcement agencies in two states, and resulting in my conviction in 1980 on
a charge of conspiracy to obstruct justice.

The Grand Inquisition into my life began in 1975 when Eugene Ehmann resigned his job as an FBI agent in Tucson and then joined the Narcotics Strike Force. He did this so that he might collect my garbage.

While Ehmann was still with the FBI, as court testimony later revealed, he and FBI agent William Christensen had discussed the possibility of operating what police call a "trash cover"—collecting someone's garbage surreptitiously. However, the two FBI agents were unable to get permission to proceed with the project. Trash covers are sensitive operations because they invade a person's privacy. If undertaken at all, trash covers need solid justification. Ehmann and Christensen had no justification whatsoever for collecting and searching through my garbage. They had no probable cause to connect me with a specific crime.

Over the years the FBI's inability to put me behind bars was seen as a great blemish on their reputation. Given this climate within the agency, it is not suprising that FBI agents have made me the object of their ambition. The FBI agent who "got" Joe Bonanno would not only preserve the agency's image but also win great recognition for himself.

On joining the Narcotics Strike Force, Ehmann received approval for his garbage collection project from strike force director Terry Grimble. The project also received the blessings of Dennis DeConcini, who, as Pima County prosecuting attorney, was the strike force administrator. Federal guidelines on trash covers are more stringent than state guidelines. As an agent for the Narcotics Strike Force, a state agency, Ehmann was therefore able to implement the same plan to collect my garbage that he couldn't put into operation with the FBI.

The trash cover began in December 1975 and was to last until April 1979. Ehmann, along with other agents, would drive by my house on garbage-collection day, very early in the morning before the regular garbage truck came by. My metal garbage cans stood outside my garden gate, where I would place them the night before. The law agents would pull alongside my driveway in a van. Then they would open the van's side door, take my garbage can inside the van, empty the garbage can and refill it with other trash the agents had brought along for that purpose. (The agents didn't want to leave my garbage can empty in case someone in my household should accidentally discover the contents were missing.) The law agents would set the refilled garbage can back on the curb and drive away.

Then the messy task began. The agents would have to sift through the refuse in the hope of finding something to build a case against me.

When Ehmann & Co. dug through my garbage looking for my torn private notes (my private thoughts on paper), they placed themselves in league with agents of a police state. They took it upon themselves—and my condemnation embraces not only Ehmann but his boss, Terry Grimble, and Grimble's boss, Dennis DeConcini—to invade my privacy, without any probable cause.

After collecting my torn-up notes from my garbage, the law agents had to piece the notes together again. Then they faced the awesome task of reconstructing my thoughts.

It is difficult enough trying to interpret the notes of an ordinary person writing in standard English. In trying to decipher my notes, the law agents faced an even more formidable task in that I sometimes write in Sicilian. Also, when I write in English, I'm capable of some pretty atrocious grammar.

This language barrier led to numerous wrong interpretations of my notes, which in another context would be funny. For example, the law agents collected a note from my garbage in which I wrote, "Call Titone work and pay scannatore." In Italian, the word *scannare* means "to cut" or "to slaughter." The law agents therefore assumed that in this note I was reminding myself to pay a man named Titone for having slaughtered someone.

However, in my Sicilian dialect, a *scannatore* is a cutting board, used by innumerable Italian housewives to cut and roll dough. That was how I used the word. Titone is not an underworld assassin. He is a carpenter in Tucson who had made a cutting board for my wife's kitchen. I was reminding myself to pay him for the work.

In searching through my garbage, these law agents turned up a lot of tidbits and scraps which titillated their imagination. If I jotted down a reminder to call someone in New York, on reading this note the law agents would assume the worst: that I was calling New York to give someone an order or to arrange an illicit deal or to demand a payoff or whatever their police mentalities came up with.

Although these vultures scavenged through my garbage for

naught for several years, they continued their search because of the many side benefits from their operation.

In discussing policemen, it is best to distinguish between street cops and paper cops. Street cops are the ones who work for a living. They're out on the streets, responding to calls, chasing criminals, settling disputes, putting their lives on the line. A man of my Tradition can have respect for a street cop.

Then there are paper cops, the bureaucrats of their profession. Paper cops spend most of their time at a desk, shuffling papers, doing research, making out reports, filing for government grants and the like. Paper cops rarely put themselves in dangerous situations. They have normal working hours, for the most part. Paper cops like to sit around and chew the fat. They are very big on holding conferences and attending crime seminars. Of course, paper cops wouldn't be seen dead in a uniform.

Eugene Ehmann was a paper cop *numero uno*. Terry Grimble was a paper attorney *numero uno*. Dennis DeConcini was a paper prosecutor *numero uno*.

The following excerpt is from an *Arizona Daily Star* article dated April 19, 1979. The article refers to events concerning the Bonanno investigation in 1976:

> By May 1976, Ehmann and Grimble knew they should share information they had obtained with other agencies. Dennis DeConcini, then Pima County attorney and now a Democratic U.S. Senator from Arizona, obtained funds to bring police intelligence agents from New York City, Los Angeles, Long Beach and San Jose, Calif., as well as from the Royal Canadian Mounted Police, the Colorado Strike Force and the FBI for a two-day meeting.
>
> "Everyone was sworn to secrecy," said a police source who attended the meeting. "Those that didn't want to participate could leave, but could say nothing about what they heard."

Barely six months after the trash cover had begun, Ehmann, Grimble and DeConcini were already hosting mini-conventions at taxpayers' expense. As I said, the garbage notes the Narcotics Strike Force had collected didn't amount to anything, but the mere fact they had been collected from Joseph Bonanno gave them ersatz value. The two-day meeting (a welcomed vacation in Arizona, I'm sure, for all those who attended) allowed Ehmann & Co. to show off before their fellow agents. It also permitted Ehmann to disseminate information based on his erroneous interpretations of my garbage notes. Thus, agents from all over the country received misinformation about me from the start.

The most interesting facet of this meeting, however, is contained in the phrase "obtained funds." To a paper cop, obtaining funds is, in a sense, more important than actually solving crimes. As long as the paper cop can obtain funds for his project or for his agency, his job is assured. One of the easiest ways for a law-enforcement agency to obtain funds is to raise the specter of organized crime.

The public-relations value of investigating Joe Bonanno gave the strike force an aura of glamour and helped it receive more government funds than it deserved or knew what to do with. It also gave someone like Ehmann celebrity status among other paper cops. Indeed, it gave him a job. Indirectly, I was putting bread in this joker's mouth.

The IRE articles concerning organized crime in Arizona began to be published in March 1977. I have already written about the shoddy job this reporting team did on me under the supervision of *Newsday* reporters Bob Greene and Tom Renner.

On March 29, 1977, Ehmann & Co. found a note in my garbage which said, "Void Bob Greene on Peter Licavoli." In the same batch of garbage they also found the note which said, "Call Titone work and pay scannatore." And they found a third note which said, "Memo for Albert Krieger. Tell I have all the bombing newspaper clips. I have all the 1970 investigation Bolles that they now continue."

I've already explained the meaning of the second note about Titone, the carpenter. The third note was a memo to my lawyer, Krieger, whom I wanted to remind that I had past newspaper clips in case I decided to sue the IRE group for libel. The first note is simple to interpret if you knew what was on my mind at the time. In that note I'm saying to myself that what Bob Greene wrote about Peter Licavoli was void, null, empty, full of hot air.

Two days after they obtained the "Void Bob Greene" note, Ehmann and Grimble flew to Long Island and presented the background of their investigation to *Newsday* editors, who agreed to keep the information confidential. On the same day, Suffolk County, New York, authorities were told that Joe Bonanno might try to have Greene murdered. Greene was placed under the protection of the Suffolk County police. Every morning for the next month police checked Greene's car for bombs and followed the journalist to work.

What a farce!

In 1976 I had traded my Cadillac Seville for a Cadillac Fleetwood at Paulin Motors, a Cadillac dealership in Tucson. The salesman who handled the transaction was Gordon Deneau, with whom I developed a friendship.

Gordon told me he had always dreamed of owning his own Cadillac dealership. He asked me if I would be his partner in such a venture. I told him no. I was retired and had no mind for this sort of enterprise anymore.

About a month after I rejected his offer to become a business partner, Gordon introduced me to the new general manager of Paulin Motors. Gordon said that the two of them were going to buy a dealership. I wished them luck. As I later found out, Gordon had introduced me to his business partner in order to make him think that I had invested money in their venture. Gordon did this to discourage people from cheating him. I was unaware of this.

During one of Gordon's visits to my house, he told me that he had learned from General Motors that a Cadillac dealership was for sale in Vallejo, California. Gordon explained how he was going to swing the deal; he even jotted down on my notepad how much money he expected General Motors to lend him and how much money he and his partners expected to raise. Gordon said he wanted the advice of someone in California who could acquire information about the Vallejo dealership. Since Vallejo is in the San Francisco Bay area, the same general area where my sons reside, Gordon suggested that my son Salvatore might be able to help him out.

As a favor to Gordon, I told him I would ask Salvatore to check into it. And later, Salvatore, through friends, located the lawyer handling the sale of the dealership. He discovered that the owner of the dealership had recently died and that the sale had to go through the executors of the man's estate, which can be a lengthy process. When I relayed this information to Gordon, he said the Vallejo dealership didn't look promising but that he was still interested in obtaining a Cadillac dealership elsewhere.

The reader might be curious to know why I was helping Gordon when I wasn't going to be his partner. What was in it for me? The answer is simple. Friendships are the fulcrum of my life. When I judge people, I don't say to myself, "Oh, he's a lawyer, he's a doctor, he's a car salesman." I first of all consider whether that man is my friend or not, whether I can trust him or not. After that, anything is possible between us because we are friends. We care for each other. We do favors for each other.

In helping Gordon, I was only doing what comes naturally. I was building goodwill. I was doing him a favor. Who knows how, or in what form, or if ever, he could return that favor? It didn't matter. If I could be of help to Gordon, someday he might be of help to me. What's so difficult to understand about that?

Shortly after Gordon began visiting me at my house, he was paid several visits by FBI agents. The lawmen tried to pump Gordon for information about me. Gordon told them I was his friend and that we never discussed anything illegal. The FBI agents kept returning to pester Gordon. It got so bad that Gordon told them he would call his lawyer if they didn't stop hounding him.

This takes us up to 1977. We must keep in mind that throughout this time, not only were law-enforcement agents surveilling me and trying to turn my friends into informants, but they also were searching through my garbage. Among the items they found during this period were notes, some of them in Gordon's handwriting, that referred to Cadillac dealerships in California.

The agents of the law naturally became suspicious of all these references to car dealerships. I must stress that these agents who sifted through my garbage lived, for the most part, in a fantasy world, in a Disneyland of the mind. To them, I was Joe Bananas. I was a mobster they had read about in mass-media accounts. I was a gangster like the gangsters they saw in the movies. Many of these agents were half my age. They weren't even alive when I was active in the Volcano. And yet they presumed to know me, to interpret my thoughts, to judge me.

On seeing references to car dealerships in my trash notes, these comic-book sleuths made the following inference:

Joe Bonanno wants to launder underworld money through Cadillac dealerships in California.

This false inference was circulated among various law agencies. The Narcotics Strike Force in Tucson told the FBI in Tucson, which in turn told the FBI in California. The more they talked about it the more they liked the idea that I was setting up "fronts." After a while, they forgot it was an assumption. They convinced themselves it was fact.

By the spring of 1977, or earlier, the Narcotics Strike Force believed I wanted to purchase Cadillac dealerships in California to launder "dirty" money. The strike force agents thought this dealership business represented a really big break, something they might prosecute me for.

The trouble was that they had no proof of anything. They had a bunch of crumpled trash notes and that's all, not the proof they needed to go to court. What they desired was a tape of a telephone conversation where I discussed this Cadillac-dealership business with someone in California. If they had that, they thought, they'd be making headway.

The agents needed court permission to wiretap my conversations. However, to get such permission, since I used public telephone booths most of the time, the agents first would have to prove to a judge that I did indeed use a specific telephone booth to make my calls.

The agents figured that if they attached a "beeper" device under my car, they could follow me and keep a record of the telephone booth I used.

In early May 1977, Ehmann & Co. recovered a trash note which disclosed that I intended to have dinner at a Tucson restaurant by the name of Scordato's. On May 18, 1977, as court testimony later revealed, an Arizona law agent by the name of Robert Lutes installed a beeper device under my car while I was dining at Scordato's.

To give you an idea of the close cooperation between the Narcotics Strike Force and the FBI, court testimony showed that while the beeper was being installed, strike force agent James Liddiard and FBI agent William Christensen were across the street in a van, watching the operation.

Five days *after* the beeper was installed, strike force agent Edwin R. Richards filed a false affidavit before a judge and received permission to install the beeper. Richards had lied simply to further the Bonanno investigation.

Also in the summer of 1977, the FBI and the Narcotics Strike Force decided they should try to obtain authority for an eavesdropping warrant so they could legally tap my telephone conversations. They submitted the necessary paperwork, but their application lingered and nothing came of it. They therefore abandoned the wiretapping application and opted instead for an application to install a "pen register" on five separate phones they believed me to be using for clandestine communications. Pen registers are electronic devices which record telephone numbers being dialed but not the conversations themselves. The lawmen hoped that through a combination of garbage notes, the beeper and the pen register they could come up with enough justification to persuade a judge to grant them an eavesdropping warrant.

Strike force agent Richards was successful in obtaining court authority for the pen registers. In the affidavit he submitted to justify the operation, Richards said the strike force investigation was aimed at my alleged plan "to set up car dealerships and leasing agencies through the Central California Valley." According to the same affidavit, my sons and I were supposed to be buying the businesses through front men who were to file false loan applications so it would not be known that the Bonannos were the true owners.

The pen registers were installed. Richards and other agents monitored the devices from the house garage of Terry Grimble, the strike force director. A few weeks after he received court authorization to install the pen registers, Richards decided to go one step further. He attached an eavesdropping device to the pen-register wires, a simple operation. This now enabled him to listen in on my conversations.

He had no authority to do this. He was breaking the law.

The agent's wrongdoing didn't surface until a Pima County sheriff's deputy reported it to his superiors in July 1977. It took a sheriff's deputy to report the illegal wiretapping. Does that mean the other strike force agents or FBI agents didn't see what was going on in Terry Grimble's garage? How odd that the agents most involved in the Bonanno case saw no wrong-doing, but a sheriff's deputy did.

Later in 1977, Edwin R. Richards, a law-enforcement official for twelve years, resigned from the Narcotics Strike Force. He pleaded no contest to a charge of illegal wiretapping and eavesdropping. Another investigator, James Liddiard, was fired from the strike force on charges of insubordination and neglect of duty. Liddiard, it was charged, knew about the eavesdropping but didn't report it to his superiors.

At the time, the incident intensified my conviction that the law agents who were snooping on me would stop at nothing to destroy me. Other than that, however, I couldn't connect the Richards wiretapping with anything else. I had no idea at the time that this was but one small segment of a Grand Inquisition into my life.

On October 5, 1977, after Richards had pleaded no contest, the following article appeared in the *Arizona Daily Star*:

The taps were reportedly aimed at Bonanno and other suspected crime figures during an investigation of drug and prostitution activities in California and Alaska.

The FBI, Pima County Sheriff's Dept., County Attorney's office and the four-county Narcotics Strike Force have spent more than a year and a half investigating local crime figures for involvement in prostitution, drug traffic and stolen property between Arizona and Alaska.

What did I have to do with prostitution, drug traffic and stolen property? Nothing.

36

AFTER GORDON DENEAU HAD LOST INTEREST IN THE CADILLAC dealership in Vallejo, California, he told me he was still interested in buying a Cadillac dealership somewhere else in the state. Salvatore had told some of his friends to keep an eye out for Cadillac dealerships that might be for sale. But the whole matter was left up in the air. It didn't press on either my mind or my son's.

This was the situation as of the summer of 1977, when one of the leading characters of this soap opera made his entrance. His name was Lou Peters. He owned a Cadillac dealership in Lodi, California, which is about seventy-five miles east of San Jose.

In June 1977, Peters was contacted by a Lodi contractor who sounded him out on the possible sale of the Cadillac dealership. The Lodi contractor—who was a friend of a friend of Salvatore's—mentioned the Bonanno name in his discussion with Peters. Perhaps thinking that he was doing Salvatore a favor but not knowing that Salvatore had no interest in locating a Cadillac dealership, the Lodi contractor told Lou Peters that he would introduce him to Salvatore Bonanno.

Two days after this initial discussion, Peters met with FBI agents and agreed to gather information for them undercover.

Even now that Lou Peters is gone (he died of brain cancer in 1981), I can't think about the man without having it churn my stomach. He is an example of a smug and deceitful do-gooder.

I've always been fascinated with the motives of people who

decide to become police informants. After all, it's a dirty business. Informants often have to lie, cheat and play duplicitous roles. Sometimes, informants become double agents, leaking information to both sides. Any way you look at it, it's an indecent occupation.

Some people become informants to save their own skin. That didn't apply to Peters. What, then, made Peters do it?

He certainly didn't need the money. I think Peters even turned down any payment for being an FBI informant. Indeed, Peters was a millionaire, according to *People* magazine.

Peters later bragged to newsmen that he became an informant because he thought it was his patriotic duty. After he agreed to become an FBI informant, Peters divorced his wife so that neither she nor their daughters would be at home. After the divorce, Peters moved to an apartment in Stockton, which the FBI outfitted with all sorts of audio and video recording equipment.

Peters would have us believe that he was so imbued with patriotic fervor that he was willing to live apart from his family and divorce his wife, all in the call of duty. There's something missing here. Why would a wealthy man with a family and status in his community undertake such an extraordinary assignment? Most normal people would have been content to let the FBI do the police work, especially when it came to "Mafia" investigations.

Peters gave away his true motivations at my 1980 trial, in which he testified. Peters admitted that he had had a lifelong fantasy of becoming an FBI agent.

After becoming an informant, Peters met and tried to ingratiate himself with my son Salvatore. However, Peters soon discovered that none of the Bonannos was interested in buying Cadillac dealerships.

In the summer of 1977, neither Salvatore nor I had any interest in Gordon Deneau's search for a dealership. I was having problems in Tucson: That was the summer the illegal wiretaps of my phone conversations were revealed. Salvatore also was having his problems. The IRS, for instance, claimed he owed them something like half a million dollars. We both had other things to worry about than Cadillac dealerships.

Now that Peters had met Salvatore, Peters had to figure out

how to keep in touch with Salvatore. Peters and the FBI, therefore, had to come up with another pretext for Peters to remain close to Salvatore and our friends. For a while Peters kept calling on Salvatore just to offer to do favors for him, any kind of favors. Peters offered to lend cars, sell cars, buy cars . . . anything at all. As a result of these visits, Peters met Jack DiFilippi.

Jack is the son of the daughter of my Uncle Giuseppe Bonanno of Sicily. That makes Jack my first cousin. But in Sicily, Jack would be referred to as my nephew. He refers to me as his uncle. Jack, who's in his middle fifties, came to this country in 1955 and became a successful commodities broker. Jack makes a living finding and packaging deals for investors. He had a spotless police record.

That's the real Jack DiFilippi, a relative and a friend. In my 1980 trial—in which Jack was a co-defendant—the prosecution depicted him as a "loyal soldier" of the Bonannos. Jack was portrayed by the government as a "Mafia money man" who supposedly attracted shady money from overseas.

Peters' acquaintance with Jack came at an opportune time. Peters couldn't turn up anything on the supposed Cadillac scheme. Therefore, Peters tried to interest my son and his friends, Jack DiFilippi in particular, in a plan to customize Pontiac automobiles and sell them under the name Barchetta.

The FBI had instructed Peters to look for large amounts of money coming in from out of the country. Peters tried to obtain financial backing for the plan by claiming to my son's friends and to Jack DiFilippi that he already had orders for the customized cars.

The truth was that Peters never had any orders for the Barchetta car. But since he didn't know Peters was a phony, Jack became interested in Peters' plan and began working on it with him.

The first time I met Lou Peters was in 1978, when I again went to California to visit my children. My sons, Salvatore and Joseph, were both in trouble with the government.

In 1978, the government capriciously revoked my sons' probation, and by the summer of that year they both were sent back to prison to serve out the remainder of their sentences on an extortion charge. Salvatore was sent to prison camp at McNeil

Island, Washington, and Joseph was sent to prison camp at Safford, Arizona.

Also that year, although I didn't know it at the time, federal agents had mounted a sweeping investigation into the activities of my sons. The investigation was being handled by the U.S. Organized Crime Strike Force in San Francisco. This was a federal strike force, as opposed to the Narcotics Strike Force, which was a state agency in Arizona.

The investigation of my sons, as I later learned, was a very general one. One of the things the federal strike force was interested in was the relationship of my sons to several businesses they were associated with, including U.S. Mattress Co. and Kachina Fashions.

When I went to California in 1978 I merely wanted to be near my sons as they faced their troubles.

In the midst of this, like a groupie hanging around a rock-and-roll band, was Lou Peters—a respectable man with impeccable credentials who acted as if being a friend of the Bonannos was for him the greatest privilege in the world. His attention flattered us. He seemed very solicitous, always asking,

—What can I do for you? Can I do anything at all?

Peters even attended Salvatore's court hearing on his probation revocation.

After Salvatore and Joseph were sent to prison, my wife and I remained a short time in San Jose in order to soften the impact of our sons' departure on their wives and children. Lou Peters kept coming to see us. Once he drove a Cadillac to San Jose and left it there for my use. When he came back to pick it up, I told Peters I appreciated his kindness but didn't need another car. Peters asked if I wanted to see his dealership in Lodi. I didn't see any reason why I should. Peters kept insisting.

He seemed well-meaning, this tall, burly man who was totally American in his manners and outlook. Both Salvatore and Jack DiFilippi were his friends. Peters had solid business credentials. I thought that one day, after Salvatore got out of prison, Peters might be of help to my son. If this Peters is a friend of Salvatore and a friend of Jack, I told myself, maybe I ought to humor him, if nothing else.

I therefore agreed to let him drive me to see his dealership in Lodi. When we got there, Peters said,

—This is the place Bill wants to buy.

I gave Peters a hard look and said,

—Salvatore doesn't want to buy your dealership. How is it possible? He's in prison. He needs money for lawyers. He owes money to the IRS. Salvatore has no money. How is he going to buy a dealership?

Peters immediately dropped the subject, and we didn't talk about it the rest of the day. Peters already knew Salvatore wasn't interested in his dealership, of course, but he wanted to draw me out on the subject, hoping perhaps that I would reveal something to take back to the FBI.

From Lodi, Peters took me to his apartment in Stockton. Although I didn't know it, the apartment was bugged by the FBI. Throughout our conversation, Peters kept asking me,

—What can I do for Bill? Is there anything I can do for Bill?

I presume that my conversation with Peters was recorded. If Peters had been my confidant in some underworld scheme to buy dealerships, that evening would have been a perfect time to discuss this business with him. But whatever was recorded apparently was of no use to the FBI. This conversation between Peters and me in his apartment was never alluded to in my 1980 trial, and the recording of this conversation was never introduced as evidence.

The next morning, Peters drove me back to San Jose. Once again he offered to leave his Cadillac with me. He said I could take it with me to Arizona. I told Peters no thank you. We parted.

I couldn't pin it down at the time, but I was beginning to feel uneasy about Peters. For one thing, he was being too nice. However, I had other things on my mind, and I stopped thinking about him.

37

IN THE FIRST WEEK OF SEPTEMBER 1978 I LEFT CALIFORNIA and returned to Tucson. Waiting for me back home, like a grim present, was a subpoena from a federal grand jury in San Francisco. The subpoena required me to produce any corporate records I had of two firms which my sons were associated with.

Because of my failing health, I was excused from having to travel to San Francisco. The subpoena, therefore, was momentarily in limbo.

That a federal grand jury in San Francisco should be seeking such corporate records from me meant that the government had opened a third front in its war against me.

The first front was the Narcotics Strike Force in Tucson. Ehmann & Co. had been rummaging through my garbage since December 1975 (unknown to me, of course). As of September 1978, these agents had found absolutely nothing of an incriminating nature. All they had found was my personal notes and memos, which they interpreted in their own biased and capricious fashion.

It was from my garbage notes that Narcotics Strike Force and FBI agents in Tucson formed the impression, among many other false impressions, that I was attempting to buy Cadillac dealerships through front men in order to launder "dirty" money. This had led to the recruitment, by the FBI in California, of Cadillac dealer Lou Peters as an informant.

Peters represented the second front. I was not aware of his undercover role either, of course. I thought Peters was a mere hanger-on. Peters became an FBI informant in 1977. A year later, he had not produced any evidence against me, despite

353

the fact that he was also stringing Jack DiFilippi along with a phony plan to sell customized cars.

In the summer of 1978 or so, the U.S. Organized Crime Strike Force in San Francisco opened the third front. This federal agency had been investigating my sons for years. Now the agency convinced itself that a link existed between me and my sons' business affairs in California.

The Organized Crime Strike Force was investigating my sons' business affairs at a time when my sons were in prison. The federal strike force was interested in obtaining the business records of such companies as U.S. Mattress Co. (which closed in 1977) and Kachina Fashions (which closed in 1978 when my son Joseph had to return to prison).

The federal strike force said it hadn't been able to find these corporate records.

After I returned to Tucson in September 1978, I received several phone calls from my daughter-in-law Karen, Joseph's wife.

Try to imagine Karen's state of mind during this period. In August 1978 her husband had been sent to prison. Karen operated a women's boutique called The Cat House, which was part of Kachina Fashions, of which her husband was an officer.

When Joseph went to prison, he had to close the business. But everything happened so quickly that he didn't have time to settle all his business affairs. For example, there were still outstanding debts. With Joseph in jail, creditors looked to his wife for satisfaction. Karen had inherited Joseph's business worries. As if that wasn't enough, Karen also was in frail health. In August of 1978 she had an operation.

The poor girl had no one to turn to for advice except her relatives, and that was the main reason for her several telephone calls to me in September 1978. Once she called to say that the IRS had informed her that Kachina Fashions owed the government about $6,000. I told her the debt had to be paid. Furthermore, I advised her that all tax and business records had to be in perfect order or the government would exploit the situation. Karen didn't have $6,000 to pay the IRS. I told her that perhaps she could get the money from her father and later I would make it up to him. I was saying all this in the interest of helping my son Joseph get out of debt.

The plight of my sons and their families preoccupied me during this period. At night, I would jot down my thoughts on notepads. These notes were ruminative and speculative. As I scribbled, I would go over things, cancel, cross out, insert, add, take out. These notes represented the pouring out of my private thoughts on paper. Once done with these notes, their purpose being exhausted, I would ordinarily tear them up and throw them in the garbage.

Here's one such note that law agents took from my garbage can on September 6, 1978:

Memo

Get all the paper for
1978 Tax Return &
Bank books etc.
& Canada book for Victor

Look for U.S. Mattress
Karen & Chuck—Papers signed
and notes of the loan

1. Bring Montreal books to Victor
2. Put bulb in front gate
3. At 1:00 pm call Karen
    at 377-9951
    Good Samaritan Hospital
4. Call barber—get dry cleaning
    Drug store to pay (yes)

None of the references in the note has any bearing on any illegal activity. The reference to U.S. Mattress, for example, refers to the promissory note for the $20,000 my wife, Fay, had lent the company in 1976. The note had been signed by Karen and "Chuck" Bonanno, Salvatore's son, who were officers of U.S. Mattress. This promissory note was Fay's (or my) personal property and not a business record.

If you didn't know this background, however, you can imagine how suggestive such a note appeared to the law agents—Ehmann & Co.—who attempted to decipher it. This note alone has references to U.S. Mattress, to tax returns, bank books, loans.

Each reference has an innocuous explanation. To give one more example, the references to bank books and tax returns refer to material I was preparing to take to my accountant Victor Tronolone for my income tax purposes.

When law agents in Tucson read notes such as the one just mentioned, they incorrectly assumed that in these notes I must have been referring to the business records of the defunct California companies being investigated by the U.S. Organized Crime Strike Force.

The Arizona law agents persuaded themselves that I was indeed hiding the sought-after records and that I also was advising Karen, and others in California, on how to thwart the government investigation in San Francisco.

The three fronts of the government's war against me were on the verge of coming together.

Later in September 1978, my daughter-in-law Karen came to Arizona to visit her husband at the Safford prison camp, some 125 miles northeast of Tucson. Karen stayed with Fay and me overnight.

On the very day Karen was to arrive in Tucson, I received a telephone call from Lou Peters. He said he was calling from Los Angeles, where he had been attending a convention. Peters wanted to know if it was all right if he could visit me. I told him that neither Fay nor I felt very well. Peters said it was only a short flight from L.A. to Tucson. He implored me to let him visit. He kept saying what an honor it would be if he could visit, and I finally relented.

The simultaneous appearance of Peters and Karen, when I look back at it, must have been more than a coincidence. Most likely, the FBI had sent Peters to Tuscon to see if he could overhear conversations between Karen and me that might link us in some sort of illegal conspiracy.

Peters was unsuccessful, although he remained with us the entire night. Peters made a total nuisance of himself. I had gotten the impression over the phone that he just wanted to pay a short visit and leave. But Peters kept hanging around the house when it should have been obvious that Fay, Karen and I had other things on our minds than entertaining him. If Peters hadn't been a friend of my son's, I would have asked him to leave.

I thought Peters was awed by the Bonanno mystique and that he was overwhelmingly curious about my way of life. As I do with many of my American guests, I showed him the portrait of my parents hanging in the family room; I showed him the Bonanno family crest and a picture of the Segesta temple near Castellammare. I rambled on about the history of my island and my race. At one point during this historical dissertation, I jotted down on a notepad these words:

"*Morte alla Francia, Italia anela.*"

As I have explained before, the words mean "Death to the French, Italy cries out." I explained to Peters that during the Sicilian insurrection against the French, the word *mafia* was used as a rebel motto because the letters in the word are the first letters of the words in the slogan.

Peters was to keep and save the note on which I scribbled this slogan. This note later turned up during my 1980 trial in San Jose. Peters identified the note as, to use his words, "the Mafia organization chart in Bonanno's own handwriting." As soon as Peters made this hilarious assessment, the prosecutor intervened and stopped Peters from making a bigger fool of himself than he already had.

Peters was a dodo. That night in September 1978 I did my best to be a good host. I thought that surely by dinnertime Peters would depart. My wife and Karen began setting the table, but Peters didn't budge or give any indication of leaving.

—Would you like to stay for dinner? I said.

—Oh, thank you, Peters gushed. That would be very nice. Thank you. Oh, thank you.

I thought for sure that if I fed him he would leave after dinner. Peters ate with gusto. Fay and Karen cleared the table. Peters smiled. Fay and Karen washed the dishes. Peters found himself a comfortable chair. Fay and Karen served fruit and coffee. Peters chatted.

Nine o'clock . . . ten o'clock . . . we watched the news on television . . . eleven o'clock . . . Fay and Karen went to bed . . . Peters lingered in the house, like a bad odor . . . midnight.

—Excuse me, I told Peters, but I have to go to bed.

Peters hemmed and hawed. He said he hadn't reserved a

room yet at a motel. I told him there was a hotel, the Arizona Inn, just two short blocks from my house and that I was sure they could accommodate him.

—But I want to see Joe tomorrow, Peters said, referring to a newfound desire to visit my son in prison.

I really didn't feel like arguing with the guy, so I told him he could sleep in the guest room, a room detached from the house next to the garage. Peters was overjoyed by the invitation.

The next morning he volunteered to drive Fay and Karen to Safford.

In October 1978, based on their faulty interpretations of my garbage notes, the FBI in Tucson requested and received authorization for a legal wiretap of my home telephone.

To justify the wiretap, the FBI presented some of my garbage notes to the federal judge who had to authorize the wiretap. As I have made clear, the notes represented nothing more than my jumbled and sometimes (to anyone but myself) incoherent scribblings, written in a combination of languages.

Nonetheless, the judge signed an eavesdropping warrant, which enabled the FBI to wiretap my phone legally from October 6 to October 31, 1978.

During this month, the FBI taped conversations between me and Karen and between me and Jack DiFilippi. In all these taped conversations, it was always Karen and Jack who called me and not the other way around. They were calling me, of course, because they were bewildered. Karen and Jack had never been through this legal grinder, this law-enforcement mangle iron. I had experienced it all my life. They were dazed by it. The FBI, the grand jury, the prosecutors . . . everyone wanted to know from Karen and Jack where these elusive records of U.S. Mattress and Kachina Fashions were. Karen didn't know. Jack didn't know. I didn't know.

I did know, however, that the government was engaged in legal gamesmanship. The law agents hounding us were not really interested in justice. They were interested in winning, in nailing the Bonannos at all costs. Most of all, they wanted me, the old man.

In my conversations with Karen and Jack, I emphasized that we should remain calm and speak the truth. The truth was that we didn't possess the business records the government sought.

At the same time, I felt that we should let the government do its own investigation and not let the government exploit us. I said this out of fatherly concern for Karen, Jack and my sons. There's nothing in the U.S. Constitution that required us to help the government destroy our lives and our family.

At the same time that my telephone conversations were being taped in October 1978, I also received another subpoena. This time the subpoena was from a federal grand jury impaneled in Tucson. Since my health had prevented me from traveling to the grand jury in San Francisco, the federal law agents decided to ask me their questions before a federal grand jury in Tucson. Once again, the subpoena ordered me to bring all business records I possessed of Kachina and other businesses.

My criminal lawyer, Albert Krieger, was busy on another case that month. Because of this and other reasons, I was successful in postponing my grand jury appearance.

In October 1978, Karen was subpoenaed to appear before the federal grand jury in San Francisco. Law-enforcement agents believed, based on their faulty interpretations of my garbage notes and telephone conversations, that I had instructed Karen to take the Fifth Amendment when she appeared before the grand jury. Based on this faulty assumption, the government filed an affidavit saying Karen had interposed her Fifth Amendment privilege. The affidavit was filed before Karen testified before the grand jury—that's how sure the government was of their scenario. As it turned out, when Karen did appear before the grand jury, she never invoked her Fifth Amendment privilege.

By coincidence, before Karen was to appear before the grand jury, she discovered where the Kachina Fashions business records were. Unknown to Karen, when Joseph went to prison he had left the business records with an associate. This man happened to be having marital problems, and he committed suicide about this time. After his death, the Kachina records were found. Alerted of this, Karen, together with Jack DiFilippi, took the business records and handed them to Jerrold Ladar, a lawyer for my sons. Consequently, when Karen appeared before the grand jury, she and Ladar brought the business records with them.

By October 1978, therefore, the government possessed the

business records of Kachina Fashions. The government also claimed to be searching for the business records of U.S. Mattress. I say "claimed" because I later learned that law agents had been very cavalier in their search for these records.

At my 1980 trial, Jerrold Ladar, a respected San Francisco lawyer, testified that federal officials had already seen these business records in the *summer of 1978*, during the probation revocation hearings for Salvatore and Joseph. Ladar said that he had all the business records in his San Jose motel room. Ladar testified that an assistant U.S. attorney with the U.S. Organized Crime Strike Force had inspected the documents for about two hours and found nothing of interest in them.

An even more telling incident concerning these documents occurred in November 1978. I didn't know this at the time, but a television reporter had offered to give copies of these records to the FBI that month. *But the FBI refused to accept them.*

The reporter in question was Marilyn Baker, who worked for a San Francisco television station. Some people might remember Baker from her reporting on the Patty Hearst kidnapping. For her investigative reporting, including her coverage of the Hearsts' adventures, Baker won the Peabody Award, the news broadcasting industry's highest award. Baker had made a name for herself through her splashy stories. In 1978, she was trying to develop a documentary on my son Salvatore— a show that never aired. While putting together the program, Baker ingratiated herself with Salvatore and his secretary, Kathy Michelis.

Before going to prison in mid-1978, Salvatore had told Michelis (a former secretary for U.S. Mattress) to hold on to the company's business records until he told her to hand them to his lawyer, who would then surrender them to the government.

Michelis testified in my 1980 trial that Salvatore's concern in giving her the records wasn't to hide anything from the FBI but to keep the FBI from harassing his friends, whose names appeared in the business records and letters of the company.

(I must again remind the reader that this information came to me after the events I'm describing occurred. In 1978, I didn't know that Michelis had received the U.S. Mattress business records from Salvatore.)

With Salvatore in prison, Michelis looked upon Baker as a confidante. Early in September 1978, Michelis received a grand jury subpoena requiring her to bring in books and records of U.S. Mattress. Michelis, a woman in her early twenties and unaccustomed to grand jury investigations, grew fearful and upset at being subpoenaed. She turned to Baker for advice.

Michelis later testified that Baker took the U.S. Mattress business records into her possession and advised Michelis that she would not be lying if she told the grand jury that she (Michelis) didn't have the business records. When Michelis appeared before the grand jury, therefore, she did not produce any documents.

While she had the records, Baker made photocopies of them. In November 1978 she offered the photocopies to Charles Hiner, an FBI agent.

FBI agent Hiner, who wasn't working on the Bonanno case, told FBI agent Adrian Coulter, who was assigned to the U.S. Organized Crime Strike Force, about these business records from Baker. Coulter refused to look at the papers Baker had, since Baker refused to turn them over unless Coulter agreed beforehand not to reveal her role. Also, Coulter didn't notify any assistant U.S. attorneys on the federal strike force.

It wasn't until July 1979—two months after I was indicted on a charge of conspiracy to endeavor to obstruct justice—that the FBI finally took possession of the photocopied business records from Baker.

On February 14, 1979, I received a call from Lou Peters. He said he wanted to wish my wife and me a happy Valentine's Day. Then he said he wanted to talk to me about an important matter. He was vague about it, and he sounded nervous. Peters said he was calling from his office. I told him I would call him back. I went out and called him from a public telephone booth.

Peters recorded this conversation at his end, as I later found out. Peters told me he had been subpoenaed to appear before a federal grand jury in San Francisco. He was vague about it all, never explaining why he should be called or what the subpoena actually said. Peters did indicate, however, that he thought the grand jury's interest in him might be over a car sale involving my son Salvatore.

All of this was new information to me. I didn't know anything about a car sale involving Salvatore. For a moment, I didn't know what to think. I was in near panic because of my concern that yet another problem was afoot to complicate Salvatore's already troubled life.

A little background will help establish the reasons for my concern. Peters told me he had given Salvatore cash for a car which Peters said belonged to Salvatore. My son was in debt to the IRS. If he had sold such a car to Peters and if he had received cash for it, Salvatore would have had to report the sale to the IRS. If he hadn't reported the sale, Salvatore would have gotten in more tax trouble.

I didn't know of such a transaction, and I didn't know whether Salvatore had reported it to the IRS or not, if it did take place. Nonetheless, I temporarily accepted Peters' disclosure. I knew Peters was a buffoon, but not that he was a liar.

Peters was lying to the hilt. As was later established in court, the true story of the car transaction is this. In June 1978, Salvatore had asked Peters to sell on consignment a Cadillac registered to one of Salvatore's businesses. The car didn't belong to Salvatore; it belonged to the company. As proceeds on the consignment sale, Peters had written out checks to the company's officers. The car transaction had been perfectly legal, and it did not compromise Salvatore with the IRS.

In my February 1979 telephone conversation, however, Peters kept stressing that Salvatore owned the car and that Salvatore had received cash for it. At one point, Peters even asked me if I wanted him to burn the records of the car transaction, records which Peters had in his possession.

My reply—and I quote from the transcript of this taped conversation—was:

"No, no. Don't burn. You save them good."

In other words, I told Peters to set aside the record of the car transaction for further discussion.

But since Peters was trying to trap me, this reply didn't satisfy him. He suggested that he fly to Tucson and discuss the matter personally.

I replied:

"No, no. That's what they're looking for, to tell everybody what to do, to charge with obstruction."

I was telling Peters not to come to Tucson because if the FBI found out about it, they would conclude that I was influencing a grand jury witness. I could be charged with obstruction of justice. I wanted to avoid any impropriety. I didn't want it to seem that I was influencing Peters, unaware, of course, that Peters was an FBI informant and that he was trying to trap me to make it seem as if I was influencing him.

By the end of February, Jack DiFilippi grew uneasy about Peters, his partner in the Barchetta plan. Unknown to me, Jack visited Peters in Stockton. Peters told him about the subpoena.

Although he knew the background of the car transaction, Jack couldn't figure out how the paperwork of the transaction could legally damage Salvatore. Jack wanted to talk to Salvatore about the records, but Salvatore was in prison; Jack couldn't just pick up the phone and chat with him. At Peters' apartment, Peters asked Jack to help him place the records of the car transaction in a bedroom closet.

After many delays, I lost my bid to quash the subpoena against me, and on March 1, 1979, I finally appeared before the federal grand jury in Tucson.

Craig Starr, an assistant U.S. attorney on the U.S. Organized Crime Strike Force, asked me a lot of questions about the business records of U.S. Mattress and Kachina Fashions. He asked me about my conversations with grand jury witnesses. I took the Fifth Amendment on all his questions.

I believe the government was not truly interested in these business records by March 1979. That was a pretext with which to make me appear before a grand jury. I think the government was hoping I would perjure myself once before a grand jury.

For example, the government already knew from its wiretap of my home phone that I had conversations with Karen in October 1978. If I had denied any such conversations before the grand jury, that would have constituted perjury. The government then would have had a clear-cut case and would have rushed to indict me. The indictment might have included other charges, but at the very least the government could have made the perjury charge stick.

When I wouldn't answer his questions, Starr became perturbed. He wanted to ask a judge to cite me for contempt. Starr conferred with my lawyer. It was decided that Starr would not seek a contempt citation if I agreed to answer just one of his questions. On my lawyer's advice I reluctantly agreed.

Starr's brilliant question was:—Are you the custodian of these business records?

It was a feeble attempt to save face.

I replied:—No.

Then the grand jury excused me.

38

A BOOK OF MY LIFE HAD BEEN GERMINATING IN MY MIND FOR some time, but it wasn't until the commotion of the late 1970s, ironically enough, that I set about the task in earnest. While most people write memoirs during periods of quiet and repose, after their battles in life are over, I began to write mine amid tumult, while I was still in the thick of life.

I did not plan it that way.

For the longest time, in fact, I opposed the writing of any book of my life, whether an autobiography or an authorized biography. Many professional writers tendered their services, but I turned them down.

My qualms stemmed from a variety of reasons. If any book about me were to be written, it had to be a book that expressed me from the inside. All too often, I detected that my would-be biographers were interested in me only as I appeared from the outside. Their point of view was all wrong, so how could they possibly write a book about me? They seemed interested only in the more sensational aspects of my exterior life. My deepest thoughts, my meditations and my philosophy did not truly interest them. Some of them simply lacked the intellect to understand me.

Much to my chagrin, I had seen what usually happened when such commercial writers wrote about men of my Tradition. The product was a cheap, trashy and sleazy book. No doubt these "Mafia" books sell well, but they are comic-book versions of reality. I did not want the book of my life to appeal to voyeurs who crave reading about crime. I wanted my book to be read by normal people.

Then too, there was the language barrier. The greatest regret of my life is that I never pushed myself to master the English language. This has proved to be a terrible disadvantage. My lack of fluency in English, for example, had forced me to be more taciturn with journalists than I perhaps would like to have been, on occasion. I know I come off poorly in interviews. Since I have a limited English vocabulary, I'm forced to simplify my thoughts. Consequently, I come off sounding crude, or needlessly obscure. My frustration is such that to avoid making a fool of myself I would rather say "no comment" and let it go at that.

Lastly, in deciding whether to write a book of my life, I always had to consider what impression such a book would make on the ordinary reader. Would the reader believe what I had to say? Would people make fun of me? Would people be interested? Oh, I knew there was interest in the sensational aspects of my life, but would people be interested in my insights about honor, family, trust? How could I possibly convince people there was another Joe Bonanno than the "Joe Bananas" they read about in the newspapers?

I am misunderstood. I had every reason to suppose that my book would be misunderstood as well. The overwhelming majority of Americans just plain don't understand what my Tradition is all about. One of their ill-informed notions concerns the so-called code of silence—*omertà*.

Many people reading this book undoubtedly believe that in writing it I have violated the code of silence and thus have broken a cardinal rule of my Tradition.

Omertà comes from the word *omu* or *omo*—which means "man." In my Tradition, *omertà* has come to describe the "manly" behavior of someone who refuses to get his friends in trouble. In the hands of the police, a captive from our Tradition ideally should remain silent. He should not cooperate. Such a man is willing to face even death rather than betray his friends to the authorities or to his rivals.

Omertà in my Tradition is a noble principle. It praises silence and scorns the informer. Try as you might, there's no complimentary way of describing an informer. All the terms are pejorative: stool pigeon, spy, rat, tattler, quisling, snitch, fifth-columnist, betrayer. It's probably true that all cultures and all languages recognize informers, no matter what side they're on, to be unsavory types.

Informers are universally scorned because they are the sort of people who betray their friends to save their own skins. In order to save himself, the informer is willing to get others in trouble. The informer is willing to *talk*. This is unmanly behavior.

Omertà is an injunction against allowing yourself to be the instrument of another man's downfall.

My Tradition has had its share of rotters. Informers such as Joe Valachi, Vincent Teresa and James Fratianno don't deserve to be called *omu*. They are louses. They bargained for their lives or their creature comforts by cooperating with the authorities, who used them for their own purposes. When a man betrays his friends, as these men did by "singing" to the cops, he betrays himself.

Out of these men's cooperation with the police came forth books: *The Valachi Papers, My Life in the Mafia, The Last Mafioso*, to name a few. All these books are bad, not so much for their inaccuracies and pretensions as for their insincerity. The books were written under duress of one form or another, most often to please the authorities. None of these men would have ever squawked about his life if he hadn't been in prison and if he hadn't had something to gain.

Omertà, however, doesn't mean that a man can't say what he feels, which is what I'm doing. I am under no coercion to write. What I say in this book about my friends or enemies I have already said to them in person. Never in my life have I provided information that would send anyone to jail. This book is not an exception.

I do not accuse others, and I do not apologize for myself. *My object is to unmask.* I do not judge conduct on the basis of legal innocence or legal guilt. I talk in terms of what is right and what is wrong, who is weak and who is strong, what makes me laugh and what makes me cry.

Having despaired of writing a book, I rejected all overtures. The matter languished. Then something quite startling, you might even say miraculous, happened. I began to write all on my own—to maintain my sanity.

My life in the late 1970s was a wreck. Everything seemed

as bad as it could get. I was under unremitting stress. I was nervous and frazzled emotionally, and in bad health physically. I was in the twilight of my life. My wife was sickly. My sons were in prison. Law-enforcement agents hunted me like a pack of jackals. Journalists buzzed around me like carrion flies. My superficial friends had abandoned me. My name was sullied. My life and my family were coming apart. I had nowhere to turn but within.

At the end of these agonizing days, I found myself seeking the solitude of my basement office, where I kept my books, my files, my clippings, my maps and photographs. The office even contained a little stereo on which I played my old Italian records. It was a pleasure to look through boxes and quite unexpectedly discover a forgotten letter, or a report card from grade school, or a banquet program with the names of bygone friends.

In trying to recall the past, I was amazed that my memory had retained so much. The miracle of memory intrigued me, especially since I was in my seventies. The older you get the more you fear the loss of memory. And yet, I could remember such distant recollections as when my grandmother Bonanno would give me eggs as a little boy in Castellammare. Grandma used to wait behind her door in the morning, waiting for me to pass by her house on the way to school. When I passed her door, she would beckon me inside and give me one of her fresh eggs for me to suck.

—Feel the egg, she would say. The shell is still warm. The hen just gave it to me.

In my basement retreat, I began to feel an overpowering need to write about my past. It was as if I had caught a fever. And so I began to write. I wrote and I wrote, paying no attention to format or style. The creative process released me into another dimension. At the same time, the things I wrote reminded me of who I truly was. They took my mind away from the slanders about me. It was a comfort, a distraction and a joy to write. Just to write.

I didn't really know where I was heading with my writing. I had never written anything like this before. But I stopped worrying about it. I stopped worrying whether I could or could not write a book. I just wrote. I stopped vexing myself with obstacles. I just wrote. I quickly discovered that I had more ideas in me than I had imagined. I kept writing, adding more and more and more. Whereas before I thought I would have to strain to think of things to say, now there seemed no end of things to say and so little time to write about them. My exterior problems spurred me to write all the more furiously. What the public would think of my book I no longer cared. It was my duty to write.

I wanted to leave something of myself behind, something my children and grandchildren and the generations to follow could return to always. I wanted them to learn who I really was.

After having filled, in a rambling hand and in two or three languages, several hundred pages on yellow legal pads, I realized I had barely begun. . . .

On March 16, 1979, Ehmann & Co. found a torn-up note in my garbage that gave them an excuse to grab the limelight away from their San Francisco cronies. The piece of paper they found in my garbage can was a promissory note, an IOU, from Kachina Fashions to me. The note was my receipt for the $20,000 loan I had made the company in the beginning of 1978. This promissory note was a perfectly legal document, signed by the company's comptroller. It was my personal property, which I could dispose of as I wished. With my sons in jail, I didn't see any point in holding on to an old debt. I never expected to be repaid anyway.

Ehmann & Co. used this promissory note to justify their request for a warrant to search my house. I believe that Narcotics Strike Force agent Ehmann and FBI agent Christensen knew that the note found in my garbage *was not* a business record of Kachina Fashions. I can't bring myself to believe that these two veteran law agents didn't know an IOU when they saw one.

These paper cops would have the world believe that Joe Bonanno was so careless as to throw away incriminating evidence in the trash. If I had documents I wanted to hide from the grand jury, would I have simply chucked them in the garbage? Wouldn't burning them have made more sense?

The simple truth is that whatever I threw away in my garbage was no more incriminating than table napkins thrown out after a meal.

On March 16, 1979, a befuddled judge, who knew nothing about my case other than what the law agents represented to him, signed a warrant authorizing a search of my house the following day. The law agents probably all had sweet dreams that night of the big splash they were going to make the following morning. They would have been pleased, of course, to find *specific* business records of U.S. Mattress and Kachina Fashions in my house. But if they did find such records—which they never did—they would have to turn them over to the San Francisco law agents.

I think Ehmann & Co. went to bed that night, however, with far more selfish expectations. Ehmann & Co. wanted the glory of capturing Joe Bonanno. Even if they didn't find any sought-after documents, the search warrant would enable them to snoop through my personal belongings and papers. That was a coup in itself. Moreover, I think what they really were hoping to find in my house was contraband. If they found an illegal substance in my house, cocaine let's say, that would have fulfilled their fondest dream. They could arrest me right away. It would be a clear-cut case. Ehmann & Co. would get all the credit.

On Saturday, March 17, 1979, Fay woke up at about five o'clock, as usual. I hadn't slept well that night. Presently, I too got up and followed the aroma of Italian cooking into the kitchen. Fay was cooking meatballs to take to our son Joseph, whom she was going to visit that day at Safford prison camp. At seven-thirty that morning, Fay's friend arrived, and both of them took off to see my son. I went back to bed.

I tried to sleep but couldn't. I felt dizzy and had a dull pain in my chest. As a survivor of three heart attacks, I didn't dismiss such symptoms lightly. My heart had served me for seventy-four years, but, what with all the pressure I was under, who knew how many more years it would continue to serve me? I sat up at the edge of the bed, about to call my doctor. I noticed it was a little after nine o'clock.

As I was picking up the phone on the nightstand, I heard voices from outside. For an instant I thought I was hallucinating. I didn't know it yet, but law agents had jumped over my front fence, entering my patio. Then they discovered that the side door of my house was unlocked. So they barged into my home.

From my bedroom I heard the voices coming closer and closer.

—Hey Joe, hey Joe. Where are you?

In the next instant a troop of law agents entered my bedroom, smirking.

—What is this? What's going on?

—Take it easy. We have a search warrant.

—What is this? I kept demanding. What in the world is this?

How can any human being take it easy in a situation like this? I felt my heart running very fast. It seemed as if a large cotton ball was stuck in my throat. The phone was still in my hand. An FBI agent asked me what I was doing. I told him I was about to call my doctor. He looked at me incredulously and said I could make the call only if I allowed him to listen to the conversation. I called my doctor.

Then law agents began going through the dressers and the closets in the bedroom. They ordered me to open my safe. In a matter of minutes, my entire bedroom was in utter disorder.

Not having the heart to watch any more, I shambled to the dining room and sat on a wooden chair. Everywhere I looked, it seemed as if a horde of vandals was sacking my house. They were overturning everything, sticking their hands everywhere —some fifteen or eighteen of them, some searching and some just standing around as if at a peep show.

Christensen and Ehmann were the prima donnas of this obscene affair. With them were other federal cops, and county cops and city cops. The county attorney was there, along with an assistant U.S. attorney. Also there was Terry Grimble, director of the Narcotics Strike Force.

Outside—my God!—there were reporters and television cameras. The law agents had it all planned. In order to get the publicity they coveted, the law agents had informed reporters ahead of time about my house search.

In the living room, I read the search warrant. All I could get out of it was that the law agents were authorized to search for business records pertaining to Kachina Fashions. Why, then, were they confiscating my personal papers? Why, then, were they looking inside my refrigerator?

They found cash and some handguns in a closet. There was nothing illegal about that. I could keep all the cash I wanted in my house. As for the handguns, I was not a felon and I could possess firearms.

Some of the law agents went downstairs to inspect my basement office. They prevented me from following them to see what they were doing. The agents said they wanted me to remain in one room of the house while they searched the rest of the house. They said they wanted me under surveillance during the search and didn't want me to follow them around. Wasn't this a violation of my rights? It was *my* house! I had a right to see what they were taking from the house.

By now my doctor had arrived. I hadn't felt good when I had gotten up that morning. Now I felt absolutely lousy. The doctor gave me an injection to calm me. We went to one of the bedrooms with an FBI agent trailing after us to see what we were doing. My utter revulsion at him and his fellow scavengers manifested itself in an uncontrollable desire to retch.

The memory of that wanton ransacking of my house is seared in my mind. Never have I felt so humiliated. I can only compare it to what a woman must feel when she's being raped. Each time one of these vandals stepped into a closet or pulled out a drawer, I felt as if he were violating me. Thank God my wife was not home. It would have killed her to see them violate her house. As the search continued through the rest of the morning, I kept telling the law agents to finish their dirty work quickly and get out before Fay returned home.

—If you people have a heart, I told them, please finish before my wife comes back and sees this. Please, my wife is very sick.

I had tried to contact my Tucson attorney, Alfred S. Donau III, but he was out of town. When another Tucson lawyer arrived, I told him to go to the basement to see what the law agents were collecting. But the law agents stopped him, as they earlier had stopped me. The lawyer was powerless. The police had cowed him. All he could do was dangle about, like a cheap suit on a hanger.

The agents left about four P.M. To this day I don't fully know what they confiscated from my house. They took reams of personal papers, personal notes, personal documents, personal letters and my incomplete memoirs.

After they left, I quickly inspected the damage. It's impossible to describe my disgust on seeing what those barbarians had done to my basement sanctuary. I'm a very neat and fastidious man. I could hardly recognize my office, such was the mess and filth the law agents had left behind. Papers and books were strewn all over the place, helter skelter. On the floor, there were crushed cigarette butts, plumes of ash, matches, chewing gum, scuff marks and spit. I slammed the door to my basement office. Only some three months later did I feel like walking in there again to clean the office.

About twenty minutes after the agents left, Fay returned home. Though I had hastily tried to straighten out the house before she arrived, it was a Herculean effort and I barely made a dent.

—Joe, Fay said, have you been having a party?

Fay sniffed the air and smelled the acrid, stale odor of cigarette smoke.

—You could have at least opened some windows.

—I had a few girls in here while you were gone, I said with dull sarcasm. I told them they had to leave before you got back.

Fay knew I was kidding, so she answered,

—As long as you enjoyed yourself, I don't have to know anything.

Then she walked into her favorite room, the kitchen, and she knew right away something was drastically wrong. From the kitchen, she dashed to the bathroom, only to come huffing out an instant later, exclaiming:

—Since when do people spit in my bathroom?

She then stormed into our bedroom. I couldn't keep up with her. I heard a shrill cry.

—What happened, Joe? Please tell me.

Fay took it badly. The devastation of her domestic haven dazed her. And she cried. Never, not in all my years as a top man of my world in New York, had any man invaded her house and defiled her home. Fay roamed around the house like a sleepwalker, sobbing and sputtering remarks such as,

—Haven't these people any heart? . . . Haven't they any children?

We had to call the doctor again later because we both needed something to calm us down. The day's events had flattened us.

—God! Fay wailed. Don't let me see things anymore.

39

SIX WEEKS AFTER LAW AGENTS RAIDED MY HOME IN TUCSON, a federal grand jury in San Francisco indicted me on a charge of conspiracy to endeavor to obstruct justice. U.S. Federal District Court Judge William Ingram was assigned my case. As a resident of Tucson I could have chosen to be tried there. That's what I favored originally. However, since my lawyers thought highly of Judge Ingram, we went to trial in California.

For the Grand Tribunal of Joe Bonanno, Ingram would have to be both judge and jury. Because of the complexity of the case, my lawyers had decided to waive a jury trial. They felt that a trained man of the law, who could sift through intricate legal issues, was more to our advantage than a jury of laymen.

Dispensing with a jury, however, had its risks. A judge, regardless of his merit, represents but one mind, while a jury represents twelve minds. With a jury, you have twelve chances. When a judge sits as the jury, you have only one chance. Lose the judge and you lose the trial.

I was not in the best of shape to travel across Tucson, much less all the way to San Jose, California. I was a seventy-five-year-old man with chronic high blood pressure and an assortment of other disabilities. Despite my poor health, I had to endure the bitter irony of being described in the mass media as a "superboss"—an ogre who ran a vast crime empire. You can imagine how ridiculous this sounded to me. To run an empire of any kind a man needs vigor. The truth was that sometimes I found it difficult to get out of bed in the morning.

My emotional state was just as precarious as my physical

health. Worries assailed me from all sides. My wife was sick again, very sick. When my trial began, my sons were still in prison. In my immediate circle of friends, I had few to turn to, few with whom to vent my feelings. I felt like a man on a desolate island. The Grand Inquisition into my life, on top of a lifetime of tribulations, had left me raw to the nerve. I became very edgy. It was not at all difficult to upset me; the jingle of a telephone could do it.

To retain my sanity, I constantly had to exhort myself not to lose control, not to give in to despair, not to burst and not to melt.

—Joe, be careful, I said in these prayers to myself. Don't let yourself down. Keep your head up. No one can help you but yourself. Do the best you can and trust in God.

I went to California to face the music.

Jack DiFilippi, who was charged with conspiring to obstruct justice with me and thus was a co-defendant in the upcoming trial, once described the grand jury investigation as "Bonanno's Ninth Symphony."

I went to California to hear a symphony which bore my name but which I had not composed.

On my first day in court in San Jose, we had a full house. I walked into the courtroom with my lawyers, Albert Krieger and Alfred Donau, a keen and sincere young man. My entourage also consisted of a clutch of reporters and cameramen. Spectators occupied every seat in the courtroom. They all had come to see me, their "silver-haired Mafia boss." They must love me very much, these people, I thought. Why else would they pay so much attention to me?

I also recognized the faces of many law agents from Tucson, both from the FBI and from the Narcotics Strike Force. I feared for Tucson's safety. The city's finest police officers were in California. Who would safeguard Tucson from criminals?

Other than the gala atmosphere, I remember only one other thing of that first day's proceedings. During the usual introductions between the lawyers and the judge, my chief defense attorney, Krieger, presented me to the bench. Judge Ingram, a half-smile on his face, shook my hand.

A judge had never shaken my hand in court like that. It put

me off. I didn't quite understand the purpose of it; it was a most ambiguous gesture.

Judge Ingram was a man in his middle or late fifties, with a round face and gray hair, of middle height, though a bit stout. He didn't move much on the bench. Once in a while he'd cross his arms. He had a deep voice, but not a loud one. He liked to rub his fingers over his nose. The judge seemed to be a very proper man, a precise man, a clear man. But he had an equivocal half-smile.

The man I hired to fight the government's calumny and vindicate my name, Albert Krieger, had been my friend for some fifteen years, ever since he had represented me in my kidnapping case. Albert started out in New York. He now had a fancy office in Miami. Albert had made it big. He traveled all over the country representing clients. At the time of my trial, he was the president of the National Association of Criminal Defense Lawyers. He lectured at Harvard Law School.

Albert was convinced that since the government's case was so tainted with misconduct, the judge would surely scuttle the case during pre-trial. Any sane person could see the government had fabricated its case and had overreached itself. The government's case, Albert said in court, represented fruit of a poison tree. He called it a "prosecutorial charade." He thought Judge Ingram would surely see this. Albert had faith in jurisprudence.

I was not so sure. I kept emphasizing the dirtiness of the government's case and how some law agents would stop at nothing to convict me. I was downright cynical about my chances of winning in pre-trial or in the trial itself. I'm sure that even to my lawyers and friends I must have sounded paranoid. I harped on the same theme. I wasn't on trial, I kept insisting, my name was on trial. My relentless protests must have tired my counselors. Their attitude was that reason would prevail. My attitude was that misunderstanding would triumph.

Before the trial proper began, Albert filed a motion to suppress evidence improperly gathered by the government. This included the wiretapped conversations and the garbage notes. If our motion had been granted, it would have effectively killed the government's case. It would have been tantamount to dismissal. Judge Ingram held a lengthy pre-trial hearing over the matter. But in the end he ruled against the defense.

I quote excerpts from Judge Ingram's pre-trial ruling, italicizing a few significant expressions:

> Notwithstanding the *stench of illegality* which, therefore, hovers over this entire proceeding, I find I must deny the motion to suppress . . .

> The trash cover, while it involves a course of conduct which I at least find to be *offensive on its face and conducted upon no real provocation*, is not apparently offensive . . .

> Notwithstanding the reek of *illegality* and *bad faith* surrounding the conduct of the pen register and the installation of the beeper, defendant has been unable . . .

I don't pretend to understand what was on the judge's mind. The overall impression I got, however, was one of great tentativeness. The judge's language was full of "notwithstanding," "while" and "apparently." I believe the judge was truly offended by the government's conduct. On the other hand, he lacked the resolve to do anything more than chide the government. In essence, then, the judge said that although the government had erred, it had not erred grievously enough. The judge recognized the government's improprieties but ultimately overlooked them, saying they did not rise to the level of flagrant wrongdoing.

From the very beginning, Judge Ingram was very fair to the government. He was very understanding of the government's difficulties, and he gave law agents who testified the full benefit of the doubt. You'd almost think the government was the defendant.

The judge's ruling permitted the prosecution to go ahead with a case which should never have come to trial in the first place.

Usually, the stronger the prosecution case is, the cleaner and simpler is its presentation. But in this trial, the prosecution case was a hodgepodge, a potpourri, a stew. It was as if the prosecution, instead of making a clean, coherent presentation, was trying to hide behind a jumble of frowzy data. At trial alone, the government introduced 286 exhibits. The transcript of the pre-trial and trial proceedings is about 4,500 pages. It was a complex case, to be sure, but the government exploited the complexity to create confusion.

No law student, no lawyer, no judge will ever study this case for its elegance. This case will go down in the annals of court history as the "trash" trial. Eugene Ehmann will go down as the "garbage" policeman. Starr will go down as the "refuse" prosecutor.

The government band marched into the courtroom, playing a dozen melodies, none of which they bothered to finish, leaving it up to the judge to make sense of the score. I was charged with trying to set up "fronts" through Cadillac dealerships, but in court the government couldn't prove that. It was contended that I was trying to "launder" money through my sons' businesses, but in court it was clearly shown that the only money I ever passed on to these businesses was perfectly legal and documented one-time loans. I was supposed to have been withholding business records sought by the grand jury, but none of these specific records were ever found in my possession; furthermore, law agents already had access to these records from other sources. I was supposed to have been telling grand jury witnesses how to testify, but when the testimony of these same witnesses was compared to what the government alleged I had instructed them to say, it was discovered that the witnesses had testified fully before the grand jury. In other words, there was no correspondence between what the witnesses actually said to the grand jury and what the law agents claimed I instructed them to say, based on their errant interpretations of my garbage notes and telephone conversations.

The government didn't have a case against me. All it had was speculation, speculation based on circumstantial evidence and faulty interpretations of my garbage notes and telephone conversations.

The prosecutors argued that their case consisted of "a progression of proof, moving from ideas on paper to the words of the co-conspirators to the co-conspirators working with the object of their criminal act."

The prosecution was wrong. Its case consisted of a progression of garbage.

* * *

Our defense maintained that the garbage notes and telephone conversations, on which the government based its case, were subject to different interpretations and the usual errors of taking words out of context.

Once, during his testimony, Jack DiFilippi, peeved at the narrow literal minds of the prosecutors, said,

"I don't know how to translate from Sicilian to English. And I was born there."

My lawyer, Krieger, also felt compelled to point out in court that although he had known me for fifteen years, he still found it difficult to interpret me:

"Mr. Bonanno is extremely difficult to understand and Mr. DiFilippi is worse . . . it requires an enormous amount of concentration."

Albert never spoke truer words.

The government often embarrassed itself with its blunders. One such awkward goof was discovered in the judge's chamber. The lawyers had repaired to the judge's room to hear a tape of a telephone conversation that the prosecution wanted to introduce into evidence. The taped conversation was between me and a man the government represented as a "California boss." As soon as the tape was played, Krieger protested, because he recognized his own voice on the tape.

The government had taped a conversation between me and my lawyer, but to the government, it sounded like a conversation between me and a mobster. The carelessness of the government's presentation, of which this is but one example, should have made the judge suspicious of the government's sincerity.

By now, the judge's rulings were beginning to form a pattern, at least to me. The judge did not countenance impropriety. However, when he encountered *proven* impropriety by the government, he had, through mental gymnastics, divorced it from the trial. When he encountered *alleged* impropriety by me and Jack, he never gave us the benefit of the doubt. It was as if I had to prove my innocence instead of the government's having to prove my guilt.

About midway through the trial, I began feeling very sick. I felt a great weight in my chest and a queasiness of the stomach. One day in court, I staggered, turned white in the face and almost passed out. Later that day, after the court session, I was examined by Dr. Dominic Campisi, a doctor for my son Salvatore's family.

My poor condition alarmed Dr. Campisi, who went on to testify as much in court. Dr. Campisi testified that he found my blood pressure to be high, "which is not good for a man with a coronary condition. . . . He [Bonanno] was quite agitated, very nervous, pacing the room. He was trembling and out of breath and complained about pressure in his chest and back of neck." Dr. Campisi also testified that I had a "serious coronary artery disease" and that I could suffer a fatal heart attack if the trial continued. "I believe his appearance in court would be life-threatening," the doctor said.

Although the judge seemed genuinely concerned over the state of my health, he rejected a motion to dismiss the case because of it. He also rejected a motion to sever my case from the trial.

In arguing against the motions, Michael Sterrett, who was on the prosecution team with Craig Starr, had said that there was no objective test of the effects of stress in the courtroom. To which my lawyer Krieger replied that "the quantification of risk is almost a ridiculous exercise . . . whether the risk is ten percent or ninety percent, the risk of a heart attack is real."

—God help me, I told Albert, but if the government wants me dead, I'll die in court. Let them enjoy the spectacle.

And so, despite my poor health, I rejected going to a hospital. I resolved to show up in court, even if I had to crawl there. At this point, I simply wanted to get the trial over with as soon as possible. The way things were going, I didn't expect any justice. Uppermost in my mind was my sick wife. She was in Tucson and I wanted to be with her very much.

The judge's handling of the situation once again indicated what an ultrarational mind he had. Since it was established that my body couldn't take the stress of a full day in court, the judge decided to hold half-day sessions. I suppose that's a mathematically sound decision, if you're worried about overloading a machine.

To spare me undue stress, the judge allowed me to view the last part of the trial from the judge's chamber on a television monitor. To me, the trial had now reached the level of the absurd. There I was, the defendant, watching my own trial on television, and I kept staring at the tube, waiting for the commercials to come on.

The trial proper lasted from April to July 1980. I had to put up with all sorts of vile accusations, fully knowing that I could not speak on my own behalf. I could have taken the stand, of course, but it would have been suicide. With my rotten English, the prosecutors would have chopped up my words and made me seem foolish. It was ironic nonetheless that in a trial in which I did not speak, everyone pretended to know what was on my mind.

In September 1980, Judge Ingram found both Jack and me guilty of conspiracy to obstruct justice. The judge later sentenced me to five years in prison. I had expected him to rule against me. He had shown himself to be too literal, too narrow in focus, too primly correct to be able to transcend the petty issues in this case and arrive at the real issues.

At the beginning of the trial, my lawyer kept saying what a good judge this man was, and that may well be. But a man may be good and yet be weak.

One of my last impressions of Judge Ingram came during a presentencing hearing in which my lawyers and I wanted to call James Fratianno to testify. Fratianno is a self-confessed "hit man." When the government arrested him, Fratianno turned informer. Subsequently, Fratianno became a key witness for the government in various cases involving alleged organized-crime figures.

On the day Ingram sentenced me, Fratianno was in San Jose, ready to testify at my hearing. The government had brought me to trial with the underlying implication that I was not only part of organized crime in California but was its top man. To show the absolute nonsense of this view, I wanted to call Fratianno to the stand. After all, if Fratianno was a good enough witness for the government, the government surely would have no objections if I borrowed its own witness.

However, the government did object. Judge Ingram, at the last minute, acquiesced to the government's wishes. In open court the judge said he didn't want to dirty the trial. His pronouncement stunned me. I became so agitated that I nearly choked. Not dirty the trial? If he didn't want to dirty the trial, why did he allow the government to bring a dumpster full of dirty garbage notes into his courtroom?

The government didn't want Fratianno to take the stand in my case because the government knew ahead of time that Fratianno had nothing bad to say about me. If he had been given the chance to testify, Fratianno would have said that he didn't know me and that the Bonannos were not part of organized crime.

In October 1980, Fratianno got to say as much anyway in the Los Angeles trial of five men implicated in the death of Frank Bompensiero.

In that trial, Fratianno said,

"Joe Bananas ain't got nothing to do with organized crime."

Attorneys kept badgering Fratianno about the Bonanno family, and at one point Fratianno blurted out,

"Sir, you've asked me that twenty times. *I never met nobody in that family. I don't know what they look like."*

The real issue in my 1980 trial is the extent to which our justice system can be corrupted by misguided prosecutors, self-seeking law-enforcement agents, arbitrary grand jury investigations and indiscriminate mass media.

Furthermore, when the dust has settled and people can look back on this case objectively, they'll see what a ridiculously trivial case this was on which to try the supposed "superboss" of organized crime in America. If I were as bad as they said I was, surely the government could have come up with something meatier.

In a complex case such as this, we can tediously argue over every point until we arrive at a level of confusion greater than when we began. The only way to get a crisp understanding of this case is through analogy—an imaginative process.

Picture an old man walking down the road. Suddenly the old man hears the roar of a mighty engine, and when he looks behind him, the old man sees a monstrous machine speeding straight at him. As old and sick as he is, the old man musters his strength to escape this menace. He runs and runs, but the monster car keeps gaining on him.

Then, just as he's approaching an intersection, the old man sees something even more horrible than the danger behind him. Across the road, the old man sees his sons, handcuffed to each other and helpless as another monster machine circles them in ever narrowing loops. The old man, forgetting his own danger, rushes across the street to help his sons.

At this critical moment, as the old man is crossing the intersection, a monster police helicopter drops from the sky. Out of this whirling machine alights a jaunty policeman, all decked out in black leather and rakish cap, who says to the old man:

—I've been watching you from the sky, Mr. Bonanno, and I'm going to have to give you a traffic ticket for crossing this here intersection on a red light.

40

THE INTERVAL BETWEEN THE END OF THE TRIAL AND MY CON-
viction about a month later I spent in Tucson with my ailing
wife. Fay's health was deteriorating as a result of a blood
disorder. She was pale and emaciated, and she seemed to be
shrinking.

I was hardly in the pink myself. In October 1980 I was
admitted to St. Mary's Hospital in Tucson. I had contracted a
bronchial infection. But as it turned out, that was the least of
my worries. When they examined me at the hospital, the doctors were aghast. They said it was fortunate that I had come
to the hospital when I had. In the course of their examination
they had discovered a cancerous tumor in my bladder. If the
tumor had been bigger, it would have ruptured the bladder and
I would have died.

This form of cancer is difficult to detect. It was this tumor
which had caused my dizziness during my trial. In any case,
I could have died in the courtroom, just as Dr. Campisi had
warned. The timely operation to remove the tumor saved my
life.

Before I had journeyed to California for my trial, I had
hoped that Fay, despite her ailments, still had several years of
life left. When I returned home I saw what a crushing effect
the trial had had on her, despite her having remained in Tucson.

Throughout our marriage I had always kept my legal problems as far away from Fay as possible. This time, however,
Fay had witnessed most of the events which led up to the San
Jose trial. She had seen the government pervert the legal process. It was she who had urged me to lend $20,000 to our son's

business, only to see the government misinterpret an act of motherly love into some sort of scam. Fay had served dinner to the miscreant Lou Peters. She had seen what a phony he was. The grand jury witnesses that the government contended I tried to influence were her relatives too. These people weren't criminal. They were people such as Karen, our daughter-in-law, and Jack DiFilippi, our nephew. Fay had seen how the government ransacked her home, her domestic temple.

On September 2, 1980—the day my conviction was announced in California—Fay's energy level had sunk so low that it was decided to take her to the hospital. A friend of Fay's and I were taking her out of the house when we were confronted by a swarm of reporters and cameramen, their cameras trained on us.

The reporters besieged my house to get my reaction to the news of my conviction—of which I was not yet aware. Since the reporters blocked our path, we could hardly get Fay out of the house. It angered me to see those camera jockeys taking pictures of my sick wife. We had no choice but to retreat into the house.

Fay, weary and sick as she felt, wasn't fully conscious of what was happening outside. The sight of the rabble and the blitzkrieg of shouting made her delirious.

—They're coming to get Joe, she kept moaning in a tremulous voice. They're coming to get my husband. They're coming for him.

In her distracted state, Fay imagined that law-enforcement agents had come to take me to prison.

I was finally able to persuade the reporters to leave us alone, and we managed to get Fay into the car. But even then the cameras rolled.

Fay had to go directly into intensive care. She was having trouble breathing. The doctors told me that Fay's stomach had not only shriveled but had twisted around itself. They had to operate.

Fay survived the operation but never recovered from the shock to her system. She was never able to return fully from that quiet, distant world which day by day was claiming her. Every so often, she would be alert momentarily. Then she would lapse back into stupor. Four days after she was admitted to the hospital, my wife died.

Her last words to me were:
—Are they coming to get you?

Greasy, a black-and-tan Doberman, lives with me today. When Greasy was a pup he'd always sniff and scamper under cars, because that's where he'd usually find Joseph, who loved auto mechanicking. The dog would get grease all over him like a greasemonkey. That's how Greasy got his name.

Greasy's in his "golden years" now, an old geezer. He sleeps all day out on the patio. Sometimes he likes to stretch himself on the grass, lying on his back and kicking his legs in the air. Then he'll saunter back to his sunny spot on the patio and take another nap.

Every morning Fay would be the first one to greet him and let him out of the house. Greasy would lie next to Fay's rocker. I would catch her scratching him behind the ear all the time. If I raised my voice at Fay, Greasy would sidle next to her and put his muzzle on her leg to give her moral support. If I tried to chase Greasy out of the room, Fay would come to his defense. Is the dog bothering you? she would ask. Greasy loved anything with Fay's smell on it.

Fay's death made Greasy very sad. He kept looking for her, and when he didn't find her he sank into depression. The day of Fay's funeral, he plopped down on the pantry floor and wouldn't move. You could yell at him, nudge him or kick him, but he wouldn't move. He was totally stuporous, in a deep melancholia for his loved one. We had to take him to the vet afterward for some pep shots.

On the Sunday after the funeral, the children and I went to the cemetery to visit Fay's grave. As we were getting into the car, Greasy jumped inside, something he has been taught not to do. But he had been so forlorn that we took him along.

When we opened the car door at the cemetery, Greasy bounded out and scanned and sniffed around. Greasy made his way to the front of Fay's grave and sat down.

Fay—the wife and the mother—had been a constant source of inner strength. Her death was an irreplaceable loss. I never gave any thought to remarrying. It came as a shock that women, after a decent interval, presented themselves at my door, as it were, with an eye toward catching a husband.

I lived alone, with Greasy. While my 1980 conviction was being appealed, I remained free on bond. Every month I was required to see my probation officer. I woke up each morning not knowing if on that day I would have to go to prison. It was—and still is—like living under the sword of Damocles.

My idleness induced me to take up domestic pastimes. In the morning I would water the fig tree, the olive tree and the flowers in the garden. Fay loved roses. I planted a row of rose-bushes along an entire side of the house.

I amused myself with plans to build a bocci court across a side lawn. Then I would berate myself. Even if I did build a bocci court, I told myself, who would come to play with me?

I continued to read the newspapers religiously, and presently I was rewarded with proof of some of my long-held suspicions. In 1981, the two Tucson newspapers began publishing stories about fiscal irregularities in the spending and account-keeping of the Narcotics Strike Force.

Since it had been established in 1974 by Dennis DeConcini, the Narcotics Strike Force had grown bigger and bigger, had hired more and more people, had received more and more money. Its budget soared into several million dollars a year. The agency had become a bureaucratic monster.

In their probe of the agency, Tucson newspapers discovered that strike force personnel were very careless, if not fraudulent, in how they spent the taxpayers' money.

In March 1981, the Pima County attorney raided the strike force's Tucson office at night and seized agency records. Strike force director Terry Grimble was suspended. Two months later, Grimble resigned, amid allegations that he had used agency money to rent an apartment and buy personal items.

The Narcotics Strike Force soon was disbanded.

It's my turn now to have the last laugh. These law agents who wanted to send me to jail so badly because I was supposed to be a grand manipulator of funds turned out to be a bunch of fiscal manipulators themselves.

41

LET US NOW SPEAK OF VIRTUOUS MEN, OR AT LEAST OF MEN who try to be virtuous. Different cultures produce different models of the virtuous man. My culture reveres a model of excellence: the prince. This word had many meanings, not just the obvious ones of son of a king, or nobleman or person of high rank. "Prince" comes from a Latin root word which means "one who takes the first part." In this sense, therefore, a prince is he who sets the example because he's the first one to show himself, the first one to take part, the first one to declare his principles.

When I was very young, watching the puppet theater in Sicily, my dream was to become a knight. Later, as a student, my ideal was to become a sea captain. When I became a man, I lost many of my romantic illusions, but I didn't lose all my ideals. As a mature man I have aspired to be a prince—a man who lives and dies by his principles.

How close have I come to my ideal?

That's not for me to say. It's not for you to say either. It's up to God.

This I know:

I have tried to be a good Father. I have helped many people. No man can say I cheated him or took away what was rightly his. I've led a productive life, not a parasitic one. I've had to protect myself and my people, but I've never been bloodthirsty. I've made mistakes, I'm not perfect, but throughout it all I've remained true to my name and scrupulous to my principles.

* * *

This book is my declaration that my Tradition has died in America. The way of life that I and my Sicilian ancestors pursued is dead. What Americans refer to as "the Mafia" is a degenerate outgrowth of that life-style. Sicilian immigrants who came to America tried to conduct their affairs as they had in Sicily, but we eventually discovered this was impossible.

American culture, with its marketplace values, made us rich for the most part, but at the same time it eroded our relationships, which had always been kinship-based.

Mafia is a process, not a thing. Mafia is a form of clan cooperation to which its individual members pledge lifelong loyalty. In other words, as corny or simple as it may sound, what makes this process work is the belief in *friendship*.

Friendships, connections, family ties, trust, loyalty, obedience—this was the "glue" that held us together. In America, however, and increasingly throughout the industrialized world, the glue that holds people together is their economic relationship. Trade and work are the basis of the new culture.

The sons and grandsons of the Sicilian immigrants absorbed the new values. Those who chose to pursue the "mafioso" way of life professed to be following the old Tradition, and yet something had changed which even they were not always aware of.

The "Mafia" phenomenon in America *today* shouldn't even be referred to by that name. I've turned my back on what I consider a debased form of my traditional life-style. Most of the names I read in the newspapers are new to me, and their activities, such as narcotics trafficking, are entirely repugnant.

What can I say about these people? They are strangers. If they engage in illicit activities, what concern is that of mine? If some of them have Italian surnames, they could just as easily have Jewish, Irish, or Puerto Rican surnames. It wouldn't make any difference. They're all trying to make money. That's all I see.

The ideals embodied in my Tradition will endure only in the hearts of men. Even in Sicily, the old Tradition is declining under the influence of the Americanization of Europe. That's the situation today, both in the New World and in the Old World. If society breaks down in the future, however, who knows if the pure mafioso spirit will blaze again?

In any case, what Americans call "Mafia" never was an

institution, an organization, a corporate body. As best as I can figure out, this fallacy continues to receive its strongest acceptance not in the minds of ordinary people but in the minds of law-enforcement agents.

Law enforcement is an endless, tedious business. There has always been and there will always be crime, either by individuals acting alone or by individuals acting in concert. Law enforcement is such discouraging work because no sooner does a policeman arrest a criminal than another criminal takes his place.

Given this monotonous and enervating flow of crime, it pleases policemen to think of some outlaws as belonging to one monolithic group, a secret society perhaps, which can be attacked and defeated, once and for all, just as one's enemy can in conventional war.

Since a policeman is a creature of a tight organization, the police bureaucracy, he tends to think, or would like to think, that his enemy also is a member of an organization. This is a psychologically pleasing projection; it gives the policeman hope he can win the war against crime if only he can destroy the "monolithic" group which he imagines controls "organized crime."

The American public is fascinated with "Mafia" for different reasons, I believe. Why did so many people flock to read *The Godfather* and to watch the movie? This work of fiction is not really about organized crime or about gangsterism. The true theme has to do with family pride and personal honor. That's what made *The Godfather* so popular. It portrayed people with a strong sense of kinship trying to survive in a cruel world.

I believe Americans are strongly attracted to such themes because they are witnessing the erosion of kinship and of personal honor in their culture. They therefore look at representations of these fading values, whether in movies, books or television soap operas, with nostalgia. I believe Americans miss the old frontier days of personal confrontation. I think Americans also miss the extended family and are having a difficult time trying to find a substitute. *Americans yearn for closeness.* Most of all, and I say this in a figurative sense, Americans yearn for a "father."

* * *

Count Camillo Benso di Cavour was asked,

—*Che cosa è la vita?*

What is life?

And the Italian statesman answered,

—*È l'ombra d'un sogno fuggente; la favola breve è finita; il solo immortale è l'amore.*

Life is the shadow of a passing dream; the story is short and finite; the only immortal truth is love.

When someone writes his memoirs and is serious about the undertaking, he cannot help realizing that aside from his other intentions, he has embarked on an odyssey to enlighten himself and his readers as to that age-old question: What is life?

The writing of these memoirs has forced me to think about what I have learned about life.

I too have something to pass on to the next generation. I consider myself luckier than the generation of today in America. I was born into a Tradition. I was born among a people whom experience had taught to cherish certain fixed values. This Tradition was the flower of our culture. It taught us right and wrong. It guided youngsters as they strove toward manhood. It guided mature men, and punished them if they deserved it. Our Tradition gave us our way of life.

That my Tradition represents a bygone era does not fill me with regret or bitterness. I'm too old for the modern world anyway. It's too late for me to change. At my age it's a blessing just to be alive. I still have my gripes, of course, but during my contemplative moments my overall mood is one of thanksgiving.

I have learned that true power comes from self-control.

I have learned that true strength comes from a clear conscience.

I have learned that true wealth comes from a good family and good friends.

INDEX

Index

Index